Islas Baleares

Ibiza, Formentera, Mallorca,
Cabrera and Menorca

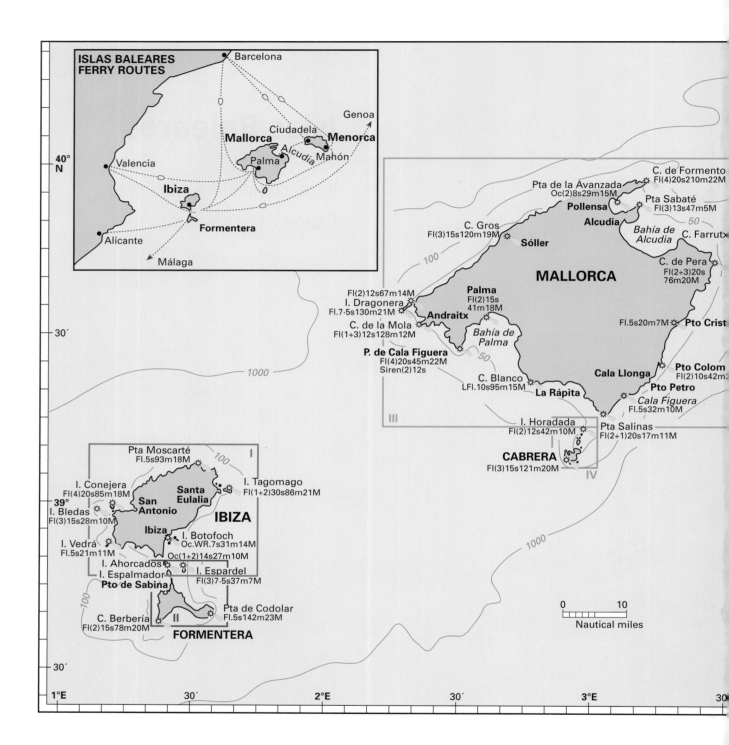

ISLAS BALEARES
FERRY ROUTES

Barcelona

Genoa

Ciudadela
Mallorca   Menorca
         Alcudia
Palma   Mahón

40°
N   Valencia

Ibiza

Formentera

Alicante

Málaga

MALLORCA

C. de Formento
Fl(4)20s210m22M
Pta de la Avanzada
Oc(2)8s29m15M
Pta Sabaté
Fl(3)13s47m5M
Pollensa
Alcudia
Bahía de
Alcudia
C. Farrutx
C. Gros
Fl(3)15s120m19M
Sóller
C. de Pera
Fl(2+3)20s
76m20M
100
Fl(2)12s67m14M
I. Dragonera
Fl.7·5s130m21M
Palma
Fl(2)15s
41m18M
Andraitx
Fl.5s20m7M   Pto Crist
C. de la Mola
Fl(1+3)12s128m12M
Bahía de
Palma
P. de Cala Figuera
Fl(4)20s45m22M
Siren(2)12s
Cala Llonga
Pto Colom
Fl(2)10s42m
C. Blanco
LFl.10s95m15M
La Rápita
50
Pto Petro
Cala Figuera
Fl.5s32m10M
III
I. Horadada
Fl(2)12s42m10M
Pta Salinas
Fl(2+1)20s17m11M
CABRERA
Fl(3)15s121m20M
IV

Pta Moscarté
Fl.5s93m18M
100
I
I. Conejera
Fl(4)20s85m18M
Santa
Eulalia
I. Tagomago
Fl(1+2)30s86m21M
San
Antonio
39°
I. Bledas
Fl(3)15s28m10M
IBIZA
Ibiza
I. Vedrá
Fl.5s21m11M
I. Botofoch
Oc.WR.7s31m14M
Oc(1+2)14s27m10M
I. Ahorcados
I. Espalmador
I. Espardel
Fl(3)7·5s37m7M
Pto de Sabina
C. Berbería
Fl(2)15s78m20M
II
Pta de Codolar
Fl.5s142m23M
FORMENTERA

1000

1000

0   10

Nautical miles

30′

30′

1°E   30′   2°E   30′   3°E   30

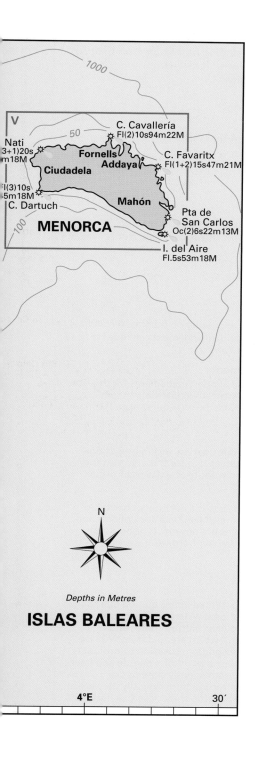

Islas Baleares

Ibiza, Formentera, Mallorca,
Cabrera and Menorca

 RCC PILOTAGE FOUNDATION

David and Susie Baggaley

Imray Laurie Norie & Wilson

Published by
Imray Laurie Norie & Wilson Ltd
Wych House The Broadway St Ives
Cambridgeshire PE27 5BT England
✆ +44 (0)1480 462114
www.imray.com
2018

© Text: RCC Pilotage Foundation 2018

© Plans: Imray Laurie Norie & Wilson Ltd 2018

© Photographs: as credited, David and Susie Baggaley,
Billy Hammond and Joanne Cotterill, Triangle Postals,
Paramotor Menorca, Geoff Williamson Photography

© Aerial photographs unless credited otherwise: Imray,
Laurie, Norie & Wilson and Patrick Roach 2011

© Thumbnail positional photos: ESA2000–2005
Balearic Islands – ENVISAT MERIS – 2 October 2004

First edition 1977 (as *East Spain Pilot: Chapter VII,
Islas Baleares*)
Second edition 1980
Third edition 1984
Fourth edition 1989 (including *East Spain Pilot Chapter I,
Introduction and General Information*)
Fifth edition 1991, updated 1995
Sixth edition 1997
Sixth edition revised 2000
Seventh edition 2003
Eighth edition 2006 (Reprinted with corrections, September)
Ninth edition 2011
Tenth edition 2015
Eleventh edition 2018

ISBN 978 184623 940 3

British Library Cataloguing in Publication Data.
A catalogue record for this title is available from
the British Library.

Printed in Croatia by Zrinski

Warning

Throughout the islands anchoring on seagrass (Posidonia)
is generally prohibited and infringement can result in
heavy fines (*see pages 14 and 21*).

Updates and Supplements

Corrections, updates and annual supplements for this title
are published as free downloads at www.imray.com.
Printed copies are also available on request from the
publishers.

Find out more

For a wealth of further information, including passage
planning guides and cruising logs for this area visit the
RCC Pilotage Foundation website at www.rccpf.org.uk

Feedback

The RCC Pilotage Foundation is a voluntary, charitable
organisation. We welcome all feedback for updates and
new information. If you notice any errors or omissions,
please let us know at www.rccpf.org.uk

CAUTION

Whilst the RCC Pilotage Foundation, the author and the
publishers have used reasonable endeavours to ensure the
accuracy of the content of this book, it contains selected
information and thus is not definitive. It does not contain all
known information on the subject in hand and should not
be relied on alone for navigational use: it should only be
used in conjunction with official hydrographical data. This is
particularly relevant to the plans, which should not be used
for navigation. The RCC Pilotage Foundation, the authors
and the publishers believe that the information which they
have included is a useful aid to prudent navigation, but the
safety of a vessel depends ultimately on the judgment of the
skipper, who should assess all information, published or
unpublished. The information provided in this pilot book
may be out of date and may be changed or updated without
notice. The RCC Pilotage Foundation cannot accept any
liability for any error, omission or failure to update such
information. To the extent permitted by law, the RCC
Pilotage Foundation, the author and the publishers do not
accept liability for any loss and/or damage howsoever
caused that may arise from reliance on information
contained in these pages.

Positions and Waypoints

Waypoints have been discontinued in this edition due to the
ubiquity of modern navigational systems which permit
navigators to define their own preferred routes and
clearance margins. Locations, which are to datum WGS 84,
are retained as an aid to recognition. Location co-ordinates
are given to the nearest decimal point of a minute and have
been placed so that they are sufficiently close to the
featured location to enable recognition. Typically they are in
the mouth of a bay or *cala* or sufficiently close to a harbour
or marina entrance that the destination is obvious, but far
enough away that a different charting system does not
show them inland. They have been established using a
Navionics electronic chart which may present differences
with other charting systems. These location co-ordinates
should not be relied upon for safe navigation.

Bearings and Lights

Any bearings are given as °T and from seaward. The
characteristics of lights may be changed during the lifetime
of this book. They should be checked against the latest
edition of the UK Admiralty *List of Lights*.

Contents

RCC PILOTAGE FOUNDATION

The RCC Pilotage Foundation was formed as an independent charity in 1976 supported by a gift and permanent endowment made to the Royal Cruising Club by Dr Fred Ellis. The Foundation's charitable objective is 'to advance the education of the public in the science and practice of navigation'.

The Foundation is privileged to have been given the copyrights to books written by a number of distinguished authors and yachtsmen. These are kept as up to date as possible. New publications are also produced by the Foundation to cover a range of cruising areas. This is only made possible through the dedicated work of our authors and editors, all of whom are experienced sailors, who depend on a valuable supply of information from generous-minded yachtsmen and women from around the world.

Most of the management of the Foundation is done on a voluntary basis. In line with its charitable status, the Foundation distributes no profits. Any surpluses are used to finance new publications and to subsidise publications which cover some of the more remote areas of the world.

The Foundation works in close collaboration with three publishers – Imray Laurie Norie & Wilson, Bloomsbury (Adlard Coles Nautical) and On Board Publications. The Foundation also itself publishes guides and pilots, including web downloads, for areas where limited demand does not justify large print runs. Several books have been translated into French, Spanish, Italian and German and some books are now available as digital versions.

For further details about the RCC Pilotage Foundation and its publications visit **www.rccpf.org.uk**

PUBLICATIONS OF THE RCC PILOTAGE FOUNDATION

Imray
Arctic and Northern Waters
Atlantic France
Atlantic Islands
Atlantic Spain & Portugal
Black Sea
Cape Horn and Antarctic Waters
Channel Islands, Cherbourg Peninsula and North Brittany
Chile
Corsica and North Sardinia
Islas Baleares
Isles of Scilly
Mediterranean Spain
North Africa
Norway
South Biscay
The Baltic Sea and Approaches

Adlard Coles Nautical
Atlantic Crossing Guide
Pacific Crossing Guide

On Board Publications
South Atlantic Circuit
Havens and Anchorages for the South American Coast

RCC Pilotage Foundation
Supplement to Falkland Island Shores
Guide to West Africa
Argentina

RCCPF website www.rccpf.org.uk
Supplements
Support files for books
Passage Planning Guides
ePilots - from the Arctic to the Antarctic Peninsula

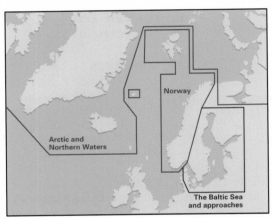

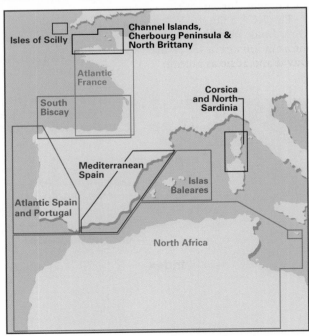

Trinity House   PATRON OF THE RCC PILOTAGE FOUNDATION

The RCC Pilotage Foundation is privileged to have Trinity House as its Patron. Trinity House, established in 1514 under King Henry VIII, is a charity dedicated to safeguarding shipping and seafarers by providing education, support and welfare to the seafaring community as well as by delivering and monitoring reliable aids to navigation for the benefit and safety of all mariners. Proud of its long history and traditions in navigation and pilotage, Trinity House is nevertheless at the forefront of technological developments and works closely with other organisations around the world to improve aids to navigation and to optimise global navigation satellite systems and e-navigation. The ongoing safety of navigation and education of mariners are common goals of Trinity House and of the RCC Pilotage Foundation.
To find out more go to www.trinityhouse.co.uk

FOREWORD

Testament to the lasting appeal of this popular cruising ground, RCC Pilotage Foundation *Islas Baleares* is now into its eleventh edition, more than forty years after the first edition, and it continues to be the best selling RCC Pilotage Foundation cruising guide.

David and Susie Baggaley (OCC/CA) have taken on the responsibility for this latest edition and the RCC Pilotage Foundation is extremely grateful to them for committing their time and effort so enthusiastically. Based on Menorca for several years, they have brought with them new depths of knowledge of the islands, their home cruising ground, including the northern and eastern coasts of Menorca which have tended to be somewhat overlooked compared to other coastlines in the islands. Fears of a sudden *tramontana* can nowadays be allayed by keeping a careful eye on the forecast winds and swell patterns, allowing enjoyment of some of the more remote and beautiful north coast anchorages during stable conditions.

The RCC Pilotage Foundation is also indebted to Tony Boas who has been a long term contributor of information about the islands and who recommended David and Susie as authors.

Much of this edition still owes itself to Graham Hutt's work, spanning twelve years, and the Foundation remains profoundly grateful to him for that enduring knowledge base.

Thanks also to all the yachtsmen and women who have contributed corrections, photographs and additional information. These contributions are fundamental to keeping Islas Baleares as up to date as possible. If you find anything which needs updating in this edition please do email us to let us know at info@rccpf.org.uk. An annual supplement will be produced each year after publication: Click through to the *Islas Baleares* page of the pilot books section of the Imray or RCC Pilotage Foundation websites where you will find any mid-season updates or corrections and links to the annual supplement available as a free download.

Finally, thanks to the dedicated team at Imray who have done their usual wonderful job in bringing this edition to publication.

Jane Russell
Editor in Chief
RCC Pilotage Foundation
June, 2018

Magnificent turquoise seas and welcoming sandy beaches around the islands *Jane Russell*

The authors Susie and David Baggaley

PREFACE

Between us, we have some 65 years' sailing experience in which we have sailed over 150,000 miles, most of which have been since our retirement in 1998. This includes extensive periods in the Caribbean, North America and the Mediterranean as well as northern Europe. We are past Roving Rear-Commodores, and current Port Officers for the Islas Baleares, of the Ocean Cruising Club and are also members of the Cruising Association.

In mid 2016 we were invited by the Royal Cruising Club Pilotage Foundation to take over the authorship of the Islas Baleares Pilot in succession to Graham Hutt, who masterminded the last three editions. Not having undertaken anything quite like this previously we were initially doubtful but quickly came to realize that this was an opportunity and challenge to bring purpose into what were increasingly becoming marine geriatric meanderings. So it has proved, and we have thoroughly enjoyed the process of cruising the Islas Baleares more comprehensively and with a spirit of enquiry. Any initial timidity was quickly overcome by the quality of help and advice from the Pilotage Foundation and Imray.

Our current yacht, the last in a longish list of marques and sizes, is a Beneteau 42 cc which we find a comfortable yacht for Mediterranean cruising, easily handled by two people. It is based in Addaya, Menorca, our favourite island in the group - a prejudice that we hope does not come through over-strongly. Our other great prejudice, perhaps a function of age, is for well-protected anchorages with good sand or mud bottoms where we can sleep soundly through wind increases and shifts.

Acknowledgements

This, the eleventh edition of the Islas Baleares Pilot, builds on the huge amount of work put in by our predecessors, especially Graham Hutt who authored the previous three editions and gave us such a fine base. The coverage, research and erudition which we inherited from him made our job relatively straightforward. As noted above a great deal of credit must also go to the team at the RCC Pilotage Foundation and the highly skilled and experienced professionals at Imray.

Feedback from other yachtsmen is an invaluable help to the production of a Pilot (*see below*). For this edition there has been input from Tony Boas, Jorge Santos, Linda Fraser, John Priestley (RCC), Ian Muir, Will Pedder (RCC), Rob Campbell, Richard Openshaw and Stephen McGibbon.

Feedback

Whilst we have assiduously visited virtually all the anchorages and harbours in the island group in 2016 and 2017, information can quickly become out of date, particularly in relation to marinas, harbours and their facilities (material for this edition was collected in 2016 and 2017 and was submitted in September 2017 for publication in early 2018). Other yachtsmen may have different experiences of the quality of holding etc. in anchorages, and it is amazing that previously unreported dangerous rocks still appear, as do new anchorages - in the Menorca section of this edition there are three 'new' anchorages and one good one which was highly underrated in earlier editions. Conversely, there may be some anchorages which might be regarded as marginal and comment on these would be equally valuable. Also it is always good to hear of clubs and marine businesses which give a high quality of support to visiting vessels. Finally, although we work really hard to make the Pilot as accurate and comprehensive as we can, it is almost inevitable there will be some, hopefully minor, errors and omissions; if you see anything you think is wrong or have any comment at all please let us know through info@rccpf.org.uk

We particularly draw attention to the caution section on page iv.

Photographs

It is surprisingly difficult to find good, high resolution photographs of anchorages and features of interest to sailors. There are a number of companies offering 'stock' photos by the thousand, but the photos are generally taken from the perspective of a beach-bound tourist rather than displaying the features or suggesting the atmosphere of an anchorage. Fortunately, some years ago Imray commissioned a major series of aerial photos which for the most part are still valid today. Graham Hutt took a number of excellent photos and we have tried to follow in his footsteps. We have obtained a number of up-to-date photos from marinas. We have also been fortunate to identify free sources for some excellent photos relating to Menorca. Triangle Postals publish an excellent guide to the Cami de Cavalls trail around Menorca (GR223) and allowed us to use a dozen of their images. Billy Hammond and Joanne Cotterill allowed us to use some photos from their private collection. Alas, we failed to find equivalent sources for Mallorca or Ibiza.

For future editions we would welcome photograph submissions from readers who reckon they have better photos than those contained in this edition or of features where there is currently no photo - no financial return but acknowledgement in the publication. In this context we would mention that a resolution greater than 2mb is needed and that deck level photos of anchorages rarely show them well; a view from a high point is generally better, whether mast head or nearby cliff - or these days, of course, a camera-equipped drone.

David and Susie Baggaley

Key to symbols used on plans

	depths in METRES
	rocks with less than 2 metres depth over them
	rock just below or on the surface
(2)	a shoal or reef with the least depth shown
	wreck partially above water
	wreck
(4) Wk	dangerous wreck with depth over it
⊙ ⊙	eddies
	rock ballasting on a mole or breakwater
	above-water rocks
	beach
	cliffs
⌘	church
♀	mosque
⚒	windmill
Ψ	wind turbine
☊	chimney
♣	pine
♠	trees other than pine
⊟	castle
⬚	ruins
▰▰	houses / buildings

⊞	fish farm
⚓	anchorage
⚓	prohibited anchorage
⚓	harbour with yacht berths
⚓	yacht harbour / marina
Ⓥ	visitors' berths
▲	port of entry
⊖	customs
⚓	harbourmaster
⚟	water
⚡	electricity
🚿	shower
⊡	waste pump-out
⛽	fuel
⊡	travel-hoist
Ⓐ	chandlers
i	tourist information
⬡	crane
⊠	post office
✈	airport
➖	slipway

⊙	beacon
⬱ R	port hand buoy
♠ G	starboard hand buoy
♣	mooring buoy

Characteristics
✳	light
◗	white light
◗	red light
◗	green light
◗	sectored light
F	fixed
Fl.	flash
Fl(2)	group flash
Oc.	occulting
R	red
G	green
W	white
M	miles
s	sand
m	mud
w	weed
r	rock
P.A.	Position approximate

INTRODUCTION

OVERVIEW OF THE ISLANDS

The Islas Baleares (Iles Balears, Ballerics, Balearics, etc.) consist of four main islands: Mallorca, Menorca, Ibiza and Formentera, along with a number of smaller islets, in three separate groups. They form probably the most attractive and varied cruising grounds in the western Mediterranean. There are many pleasant anchorages and harbours, ranging from large cosmopolitan ports such as Palma de Mallorca, to tiny anchorages in exquisitely beautiful bays.

The islands are under Spanish sovereignty and therefore within the European Union. The distances between islands are not great and those between ports, harbours and anchorages are often only a few miles, making the islands suitable for cruising throughout the year. Shelter is never far away.

Although Ibiza and Mallorca developed a reputation for out of control development to capitalise on tourism, most parts of the islands are unspoiled, although coastal regions are universally crowded in July and August.

Menorca, though possibly less spectacular, has managed to preserve a great deal of its rural charm. Driving along the coastal roads, which wind their way inland around areas of gently rolling hills through thick pine forests, is very pleasant. Far out to sea you can smell the rich pine forests.

The western group of islands lies less than 50 miles east of the Spanish mainland at Cap de Nao near Denia. This group includes Ibiza, Espalmador, Formentera and half a dozen smaller islets (*islotes*) separated from the mainland and Mallorca by deep channels. These islands were recognised as a separate group in Roman times when they were called Pityusae (Pine Islands) and are still sometimes referred to as the Islas Pitiusas. They offer many secluded bays and *calas* (coves) where it is possible to anchor. The northern areas are generally high and rocky whereas the south is low-lying with sandy bays.

The second group, consisting of Mallorca, Cabrera, Menorca and some small inshore islands, was known by the Romans as Insulae Baleares, possibly from the Phoenician baal laaron meaning 'a man who throws stones. Apparently the sling-shot was the islanders' weapon of choice for resisting attack. The names Mallorca and Menorca are derived from the Latin 'Major' and 'Minor.' Mallorca, the largest island of the group, is approximately 45 miles northeast of Ibiza. It has a major port, Palma de Mallorca, several harbours and many bays and *calas* where it is possible to anchor. The northern part is mountainous and the northwest, where the highest mountains rise straight from the sea, is truly spectacular. One large offlying island to the south, Cabrera, has a well-protected bay, several *calas* and a number of islets around its coastline. It is a national park with restricted access. Anchoring is forbidden but mooring buoys have been laid to accommodate a limited number of yachts (maximum 50).

Menorca lies 25 miles northeast of Mallorca and is much lower and flatter than its neighbour. It is some 30 miles long, with few harbours but numerous *calas* where anchoring is possible. As in Mallorca, the northern part is higher and more rugged than the south. Menorca tends to have different weather patterns to the rest of the Balearics, being more exposed to the stronger winds generated in the Golfe du Lion.

The islands are attractive and form an excellent cruising ground with the possibility to sail throughout the year. Outside of the summer season, deserted anchorages and quiet nights await those still wanting to sail, a completely different experience to the summer season when anchorages and mooring buoys are full and booking online for a marina place or a buoy is essential.

Changes to the buoyage around the islands are a frequently reported item. The Posidonia project (described on page 21) has made a big impact on yachtsmen, mainly because of the necessity to book moorings in advance through a website that has in the past often been dysfunctional. The lack of internet information in a language other than Spanish and Catalan is a problem for many yachtsmen. Furthermore, buoyed areas and those marked as anchorages change, as does the period in which they are laid. Some are only in place for the summer high season, whereas others remain

Cala Pinar, Bahia de Pollensa, Mallorca. Rich pine forests stretch from the sea to the mountains

Traditional farming: near Montuiri, Mallorca
Geoff Williamson

throughout the year. Some areas marked as anchorages are only available as such for part of the year.

Whatever the buoyage or anchoring situation, anchoring in the 'sea meadows' is generally forbidden, but may be possible in some contiguous areas of sand. Yachts have often anchored without being challenged in prohibited areas, an inconsistency making it difficult to be precise. Where buoys are laid, anchoring information is therefore still included, even if anchoring is not permissible at a particular time of year. The majority of *calas* now have buoyed-off areas for swimmers and indeed in some cases the whole *cala* may be inaccessible for anchoring. Usually there is an identified channel for pedalos, canoes, etc. to be launched from the beach, and this can be used for dinghy access to the shore.

The islands are popular amongst the Germans, Italians and French, especially in July and August, and of course the Spanish. In recent summers the number of French yachts in particular has increased enormously and the French flag has been the most common after the Spanish. British and French yachtsmen are often seen sailing well outside the summer season.

For those who can choose, it must be emphasised that visiting the islands outside of the peak summer season is a totally different experience to visiting in that peak period. Although it is possible to sail most of the year round, the majority of Europeans take their annual vacations in July and August when prices have been raised, often doubled, and marinas are full. Many yachtsmen based in the Mediterranean fly back to northern Europe at this time of year to avoid the crowds and heat. Outside the holiday season, anchorages are relatively empty, marina prices halve, restaurants do not need booking well in advance and the extreme heat of July and August is avoided. Sea temperatures are very comfortable for swimming by the end, if not the beginning, of May and remain so until perhaps late October.

List of ports

Ports IB has taken over the concessions previously managed by the Port Authorities and now runs several marinas throughout the islands, usually charging less than half the price of the privately run *club náuticos*. They do, however, tend to be quite small and it is still almost impossible to find a *club náutico* or Ports IB marina with a mooring available in July and August without booking well in advance. The online booking systems used by Ports IB and Posidonia were awkward and often dysfunctional at first, but now seem to run more smoothly.

Most of us have now got used to the exchange of anchorages for buoyed areas which Posidonia initiated with environmental justification. Many of the best anchorages actually give poor holding because they are constantly being ploughed up, a factor often not appreciated until the middle of the night when katabatic winds come howling through the *calas* in the darkness, causing mayhem for inexperienced charterers. Being secured to a buoy and not having to worry about dragging anchor is a reasonable trade off, not to mention the salvation of the sea-grass meadows, a message that is beginning to be communicated. Conservation is a big issue – and big business. Protected areas are often changed from one part of the coastline to another, so it is only by viewing the online sites that current information can be updated.

Climate and seasons

For those accustomed to more northern latitudes a winter cruise has its attractions. There are many days with a good sailing breeze and the weather is often warmer and sunnier than an English summer. Storms and heavy rain occur in winter, but in general the climate is mild compared with northern Europe and, particularly from January to March, reasonably pleasant most of the time. Menorca is more exposed to weather coming down from the Golfe du Lion and February/March are sometimes cold, wet and windy.

Offshore, the Mediterranean weather in winter can be fearsome, but in the Balearic Islands it is feasible to dodge bad weather and slip from harbour to harbour as they are seldom far apart. Sailing out of season not only has the great advantage that there are no crowds, but the shops and services are freer to serve the winter visitor. Local people can be met, places of interest enjoyed and the empty beaches and coves used in privacy. Many *club náuticos*, which in summer have to turn away cruising sailors, welcome visitors off-season.

Local economy

Tourism is now the most significant contributor to the local economy, but agriculture and light industry manage to co-exist in the islands. There is an established boat building industry, drawing skilled labour from the industrial sectors. The yachting industry in the Islas Baleares generates about a billion Euros each year.

Language

The islands have two official languages: Spanish (Castilliano) and Catalan. The latter is transformed into local dialects, referred to as *Mallorquín*, *Menorquín* and *Ibicenco*, in Mallorca, Menorca and Ibiza. Examples of Catalan alternatives for Castilliano Spanish phrases include: *bondia* – good morning (rather than *buenos días*), *bona tarde* – good afternoon (*buenos tardes*), *s'es plau* – please (*por favor*). Many French and Italian words are integrated into the local dialects.

Ancient church in Banys de la Font Santa, Mallorca
Graham Hutt

Most local people now speak English or German, albeit with varying degrees of fluency, often learnt from tourists. Mallorca is virtually a German island to the extent that the menus in many restaurants are presented primarily in German. The same is true of English in Menorca.

Holidays and fiestas

As on the Spanish mainland, most inhabitants of the islands are Roman Catholic, though, as on many islands throughout the Mediterranean, practice may be more cultural than religious and quite different from that on the mainland. Perhaps the most overt manifestation of religious practice is the celebration of saints' days. There are literally hundreds of these throughout the islands and they can be a huge affair – always with a procession during which the saint, or an effigy of the Virgin Mary will be paraded down the main street or taken by boat, effectively closing down the town for several hours. One of the largest, *Fiesta del Virgen de la Carmen* is celebrated in many harbours during mid-July. When a national holiday falls on a Sunday it may be celebrated the following day.

Fiestas usually culminate with a firework display. Every city, town and village has its own saint's day and corresponding fiesta. Other celebrations are of historic events, commemorating the rich history of the islands.

A useful *Fiestas Guide* is published annually by the Balearic Tourist Institute and is available from tourist offices. There is also a monthly update including cultural events taking place locally, also available from tourist offices and from many hotel lobbies.

See Tourist offices page 25.

METEOROLOGY

Regional weather in the Western Mediterranean

The weather pattern in the western Mediterranean basin is affected by many different systems and local topography. It is largely unpredictable, quick to change and often very different at places only a short distance apart.

Winds most frequently blow from the west, northwest, north and east but are considerably altered by the effects of local topography. Winds on the east coast of Mallorca seldom seem to match those on the west side. Winds with a westerly component are relatively rare around Menorca in summer when winds between north and southeast dominate. The Mediterranean is an area of calms and gales and the old saying that in summer there are nine days of light winds followed by a gale, is very close to reality. Near to the coast normal sea and land breezes are experienced on calm days. Afternoon sea breezes often rise to F4 or 5 in late afternoon: a factor worth noting when entering a marina and encountering a cross wind. It usually drops suddenly around sunset. Winds often curve round the coasts of the islands.

It should be noted that when there is a high pressure system over northern Europe, a low pressure system may come barrelling through the Straits of Gibraltar before heading northeast towards Corsica and the Ligurian Sea, sometimes stalling for a few days and bringing wet and windy weather to the Islas Baleares.

The winds in the Mediterranean have been given names dependent on their direction and characteristics. Those which affect this area are detailed below.

Winds

Northwest *Tramontana*

This wind, also known as the *mestral* or *maestral* near Río Ebro and the mistral in France, is a strong, dry wind, cold in winter, which can be dangerous. It is caused by a secondary depression forming in the Golfe du Lion or the Golfo di Génova on the cold front of a major depression crossing France. The northwesterly airflow generated is compressed between the Alps and the Pyrenees and flows into the Mediterranean basin. In Spain it chiefly affects the coast to the north of Barcelona, the Islas Baleares, and is strongest at the latitude of the northern end of the Costa Brava.

The *tramontana* can be dangerous in that it can arrive and reach gale force in as little as 15 minutes on a calm sunny day, with virtually no warning. Signs to watch for are brilliant visibility (sometimes two or three days in advance of a storm), clear sky – often with cigar-shaped clouds, very dry air and a steady or slightly rising barometer. On rare occasions the sky may be cloudy when the wind first arrives, although it clears later. Sometimes the barometer will plunge in normal fashion, rising quickly after the gale has passed. If at sea and some way from land, a line of white on the horizon and a developing swell give a few minutes' warning. The only effective warning that can be obtained is by radio – Marseille (in French) and Monaco (in French and English) are probably the best.

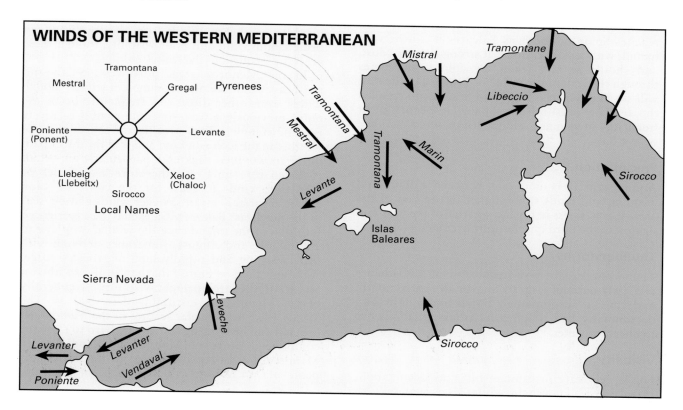

WINDS OF THE WESTERN MEDITERRANEAN

Local Names (compass): Tramontana, Mestral, Gregal, Pyrenees, Poniente (Ponent), Levante, Llebeig (Llebeitx), Sirocco, Xeloc (Chaloc)

Mistral, Tramontane, Libeccio, Tramontana, Mestral, Marin, Levante, Sirocco, Islas Baleares, Leveche, Sierra Nevada, Levanter, Vendaval, Poniente

The *tramontana* normally blows for at least three days and, on occasions, may last for a week or longer. It is very frequent in the winter months, blowing for a third of the time, and on occasions can reach Force 10 (50 knots) or above. In summer it is neither as frequent nor as strong, although it can still make untenable most parts of the north coast of Menorca.

West *Vendaval*

A depression crossing Spain or southern France creates a strong southwest to west wind, the vendaval or *poniente*, which funnels through the Strait of Gibraltar and along the south coast of Spain. Though normally confined to the south and southeast coasts, it occasionally blows in the northeast of the area. It is usually short-lived and at its strongest from late autumn to early spring.

East *Levante*

Encountered from Gibraltar to Valencia and beyond, the easterly *levante*, sometimes called the *llevantade* when it blows at gale force, is caused by a depression located between the Islas Baleares and the North African coast. It is preceded by a heavy swell *(las tascas)*, cold damp air, poor visibility and low cloud which forms first around the higher hills. Heavy and prolonged rainfall is more likely in spring and autumn than summer. A *levante* may last for three or four days or more. It is usually preceded two or three days in advance by brilliantly clear weather and the formation of cigar or huge layered saucer-shaped clouds.

South *Sirocco*

The hot wind from the south is created by a depression moving east along or just south of the North African coast. By the time this dry wind reaches Spain or the Islas Baleares it can be very humid, with haze and cloud. If strong it carries dust, and should it rain when the cold front comes through the water may be red or brown and the dust will set like cement. This wind is sometimes called the *leveche* in southeast Spain. It occurs most frequently in summer, seldom lasting more than one or two days.

Precipitation

Annual rainfall is moderate, between 450mm and 500mm, and tends to be higher in the east of the area. It is heaviest in the last quarter of the year and lightest in the third quarter: July averages 4–5mm.

Thunderstorms

Thunderstorms are most frequent in the late summer and early autumn – up to four or five each month, and can be accompanied by strong squalls and occasionally hail. High level cumulus clouds are frequent in winter.

Visibility

Fog is very rare in summer but may occur about three times a month in winter. It is generally in relatively narrow banks and burns off very quickly. On occasions dust carried by the southerly *sirocco* can reduce visibility (and make an awful mess of your deck!).

Temperature

Temperatures drop to around 10–15°C in winter, rising steadily after March to around 20°C or more in Spring. Afternoon temperatures frequently reach 30–33°C in the summer, with occasional days higher, most likely in late July and early August. The usual afternoon sea breeze keeps the temperature from reaching mainland highs of around 40°C, although this level was seen over some weeks in the great heat surge experienced by most Mediterranean countries in 2017.

Humidity

With winds from west, northwest, north and south relatively low humidity is the norm. An easterly levante wind brings with it high humidity, often around 95%. The relative humidity increases throughout the night and falls by day.

Local weather in the Islas Baleares

The southwestern area is influenced by the weather over mainland Spain – winds are variable but, in general, those from the southeast semicircle prevail in summer and those from the northwest in winter. Gales are rare in summer (though sudden short term squalls are becoming increasingly common), but may blow for 5–10% of the time in winter. These are generally the result of a *tramontana*, though they may blow from anywhere between west through north to northeast. Winds from the southeast can bring clouds, rain and poor visibility, though these are more frequent in the winter months.

In the Menorca area, northwest, north and northeast winds are most common in winter, though winds from other directions frequently occur. As noted previously, a westerly component is relatively rare in summer. This area is influenced by the weather in the Golfe du Lion and is in the direct path of the *tramontana*, making it particularly important to listen to regular weather forecasts. Gales or increased winds forecast for the Golfe du Lion almost invariably mean stronger winds and big seas in the northeast Baleares. Gales may be experienced for 10% of the time during the winter, dropping to 2% in July and August, sometimes arriving with little warning and rapidly building to gale force. Although there is more rain than in the southwest sector of the archipelago, visibility is generally better. Menorca is justifiably described as 'The Windy Isle.' A particular feature of the *tramontana* is that it can be blowing sufficiently hard to close the commercial ports of Mahón and Ciudadela in Menorca, but by ten miles west of the Formentor peninsula on Mallorca there is little or no wind,

Andraitx sunset from the anchorage SE of the entrance *Graham Hutt*

protection presumably being created by the alignment of the Costa Brava.

Throughout the area, in calm weather a sea breeze (*brisa de mar*) will be experienced near the coast, blowing more strongly where it is channelled into a large bay such as the Bahías de Palma, Pollensa or Alcudia. It usually gets up at around 1300, is at its maximum between 1500 and 1600 and drops towards dusk. It can reach Force 5 (20 knots) or more at times. In spite of its name it seldom blows directly onshore – more often at 45° to the coast or even parallel to it.

A land breeze is sometimes present during the latter half of the night and lasts until the sun has had time to warm the land. This breeze can be quite strong where there are valleys leading inland.

Precipitation and visibility

Annual rainfall at Palma averages 460mm, the wettest period being October to December. Fog sometimes occurs in winter but is almost unknown in summer.

Weather forecasts

It should be noted that visual signs and methods of forecasting using clouds and barometer, as is usual in Northern Europe, usually do not give the same indications in the Mediterranean. This is more noticeable as you travel east from the Strait of Gibraltar. It is common to see a fast falling or rising barometer, with no resulting change in conditions. Similarly, cloud formations that would normally indicate rain or storms approaching, often clear in minutes, leaving blue skies. Sudden winds or squalls can appear very quickly without any warning whatsoever and from a clear sky. The good news is that these unannounced changes are normally short-lived.

See *Appendix* for a glossary of Spanish meteorological terms.

Radio and other weather forecasts

Details of coast radio stations, weather forecasts, Weatherfax and Navtex follow. See individual harbour details for port and marina radio information. All times quoted are UT (universal time) unless otherwise specified. Only France Inter, Radio France International, BBC Radio 4 and one of the two Monaco stations observe local time (LT), thus altering the UT transmission times when the clocks change.

VHF radio weather forecasts in english and spanish

Throughout the Baleares Islands, weather information is given for your local area approximately every 2 hours (though often late). After the call on VHF Ch 16: 'All ships, all ships, all ships,' a list of channels for each local area is given directing you to your nearest local coastal weather information centre. Most broadcasts are in English, followed by Spanish.

From Menorca eastwards, the Italian military weather station 'Meteomar' can be picked up on VHF Ch 68. This gives continual 24 hour weather information alternating in English and Italian for the area from the Balkans to France and the Spanish mainland, including the Baleares. Once accustomed to the nomenclature and system, this is one of the best stations, with regular updates and good outlook forecasts, covering 48 hours split into 6 hour intervals. Early warning of a possible Tramontana (a strong N gale), is also given.

French and English forecasts can also be heard around the S Baleares from the Algerian coastal stations approximately every 2 hours and notified on Ch 16 with 'Pan, Pan, Pan.'

Non-radio weather forecasts

A forecast in Spanish can be obtained from the airport Met Office on each island (ask for *meteorologia*). The pre-recorded weather phone service has been superceded by an excellent web service at www.aemet.es, the easy to read pictorial page being fast to download.

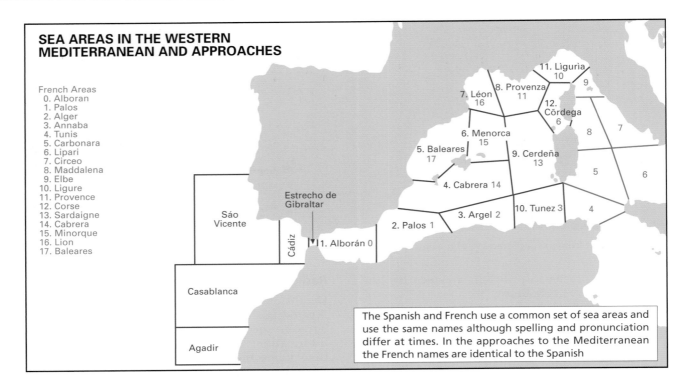

SEA AREAS IN THE WESTERN MEDITERRANEAN AND APPROACHES

French Areas
0. Alboran
1. Palos
2. Alger
3. Annaba
4. Tunis
5. Carbonara
6. Lipari
7. Circeo
8. Maddalena
9. Elbe
10. Ligure
11. Provence
12. Corse
13. Sardaigne
14. Cabrera
15. Minorque
16. Lion
17. Baleares

The Spanish and French use a common set of sea areas and use the same names although spelling and pronunciation differ at times. In the approaches to the Mediterranean the French names are identical to the Spanish

An excellent forecast is given on all Spanish TV channels following the main morning and evening news. This is produced by the meteorological department of the Spanish military and is generally accurate. Channel TV1 gives best coverage with a full synoptic forecast, wind direction and 3-day outlook. News broadcast times vary depending on which channel is used and the length of the preceding adverts. Most national and local newspapers also carry some form of forecast.

Most marinas and yacht harbours display a synoptic chart and/or a forecast, generally updated daily (though often posted rather late to be of use if you want to get away early). Additionally they often display a forecast for several days ahead from either Windfinder or Windguru, although this forecast will be for the specific location of the marina or harbour.

Weatherfax

Rome broadcast weatherfax transmissions covering the Islas Baleares and suitable for reception via SSB

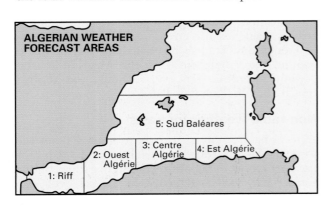

ALGERIAN WEATHER FORECAST AREAS

5: Sud Baléares
2: Ouest Algérie
3: Centre Algérie
4: Est Algérie
1: Riff

and computer or dedicated weatherfax receiver. Refer to the *Admiralty List of Radio Signals Vol 3 Part 1* (NP 283(1)) for times and frequencies.

Navtex

Navtex is transmitted on the standard frequency of 518kHz. The Mediterranean and Black Sea fall within NAVAREA III.

Valencia (Cabo de la Nao), Spain (Identification letter X)
Weather messages: 0750, 1950 (gale warnings, synopsis and 24-hr forecast, in English, for areas 8–12).
Navigational warnings: 0350, 0750, 1150, 1550, 1950, 2350 in English, for the Mediterranean coast of Spain and Islas Baleares.
La Garde (CROSS), France (Identification letter W)
Storm warnings: On receipt and at 0340, 0740, 1140, 1540, 1940, 2340, in English, for areas 14 (eastern part) 13, 6, 8, 9 and 10.
Weather messages: 1140, 2340 (gale or storm warnings, synopsis and 24-hr forecast, in English, for areas 514 eastern part-523, 531-534): see diagram for areas covered.
Navigational warnings: in English, for the northwestern Mediterranean only.

Internet weather forecasts and GRIB files

Grib files are low resolution (fast to download) weather data files suitable for all computers from desktops to Android mobile phones. They are excellent, and when viewed via a GRIB viewer app they are easy to interpret and can give long range information as well as current local information. Many apps have been developed specifically for mobile phone use and most are free.

Many hundreds of internet weather sites exist for all areas of the world. Most skippers will be familiar with sites and will have their own favourites. However, for those new to it, here is a start:

www.aemet.es/es/eltiempo/prediccion/maritima
Select the area (Baleares Islands)

www.eltiempo.es/viento/ Excellent fast loading site with 2 and 3 day forecast of Baleares

www.windfinder.com English site with wind up to 7 days, precipitation and swell forecasts

www.passageweather.com As above, but more in-depth analysis

www.windguru.cz select any port

www.weatheronline.co.uk Sailing forecast under 'sports'

www.predictwind.com Dramatically coloured wind arrow display, 3 months free

www.accuweather.com Contains an hour-by-hour forecast which is sometimes useful for short-term planning, but of course of doubtful value beyond perhaps 36 hours)

The latter three forecasts are favoured by the authors with aemet also being useful.

Inmarsat

Broadcast times for weather for METAREA III are 1000 and 2200.

SEA CONDITIONS

Currents

The current around the islands normally sets southeast, south or southwest at a rate of 0·5–1 knot, though stronger in the channels between them and off promontories. Its direction and strength can also be modified by the effects of strong or prolonged winds, those from the south tending to reduce or reverse the current and those from the north increasing the rate of flow.

Tides

Even at springs, tidal range is less than 0·3m, so can be disregarded. Sea level is more affected by the strength, direction and duration of winds and by variations in barometric pressure. In general, winds from the north combined with high pressure cause a fall in sea level and those from the south with low pressure cause a rise in the level. In addition, the levels in harbours or *calas* facing an onshore wind will be higher than in those experiencing offshore winds.

Even with these factors, the range of sea level is most unlikely to exceed 1m, other than during a phenomenon known as *resaca* or *seiche*. This occurs rarely: usually when a depression and spring tide coincide. This causes a rise and fall of sea level by as much as 1·5m every ten or fifteen minutes; an oscillation which may last for several days. *Resaca* most often affects Puerto de Ciudadela, Menorca and the deeply indented harbours and *calas* on the southeast coast of Mallorca, but has also been experienced as far west as Puerto de Arenal in the Bahía de Palma.

For interest, an earthquake during 2004 in Al Hocïema, Morocco, 400 miles away, caused a lot of damage in several marinas in the islands. Advance warning was given – though few understood its significance – when some harbours, most notably Mahón, suddenly dried out. The resultant surge of incoming water half an hour later was traumatic, leaving some boats several hundred metres inland and many trapped under pontoons.

Swell

Swell is not usually a major problem in summer: winds are local and form a daily pattern of sea or land breezes, dropping at sunset. However, there are occasional gales which can quickly whip up high steep seas, though these usually are short lived. In early 2005, a large passenger ferry encountered 40-foot seas between Menorca and Corsica and sustained severe damage when the bridge windows were smashed and electrics disabled, but these conditions are rare. In July and August periods of flat calms are more often experienced. Swell from any direction can affect the Islas Baleares, and particularly the *cala* anchorages. A gale in the Golfe du Lion – common in winter – is likely to send a north or northeast swell of up to 2m down into the islands, possibly before the wind itself arrives. Northwest to east winds can set in for days, making the north and east facing *calas* uncomfortable. It is advisable to monitor swell forecasts, which are now readily available on many of the weather websites.

Scouring and silting

In passages and anchorages where the bottom is of loose sand, depths may change due to the effects of rainfall and wind.

Sea temperature

Sea temperature ranges from around 14°C in February to 25°C or even low 30s in some places in August. Winds from the south and east tend to raise the temperature and those from the west and north to lower it.

Waterspouts

Waterspouts may occasionally be encountered, usually in spring and autumn, usually near promontories and often associated with thunderstorms.

FLORA AND FAUNA ON THE ISLANDS

Much as on the Spanish mainland, pine trees and lavender can be smelled from miles offshore. Olive trees, honesuckle and several species of orchid abound. *Adelfa* (oleander) grow well in riverbeds, bringing colour throughout the summer season.

Birds

The Audouins Gull (rare elsewhere) can often be seen, particularly at San Antonio (Ibiza), Puerto de Andraitx, Puerto de Pollensa and Porto Colom

(Mallorca), around Cabrera, and Mahón (Menorca). They are somewhat smaller than herring gulls, and have a large red beak with black tip and dark legs. Viewed from below in flight, the wingtips appear considerably blacker than those of a herring gull. The cry is a nasal 'gee-ow'. Herring gulls are common (though with yellow legs rather than the pink of their northern relatives), together with shearwaters and many land birds.

Birds of prey such as osprey and both species of peregrine and the very rare Eleanora's falcon favour the more wild and rocky stretches, including parts of Mallorca's north coast and that of the Cabrera group. Several species of owl, eagles, hawks and kites and the rare black vulture can be seen on the Formentor peninsula ridges. Bee-eaters are found in sandy areas. There are many hoopoes, said to be the only bird in the world for which there is only one species. Their name reflects their call 'hoo, hoo, hoo'.

The Albufera Nature Reserve, 4km south of Alcudia, is home to many rare waders and other water birds; a visit is recommended (and it is free!).

The publication *Essential Mallorca, Ibiza and Menorca* includes a particularly interesting section entitled 'Countryside and Wildlife on the Balearic Islands', detailing bird migration as well as the flora and fauna of the various habitats.

Animals

Sheep, goats, ferrets, rabbits and horses are found throughout the islands and, though seldom seen, there are many pine-martens too. A rare frog-ferret can be found only on Formentor, Mallorca. Several different species of lizard abound on the islands, some being rare or non-existent elsewhere. Menorca is renowned for its dairy herds and its cheeses are in great demand throughout Spain.

Marine life

Several parts of the islands have been declared nature reserves and fishing is not permitted in those areas. This has done a lot to preserve fish stocks. Tuna and dolphins are often seen, along with grouper and sunfish. Whale sightings include fin whales, as well as the more common pilot whales.

NAVIGATIONAL INFORMATION

Buoyage

Buoys in the Baleares adhere to the IALA A system, based on the direction of the main flood tide. Yellow-topped black or red rusty buoys some 500m offshore mark raw sewage outlets.

Yellow or white buoys in line mark the seaward side of areas reserved for swimming. Narrow lanes for water-skiing and sailboarding, also buoyed, may lead out from the shore.

Harbour traffic signals

Traffic signals are rare, and in any case are designed for commercial traffic and seldom apply to yachts.

Storm signals

The signal stations at major ports and harbours may show storm signals, but many do not. With minor exceptions they are similar to the International System of Visual Storm Warnings.

Lights

The four-figure international numbering system has been used to identify lights in the text and on plans, the Mediterranean falling into Group E. As each light has its own number, correcting from Notices to Mariners or the annual *List of Lights and Fog Signals*, whether in Spanish or English, is straightforward.

Positions correspond to the largest-scale British Admiralty chart of the area currently available. All bearings are given from seaward and refer to true north. Where a visibility sector is stated this is always expressed in a clockwise direction.

Harbour lights, which in the Islas Baleares adhere to the IALA A system, are normally listed in the order in which they become relevant upon approach and entry.

Radio beacons

Many radio beacons are no longer maintained. Since the accuracy of GPS – even given the cautions below – is well above that which can be derived from radio beacons, this information is no longer included.

Depths around harbour entrances

Depths where known are shown on the harbour plans. It should be noted, however, that these can and do change, especially following onshore gales and if harbour entrances are open towards the prevailing wind sector. It also applies near rivers. Although most ports and harbours are dredged, there is no certainty about the depth to which dredging has taken place or when it was last done. Always proceed with caution, paying attention to the depth sounder on entry to any harbour and, if in doubt, call the marina or port authority to establish the likely depths.

Location coordinates

The World Geodetic System 1984 is now the standard datum for all new charts and is used for all coordinates throughout this volume. Apply the appropriate correction as stated on your chart, if necessary.

Positions given in the text and on plans are intended purely as an aid to locating the place in question on your chart if necessary.

Magnetic variation

Magnetic variation throughout the Baleares is less than 001°E.

Charts

Current British Admiralty information is mostly obtained from Spanish sources. The Spanish Hydrographic Office re-issues and corrects its charts periodically, and issues weekly *Notices to Mariners*. Corrections are repeated by the British Admiralty, generally some months later. Spanish charts tend to be short on compass roses, so carry a chart plotter or rule which incorporates a protractor.

Before departure

Spanish charts can be obtained through certain British agents, notably:

Imray Laurie Norie & Wilson Ltd
    ☎ +44 (0)1480 462114
    www.imray.com

Orders can be made direct from:

Instituto Hidrográfico de la Marina, Cádiz
    ☎ +34 956 59 94 12
    www.armada.mde.es
Suisca SL, Algeciras
    ☎ +34 902 22 00 7
    admiraltycharts@ suiscasl.com

In Spain and the Islas Baleares

The only British Admiralty chart agent in the Islas Baleares is:

Rapid Transit Service SL, Network Yacht Team,
    Edificio Torremar, Paseo Marítimo, 44 – 07015,
    Palma de Mallorca ☎ 971 40 12 10
    charts@rapidtrans.com

In Mallorca, Spanish charts are stocked by:

Libreria Fondevila, C/Costa de las Pols 18, Palma
    ☎ 971 72 56 16
Libreria del Náutico, Aragon 28, Bajo, Palma
    ☎ 971 90 90 60
    www.libreriadelnáutico.com

Listing of a chart under both *Approach* and *Harbour* headings normally implies that a large-scale harbour plan appears as an insert on a smaller-scale approach chart. Information on available charts is included in the *Appendix*.

Pilot books

Details of principal harbours and some interesting background information appear in the British Admiralty Hydrographic Department's *Mediterranean Pilot Vol 1 (NP45)*.

PRESENTATION OF INFORMATION

Chart spellings, nomenclature and language

Charts and pilots are inconsistent in their spellings. Names appear in Castillano, French, Catalan and English, often mixed or transliterated on the same chart.

An attempt has been made to standardise spellings to appear in Castillano Spanish form where possible with local alternatives in brackets. Where there is no Castillano form, the local name is used.

Many enterprises, including marinas, use different nomenclature to describe themselves. So, 'Puerto, Puerta and Port' can all be found along with 'Marina'. Since these are commercially registered names, these have been used. Many marine commercial enterprises are not quite what they seem. Several 'Marinas' are no more than a pontoon or two, with few facilities other than water and electricity. Some open beaches or *calas* (bays or coves) are also titled harbour, puerto or even sometimes, marina. To avoid confusion, since these are official names, they are named likewise here regardless of what they offer.

Words used to describe nautical locations are also variable, depending on which chart is used and even within the same chart. A cape may be called a 'point, punto, punta, pta, cabo, c', etc. As with island, which may be isl, isla, isloto, islota, islote, the title used is as per the chart.

Bearings are true and from seaward. Depths are in metres.

Information layout

Port information for each island begins at the relevant main port, Palma de Mallorca, Puerto de Ibiza, Puerto de Sabina and Mahón, and moves in a clockwise direction around the island. With excellent international airports located close to these ports (except Sabina), this will be a natural starting point for the many who charter from, or keep their yachts in the islands.

Harbour information

Co-ordinates of ports are usually located in the approach well clear of the harbour entrance but sufficiently close to enable recognition (see *Caution* on *page iv*). These should not be taken as waypoints.

Prices for harbour dues and hauling out etc are usually available on websites. Where known, web addresses and or email contacts are included.

Positions and waypoints

Waypoints have been discontinued in this edition as they are unnecessary with modern navigational systems which permit navigators to define their preferred routes and clearance margins easily and accurately. Locations, which are to datum WGS84, are retained as an aid to recognition.

Co-ordinates are given to the nearest decimal point of a minute and have been placed so that they are sufficiently close to the featured location to enable recognition. Typically they are in the mouth of a bay or *cala* or sufficiently close to a harbour or marina entrance that the destination is obvious, but far enough away that a different charting system does not show them inland. They have been established using a Navionics electronic chart which may present differences with other charting systems.

These location co-ordinates should not, of course, solely be relied upon for safe navigation.

PLANNING YOUR CRUISE

Time zone

Spain keeps Standard European Time (UT+1), advanced one hour in summer to UT+2 hours. Changeover dates are now standardised with the rest of the EU as the last weekends in March and October respectively.

Budgeting and finance

Though the islands are not cheap if harbours and marinas are used, most anchorages are free and reasonably cheap eating places can be found everywhere ashore. A Spanish custom, written into law, is that every restaurant must offer a *menu del dia* (lunch at a reasonable price). This is often a substantial meal with a set menu for, typically, €8–€18, including wine. This law goes back to the Franco era when the country was poor. There are many excellent restaurants and the islands' facilities cater for cruising yachtsmen on a tight budget as much as to those on superyachts, the latter abounding in places like Palma and Puerto Portals.

Credit and debit cards can be used almost everywhere to draw cash from banks on presentation of a passport and are almost always acceptable for payments in shops and restaurants. ATM machines are fitted in most banks. Some banks make high charges for use of their ATMs and it is worth checking whether your own bank card issuer has an arrangement with one of the Spanish ATM networks, of which the two most common are Telebanco and Servired. Travellers cheques are taken in most banks. Cash in Dollars or Pounds Sterling is acceptable almost everywhere in banks and in some shops. €500 notes are not always accepted due to the prevalence of counterfeit notes or the difficulty of giving sufficient change.

The unit of currency is the Euro. Bank hours are normally 0830 to 1400, Monday to Friday, with a few also open 0830 to 1300 on Saturday.

Medical advice

Vaccinations are not required. Take along any personal medicines or enquire about generic availability abroad via the internet. Many drugs normally restricted in the UK are available in Spain without prescription.

Though not a requirement, limited health insurance can be inexpensive and many yacht insurance policies include health over for crew, particularly in the event of injury while on board. This can include repatriation to your home country for treatment.

Minor ailments may best be treated by consulting a *farmacía*, or by contacting a doctor (recommended by the *farmacía*, marina staff, a tourist office, the police or possibly a hotel). Medicines generally are not expensive in Spain and often have different brand names from those used in Britain.

Apart from precautions against the well-recognized hazards of sunburn and stomach upsets, heat exhaustion (or heat stroke) is most likely to affect newly joined crew not yet acclimatised to Mediterranean temperatures. Carry Dioralyte or similar to counteract dehydration, and of course drink lots of water. Insect deterrents, including mosquito coils, can be obtained locally.

Emergency medical treatment for EU/EEA nationals

The European Health Insurance card (EHIC) should always be carried - check that is still in valid date. This facilitates reduced cost or free emergency medical treatment under a reciprocal agreement between the countries of the EEA which in 2017 include the 28 EU member states plus Iceland, Norway and Lichtenstein. The card is not an alternative to travel insurance. If you are an EU/EEA national and qualify for a card, which is free, apply via the websites below:

www.gov.uk/european-health-insurance-card

www.ehic.org.uk/Internet/startApplication.do

If you're from the UK, EEA or Switzerland you can also apply by post or by phoning an automated service ☎ 0300 330 1350.

For further details of Spanish medical protocols and emergency treatment search the nhs.uk webpage.

For further advice, contact the Overseas Healthcare Team at the Department of Work and Pensions:

Overseas Healthcare Team
Room MO601, Durham House
Washington
Tyne & Wear
NE38 7SF

☎ 0191 218 1999

Medical emergency telephone numbers are ☎ 112 and ☎ 061. If you have an EHIC card, be sure to inform the medical authorities of this when first contacting them for emergency treatment or you may have to pay full private rates which might not not be reimbursed.

It is not yet known how Brexit might affect medical insurance but there is unlikely to be any change before 2021. Check the latest before travel.

CRUISING THE ISLANDS

The whole island chain is a suitable cruising ground, though some areas have restricted access having been declared conservation zones in which anchoring is forbidden. For example the island of Cabrera is one such zone where buoys have been laid which must be used in lieu of anchoring. These zones are noted on the plans.

Anchorages

One of the main charms of the island has been the large number of attractive *cala* anchorages, although many are often crowded in summer. A down-sun approach using eyeball navigation with a lookout on the bow, equipped with Polaroid sunglasses greatly assists anchoring. Note that most of the anchorage plans (as opposed to those of marinas and commercial harbours) are derived from observation and virtually no official data is available and therefore depths, shapes, distances, etc. should be taken as approximate. Many popular anchorages are grossly overcrowded from late morning to early evening in the peak summer period but then become peaceful overnight when most motorboats and many local yachts return to their nearby home ports.

Over recent years, many *calas* have been wholly or partly closed off by a line of buoys to define areas reserved for swimmers and even where the *cala* is

Harbours of refuge

The following harbours and anchorages can be entered in severe weather, albeit with some difficulty.

IBIZA
Puerto de Ibiza
Puerto de San Antonio

MALLORCA
Puerto de Palma
Puerto Portals
Puerto de Andraitx
Puerto de Sóller
Anchorage NW of Punta de la Avanzada, Bahía de Pollensa
Puerto de Alcudia
Porto Colom
Cala Llonga

CABRERA
Puerto de Cabrera (other than in a northwesterly gale)

MENORCA
Puerto de Mahón
Puerto de Fornells
Puerto de Ciudadela (except in a southwestly or westerly gale)

Many other harbours and anchorages can safely be entered in strong offshore winds and even gales, and even more provide excellent shelter from most directions once inside.

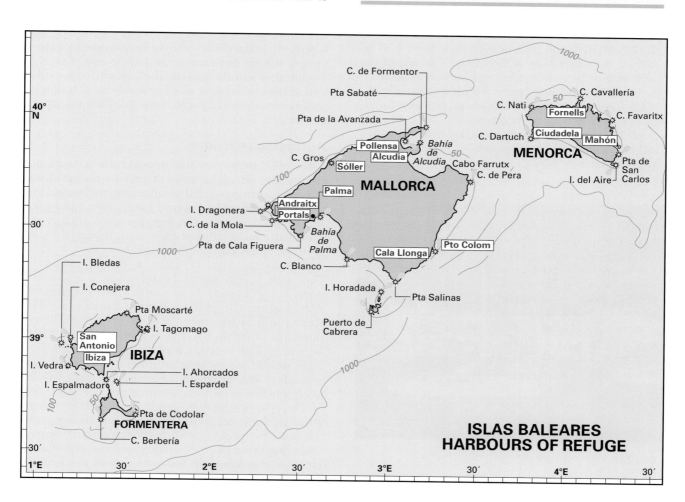

ISLAS BALEARES
HARBOURS OF REFUGE

only partly closed yachts are in consequence forced out into deeper and perhaps less sheltered water. Also, in many anchorages buoys have been laid to protect the posidonia sea-grass (*see page 21*). There is an extant proposal (2017) before the Balearic Islands Parliament to place buoys in a further 33 anchorages, the list being as follows:-

Ibiza and Formentera Puerto de San Miguel, Portinatx, Tagomago, Coneja Island, Sant Antoni Abad, Trocador, Rocabella, Estany des Peix, and *Calas* San Vicente, Pada, Moli, Bassa, and Saona.

Mallorca Puerto Portals, Magaluf, Las Illetas, Cala Mondrago, Pollensa, Camp de Mar, Andratx, Portals Vells, Santa Ponsa and Sóller.

Menorca *Calas* Alghaiarens, Pregonda, Caldés, Addaya, Es Grau, Arenal d'en Castell, Mitjana, Macarella, plus Isla del Aire.

The selection of anchorages is rather strange as it includes some which have little or no posidonia, others which have some posidonia but also large areas of sand, and some which are so small as to be barely worth bothering with! However, if the principle is applied sensibly to avoid anchoring on posidonia, whilst permitting free anchoring on sand, then there is no real basis for complaint. A good example of this approach is the anchoring area between Isla Colom and the mainland of Menorca. Some thirty buoys have been laid in a posidonia area down the western side of Isla Colom and several in the mouth of Cala Tamarells d'es Sud. In the inner part of this *cala* and the whole of Cala Tamarells d'es Nord, conservation area buoys have been laid to indicate that anchoring is forbidden. The rest of the large area of predominately sand bottom in between the island and the mainland is left for free anchoring.

Charges for the use of buoys can be substantial, €30 or more not being uncommon.

Effectively, anchoring on sea grass is now banned and heavy fines can be imposed on yachts doing so (*see Posidonia on page 21*).

Andraitx. Moorings now laid in the outer harbour
Graham Hutt

A number of *calas* have more than one name, both naturally and as a function of language (Castillano, Catalan/Menorquin/Mallorquin/Ibiceno) and each name within the local language may have more than one spelling. Popular names, such as Cala Figuera, crop up several times.

The weather in the Islas Baleares can be unexpectedly changeable and can deteriorate very quickly. During the day the sea breeze can be strong, especially if there is a valley at the head of an anchorage. Similarly a strong land breeze can flow down a valley in the early hours of the morning. If anchored near the head of a *cala* backed by a river valley, should there be a thunderstorm or heavy downpour in the hills above, take precautions against the flood of water and debris which will descend into the *cala*. Thunderstorms are most common in late summer and early autumn and as well as heavy rain may bring fierce squalls and violent wind-shifts.

Many *cala* anchorages suffer from swell even when not open to its apparent direction. This is because swell tends to run along the coast, curling around all but the most prominent headlands into the *cala* behind. Wash from boats entering and leaving, as well as from larger vessels passing outside, adds to the discomfort. If considering a second anchor or a line ashore in order to hold the yacht into the swell, first calculate the swinging room required by yachts on single anchors should the wind change.

In a high-sided *cala*, winds are often fluky and a sudden blow, even from the land, may make departure difficult. Plans for a swift and orderly exit – possibly in darkness – should be considered, even if simply noting the course for a clear exit. Exposed anchorages should only be used in settled weather and left in good time if swell or wind rise. It is unwise to leave an anchored yacht unattended for any length of time.

Anchoring technique

Choice of anchor: many popular anchorages are thoroughly ploughed up each year by the hundreds of anchors dropped and weighed by visiting yachts. Others are of weed-covered compacted sand and, not without reason, the four-pronged grab is the favourite anchor of local fishermen, though difficult to stow. A fisherman-type anchor is easier to stow and a useful ally. If using a patent anchor – Danforth, CQR, Bruce, Fortress, etc. – an anchor weight (or Chum) is a worthwhile investment, encouraging the pull to remain horizontal. The Rocna and Spade anchors have been particularly noted as suitable for the conditions around the Baleares. The Fortress has the advantage of very light weight for its strength, making it useful as a secondary anchor which is easy to row out. A Delta anchor is fine in most circumstances.

Once in a suitable depth of water, if clarity permits, look for a weed-free patch to drop the anchor. In rocky or otherwise suspect areas, including those likely to contain wrecks, old chains, etc., use a sinking trip line with a float (an inviting buoy may be picked up by another yacht). For overnight anchoring, chain scope should be at least four times the maximum depth of water measured from the bow rather than waterline; for nylon scope double this. It is always worth setting the anchor by reversing slowly until it holds, but on a hard or compacted bottom this must be done very gently in order to give the anchor a chance to bite – over-enthusiasm with the throttle will cause it to skip without digging in.

Rescue and emergency services

In addition to VHF Ch 16 or 2182kHz on MW (MAYDAY or PAN PAN as appropriate) the marine emergency services can be contacted at all times on ☎ 900 202 202. Note that a recorded message in Spanish invites you to leave a message stating the nature of your emergency and your telephone number and that they will reply immediately (in practice within up to ten minutes).

The National Centre for Sea Rescue is based in Madrid but has a string of communications towers, including one at Palma, Mallorca. On-the-spot responsibility for co-ordinating rescues lies with the Capitanías Marítimas with support from the Spanish Navy, Customs, Guardia Civil, etc. Lifeboats are stationed at some of the larger harbours but not all appear to be all-weather boats.

The other emergency services can be contacted by dialling 003 for the operator and asking for *policía* (police), *bomberos* (fire service) or *Cruz Roja* (Red Cross). Alternatively the police can be contacted direct on 091.

Sea rescue/Rescate en alta mar emergency Salvamento notes

Search, rescue and salvage services at sea, as well as clean-up operations and the prevention of pollution, are undertaken by the National Society for Maritime Rescue and Safety (Salvamento y Seguridad Marítima: SASEMAR). SASEMAR is co-ordinated by joint collaboration agreements between the following bodies: The Spanish Navy, the Air Force SAR service – the Customs Coastguard Service, the Guardia Civil Maritime Services, the regional governments, the national telephone company's Maritime Service and the Spanish Red Cross.

SASEMAR works in close collaboration with the coastal stations of each town around the coast. These are equipped with rescue launches, 15m and 20m rapid intervention craft, small sized antipollution craft and rescue helicopters.

Anyone on shore who sees a boat in difficulties (signalling by waving arms or setting off flares, smoke or fire, etc.) should report to the appropriate rescue centre by calling Freephone ☎ 900 202 202 (*see note above*).

Persons on board a ship in distress should radio for help on VHF Ch 16 or 2182kHz on MW. The correct procedure in Spanish is as follows:

1. MAYDAY … MAYDAY … MAYDAY …
2. AQUI LA EMBARCACION … (The name of your boat repeated three times)
3. ESTA EN LA SITUACION … (Give your position) or ME ENCUENTRO A … MILLAS DE … (Give position as regards distance in miles or in journey time from any given point) Una (1), dos, tres, cuatro, cinco, seis, siete, ocho, nueve, diez (10))
4. NECESITO AYUDA URGENTE A CAUSA DE … (Indicate nature of emergency)
   fire – *tengo fuego en mi barco*
   sinking – *mi barco esta hundimiento*
   man overboard – *hombre en agua*
   medical emergency – *urgencia medical*

The rescue centres lay particular emphasis on proper preparation as the best means of avoiding dangerous situations. It is essential to have the correct equipment, to have the necessary skill and experience, and to keep informed about weather conditions.

Palma Sea rescue centre ☎ 971 728322 / 722011.

HAZARDS

Restricted areas

Anchoring and fishing is banned in the following areas due to submerged cables: Cala de Puerto Roig, Punta Grosa and north of Isla Vedrá in Ibiza, south of Cabo de Pera on the east coast of Mallorca and off Cabo Dartuch in southwest Menorca. Spanish naval vessels and submarines exercise around Isla de Cabrera and in the Bahía de Pollensa, Mallorca. There are also several marine reserves around the islands which are restricted areas. Information about these can be found at www.magrama.gob.es/.

Night approaches

Approaches in darkness are often made more difficult by the plethora of background lights – fixed, flashing, occulting, interrupted – of all colours. Though there may be exceptions, this applies to nearly all harbours backed by a town of any size. Powerful shore lights make weaker navigation lights difficult to identify and mask unlit features such as exposed rocks or the line of a jetty. If at all possible, avoid closing an unknown harbour in darkness. A particular hazard is the green flashing light of the local pharmacy, which can be very confusing, as can the yellow strobe of a refuse vehicle…personal experience!

Skylines

Individual buildings on these developing islands, particularly prominent hotel blocks, do change with surprising frequency.

Swimming areas

Many *calas* and beaches have large areas from the shoreline roped and buoyed off during the summer. These areas are exclusion zones for all vessels and large penalties are extracted in fines for crossing them. They may be sufficiently extensive effectively to close *calas* to anchoring vessels. Often a marked channel is left for beach launched pedalos, dinghies, jet skis etc. to operate and these channels may also serve to enable a yacht's tender to access the beach area.

Tunny nets

In the past during summer and autumn, these nets anchored to the sea bed and up to six miles long, were a substantial hazard to yachts. Due to dwindling fish stocks and conservation zones, they no longer seem to be a problem around the Baleares Islands.

Commercial fishing boats

Commercial fishing boats should be given a wide berth. They may be:

- trawling singly or in pairs with a net between the boats
- laying a long net, the top of which is supported by floats
- picking up or laying pots either singly or in groups or lines
- trolling with one or more lines out astern
- drifting, trailing nets to windward.

Do not assume they know, or will observe, the law of the sea – keep well clear on principle.

Small fishing boats

Small fishing boats, including the traditional double-ended *llauts*, either use nets or troll with lines astern and should be avoided as far as possible. At night many fishing boats use powerful electric or gas lights, to attract fish to the surface. When seen from a distance these lights appear to flash as the boat moves up and down in the waves and can give the appearance of a lighthouse.

Speedboats, etc.

Paragliding, water skiing, speed boats and jet-skis are all popular, and are sometimes operated by unskilled and thoughtless drivers with small regard for collision risks. In theory they are not allowed to exceed 5kn within 100m of the coast or within 250m of bathing beaches, but may still speed through anchorages to the peril of people swimming from their yachts. Regretably, sizeable tenders from large yachts may be among the worst offenders. Water-skiing is supposed to be restricted to buoyed areas but this restriction does not appear to be enforced.

Scuba divers and swimmers

A good watch should be kept for scuba divers and swimmers, with or without snorkel equipment, particularly around harbour entrances. If accompanied by a boat, the presence of divers may be indicated either by International Code Flag A or by a square red flag with a single yellow diagonal. Many deeper water snorkellers sensibly tow orange floats and a good watch should be made for these, especially close in to cliffs and points.

PREPARATION AND PRACTICAL TIPS

Yacht and equipment

The type of yacht suitable depends entirely on the type of sailing envisaged, from a small motor yacht for coast hopping in good weather, to more adventurous voyages around the islands and to the mainland. Do bear in mind that there are often light winds, decreasing to no wind at night, or the occasional possibility of sudden strong or gale force winds, even in summer.

A yacht properly equipped for cruising in northern waters should need little extra gear, but the following items are worth considering if not already on board.

Ventilation Modern yachts are, as a rule, better ventilated than their older sisters though seldom better insulated. Consider adding an opening hatch in the main cabin, if not already fitted, and ideally another over the galley. A wind scoop for the forehatch helps increase the draught, particularly if the open hatch is not forward facing. Small fans of the Hella variety take little power and can be reasonably used in sleeping cabins at night-time, also around the galley to make life more comfortable for the galley-slave of the day!

Awnings An awning covering at least the cockpit provides shade and protection for the crew, while an even better combination is a bimini which can be kept rigged whilst sailing, plus a larger 'harbour' awning, preferably at boom height or above and extending forward to the mast.

Cockpit tables It is pleasant to eat in the cockpit, particularly while at anchor. If nothing else can be arranged, a small folding table is an advantage.

Refrigerator/ice-box If a refrigerator is not fitted it may be possible to build in an ice-box (a plastic picnic coolbox is a poor substitute), but this will be useless without adequate insulation. An ice-box or refrigerator designed for northern climes will almost

Swimming area demarcation buoys off almost every beach: do not venture closer inshore beyond them *Graham Hutt*

certainly benefit from extra insulation, if this can be fitted; 100mm (4") is a desirable minimum, 150mm (6") even better. Even the better quality yachts seldom have sufficient insulation for tropical or even sub-tropical temperatures. A drain is also essential and should drain overboard rather than to the bilge. If a refrigerator is fitted but electricity precious, placing ice, especially in block form, inside will help minimise battery drain.

Mosquito nets Some advocate fitting screens to all openings leading below. Others find this inconvenient, relying instead on mosquito coils and other insecticides and repellents. For some reason mosquitoes generally seem to bother new arrivals more than old hands, and anchoring well out will often decrease the problem. The Islas Baleares are generally very dry in summer; mosquitoes are particularly associated with stagnant water and are most likely to be a nuisance where there are brackish lakes near the anchorage.

Water A large extra water container or two should be carried in summer in case harbours are unable to offer a berth. Low cost 12v watermakers are now available and could be considered.

Hose At least 25m. Standpipes tend to have bayonet couplings of a type unavailable in the UK so purchase them on arrival.

Deck shower A rinse-off on deck after swimming is important for keeping salt out of clothes and furnishings. If you don't have a deck shower, lay a black walled 'solar shower' on deck to warm in the heat of the day then hang in the rigging to use.

Tools and spares

Carry tools and equipment to hook up to continental-type electrical fittings. A selection of fittings and jubilee clips. Sufficient paper charts to back up electronic navigation systems in the event of failure, to be used in conjunction with pilot books, maps, guidebooks, and a Spanish dictionary.

Fenders and fender plank

In marinas, mooring is usually bows- or stern-to a quay or pontoon with a line tailed from the quay, so good clean fenders are required as it is often a tight squeeze; fender 'socks' reduce irritating squeaks in this situation. A fender plank is very useful alongside uneven quay walls. It will also double as a boarding plank when moored bow- or stern-to if your vessel is not already fitted with a *passarelle*.

Clothing

The sun's rays at sea, especially in summer, are easy to underestimate and present a serious risk of burning as well as of skin cancers. Direct sunlight and reflected light from the sea combined with salt air and wind, constitute a hazard to be avoided.

Lightweight, loose fitting, patterned cotton clothing is handy in this context – it washes and dries easily and the pattern camouflages the creases.

Non-absorbent synthetic materials are best avoided. Until a good tan has been built up it may be wise to wear a T-shirt when swimming.

Some kind of headgear, preferably with a wide brim, is essential. A genuine Montecristi hat can be rolled up, shoved in a pocket and doesn't mind getting wet (they come from Ecuador, not Panama, which has usurped the name). A retaining string, tied either to clothing or around the neck, is a wise precaution whilst on the water.

Footwear at sea is a contentious subject. Many experienced cruisers habitually sail barefoot, but while this may be acceptable on a familiar vessel it would be courting injury on a less intimately known deck. In either case, proper sailing shoes should always be worn for harbour work or anchor handling. Decks (especially teak decks) may become unexpectedly hot and very painful to unprotected feet. It is a good idea to keep a pair of shoes (which may be as basic as 'Crocs') solely to wear on board. If wearing sandals ashore, the upper part of the foot is a prime area for sunburn. Shoes give necessary protection against sea-urchin spines when swimming or landing the dinghy.

Winters can be wet and cold, and foul weather gear as well as warm sweaters, etc. will be needed. Even night sailing in summer can be unexpectedly cold when it rains.

Shore-going clothes should be appropriate – beachwear is not usually acceptable in restaurants and yacht clubs.

SUPPLIES AND PROVISIONS

Fuel

Diesel (*gasoleo*, *gasoil* or simply diesel) is available in most marinas and yacht harbours in the Islas Baleares. A limited number also have a pump for petrol (*gasolina*). *Petróleo* is paraffin (kerosene). Credit and debit cards are widely, but not universally, accepted – if in doubt, check before filling.

A concession for fishing boats that benefited yachts, was the provision of Gasoleo B. This carried a lower rate of tax making it considerably cheaper than the usual Gasoleo A. However, this tax exemption has been phased out to comply with EC tax laws.

Water

In many places drinking water (*agua potable*) is scarce and becoming increasingly more so each year. It is usually available at every berth, but expect to pay for it, particularly if supplied by hose, and do not wash sails and decks before checking that it is acceptable to do so. Many marinas insist on hoses being connected to a 'pistol' rather than being open-ended. In those harbours where a piped supply is not available for yachts a public tap can often be found.

Water quality in Mallorca and Menorca is generally good. However, water quality throughout all the islands varies from year to year. Locals nearly always drink bottled water, not so much because the *agua potable* is contaminated, but because it tastes better. Always check verbally and taste for salinity or over-chlorination before topping up tanks – the ideal is to have a tank specifically reserved for drinking water, with other tanks for general use. Failing this, earmark some cans for the purpose, but stow them in a dark locker to discourage algae. As most of the water in the islands is desalinated it can be quite corrosive, especially to stainless steel tanks and pumps, and a pre-tank in-line filter is highly recommended. Bottled water is readily available in bars and supermarkets.

Note Water quality in Ibiza is not always good and advice should be obtained from marina staff before filling tanks.

Ice

Block ice for an icebox is widely obtainable (use the largest blocks that will fit) while chemical ice is sometimes available in blocks measuring 100x20x20cms. Don't use these in drinks. Cube or 'small' ice is widely obtainable and generally of drinks quality, particularly if bought in a sealed bag. An increasing number of marinas and yacht clubs now have ice machines.

Gas

Camping Gaz is widely available from marinas, supermarkets or *ferreterias* (ironmongers); the 1·9kg cylinders are identical to those in the UK. Its availability is therefore not usually listed in the text under individual harbour facilities.

REPSOL/CAMPSOL depots in Spain will not refill any UK (or any other country's) Calor Gas cylinders even with a current test certificate. It is therefore essential to carry the appropriate regulator and fittings to permit the use of Camping Gaz cylinders. Yachts fitted for propane systems should certainly follow this course. If in doubt consult the GasBOAT website at www.whayward.com.

Electricity

It is a good idea to be at least partly self-sufficient with solar panels and/or a wind generator and an inverter if planning to anchor a lot, or be prepared to run your engine on a regular basis.

Electricity is provided at most marina berths, the standard being 220V, 50Hz, generally using the standard 'marinco' style sockets. It is a good idea to carry an adaptor for the larger 32 amp shore supply and also a 'splitter' to enable two yachts to connect to one shore supply socket. On rare occasions the shore end may be a two-pin socket and again it is useful to have an adaptor system ready for this. Some marinas provide 380V supplies to berths for yachts over 20m. If using American 110V 60Hz equipment seek advice – cycles may be a greater problem than volts for some equipment, particularly those using motors. Even if the yacht is not wired for mains, a 25m length of cable and a trickle charger may be useful.

Provisioning

There are many well stocked stores, supermarkets and hypermarkets in the larger towns, often on the outskirts or industrial estate (*poligano*) and it may be worth doing the occasional major stock-up by taxi. It is useful to have a wheeled shopping bag on board. Conversely, many isolated anchorages have nothing ashore - a major part of their attraction. As a rule, availability and choice varies in relation to the size of the town. Even the smallest has something and most older settlements (though not all tourist resorts) have a traditional-style market offering excellent local produce at very reasonable prices. Alcohol is cheap by UK standards with, not surprisingly, Spanish wines and spirits of particularly good value. Shop prices generally are noticeably lower away from tourist resorts.

Most shops, other than the large supermarkets, close for siesta between 1400 and 1700 and remain closed on Sunday, though some smaller food shops do open on Sunday mornings. In larger towns the produce market may operate from 0800 to 1400, Monday to Saturday; in smaller towns it is more often a weekly affair.

Local gastronomic specialities include *ensaimadas*; flat spirals of flaky pastry ranging from one-person size to family-size nearly two feet across! Everyone is familiar with *mahonésa* (mayonnaise), but possibly not with its cousin *aïoli* or *alioli*, a more powerful version made with garlic. An excellent way to sample unfamiliar delicacies in small portions is in the form of bar snacks or tapas, once served gratis but now almost invariably charged for, sometimes heavily.

Mallorca produces some local wines, including Binisalem and Felanitx, and Menorca too has a growing production, the main brand being Binifadet, but most wine is imported from the mainland. Some of the vineyards have attractive bodegas and restaurants attached. Each island has its own apéritifs and liqueurs. Ibiza produces Hierbas, Rumaniseta and La Frigola, all made from herbs. Mallorca makes Palo from carob nuts, and Menorca specialises in gin, with Xoriguer the best known brand. Menorca also has varieties of Hierbas.

Eating out

Every marina, port, harbour, village and even most semi-deserted bays have eating facilities too numerous to mention. In summer, *chiringuitos* spring up on some beaches, offering basic food and sometimes fresh fish at decent prices. Restaurant quality has improved substantially in recent years and all the islands now have some excellent examples. Do consult some of the excellent guidebooks on the Baleares for more information.

MARINAS AND MOORINGS

The rapid growth of marinas in the 1990s was suddenly halted in 2000 because of environmental concerns. There are nearly 30,000 yacht berths in the islands and many more boats are cruising there in summer than there are berths. During July and August, it is almost impossible to find a mooring in any of the harbours. Thus it is essential to radio (VHF Ch 09 for marinas or Ch 08 for Ports IB) or phone before arrival at a port to check if a berth may be available, or for the greatest chance of success book online or by email well in advance.

Future plans for new marinas or extensions

Although a number of plans for new marinas have been proposed, it seems unlikely that any further major developments or new marinas will be permitted in the foreseeable future, though existing facilities may be improved.

Berthing

Due to the vast numbers of yachts and limited space available, berthing stern-to the quays and pontoons is almost universal (and allows easiest shore access). For greater privacy berth bow-to, which has the added advantage of keeping the rudder away from possible underwater obstructions near the quay and making the approach a much easier manoeuvre. An anchor may very occasionally be needed, but normally a bow (or stern) line will be provided, usually via a lazyline to the pontoon, though sometimes buoyed. This line is likely to be both heavy and dirty and gloves will be useful. Either way, have plenty of fenders out and lines ready.

Most cruising skippers will have acquired some expertise at this manoeuvre before reaching the Islas Baleares, but if taking over a chartered or otherwise unfamiliar yacht it would be wise both to check handling characteristics and talk the manoeuvre through with the crew before attempting to enter a narrow berth. Detailed instructions regarding Mediterranean mooring techniques will be found in Imray's *Mediterranean Almanac*.

Mooring lines

Surge in harbours is not uncommon and mooring lines must be both long and strong. It is sometimes useful to have a loop of chain made up at the shore end to slip over bollards, though in other places rings are in use. Steel spring or rubber surge dampeners will help to protect from the more violent surges.

Moorings

In order to capitalise on income many marinas and harbours have laid moorings and prohibited the use of anchors. This has now been extended to many of the *calas* around the islands.

There are several buoy concession holders around the islands. These are:
1. Those run by private marinas or Ports IB (generally cheaper)
2. Buoys specifically for the island of Cabrera
3. Private moorings leased to residents
4. Posidonia buoyed conservation areas.

The general colour convention is orange for vessels up to 8m and white up to 15m. Some buoys have the max length written on them. However, a different colour system is used on Cabrera island, as noted in the relevant section (page 209) and some red buoys denote a mooring less than 10m. These differences are noted in the text where known.

Each concession has its own methods of charging and rates. Buoys are usually removed and stored during winter months, or can be used without charge: most only charge between 1 June and 30 September. Rates within these months may vary, with August attracting the highest charge.

Yacht clubs

Most harbours of any size support at least one *club náutico*. However, some of the grander ones in particular may be social as well as sailing clubs – often with tennis courts, swimming pools and other facilities – and may not welcome the crews of visiting yachts. There is usually both a marina and a club, and unless there are special circumstances, the first option for a visitor is the marina. That said, many *club náuticos* have pleasant bars and excellent restaurants which appear to be open to all, and are usually helpful and friendly to visitors.

Sunset over the anchorage at Andraitx *David Russell*

PORTS IB

www.portsib.es

The Spanish government holds the freehold to all its coastal waters and leases the concession to run marinas or rent out mooring buoys on a contract basis. Ports IB runs its facilities at a very much cheaper rate than the private marinas. In the high season, the difference is often better than half the price.

As with Posidonia, registration must be made online at the website above. The Ports IB website is only in Spanish, but is easy to get around. (*See page 296 for a glossary of Spanish terms.*) Acknowledgement takes about 2 days. Once registered, a booking may be made by Visa for two or more days ahead. This will be accepted immediately if there is a space. Once paid for, the booking cannot be refunded.

A map listing all the Ports IB moorings is available from their offices and on their website, along with contact information for all the marina facilities around the islands. Unofficially, a call on Ch 08 outside the peak summer season, may produce a berth.

Once booked, a mooring can be accessed after 1200 and must be used before 1800 or it will be considered vacant and available for anyone to use.

Ports IB staff are helpful and courteous.

Posidonia and Ports IB mooring buoys are generally removed during the winter months.

If during the high season the mooring buoy area is full, it is permissible to anchor in a sandy area away from the sea grass provided there are no exclusion zone buoys (usually dark red with a white square on each side). The authorities have RIBS which regularly patrol their areas to collect mooring fees and which can levy fines for those infringing the rules.

Charges and payment for marinas and moorings

All marinas and most laid buoyage areas charge for their use on a daily basis. Some marinas charge separately for water and electricity. Charges, especially in summer, change from week to week and it is impossible to keep up with the changes. Many will charge extra when a regatta or other special event is taking place. Most consider the high season from 30 June to 30 September and some have 'shoulder' season pricing outside this period. Many have varying rates even within this time frame, with August always being the highest month. Ports IB moorings, (formally Port Authority) are usually cheaper, generally having a fixed summer rate of under €50 in high season for a 12m berth, including water and electricity. Their marinas are usually excellent and often closer to the town centre than the private marinas. Booking has to be made online as described in the Ports IB box above.

As a general indication: a marina berth for a 12m yacht will cost between €50 and €200 in the high season per day, and less than half that off season.

Winter rates fall dramatically and for those laying up for several months, are usually negotiable, especially if payment is made in advance.

Those Posidonia buoys left in situ during the off season, are currently not charged for.

Up to date availability and pricing information is on the web, with contact information in the header section of each marina in this volume. Payment by credit/debit card is accepted throughout the islands.

Large yachts

Many harbours in the Islas Baleares are too small, or too shallow for a large yacht, which must anchor outside whilst its crew visit the harbour by tender. It is essential that the skipper of such a yacht, wishing to enter, telephones or radios the harbour authorities well in advance to reserve a berth (if available) and receive necessary instructions.

Laying up

Laying up either afloat or ashore is possible at some marinas, though many have little or no hard standing. Facilities and services provided vary considerably, as does the cost, and it is worth seeking local advice as to the quality of the services provided and the security of the berth or hard standing concerned. Hard standing, when available, may be considerably more expensive than laying up afloat.

The northwesterly *tramontana* (*mestral*) can be frequent and severe in winter and early spring, and this should be borne in mind when selecting the area and site to lay up. Yachts with wooden decks and varnished brightwork will need protection from the winter sun, and ideally arrangements should be made for the former to be hosed down each evening or covered with a tarpaulin.

It may well prove cheaper to return to mainland Spain rather than to lay up in the Islas Baleares.

Repairs and chandlery

Many marinas are equipped to handle all aspects of yacht maintenance from laying up to changing a washer. Nearly all have travel-hoists and the larger marinas have specialist facilities – GRP work, electronics, sailmaking, stainless welding, etc. Charges may differ widely so, if possible, shop around.

The best-equipped chandleries will be found near the larger marinas, where they may equal those of the UK (though generally with higher prices). There do not appear to be any of the really really large mail-order chandleries like those that now dominate the UK market. Smaller harbours or marinas are often without a chandlery, though some requirements may be found in the associated town. Basic items can sometimes be found in *ferreterias* (ironmongers) and fishing tackle shops.

Chartering

Chartering is a well-regulated business in the Islas Baleares with somewhat different regulations to those applied in mainland Spain, notably that there is no blanket restriction on foreign-owned and/or

POSIDONIA

www.balearslifeposidonia.eu

The Islas Baleares Government, through the Environmental Ministry and the pressure group Ophiusa Iniciatives Nautiques, has established the company Posidonia to protect the coastal environment and particularly the vast expanses of *Posidonia Oceanica*, (commonly known as seagrass), which are found around the islands.

Conservation areas have been established in many calas and buoys belonging to the Posidonia organisation have been placed to prevent anchoring, whilst giving an alternative method of mooring, with the idea of protecting the natural underwater environment. It is postulated that disturbing the roots when anchoring is the cause of long term environmental damage. These plants are essential to the ecology of the islands. The seagrass is also suffering from a disease supposedly caused by the pollution from yachts. Since the plant is believed to have a huge impact on the sea environment, from water clarity to the health of the beaches, and as a breeding nursery for many species of fish, something had to be done to protect the future tourist industry of the islands. The Posidonia project has UNESCO backing. To help yacht crews to better understand the needs and philosophy of the Posidonia project, a well written pamphlet, *Posidonia Survival*, is available from marina offices.

Booking moorings in advance online after registration with the organisation is essential.

Registration, bookings, charge rates and rules for the use of Posidonia buoys are explained on their website.

Note that the first step is to register your yacht with the organisation and then wait to activate the registration by uploading a pdf or jpg of your ship's document. The online booking system works well (after three years of problems) and is in English as well as Spanish. Posidonia areas can be seen on the website. The system changed in 2017 and it is now necessary to register each year. Yachts that have not registered but are seeking a mooring buoy may try calling Posidonia on Ch 77 (and some yachts have been heard making contact on Ch 9) to see if there are any spare buoys.

Note that according to Spanish law, anchoring is technically prohibited within 200m of the shoreline. This is rarely enforced, but has been in Sóller on occasions, with fines for non-compliance when yachts swung closer to the shore as a result of a wind shift. Strict application would eliminate many anchorages.

Areas prohibited from anchoring at all times are: Cala Gat and Cala Olla (Mallorca), Calas Tamarells (Menorca).

Marine reserves are at:

- Son Moll
- Cala Agulla
- Cala Moltó
- Cala Mesquida
- Cala Mitjana
- Cala Matsoch
- Cala Font Salada
- Es Caló

See also comments on Anchorages (pages 13-14) regarding proposed legislation being considered by the Balearic Parliament.

Buoys indicating prohibited and restricted areas should be in place as indicated in their brochures. However, the organisation does not currently have the funds to plant buoys everywhere their literature says they are placed.

In 2017 the Balearic Government made additional funds available to the Posidonia organisation specifically to finance new patrol RIBs and a number of fines of up to 6,000€ have been imposed.

skippered vessels applying for charter authorisation. However the necessary paperwork is time-consuming and involved. The islands are virtually free of the large flotilla fleets found in the eastern Mediterranean.

Security

Crime afloat is not a major problem in most areas, and regrettably much of the theft which does occur can be laid at the door of other yachtsmen. It is sensible to take much the same precautions as at home: lock up before leaving the yacht, padlock the outboard to the dinghy, and secure the dinghy (particularly if an inflatable) with chain or wire rather than line. Folding bicycles are particularly vulnerable to theft, and should be chained up when not in use, even when on deck. As they say, 'Lock it or lose it!'

Ashore, use common sense as to how handbags are carried, where not to go after the bars close, etc. and there should be no problems.

FORMALITIES AND DOCUMENTATION

The officials most likely to be seen are the *Guardia Civil*, who wear olive green uniforms and deal with immigration as well as more ordinary police work, the *Aduana* (customs) in navy blue uniforms, and the *Policía local*, also in blue uniforms, who deal with traffic and civil disturbances rather than criminal matters. However, over the past few years arrival procedures have been standardized and simplified. Marinas now handle all paperwork on entry, and they pass on information to the *Guardia Civil* who usually take no further action. A simple form is required to be completed on checking in, giving ships details, captain's address and crew passport details and nationality. A copy of passports and ships papers are often copied, along with yacht insurance certificate. Third party insurance is sufficient and this is now mandatory in almost all Spanish marinas.

If any of the crew are not EU citizens, or if you have arrived from outside of the EU Schengen countries, a visit later from the immigration police or *Guardia Civil* may ensue, but this is rare.

It is always a good idea to carry proof of VAT status, a copy of the captain's certificate of competence and radio licence, but these things are almost never asked for.

Brexit

The United Kingdom will secede from the European Union in March 2019. A period of transition or implementation will follow the secession lasting to the end of 2020, during which there will be little or no change to the formalities and documentation affecting British yachtspeople and British-flagged yachts visiting, or based in, EU countries. Subsequent change seems inevitable but the nature and extent of that change cannot be predicted at the time of finalising the content of this pilot book in early 2018. Once the position is clear, factual information, and possibly guidance, will be published in the online annual supplement (*see page iv*).

Flag etiquette

A yacht in commission in foreign waters is legally required to fly her national maritime flag, normally the Red Ensign for a British yacht. If a special club ensign is displayed, it must be accompanied by the correct burgee. The courtesy flag of the country visited (in this case Spanish) should be flown from the starboard signal halliard – note that in Spain, as in the UK, the maritime ensign and national flags are not the same; strictly, the Spanish maritime flag defaced with a crown should only be flown as an ensign by a Spanish registered vessel. The Islas Baleares each have their own regional flags which may be flown below the national courtesy flag if desired.

Under EU regulations, EU-registered vessels are not required to fly the Q flag on first arrival unless they have non-EU nationals or dutiable goods aboard. Nevertheless, clearance should be sought either by a visit to or from officials or through the offices of the larger marinas or yacht clubs.

Visas

As Spain is a member of the European Union, other EU nationals may now stay indefinitely.

Non-EU nationals wishing to remain in Spain may apply for a *permiso de residencia* and subsequent 90-day extensions.

With the high rate of illegal immigration and smuggling taking place throughout the Mediterranean, all yachts are now tracked by satellite. On entering harbour, a form is completed which serves as the entry formality, with no officials involved.

Pet 'passports', along with up-to-date health check documents, are required but are rarely asked for.

In 2016 and 2017 there has been a huge increase in illegal immigration by sea from North Africa (particularly Morocco) and it is likely that yachts approaching Spain from a southerly direction will have an increased probability of inspection and should be doubly sure that their paperwork is in order.

International Certificate of Competence

A Certificate of Competence is a requirement for skippers of all Spanish vessels, and may be asked of foreign visitors. Production of the RYA ICC certificate is sufficient in most marinas for the form-filling if demanded. Some of the charter companies now require proof of competency to RYA Coastal Skipper level or equivalent.

VAT on yachts

A boat registered outside the EU may stay in an EU port for up to six months before VAT must be paid, although this time period can often be extended. Value Added Tax (IVA – *Impuesto sobre el valor añadido*), subject to certain exceptions, is levied at 21% of the value of the vessel unless it can be shown to have been paid or has an exemption certificate.

Note that for VAT purposes the Canaries, Gibraltar, the Channel Islands and the Isle of Man are outside the EU fiscal area.

Any boat purchased outside the EU by an EU resident is liable for VAT on import to the EU.

The rules are open to differing interpretations and flexibility and the practices vary considerably from one country to another, and often from one harbour to another in Spanish waters.

The Almudaina palace, Palma, displaying splendid Arab-style architecture from a bygone era *Geoff Williamson*

Impuesto de Matriculation

Impuesto de Matriculation (IM) is a registration tax and is similar to that paid on motor vehicles when the owner has been in Spain for more than 183 days. Please note that this has nothing whatsoever to do with VAT.

The tax may be applied to foreign residents of Spain with a yacht if they are deemed 'Fiscally resident for the purposes of this tax'.

Insurance

All marinas require vessels to have insurance cover, though third party only is usually all that is required. Many UK companies are willing to extend home waters cover to the Mediterranean, sometimes excluding certain areas.

All foreign yachts sailing in Spanish waters are required to carry third party insurance cover of at least £2,000,000 with all the details on the correct form in Spanish. UK insurance companies will issue, on request, the relevant document in Spanish. All kinds of unpleasantness, from a heavy fine to confiscation of the yacht can technically result from non-compliance.

T-0 de Faros y Salvamiento Maritimo

Originally a charge for light dues, this charge has been increased substantially and now includes a notional contribution to the cost of the lifeboat and other rescue services. The charge, known as Tarifa G5, is supposedly levied on all vessels in the islands. Locally-based pleasure craft pay at the rate per square metre per year (area being calculated as LOA x beam). In theory, visiting pleasure craft should pay one tenth of that sum on arrival, which covers a 10-day period, after which it is again due. The status of a charter yacht is not clear.

In principle it should be paid to the Customs authority but it is generally wrapped up in marina and harbour charges; although it is supposed to be shown separately on the invoice or receipt. It is likely, that in practice, marinas and harbours have a 'block' deal with the authorities to simplify collection and accounting.

T-5

This is the charge for harbour dues which is collected by private marinas and harbour authorities and included in their overall charges; again this should be clearly shown on the invoice.

MARITIME REGULATIONS AND RESTRICTIONS

Speed limit

All harbours have speed limits, usually 3kn or less. There is a blanket 5kn speed limit along the whole coast extending 100m offshore, increasing to 250m off bathing beaches.

Buoys

Yellow (usually) buoys are placed parallel to beaches in summer to indicate swimming areas. These can extend up to more than 100m off the beach, but are usually less, depending partly on the topography. Anchoring or venturing beyond these towards the beach is strictly prohibited with heavy fines levied if contravened. Often a buoyed channel is in place to enable pedalos and other beach-hire craft to be launched, and the same channel can be used to enable yacht tenders to access the beach and any restaurants etc.

Swimming areas often have a buoyed channel giving dinghy access to the beach *Jane Russell*

Water-skiing and jet-skis

There has been an explosive increase in the use of high powered outboards for water-skiing over the past decade, accompanied by a significant increase in accidents. In most of the main ports and at some beaches it is now controlled and enquiries should be made before skiing. It is essential to have third party insurance and, if possible, a bail bond.

If water skiing areas are buoyed, yachts are excluded.

Due to the number of fatal accidents in recent years, the use of jet-skis is now prohibited without a specific license to operate one.

Snorkelling

Spearfishing while using a snorkel is controlled and, in some places, prohibited.

Scuba diving

Inshore scuba diving is strictly controlled and a licence is required from the Comandancia Militar de Marina. This involves a certificate of competence, a medical certificate, two passport photographs, the passport itself (for inspection), knowledge of the relevant laws and a declaration that they will be obeyed. The simplest approach is to enquire through marina staff. Any attempt to remove archaeological material from the seabed will result in serious trouble.

Garbage

It is an international offence to dump garbage at sea and, while the arrangements of local authorities may not be perfect, garbage on land should be dumped in the proper containers. There are often facilities to segregate glass, paper and cardboard, plastic bottles etc. and these should be used to the greatest extent possible - as with most islands, and tourist islands at that, garbage disposal is a major problem for the local authorities and much is transported to the mainland. Many marinas now have facilities for the removal of holding tank waste (*agua negra*) and old engine oil.

COMMUNICATIONS

WiFi

The majority of marinas in Spain and the Baleares (apart from Ports IB facilities) have WiFi. Unfortunately, more often than not they do not work properly as the yacht is in a 'dead' spot or there are too many people logged in, reducing bandwidth.

It is now almost impossible to cruise the Balearics without the internet; even booking a mooring requires it, so if you need an alternative to marina WiFi, you could use a commercial provider (examples of these often pop up when you try to access the internet) or take your laptop, tablet or smartphone to a local café and use the WiFi there.

The authors use a Vodafone modem (about 4 x 2") which gives 15Gb per month at a cost of €45; the contract can be cancelled when not required and subsequently re-activated (alas, rather a hassle). This generally receives a signal in locations where telephone signal is available.

Telephone

International code +34
Local code for Baleares 971

Mobile phones work throughout the islands. The mobile phone system often functions several miles out to sea providing a link to the world. With a computer interface, this can also provide internet and email facilities. Ensure that the International Roaming facility is activated for use abroad. Telephone kiosks are available (but becoming less common), both local and *teléfono internacional*, and most carry instructions in English. Both coins and phonecards (available from tobacconists) are used – most kiosks accept either. American Express and Diners Club cards can also be used in some phone boxes, though oddly enough not VISA or Mastercard.

Calls to the United Kingdom begin with the prefix 0044, followed by the area code (without the initial zero) and number; calls to North America with the prefix 001, plus area code and number. It may be necessary to pause after dialling the initial 00 to await a second dialling tone. The European International Operator can be accessed on 1008 and the Worldwide International Operator on 1005.

To call a Spanish number from abroad, dial that country's international access code (00 in the UK, 011 in North America) followed by 34, plus area code and number. If dialling within Spain it should be noted that the area code forms part of the number, with no digits dropped when dialling from abroad. A number prefixed with 6 denotes a mobile phone, e.g. 608 or 609.

Mail

Letters may be sent *poste restante* to any post office (*oficina de corréos*). They should be addressed with the surname of the recipient followed by *Lista de Corréos* and the town, island and Islas Baleares. Addresses of harbours can be found on the internet using the web address given in the text. Collection is a fairly cumbersome procedure and a passport is likely to be needed. Alternatively, most marinas and some *club náuticos* will hold mail for yachts, but it is always wise to check in advance if possible.

Uncollected letters are seldom returned.

Mail to and from the UK usually takes about six days. If speed is important ask for 'express', which for extra cost expedites dispatch from Spain and may save two or three days. Generally, mail speed within Spain is excellent, though some pockets of poor service remain. Post boxes are yellow, and stamps are available from tobacconists (*Estancos or*

The spectacular ancient city of Mahón, Menorca *Jane Russell*

Tabacos) as well as post offices. Every town has a post office, so these are not listed under individual harbour facilities in the text.

Tourist offices

There is at least one tourist office in every major town or resort and a great deal of information is available on the internet.

Of the many free publications available, the A4-sized *I'd like to see you!* series published by The Balearic Institute for the Promotion of Tourism (IBATUR) is worth seeking out. Four beautifully-illustrated booklets cover the main islands, giving a smattering of history, places to visit, fiestas, local folklore, island statistics and useful telephone numbers. Excellent value!

See *Appendix* for further reading about the islands.

www.illesbalears.travel
www.infomallorca.net
www.illesbalears.es

Transport and travel

International airports Information is given in each island section. The three larger islands each have an international airport, Mallorca's being one of the busiest in Europe during the holiday season. There are still some real bargains to be found amongst charter flights from the UK.

Ferries Listed under each island. Ferries run to mainland Spain, France and Italy and there are inter-island ferry and hydrofoil services. The largest ferry

companies are Trasmediterránea with offices at Palma, Ibiza and Mahón, and Balearia. There are various internet ferry comparison sites to compare prices.

Almost every community has some form of public transport, if only one *autobús* a day.

Trains Surprisingly, Mallorca boasts two railway lines – one is narrow-gauge, dating back to Victorian times, which links Palma to the town of Sóller in the north, the final connection to Puerto de Sóller being completed by vintage tram. The other line runs from Palma to Inca, about halfway to Alcudia. Both are recommended for the experience and as a means of seeing some of Mallorca's unspoilt interior.

Taxis and car hire Are easily found in the tourist resorts though less common outside them, but can always be ordered by telephone. Car hire is simple, but a full national driving licence with a photo, must be shown. Marina staff are usually happy to arrange.

Consulates

British Consulate
www.gov.uk/world/organisations/british-consulate-palma-de-mallorca

US Consulate
https://es.usembassy.gov/u-s-citizen-services/u-s-consular-offices/consular-agency-palma-de-mallorca/

A list of other consulates in Mallorca is given at: www.mallorca-now.com/consulates.html
For contact details see Appendix page 295.

APPROACHES TO THE ISLAS BALEARES

General

With the exception of a few inshore rocks and islands, and shallow water at the heads of bays, there is generally deep water up to the coast with few offshore dangers. The islands, by virtue of their height and the usual good visibility, can often be seen from many miles away and are well lit at night. The channels between the islands are free from obstructions, but in the strong winds that blow between Mallorca and Menorca, the sea can be rough due to a shallow and uneven bottom. The passage from the mainland to the islands presents no particular problems with the one exception of the north or northwest *tramontana* or *mestral* which can be dangerous in winter and unpleasant in summer.

From the Spanish coast

From west and southwest The shortest passage from mainland Spain is from Puerto de Jávea or Puerto de Denia to Puerto de San Antonio, Ibiza, at about 55 miles. Should a *tramontana* arise during the crossing it will be on the beam or the quarter and San

DISTANCES BETWEEN PORTS IN NAUTICAL MILES

MALLORCA	MENORCA	MENORCA	MENORCA	IBIZA	IBIZA	FORMENTERA
	Ciudadela	Fornells	Mahón	Ibiza	S Antonio	Puerto de Sabina
Palma	87	106	100	69	77	78
Cala Bona	32	50	49	106	115	112
Cala d'Or	47	65	61	90	99	96
Cala Figuera	66	85	79	74	84	82
Cala Gamba	85	104	98	70	78	79
Cala Nova	87	106	100	67	75	76
Cala Ratjada	25	43	44	112	121	118
Ca'n Pastilla	84	103	97	70	78	79
Ca'n Picafort	34	51	56	121	125	129
Colonia San Jordi	63	82	76	77	87	85
Colonia San Pedro	32	49	54	122	126	130
El Arenal	82	101	95	71	79	80
Bonaire	35	51	62	119	123	127
Molinar de Levante	86	105	99	69	72	78
Islote El Toro	84	108	102	60	69	69
Estanyol	70	89	83	70	80	79
Palma Nova	87	106	100	65	73	74
P. d'Alcudia	35	51	60	119	123	127
P. Andraitx	81	96	108	59	63	67
P. Pollensa	35	61	62	119	123	127
P. Sóller	56	71	83	81	85	89
Portals Vells	86	105	99	61	69	70
Portixol	86	105	99	69	77	78
Porto Colom	44	62	60	93	101	99
Porto Cristo	36	54	52	101	110	107
Porto Petro	48	66	62	89	98	95
P. de la Rapita	67	86	80	74	84	82
Sta Ponsa	92	111	105	61	69	70
Serra Nova	32	49	54	122	126	130
Ciudadela		22	33	136	147	144
Fornells	22		20	155	166	163
Mahón	33	20		149	160	157
Ibiza	136	155	149		27	11
S Antonio	147	166	160	27		25
Puerto de Sabina	144	163	157	11	25	

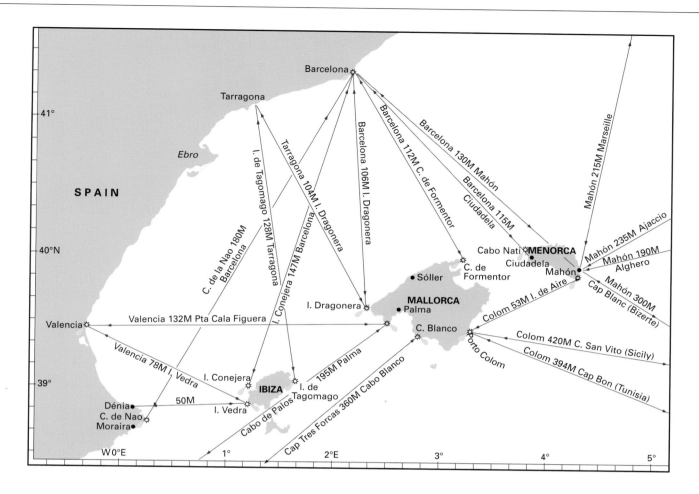

Antonio can, if necessary, be entered under gale conditions. For a flatter approach and better protection once in harbour, it would be wise to continue around the island to Puerto de Santa Eulalia or Puerto de Ibiza, (but accurate navigation through Freu Grande between Ibiza and Espalmador would be critical.)

From northwest and north From the Spanish coasts between Valencia and Barcelona, a choice of islands is offered at distances of 80 miles plus. The usual route is to leave the Spanish coast near Barcelona and to sail for Puerto de Andraitx (110 miles). If the *tramontana* or *mestral* blows it will be on the stern or quarter. Puerto de Andraitx can be entered in almost any conditions. In good and settled weather Puerto de Sóller is nearer but, because the coast on either side is very dangerous, accurate navigation is vital. Note also the *Caution* opposite.

From the French coast

Menorca is the nearest island to the French coast, being 170 miles from Port Vendres, 210 miles from Sète and Toulon and 270 miles from Nice. Probably the safest route is from the area of Cap Béar to Mahón, which can safely be entered in gale conditions. Should a *tramontana* blow it will be on the stern or quarter, and should this occur in the early part of the voyage the Spanish coast can be closed for shelter. Again, note the *Caution* below.

From the eastern Mediterranean

For yachts on passage from Sardinia, Tunisia, Malta or further east, Mahón is the obvious choice for arrival. Distances are approximately 200 miles from the west coast of Sardinia, 360 miles from Tunis and 550 from Valletta, Malta. Should a *tramontana* affect the last part of the passage it will of course be directly on the nose but the landfall will be relatively sheltered. Conversely a southerly *sirocco* will be on or aft of the beam but may give rise to poor visibility.

Caution

The two lights marking the north end of the channel between Mallorca and Menorca have similar characteristics and are easy to confuse. Cabo Formentor (Mallorca) shows Fl(4)20s while Cabo Nati (Menorca) is Fl(3+1)20s. When running towards the islands in a *tramontana*, mistaken identification could lead to a dangerous situation.

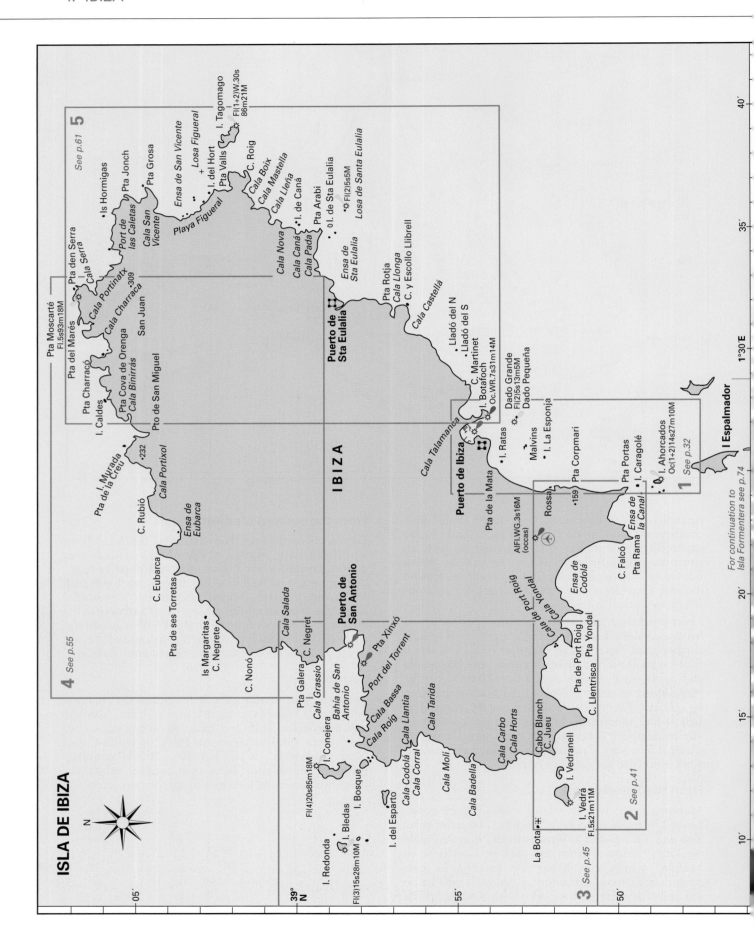

ISLA DE IBIZA

N

I B I Z A

Puerto de Ibiza

Puerto de San Antonio

Puerto de Sta Eulalia

39° N

I Espalmador

Pta Moscarté
Fl.5s93m18M

Pta den Serra
Pta del Marés
Pta Charracó
Pta de la Creu
I. Murada

I. Caldes
Pto de San Miguel
San Juan
Cala Binirás
Pta Cova de Orenga

· Is Hormigas
Pta Jonch
Port de las Caletas
Cala San Vicente
Ensa de San Vicente
Pta Grosa
Playa Figueral

Cala Serrà
Cala Portinatx
·309
Cala Charraca

Losa Figueral
I. del Hort
Pta Valls
C. Roig
Cala Boix
Cala Mastella
Cala Lleña
I. de Caná
Pta Arabi

I. Tagomago
Fl(1+2)W.30s
86m21M

·232

C. Rubió

Is Margaritas
C. Negrete
C. Nonó

C. Eubarca
Pta de ses Torretas

Ensa de
Eubarca

Cala Portixol

Cala Salada
C. Negret

Cala Nova
Cala Caná
Cala Pada

ol. de Sta Eulalia
Fl(2)5s5M
Losa de Santa Eulalia

Ensa de
Sta Eulalia

Pta Rotja
Cala Llonga
C. y Escollo Llibrell

Cala Castellá

Lladó del N
· C. Martinet
Lladó del S

Cala Talamanca
· C. Botafoch
Oc.WR.7s31m14M

Dado Grande
Fl(2)5s13m5M
Dado Pequeña

· I. Ratas
Malvins
· I. La Esponja

I. Caragolé
I. Ahorcados
Oc(1+2)14s27m10M

Pta Corpmari

Pta Portas

·159
Rossa

Pta de la Mata
AlFl.WG.3s16M
(occas)

Pta Ram de
la Cala
Ensa de
la Canal

C. Falcó

Ensa de
Codolá

Cala de Port Roig

Cala Yondal

Pta de Port Roig
Pta Yondal
C. Llentrisca
Cabo Blanch
C. Jueu

I. Vedranell

I. Vedrá
Fl.5s21m11M

La Bota

Cala Carbo
Cala Horts

Cala Badella

Cala Molí

Cala Tarida

Cala Roig
Cala Bassa
Cala Llantia
Cala Corral
Cala Codolá

Pta Galera
Cala Grassio
Bahía de San
Antonio
Pta Xinxó
Port del Torrent

· I. Conejera

Fl(4)20s85m18M
I. Bosque
I. del Esparto

· I. Bledas

· I. Redonda
Fl(3)15s28m10M

See p.61 **5**
See p.55 **4**
See p.45 **3**
See p.41 **2**
See p.32 **1**
For continuation to
Isla Formentera see p.74

40´
35´
1°30´E
20´
15´
10´

05´
55´
50´

I. IBIZA

Although a magnet for nightclubbers and hordes of summer holiday-makers, Ibiza is a World Heritage site, not for its famed nightlife but its architecture, archaeology and marine ecosystem. There are a number of scenic anchorages and all facilities are available at the major marinas of Puerto de Ibiza and Puerto de San Antonio. The pine forests inland inspired the Romans to name the group Pityusae: the Pine Islands.

The coastline is considered in a clockwise direction around the island beginning at Puerto de Ibiza.

The ancient Moorish castle and D'Alt Vila (old town), at the head of Ibiza port *Geoff Williamson*

Navigational information for approaches to Ibiza

All offlying dangers, including Islas Bledas and Isla Vedrá to the west and Isla Tagomago to the east are well covered in this chapter.

Magnetic variation
Less than 001°E

Approach and coastal passage charts
Imray	M3, M12, M13	Spanish	7A, 478, 479
Admiralty	1701, 1702, 2834	SHOM	5505, 7114

Approach lights
Aeropuerto 38°52'·7N 01°22'·3E Aero AlFl.WG.3s16m
Control tower 9m Occas Situated 1M inland
Isla Vedrá 38°51'·9N 01°11'·5E Fl.5s21m11M
White conical tower 3m 262°-vis-134°
Islote Bleda Plana 38°58'·9N 01°10'·5E Fl(3)15s28m10M
White round tower 8m 349°-vis-239°
Isla Conejera 38°59'·7N 01°12'·9E Fl(4)20s85m18M
White tower and building 18m
Punta Moscarté 39°06'·8N 01°32'E Fl.5s93m18M White round
tower, black diagonal stripes 52m 074°-vis-294°
Islote Tagomago 39°02'·1N 01°38'·9E Fl(1+2)W.30s86m21M
White octagonal stone tower on building
Islote Botafoch Oc.WR.7s31m14M
White round tower on white dwelling
Isla Ahorcados Oc(1+2)14s27m10M
White tower, black bands, on white building

INTRODUCTION

Ibiza, the most westerly of the Islas Baleares, lies 50 miles off Cabo de la Nao on the Spanish mainland. It is 26 miles long and 16 miles wide and covers an area of some 250 square miles. The northern half and the southwestern extremity are hilly, the highest point being Atalayasa at 475m. There are three true harbours (Ibiza Town, San Antonio and Santa Eulalia) and many small anchorages around the coast which, with the exception of some stretches of low sandy beaches on the south and southeast sides, is very rugged and broken. Rocky cliffs are interspersed with *calas* (literally coves, but in practice often wide bays), many with small sandy beaches at their heads.

The Romans named the island group the Pityusae (Pine Islands), which is as appropriate today as it was 2,000 years ago. Inland, Ibiza is green and fertile with carpets of flowers in the spring and many pine forests throughout, although agriculture is rather less in evidence than in the other main islands. In common with the rest of the archipelago, Ibiza receives huge numbers of holidaymakers each summer and many of the formerly deserted and beautiful *calas* are now surrounded by hotels and holiday apartments as is common in much of the Mediterranean. The permanent population of Ibiza is around 150,000 about a third of whom live in the capital, Ibiza (Eivissa). Hotels, apartments and guest houses throughout the island have the capacity to accommodate a further 230,000 visitors.

History

Like many parts of the Mediterranean, Ibiza has experienced waves of invasion and settlement throughout its history.

Neolithic pottery discovered in a cave near Cala Vicente indicates that the inhabitants at the time of the early Bronze Age were Iberian; this is borne out by drawings on the walls in a cave at the foot of Cabo Nono. By 1200BC the civilisations of the eastern Mediterranean were spreading westwards and there are many objects of Phoenician and Carthaginian origin, such as bronze axes and discs from San Juan, Salinas and Formentera, as well as figures from the Cave of Es Cuyeram, once a temple dedicated to the goddess Tanit.

The city of Ibiza was founded during the 6th century BC by the Carthaginians, who are thought to have fortified the hill now known as D'Alt Vila (The Old Town) and to have given both town and island the name Ibasim. There is evidence to show that agriculture was improved, tunny fishing and olive cultivation were introduced and the manufacture of purple dye from murex molluscs commenced. By the 3rd century BC the island was minting its own coinage.

It is claimed that Isla Conejera, off the west coast of Ibiza, was the birthplace of the Carthaginian general Hannibal. Certainly the inhabitants of the Islas Planas, part of the Islas Bledas group, were known for their skill at stone slinging and a number of slingers were recruited for the armies of Hannibal in his fight against Rome. As Rome gradually became the victorious power, both Ibiza and Formentera recognised her sovereignty and became city states within the Roman Empire under the name Pityusae (the Pine Islands), as mentioned above.

Other than the name Ebysos there is little remaining evidence of the Greeks in Ibiza, but the Romans brought prosperity to the island, later renamed Ebusus, founding saltworks at Salinas and lead mines at San Carlos. They boosted agriculture by taking shipments of corn to Rome, also built an aqueduct, and a new citadel on the site of the old Carthaginian fortress.

With the fall of Rome, Ibiza suffered the same fate as other satellite countries, being occupied throughout the centuries by various different groups. Raids by the Vandals drove many inhabitants away to seek refuge on the mainland. In AD 426 a Barbarian tribe called the Gunderic occupied the island until the great Byzantine sailor Admiral Belisarius captured it in 535.

The Moors, who at first found the island useful as a base for raids on shipping and the mainland, arrived from North Africa in 707 and remained for more than 500 years. To them the island was Yebisah. The Vikings attempted an invasion in 857 as did Charlemagne in 798–801, but the Moors managed to hold on until 1235 when Ibiza was eventually reconquered by a force under Guillem de Montgrí, Bishop of Tarragona, backed by King Jaime I of Aragon. The Moorish influence is still evident in the architecture, customs and traditional dress of the islanders and the reconquest by Aragon in the presence of Catalonian in their language, from which the Ibizan *Ibicenco* dialect is derived, and the origin of the island name Eivissa.

Ibiza's return to Christian rule failed to bring peace, and the island was subject to much fighting during the period of Spanish internal strife. In 1492 the whole of Spain, including Ibiza, became united under King Ferdinand and Queen Isabella, but for another two centuries attacks on the island by Barbary pirates, Moors and Turks were frequent. Watchtowers were kept permanently manned, the present city walls were built and cavalry patrols were established. Even village churches were fortified.

After a period being part of the Kingdom of Mallorca, Ibiza reverted to Catalonian rule, but then backed the losing side in the War of the Spanish Succession (1702–14) and was made into a Spanish province as a result. It gradually became a cultural and economic backwater, emigration adding to a population decline begun by the Black Death plague 400 years earlier.

Recent history

During the Spanish Civil War Ibiza declared allegiance to General Franco, only to be rebuffed by the Republicans and occupied for a six-week period when considerable damage was done to churches and other buildings.

In the past, Ibiza's main wealth came from the export of 'red' salt which was particularly valued. Even today some 70,000 tons of salt are exported each year. Fruit, grain and shellfish were other exports of importance. However, during the last fifty years the tourist trade has expanded into a major industry. The island was a haven for the simple life and values, in particular both Ibiza and Formentera became favourites with the so-called 'hippie' culture, a legacy still evident in a marked tolerance towards non-mainstream lifestyles. But the 1970s saw the emergence of a club culture which has retained its international status. Nevertheless, the construction of apartment blocks for tourists has finally slowed, together with large numbers of tourist shops, cafés, bars, restaurants and related services. The local authorities have realised, perhaps a little late, that ever-expanding tourism brings with it a heavy environmental price and consequently a renewed focus on historic culture is being encouraged.

Tourist information

Places of particular interest on Ibiza

The church of Nostra Señora in the small village of Jesús just north of Ibiza city contains a famous (and very beautiful) altarpiece dating back to the early 16th century.

In the northern part of the island lie Balafia, a fortified Moorish village just outside San Lorenzo, and the Es Cuyeram cave which was once a Carthaginian temple to the goddess Tanit (also accessible from the anchorage at Cala de San Vicente). In the southwest, the Carthaginian and Roman remains at Ses Païses de Cala d'Hort (near Cala Horts) make an interesting visit. Inland lies Ibiza's highest point, Atalayasa, near the village of San José. Further east, on the road to Ibiza, are the caves of Cova Santa, also accessible via a track from Cala Yondal.

Cala Llonga. Good shelter in all but E winds *Graham Hutt*

I. IBIZA

1. PUERTO DE IBIZA TO PUNTA PORTAS (INCLUDING PASSES BETWEEN IBIZA AND ESPALMADOR)

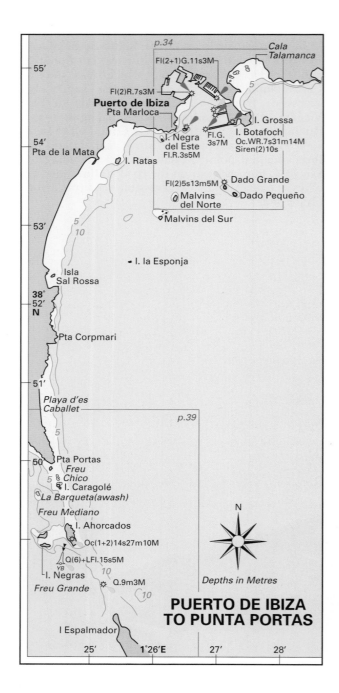

p.34

Cala Talamanca

Fl(2+1)G.11s3M

Fl(2)R.7s3M

Puerto de Ibiza
Pta Marloca

I. Grossa
I. Botafoch
Oc.WR.7s31m14M
Siren(2)10s

I. Negra
del Este
Fl.G. 3s7M
Fl.R.3s5M

Pta de la Mata

I. Ratas

Fl(2)5s13m5M — Dado Grande
Malvins del Norte — Dado Pequeño
Malvins del Sur

I. la Esponja

Isla Sal Rossa

38° 52' N

Pta Corpmari

Playa d'es Caballet

p.39

Pta Portas
Freu Chico
I. Caragolé
La Barqueta(awash)
Freu Mediano
I. Ahorcados
Oc(1+2)14s27m10M
Q(6)+LFl.15s5M
I. Negras
Freu Grande
Q.9m3M

N

Depths in Metres

PUERTO DE IBIZA TO PUNTA PORTAS

I Espalmador

25' **1°26'E** 27' 28'

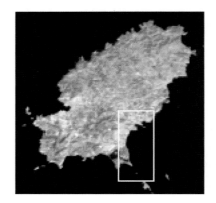

View along the southwest harbour wall towards the ancient town of Ibiza (D'Alt Villa) and the Cathedral of Our Lady of the Snows
Geoff Williamson

Puerto de Ibiza (Eivissa)

38°54'·1N 01°26'·7E

An easy-to-enter harbour in almost any conditions, offering good shelter, with several commercial yachting facilities. Berthing for over 1,200 yachts up to 30m.

Communications
Pilots (Ibiza Prácticos) VHF Ch 12, 13, 14, 16
Port Authority Ch 08,16 ☏ 971 31 33 63
See text for further information on other options

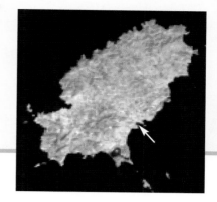

The port

Puerto de Ibiza is a large port offering excellent facilities for over 1,200 yachts. The harbour accommodates four separate marinas - Marina Botafoch, Marina Ibiza, Club Náutico de Ibiza and Marina Ibiza Magna - and is easy to enter under most conditions, giving good shelter. Swell which used to enter the port has been considerably reduced by the extension of the breakwater extending west-southwest from Islote Botafoch. The harbour is expensive and in season a berth will be hard to find. To put the cost into perspective, in high season 2017 the cost for a 12m yacht in Marina Ibiza was €236 per night plus charges for water and electricity; in Ibiza Magna which then had no facilities whatever, and a construction site alongside, the nightly cost was €200, again plus water and electricity. The charges reduce by a half or more in the shoulder season and in winter good deals may be available.

Depending on wind direction, the port, and in particular the outer part, is directly under the landing flight path for the nearby airport and noise levels from the aircraft are substantial in the outer marinas. When taking off to the north, aircraft are banked to take them offshore and there is little noise. Marina de Botafoch also suffers at times from considerable noise from the ships in the new ferry

Puerto de Ibiza looking northwest. Marina Botafoch with Marina Ibiza and commercial dock beyond

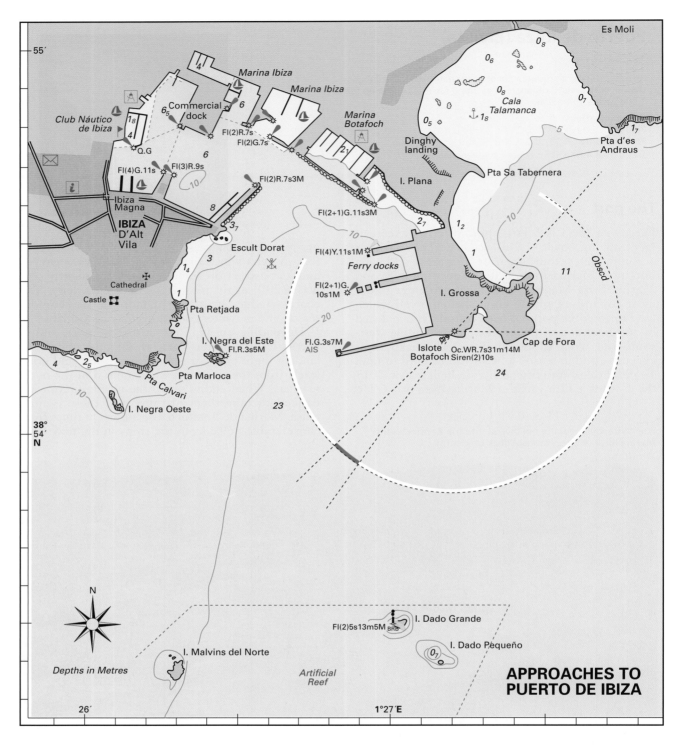

APPROACHES TO
PUERTO DE IBIZA

terminal and the heavy goods vehicles which access them. Whilst on the subject of noise it is worth noting that Marina Ibiza has a large new restaurant/cabaret/disco which is open-fronted onto the harbour.

The north side of the harbour including Marinas Botafoch and Ibiza and the surrounding area are reminiscent of Puerto Banús and Marbella on the Costa del Sol.

Pilotage

Approach

From south Several potential hazards litter the southern approach (*see plan page 32 and above*). These are: Islote La Esponja (10m), one mile east of Isla Sal Rossa; Malvins del Sur (20m) and Malvins del Norte (12m), 1·1 and 0·9 miles south of Pta Marloca; Dado Grande (7m) and Dado Pequeño (9m) about 0·8 miles south of Isla Botafoch. All lie near or outside the 20m contour and in daylight can be left on either hand. Dado Grande is lit (*see below*), the light being at 38 53'·5N 01 27'·2E.

If approaching at night it is wise to pass outside (east) of all these hazards – a bearing of 345° or less on Islote Botafoch ensures safe water. There is a light on Dado Grande and a light at the head of the newly extended breakwater (*see plan opposite*).

From northeast Coastal sailing from the northeast end of the island, or approaching from the direction of Mallorca, *see page 64* for details of the passage inside Isla Tagomago and *page 67* for Isla de Santa Eulalia. After passing Puerto de Santa Eulalia, Cabo Llibrell should be given a least offing of 200m, then the two small islands Lladó del Norte (10m), and Lladó del Sur (6m) identified just under a mile northeast of Cabo Martinet. Once spotted they can safely be passed on either side. Cabo Martinet, Isla Grossa and Isla Botafoch are all steep-to, though the latter now has a 400m breakwater running west-southwest from the lighthouse, which is left to starboard.

Anchorages in the approach

Anchoring on the northeast of the peninsula (east of the cathedral and north of Pta Retjada) is now prohibited. Since it is difficult to find a berth in the high season, bear this in mind if you are intending to pick up crew, as there are now no anchorages in the vicinity. A fine of up to €6,000 can be levied for anchoring. Cala Talamanca (*see page 73*) is now the closest anchorage, giving reasonably convenient access to the town via the Marina Botafoch ferry.

Entrance

The outer harbour is entered on passing between the extended breakwater and Islote Negra del Este. An inner harbour half a mile further north is formed by another mole (Dique Sur) on the west side; and Marina Botafoch to the northeast. Marina Ibiza, the Club Náutico and Marina Ibiza Magna lie within this inner basin.

Large commercial ships and many ferries use the harbour; they have right of way and must not be obstructed. For this reason it is advisable to keep to the starboard side of the entrance but there are no other navigational hazards. Islote Negra del Este and the breakwater head are both steep-to and there are good depths (i.e. more than 5m) in the entrance and throughout the commercial harbour. Note that to starboard (east) on entering the harbour there is now a major new ferry terminal with two large jetties which seem to be dedicated to the big Trasmediterranea and Balearia ferries which ply between the islands and to the mainland. These may not be shown on older charts. The two flashing green buoys, shown near the ends of these jetties on recent charts, were not in place by 2017, nor a third green buoy just SE of Marina Botafoch. The dock development means that the entrance to Marina Botafoch is largely obscured until close in, however the outer mark for the marina is a very clear beacon, *see plan opposite*. The numerous ferries of varying sizes which carry traffic to and from Formentera still operate from an area close to the Club Náutico. These ferries depart and arrive at relatively high speed and so a good lookout and caution are needed throughout the harbour.

Berthing

Once in the harbour there are four options for berthing, though as noted above all are likely to be crowded and very expensive in the high season.

1. Marina de Botafoch

An upmarket marina with 428 berths, able to take yachts of up to 30m, with excellent facilities. The office staff are helpful and several speak English. There are numerous restaurants and shops on site including a small supermarket and also a laundry which will collect and deliver to the boat.

Although reasonably wide, the entrance does not open up until past the ferry docks and can therefore be difficult to identify. The fuel and reception berth is on the starboard side on entry, with the marina offices nearby. When berths are not available, secure alongside the fuel

Puerto de Ibiza viewed southwest across Marina Botafoch towards the old town   *Geoff Williamson*

Marina Botafoch and the new ferry terminal from D'Alt Vila *Susie Baggaley*

dock when it closes. The fuel dock is open 0900–2100 in high season and 0900–1400 and 1600–1800 outside that period (closes 1400 at weekends). You must leave the dock before it opens again at 0900 the next morning unless purchasing fuel. A ferry plies across the harbour into town every half hour; in 2017 this was at quarter to and quarter past the hour.

VHF Ch 09
☎ 971 31 17 11/31 30 13/31 22 31
info@marinabotafoch.com
www.marinabotafoch.com

2. Marina Ibiza
(formerly Deportivo Ibiza Nueva)

Extending into the old commercial basin to the west has made Marina Ibiza the largest marina in the port, with 536 berths for yachts up to 55m on two pontoons. The northwest basin accommodates boats of 8–15m, providing optimum protection for vessels of that length. The southeast basin caters to vessels 18–55m in length. Work has been carried out recently - see the website for details. This includes parking, gardens, social club, fitness centre, restaurant, hairdressers, upmarket shops, TV and conference rooms. Facilities for yachts include water and electricity, (400A/380V) internet, TV, bilge and sewage pumps, fuel station, dry dock for small vessels and small scale repairs, as well as provision of a security service.

The dogleg entrance to the right of the yellow marina complex buildings presents no particular problems and has 3·5–4m depths. Secure on the north side of the north mole (where fuel is also available) to await allocation of a berth. There is a ferry service into town.

Note Berths near the commercial dock can be noisy with ships sometimes unloading all night.

Marina Ibiza VHF Ch 09
☎ 971 318 040
info@marinaibiza.com
www.marinaibiza.com/index_i.html

3. Club Náutico de Ibiza

Situated at the head of the harbour where there is berthing for 300 vessels. The club normally reserves 30 outside berths for visiting yachts of up to 15m (berths inside the marina are private). These outer berths can be oily and are exposed to ferry wash, so the use of 'spring coil'-type shock absorbers is recommended or use the Club Náutico lines which have car tyres as springs. It is said that the conditions are relatively quiet at night. The facilities are pleasant and welcoming, if less glitzy than the other marinas.

Club Náutico de Ibiza VHF Ch 09
☎ 971 31 33 63
info@clubnáuticoibiza.com
www.clubnáuticoibiza.com

4. Ibiza Magna
(formerly Port Authority pontoons)

This marina is situated in the extreme southwest corner of the harbour (at the foot of the historic D'Alt Vila, south of the Club Náutico) and has 85 moorings for yachts up to 60m length and 10m draught. It consists of two pontoons for vessels of up to 15m, of which 15 are kept for visitors, and a wall with about 12 positions for vessels of up to 60m. No depth restrictions. In 2017 the old office and facilities on the adjacent pier had been demolished and the whole area was a construction site. The Marina staff had a tiny office opposite and there were no facilities for those staying in the marina other than water and electricity on the pontoons. It is clear that the new works will not be completed in 2017 and perhaps not 2018. The Marina Magna website should be checked or the office contacted by those thinking of using the marina.

The picturesque cobbled streets of the old town (D'Alt Vila), leading to the cathedral and Punic necropolis, are close by. Be aware that in places the cobbles have worn to the point of being very slippery and care may be needed when descending some of the steeper streets and alleys.

Note This marina used to be one of the few collecting light dues on first entry to the islands, on behalf of the government but recent reports suggest they no longer do so. *See notes on Tarifas T-5 and T-0 on page 23.*

Ibiza Magna VHF Ch 09 (24 hours)
① 971 193 870
info@ibizamagna.com
www.ibizamagna.com

Facilities

Water At all berths listed above. The water in Ibiza may not now be suitable for drinking, so if possible consult other yachtsmen before filling tanks.

Electricity At all berths. Normally 220v, but 380v available at large yacht (25m) berths in the two marinas.

Fuel At Marina Botafoch and Marina Ibiza which has two fuelling points.

Bottled gas Camping Gaz exchanges at chandleries or in town. Note that Calor Gas bottles are not refillable on the islands now.

Provisions Supermarkets at the marinas plus an excellent choice in the town. All-day market on Fridays in summer.

Ice In the supermarkets at the marinas and in the Club Náutico bar.

Chandlery Well-stocked chandleries at Marina Botafoch and across the road from the Club Náutico.

Repairs The largest boatyard is situated just north of the Club Náutico but is actually part of the Marina Ibiza, as is the yard at the head of their west basin ① 971 310617. A smaller concern at Marina Botafoch. There are 160-tonne (max beam 10m) and 27-tonne travel-lifts at Marina Ibiza yards, 62-tonnes at Marina Botafoch and a slipway close north of the Club Náutico. Ibiza Yacht Service ① 971 312920/ 655626068/ 695888287
agency@ibzyachtservices.com
vicent@ibzyachtservices.com

Engineers Marina Botafoch and Marina Ibiza boatyards, also Yates Ibiza ① 971 19 03 26 just north of the Club Náutico and Ibiza Yacht Service ① 971 31 06 17 at the head of the Marina Ibiza west basin.

Official service agents include:
Auto Recambios Isla ① 971 31 10 12, *Yamaha*
Ibiza Yachting ① 971 191622, www.ibizayachting.com *Johnson*
Marina Marbella Ibiza SA ① 971 31 32 10, www.marinamarbella.net *Mercury/MerCruiser, Volvo Penta*
Motonautica ① 971 30 66 65/ 666 58 89 98 *Honda, Mercury/ MerCruiser, Soler, Suzuki, Yanmar*
Servinautic ① 971 19 13 18 www.servinauticibiza.com *Mariner, MerCruiser, Volvo Penta*

Electronic and radio repairs Both marina boatyards, Nautronic at Marina Botafoch, Yates Ibiza and Ibiza Yacht Service. Dews Marine.

Sailmaker Velamar Sailmakers, c/Capitan Guasch, Puig d'en Valls. ① 971 31 86 73/ 667205432

Yacht club Club Náutico de Ibiza has a bar, lounge, terrace, showers and restaurant.

Showers At the marinas and the Club Náutico.

Launderettes At the marinas and in the town.

Banks Several in the town.

Post office In the town.

Hospital/medical services In the town.

Transport

Car hire/taxis In the town, or arrange through marina offices.

Buses Regular services over most of the island.

Ferries Car ferries to mainland Spain and Mallorca. Frequent tourist ferries and hydrofoils to Formentera and various beaches.

Air services International airport three miles south of the harbour. The hourly bus service from the airport to the terminus on Avenida Isidoro Macabich in the centre takes 20 minutes and runs between 0730–2230 from the airport.

Ashore

Although a small part of the old town (D'Alt Vila) and citadel is still unspoilt, the city has become very overcrowded in the summer, and even in winter the locals are outnumbered by foreign visitors and

Marina Ibiza Magna

I. IBIZA

residents. However, both the old town and the wider city are well worth a visit and contain, amongst many other interesting buildings, the cathedral and the Archaeological Museum.

On the western slopes of the hill is the Puig des Molins necropolis, a subterranean burial place which served the city from the Phoenician era (7th century BC) until Roman times. It is open to the public, together with a museum. Parts of the cathedral date back to the 13th century, shortly after the island was reconquered for Spain, but the great citadel walls were built in the late 16th century and bear the arms of King Phillip II.

If hiring a car, take the road north from Ibiza city towards San Juan Bautista and Cala Portinatx or to the tranquil Cala San Vicente, a pleasant drive along winding coastal roads, where you will find a shrine to the goddess Tanit who was worshipped by the Phoenicians at the Cueva Cuyeram.

Local events

Fiestas are held on the Friday night of Holy Week (Good Friday), on 24 June to celebrate the old king's name saint (San Juan), and 1 August in honour of La Virgen de las Nieves, patron saint of the island. On 16 August there is a sea procession as part of the Fiesta del Virgen del Carmen.

Eating out

There are restaurants and bars in the marinas, and a vast number in the town, many of them excellent. One place of note for something very different is El Zaguan – a tapas bar in Avda Bartolome Rosello, 15. Not by any means a normal tapas bar, but with a constant stream of high quality tapas the likes of which you will probably never have experienced before - and not expensive. Well worth the inevitable wait for a table: no advance bookings possible.

Islets south of Puerto de Ibiza

Several small islets lie in the bay south of Puerto de Ibiza (see *Approach* above). From north to south these are: Dado Grande (Dau Gran) (7m) and Dado Pequeño (Dau Petit) (9m) about 0·8 miles south of Islote Botafoch; Malvins del Norte (12m) and Malvins del Sur (20m) 0·9 and 1·1 miles south of Pta Marloca; and Islote La Esponja (10m), one mile east of Isla Sal Rossa. All lie near or outside the 20m contour and can be left on either hand.

Anchorages and features south of Puerto de Ibiza

⚓ Punta de la Mata (Playa d'en Bossa)
38°53'·7N 01°25'E

A small and shallow harbour of little use to yachts about one mile southwest of Puerto de Ibiza, (see *plan page 32*) tucked southwest of the punta and partially enclosed by a rough breakwater and short jetty. Small fishing boats and motor boats lie to crowded moorings in ±1m over sand and weed.

It is overlooked by hotels and high-rise tourist apartments, with a main road nearby.

⚓ Calas de Sal Rossa
38°52'·3N 01°24'·5E

Two small anchorages either side of Isla Sal Rossa (see *plan page 32*) open northeast–east–southeast. Anchor in 2–3·5m over weed, sand and rock. The conspicuous (28m) Torre Sal Rossa stands to the northwest.

The area is still unspoilt, with only some local fishing craft and net stores ashore. Ibiza airport is little more than a mile away (see *plan page 28)* but noise is not really a problem as the anchorage is away to the side of the flight path. There is a rough track to the main road.

⚓ Playa d'es Caballet (Es Cavallet)
38°51'·2N 01°24'·3E

A long sandy beach open north–east–south. There are developments at either end, a small jetty to the north and a track to the road. Anchor in 5m or less over sand and rock.

Isla Espalmador
38°47'·8N 01°25'·3E (N tip)

This 1·5M long rocky island is the largest of a chain forming the long south-southeast-going reef and shoals that connect Ibiza with the island of Formentera. Anchorages and features around Espalmador and Espardel are described separately under *Formentera* on *page 80*.

Passes between Ibiza and Espalmador

There are three possible passes (*freus*) between Isla de Ibiza and Isla Espalmador; only one, the Freu Grande, is usable in all conditions, day or night, although Freu Mediano makes a useful short cut in good weather in daylight. The lights in the area are reliable and a night passage through Freu Grande should not present any problems. *See plan opposite.*

This whole area is a marine reserve (effectively meaning no fishing or anchoring) and was marked by six yellow conical buoys Fl.Y.5s with x topmark, but these do not seem to be still present. Three were to the east and three to the west of the chain of islands. (If they reappear, feedback would be appreciated.)

Approach

See plan page 28

From east or northeast Approach the *freus* on a southwest course following the coast of Ibiza and leaving Isla Espardel (lit) to port. Two hills, Corpmari (159m) and Falcón (145m), lie near the southern extremity of Ibiza though Punta Portas itself is low. The black-and-white-banded

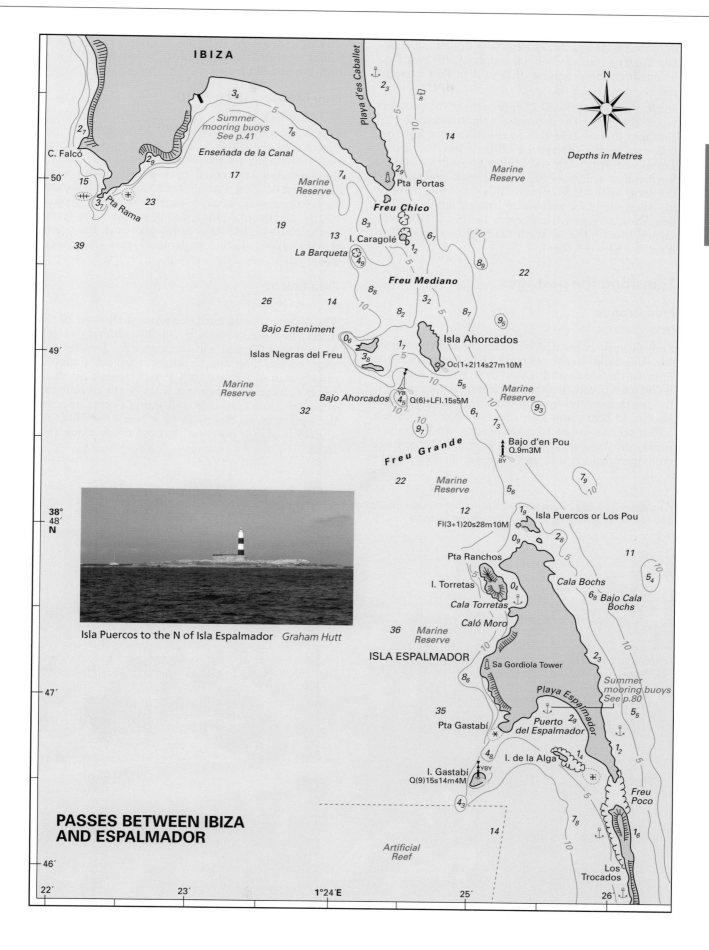

IBIZA

C. Falcó

2₇

2₉

15

3₇

Pta Rama

23

39

3₄

Summer
mooring buoys
See p.41

Enseñada de la Canal

17

7₆

7₄

Marine
Reserve

19

5

Playa d'es Caballet

2₃

R

Pta Portas

2₉

Freu Chico

8₃

13 I. Caragolé

La Barqueta

4₉

8₈

1₂

6₇

Freu Mediano

26

14

8₂

3₂

8₇

Bajo Enteniment

0₆

1₇

Islas Negras del Freu

3₈

5

Isla Ahorcados

Oc(1+2)14s27m10M

9₅

Marine
Reserve

Marine
Reserve

14

Depths in Metres

N

I. IBIZA

50′

49′

10

8₉

22

9₃

5₅

6₁

7₃

Bajo Ahorcados

YB
4₅ Q(6)+LFl.15s5M

32

10

9₇

Freu Grande

22

Marine
Reserve

5₆

Bajo d'en Pou
Q.9m3M
BY

7₉

10

12

Fl(3+1)20s28m10M

1₉ Isla Puercos or Los Pou

0₉

2₈

11

5₄

Pta Ranchos

Cala Bochs

I. Torretas

0₄

6₈ Bajo Cala
Bochs

Cala Torretas

Caló Moro

36 Marine
Reserve

ISLA ESPALMADOR

Sa Gordiola Tower

2₃

8₆

Summer
mooring buoys
See p.80

35

Pta Gastabí

Puerto
del Espalmador

2₉

5₅

4₈

I. de la Alga

1₄

1₂

I. Gastabí
Q(9)15s14m4M

YBY

4₃

Freu
Poco

14

7₈

1₆

Artificial
Reef

Los
Trocados

38°
48′
N

Isla Puercos to the N of Isla Espalmador *Graham Hutt*

48′

47′

46′

22′

23′

1°24′E

25′

26′

PASSES BETWEEN IBIZA
AND ESPALMADOR

lighthouses of Isla Ahorcados (Illa des Penjats) and Isla Puercos (or Los Pou) are unmistakable, with the lit north cardinal beacon of Bajo d'en Pou between them.

From west or northwest If approaching the passages from the Spanish mainland, the mountains of southern Ibiza will be first to rise above the horizon, followed by the spectacular cliffs of Isla Vedrá (lit). On closer approach the higher southern parts of Formentera will be seen, but the smaller islands of the *freus* will not become visible until much closer in, when the black-and-white-banded lighthouses of Isla Ahorcados and Isla Puercos (or Los Pou) can be identified with the lit north cardinal beacon of Bajo d'en Pou between them.

Transiting the passages

Freu Grande

38°48'·5N 01°24'·8E

Freu Grande is located between the lighthouses of Isla Ahorcados to the north and Isla Puercos (or Los Pou) to the south and is just over a mile wide and 6–7m least depth. Slightly to the south of its centre is the north cardinal beacon marking Bajo d'en Pou, also lit. In heavy seas keep clear of Bajo Ahorcados, 550m southwest of Isla Ahorcados, and pass just north of Bajo d'en Pou. It is the only passage recommended for use after dark, but in that case be careful to avoid the two Islas Negras del Freu, about 500m west of Isla Ahorcados, which are unlit and only 2m and 4m high.

Freu Mediano (Freu Petit)

38°49'·4N 01°24'·6E

Freu Mediano lies between Isla Ahorcados (Illa des Penjats) to the south and Islote Caragolé, a small rock 8m high, to the north. Watch out for La Barqueta, an unmarked rock awash 500m west-southwest of Islote Caragolé: though often indicated by breaking seas, in calm weather it does not show clearly. Depths of 3–4m are to be found in the centre of the channel. Isla Ahorcados was once the site of the gallows where condemned prisoners were executed.

Freu Chico

38°49'·8N 01°24'·4E

The furthest north, narrowest and shallowest of the three *freus*, for use only by shallow-draught vessels in calm weather and with extreme care. Depths may shoal to less than 1m. Careful eyeball navigation is required in order to avoid a rocky patch north of Islote Caragolé; a course a little north of halfway between Islote Caragolé and Punta Portas appears the optimum. La Barqueta rock (see *Freu Mediano* above) is also a potential hazard when using this freu.

Freu Grande passage from the southwest. Lighthouses on Isla Puercos (right) and Isla Ahorcados (left) are clear for a night passage

2. ENSENADA DE LA CANAL TO ISLA VEDRÁ

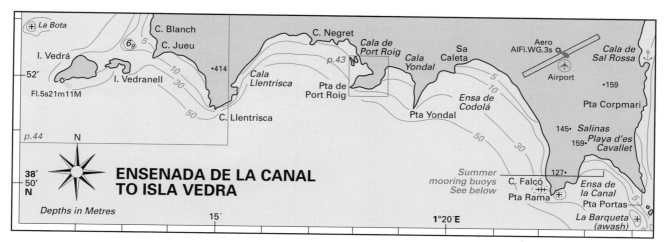

⚓ Ensenada de la Canal

38°50'·3N 01°23'·2E

A large sandy bay south of the National Park Ses Salines, between Punta Portas and Punta Rama; on the southern tip of Ibiza. A pier for loading salt is sited in the northwest corner, backed by a factory complex ashore. Mooring buoys have been placed along this stretch, managed by Posidonia, but nevertheless there are still places to anchor outside of the buoyed area taking care to avoid the sea grass. See www.balearslifeposidonia.eu. Buoys can be reserved from 1 June to 30 September, although the busy time is in July and August, and moorings can be found with little difficulty outside of those months. See also the *Moorings* section on *page 19*.

The bay is relatively undeveloped ashore other than a few beach restaurants, but the beach itself (Playa de Mitjorn) can get very crowded, due to frequent ferries and buses from Ibiza. The nearby *salinas* (salt pans) are a protected area, attracting many migrating birds in spring and autumn.

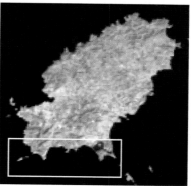

Punta Rama and Cabo Falcó

38°49'·8N N 01°22'·3E

A prominent double headland with various offlying hazards. The isolated Bajo Morenallet lies 350m east of Punta Rama, several islets lie to the south and there is a wreck some 100m west of the punta. Allow an offing of at least 500m.

Ensenada de la Canal anchorage. Note the salt loading pier

Sa Caleta, looking NNW

⚓ Ensenada de Codolá (Sa Caleta)

38°51'·9N 01°20'·4E

A long bay shielded by Punta Yondal and Cabo Falcó at either end, with a smaller bay, Sa Caleta, at its western end. Anchor in 5m over sand at Sa Caleta, off the beach with a restaurant above, or further east in 10m over sand and weed off the sand and stone beach. The village of Sa Caleta is backed by several tower blocks. Phoenician remains have been found on the peninsula west of Sa Caleta, including the foundations of a village dated at around the 7th century BC.

The centre of the bay lies under the airport flight path, making the area noisy – it is 1·5 miles from Sa Caleta to the terminal buildings. The area south of the airport is salt pans.

Punta Yondal (des Jondal)

38°51'·4N 01°19'·3E

A serrated headland running out to a low promontory with a hole through it. Rocks extend up to 300m south of the point.

Cala Yondal

⚓ Cala Yondal (des Jondal)

38°51'·4N 01°19'·2E

A wide but relatively sheltered bay lying between Punta de Port Roig and Punta Yondal, open south and southwest. Anchor about 100m off the beach in 6–10m over sand and weed. Beach café and other buildings inland, and a track to the road. This *cala* has become very crowded in summer. Dinghies are not welcome here. In fact, landing can be quite difficult as the beach is steep-to. Probably the best place is the northwest corner close to a small landing stage which is for the Es Xarca restaurant customers. The restaurant (☎ 971 187867) has a water taxi service for anchored yachts.

Punta de Port Roig (Punta Porroig)

38°51'·7N 01°17'·8E

A relatively low flat point with a hole through it and some scattered buildings on the summit.

⚓ Cala de Port Roig (Cala Porroig)

38°52'·1N 01°18'·0E

In no way a port, but rather a delightful sheltered anchorage between Punta de Port Roig and Las Isletas, surrounded by sloping reddish cliffs and well protected from all winds except southwest. Anchor in 6–10m over sand, weed and rock, taking care to avoid cables from the Spanish mainland which come ashore in the bay.

Fisherman's huts line the eastern shore, but there are few other buildings. Many private buoys are placed in the bay in summer, depleting the anchorage possibilities. A short dinghy trip around Las Isletas takes you to a lovely (nudist) beach, Cala es Torrent, which has a *chiringuito*/bar.

Cala es Torrent, north of Cala de Port Roig: a remarkably tranquil anchorage. Note Illeta Petita and Illeta Grossa to the right

⚓ Cala Llentrisca

38°51'·8N 01°15'·4E

A small anchorage with a stony beach tucked under scrub-covered cliffs on the east side of Cabo Llentrisca. Exposed from northeast to southeast and to swell from the south. Anchor in 4–6m over sand and stone, although there are depths of up to 23m off the entrance. Boats and fishermen's huts line the beach, with a steep track up to the road.

This is a useful anchorage while awaiting favourable weather for the passage to the mainland but keep well clear of the fishermen's moorings.

Cabo Llentrisca

38°51'·3N 01°14'·9E

A steep, white-cliffed headland (148m) free of off-lying dangers.

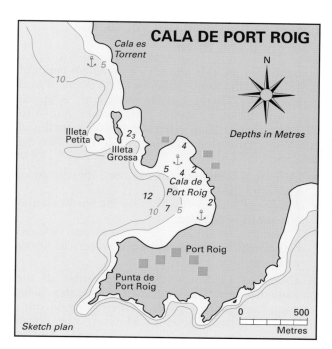

Sketch plan

CALA DE PORT ROIG

Cala es Torrent

⚓ 5

10

Illeta Petita

Illeta Grossa

2₃

N

Depths in Metres

4

5   4   2

Cala de Port Roig

12

10   7   5   2

Port Roig

Punta de Port Roig

0   500

Metres

Cala Llentrisca: a small sheltered anchorage northeast of Cape Llentrisca

Isla Vedra, Isla Vedranell, with Cala Horts above Vedranell, and the passages to the mainland *Geoff Williamson*

⚓ Isla Vedrá

38°51'·8N 01°11'·3E (light)

A lofty (382m), spectacular, rocky island, steep sided and steep-to, of a reddish colour. The lighthouse (white conical tower, 3m) is on the south coast and obscured when bearing between 134° and 262°.

There are two possible anchorages: one close north of the island in 12m tucked in to the east of Isla Galera, with landing feasible in a small inlet, the other off the northeast coast in 15m, just west of a group of rocks. Both have poor holding over stone and rock. Approach with care, and only in good conditions. The island was used as a location for the South Pacific 'Bali Hai' photography.

⚓ Isla Vedranell

38°52'·1N 01°12'·9E (E. Point)

Considerably lower (125m) and smaller than its neighbour, but equally steep-to, particularly to the south. Anchor in 12m over sand and rock close off the north coast. Again, a strictly fair weather spot.

Isla Vedranell with deep-water passages either side

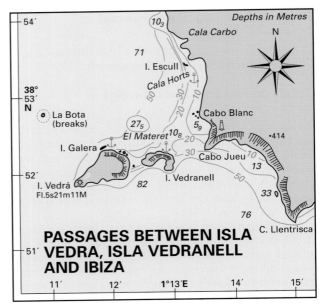

PASSAGES BETWEEN ISLA VEDRA, ISLA VEDRANELL AND IBIZA

Passages between Isla Vedrá, Isla Vedranell and Ibiza

A channel 750m wide and with a minimum depth of more than 10m runs between Isla Vedranell and Cabo Jueu (l'Oliva) on the mainland. A much narrower passage, some 200m wide but also carrying a good 10m, separates Isla Vedranell and Isla Vedrá. Attention must be paid to the following dangers:

- La Bota, a breaking rock 1M north-northwest of Isla Vedrá light
- A series of small rocky islets on the northeast and east coasts of Isla Vedrá
- El Materet, 10·8m deep, 800m southwest of Cabo Blanc, which creates turbulent waters in heavy weather.

A course of 125°/305° down the centre of the passage between Isla Vedranell and Cabo Jueu, keeping the point of Cabo Llentrisca equidistant between the two, clears El Materet. The inside passage is prone to sudden, strong gusts, and in heavy weather it is advisable to pass well outside Isla Vedrá and La Bota.

3. CABO JUEU (L'OLIVA) TO PUERTO DE SAN ANTONIO

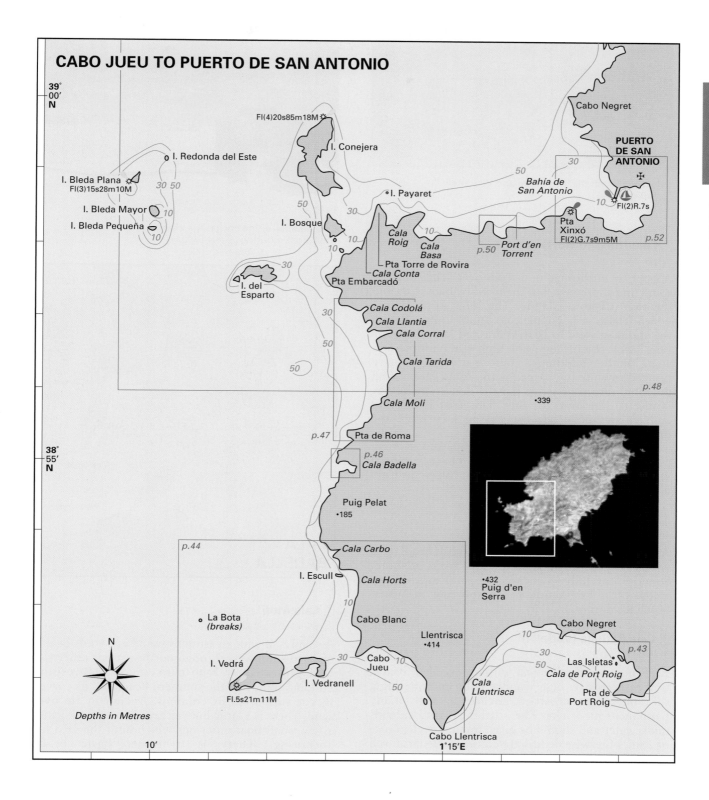

CABO JUEU TO PUERTO DE SAN ANTONIO

39°00'N

Fl(4)20s85m18M

I. Conejera

I. Redonda del Este

I. Bleda Plana
Fl(3)15s28m10M

30 50

I. Bleda Mayor
10

I. Bleda Pequeña
10

I. Payaret

I. Bosque

50

30

Cabo Negret

PUERTO DE SAN ANTONIO

30

50

Bahía de San Antonio

10

Fl(2)R.7s

Cala Roig

Cala Basa

10

Port d'en Torrent

p.50

Pta Xinxó
Fl(2)G.7s9m5M

p.52

Pta Torre de Rovira

Cala Conta

Pta Embarcadó

10

30

I. del Esparto

Cala Codolá

Cala Llantia

Cala Corral

30

50

Cala Tarida

50

p.48

Cala Moli

•339

p.47

Pta de Roma

p.46
Cala Badella

38°55'N

Puig Pelat
•185

p.44

Cala Carbo

I. Escull

Cala Horts

10

La Bota
(breaks)

Cabo Blanc

Llentrisca
•414

I. Vedrá

30

Cabo Jueu

10

I. Vedranell

50

Fl.5s21m11M

N

Depths in Metres

10'

Cala Llentrisca

Cabo Llentrisca

1°15'E

•432
Puig d'en Serra

Cabo Negret

10

30

50

Las Isletas

Cala de Port Roig

p.43

Pta de Port Roig

Cala d'Hort with the Islas Vedra and Vedranell
Susie Baggaley

Cala Badella, a fine anchorage albeit partly taken up by
small boat moorings *Susie Baggaley*

⚓ Cala Horts (d'Hort)

38°53'·3N 01°13'·4E

A popular anchorage in 5–10m over sand, open to
south and southwest, but sheltered by high cliffs and
the two offshore islands. The long stony beach,
which is also very popular, no doubt in part due to
the stunning view to Islas Vedra and Vedranell, has
two beach restaurants, one high-rise building and
some smaller buildings. There is a very extensive
buoyed swimming area with some anchoring
potential directly outside but the largest anchorage
is just to the south of this. This *cala* is another
convenient anchorage for passages between the
mainland and Ibiza.

Remains from the Carthaginian and Roman
periods, including the foundations of a substantial
villa, have been excavated at Ses Països de Cala
d'Hort, a short distance inland.

⚓ Cala Carbo

38°53'·7N 01°13'·0E

A small angled *cala* between low reddish headlands,
which may be difficult to identify from offshore.
Sound-in carefully to anchor in ±3m over sand and
weed, off a fine sandy beach sporting the usual
beach restaurant.

⚓ Cala Badella (Vadella)

38°54'·8N 01°13'·1E

A deep and attractive *cala* with an excellent beach,
well protected by high wooded cliffs and offering a
safe but often crowded anchorage with many
permanent moorings. The north headland extends
underwater and should be given minimum clearance
of 25m, otherwise depths are considerable until well
inside the *cala*. Anchor in 3–10m as space permits
over sand and weed; it may be necessary to use two
anchors to limit swinging. Larger yachts sometimes
moor with a line to the rocks on the southern
headland. No shortage of restaurants, cafés and bars
behind the beach. Small supermarket in the village.

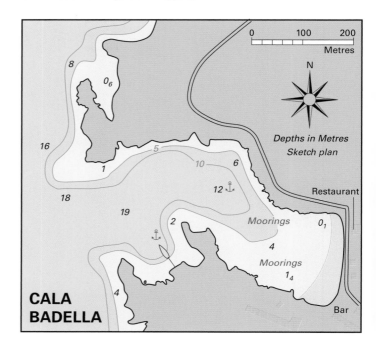

CALA BADELLA

⚓ Cala Moli

38°55'·9N 01°13'·8E

A small *cala* with an attractive sand and stone beach,
open to southwest through northwest but otherwise
well protected by high cliffs. A distinctive pink
building stands on the southern headland, its curved
façade supported by columns. Anchor in 5m over
sand. There is a large buoyed area for swimming and
a few small boat moorings which limit the area for
anchoring. There is a rather basic beach
bar/restaurant ashore, catering for the tourist boats
from San Antonio, plus some new development to
the north.

Cala Moli *Susie Baggaley*

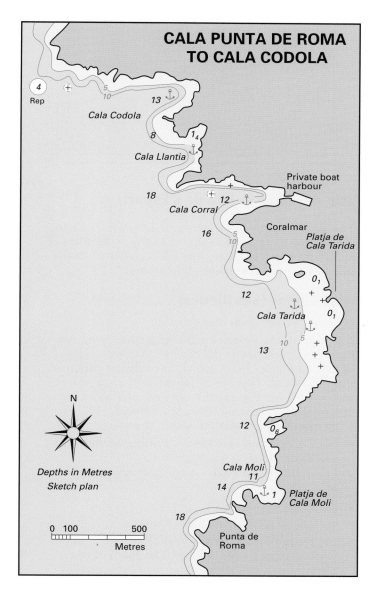

**CALA PUNTA DE ROMA
TO CALA CODOLA**

4
Rep

5
10

13

Cala Codola

8

1₄

Cala Llantia

18

12

Cala Corral

16

5
10

Private boat
harbour

Coralmar

Platja de
Cala Tarida

0₁

12

Cala Tarida

0₁

13

10   5

12

0₆

Cala Moli
11

14   1

Platja de
Cala Moli

18

Punta de
Roma

N

*Depths in Metres
Sketch plan*

0   100   500

Metres

I. IBIZA

⚓ **Cala Tarida**
38°56′·3N 01°14′E

A long bay with two sandy beaches separated by a substantial rocky outcrop thus forming Calas Tarida del Sur and del Norte, and with two low, inshore islands. Cala Tarida is easily identified by the extensive tourist developments around both north and south. Anchor in 4–5m over sand, weed and rock. There are many beach restaurants and cafés ashore, together with some shops. A submarine cable shown extending WSW from the E shoreline in the *cala* on some earlier charts has been removed on updated plans.

⚓ **Cala Corral**
38°56′·7N 01°13′·8E

A rocky-sided *cala* open southwest through northwest and with a small and shallow private harbour (Coralmar) tucked behind a rocky wall at its head. Anchor in 5–6m over sand and rock. A large tourist development (confusingly, a part of Cala Tarida del Norte) stands behind and somewhat above the beach, itself fringed by fishermen's huts. A restaurant and supermarket will be found amongst the buildings to the north.

Cala Tarida *Lukasz Janyst / 123RF*

Cala Corral *Susie Baggaley*

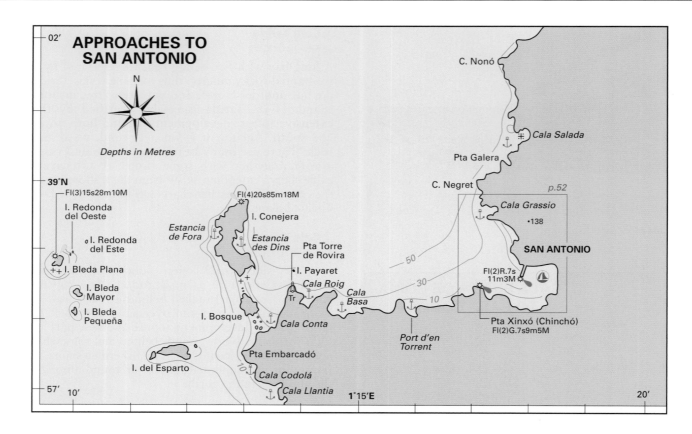

⚓ Cala Llantia

38°56'·8N 01°13'·7E

A rocky-sided *cala* open southwest and west, with a beach at its head and a line of white houses on a cliff to the northwest. Anchor off the beach in 5m over sand.

⚓ Cala Codolá (Codolar)

38°57'N 01°13'·5E

A cliff-sided *cala* with a stony beach at its head, open to southwest through northwest. The north side of the *cala* is roped off for swimming. Although it is possible to anchor just outside the swimming buoys, this is rather close to the rocks and to allow sufficient swinging room for comfort it is better to anchor further out over sand, weed and rock in about 8m. Low-rise white houses line the clifftop to the north, together with a few shops. Tourist boats visit daily in season.

Isla del Esparto (Illa de s'Espart)

The north–south pass between Isla del Esparto (68m) and Ibiza is more than 1,000m wide with a minimum depth of 30m. A small rocky islet stands just off the northeast point of the island.

Islas Bledas (Ses Bledes)

38°58'·8N 01°09'·6E (Bleda Plana lighthouse)

A group of five uninhabited rocky islets lying two miles northwest of Isla del Esparto. At their centre is Isla Bleda Plana (23m), which has offlying rocks to the southwest. There is a lighthouse (white round tower, 8m) on the northwest side of this island, obscured when bearing between 239° and 349°. The other islands, from north to south, comprise:

- Isla Redonda del Este (13m), 1,000m northeast of Isla Bleda Plana
- Isla Redonda del Oeste, close northeast of Isla Bleda Plana
- Isla Bleda Mayor (Na Bose) (39m), 1,000m south-southeast of Isla Bleda Plana
- Isla Bleda Pequeña (Na Gorra) (29m), sometimes referred to as Porros, about 400m south of Isla Bleda Mayor and with foul ground between the two.

Explore the area with care and a bow lookout. In settled conditions it is reported possible to anchor in 5m near the lighthouse landing on Isla Bleda Plana, taking a sternline ashore.

Pass between Isla Conejera (Sa Conillera) and Isla Bosque (de Bosc)

A pass 200m wide exists between Isla Conejera (69m) and Isla Bosque (67m). It is generally deep, except where a narrow bar of rocks and sand links the two islands, leaving previously reported minimum depths of 2·3m midway between islands, clearly visible on the photo below. However, more recent reports have given 4·5–4·8m, which is consistent with Spanish charts. It is still recommended that this pass should only be attempted in reasonably flat sea conditions and good light. Do note that this bar also contains rocks along its length. In good light the paler colours of the bar should be clearly visible. Rocks extend from both islands, those off Isla Conejera barely breaking while those off Isla Bosque stand well above the water (though with a few breaking outliers).

Take the pass in an east–west direction halfway between the two islands with a bias towards Isla Bosque. It becomes unsafe with any sea running, when it would be much more sensible to pass outside Isla Conejera . There is an excellent small anchorage on the NE side of the bar tucked in under the cliff: take lines to the shore to avoid swinging. Note that park rangers patrol the island and often prohibit landing, but not anchoring. Their rib is marked as Islas Verdi.

Pass between Isla Bosque and Ibiza

The pass between Isla Bosque and Ibiza is a dangerous mass of awash and barely-covered rocks (*see photo*) and really only suitable for dinghies in calm conditions, though a 2m passage is said to exist - definitely for use only with local knowledge.

Anchorages and features between Isla Conejera and San Antonio

⚓ Estancia de Fora, Isla Conejera
38°59'·1N 01°12'·4E

A small *cala* on the west side of Isla Conejera. Strictly a fair-weather spot. Anchor in 5–7m over sand and rock.

⚓ Estancia des Dins, Isla Conejera
38°59'·1N 01°12'·8E

A large sandy bay on the east of the island, open to the northeast and with a three mile plus fetch to east and southeast. Anchor in 3m or more over sand and rock. There is a landing and miniature boat harbour at the north end of the bay, with a track to the lighthouse (white tower and building, 18m) which stands at the north end of the island.

There are no facilities ashore, though temporary beach restaurants do set up in summer when the island is a popular destination with tourist boats. The protected green lizard abounds.

⚓ Cala Conta (Comte)
38°57'·9N 01°13'·4E

A small but exposed *cala* on the mainland shore just north of the shoals running out to Isla Bosque. Anchor in 5–6m over sand, off a fine beach fringed by fishermen's huts. An alternative anchorage is W of the shoals between Isla del Bosque and Ibiza.

⚓ Cala Roig (Roja)
38°58'·3N 01°14'·1E

A rocky-sided *cala* open to the north sector, not recommended unless conditions are good. The impressive Torre de Rovira, built in 1763 to protect Ibiza's west coast, stands on the headland of that name west of the *cala*. Shoals run out towards Isla Payaret some 200m northeast of the point.

Isla Conejera (larger island) and Isla Bosque: the bar clearly visible

Port d'en Torrent *Susie Baggaley*

Cala Basa: yachts anchored on west side. Note the swimmers' buoys *Geoff Williamson*

Port d'en Torrent: a *cala* offering shelter deep inside

⚓ Cala Basa (Cala Bassa)

38°58'·1N 01°14'·5E

A large and attractive *cala* with a sandy beach at its head, surrounded by pine woods and low cliffs, open to north and northeast. Anchor in 5–8m over sand and rock. There is a landing stage used by tourist boats, several beach restaurants and cafés, and a nearby camp site. Though often crowded during the day, the beach is usually deserted by evening.

The entire *cala* shoreline is now owned by Cala Bassa Beach Club, a company with links to Andorra. Bars, restaurants, boutiques and a Taittinger Lounge are here and it is very crowded in summer. Reports of difficulty breaking out anchors from the rocks have been filed. It may be better to anchor in deeper water not less than 12–15m, where rocks give way to a sand and weed bottom with good holding, although this holding may be patchy.

⚓ Port d'en Torrent

38°58'·2N 01°15'·9E

A large angled *cala* with low rocky sides and a sandy beach at its head, open to the north sector. Anchor in 4–6m over sand, rock and weed. Small yachts may be able to tuck into the sheltered east arm, though this is now partly occupied by permanent moorings, leaving room for probably only one yacht to have reasonable swinging room. A careful watch should be kept for swimmers and water-skiers, as well as on the depth. Larger vessels should anchor further northwest (*see plan*) where the holding is also somewhat better, but be ready to depart at the threat of onshore winds.

There are beach bars and restaurants near the *cala* but rather less than is suggested by the sobrequet 'Port'. The original large supermarket closed and two smaller ones opened, giving basic provisions. The beach officials object to yacht dinghies being left during shopping trips. Jet-skis are banned in the area.

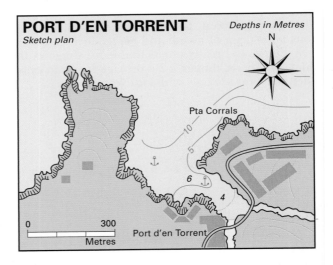

PORT D'EN TORRENT
Sketch plan

Depths in Metres

N

Pta Corrals

10
5
6
4

0   300
Metres

Port d'en Torrent

Punta Xinxó (Chinchó)

38°58'·5N 01°17'·0E

A very low, rocky-cliffed promontory, difficult to identify except for the lighthouse on the point (Fl(2)G.7s9m5M green column on white base displaying a green triangle). A road and buildings lie behind.

Puerto de San Antonio
(Sant Antoni de Portmany)

38°58'·6N 01°17'·5E

A safe harbour, easy to enter in all conditions tucked into the N end of a large bay. There is berthing for over 500 yachts up to 50m at Club Náutico and around 250 with Ports IB, with several transit visitors' berths available.

Communications

Es Naútic San Antonio
(Previously Club Náutico and still a members' club)
    VHF Ch 09 Marineros and office
    VHF Ch 11 Fuel berth
    VHF Ch 12 Visitors short stay (up to 2 hours)
    ☎ + 34 971 340645
    info@esnautic.com
    Reservations via www.amarreibiza.com (except in August) or www.esnautic.com

Ports IB
    Ch VHF 14, 8
    ☎ +34 971 340503
    port.santantoni@portsib.es
    www.portsib.es

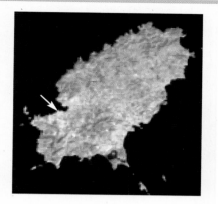

I. IBIZA

The harbour

A large yacht and fishing harbour deep inside a bay protected by a short breakwater. The facilities are well used, with many private moorings also in the bay. The two marinas have a total of nearly 800 berths, but it is difficult to find a space in July and August.

Moorings with Ports IB (see below) are cheaper than Es Náutic, but these must be booked online in advance in high season. The number of transit berths available is reduced off season.

Es Naútic is a modern, well run marina with excellent facilities whose prices are not unreasonable by Balearic standards, at least outside high season; in May 2017, a 13·2m yacht was €45 per night including water and electricity.

Pilotage

Approach

From northeast and north From northeast and north Cabo Eubarca, which has a cone-shaped top, and Cabo Nonó, which is covered with pine woods, are high, steep headlands and easy to identify (*see plan on page 55*). The Islas Margaritas can be left on either side. Enter the bay of San Antonio on a southerly course, steering initally towards a group of distant mountains. When well inside the bay the head of the breakwater with its red column and white base will open up.

Bahía de San Antonio

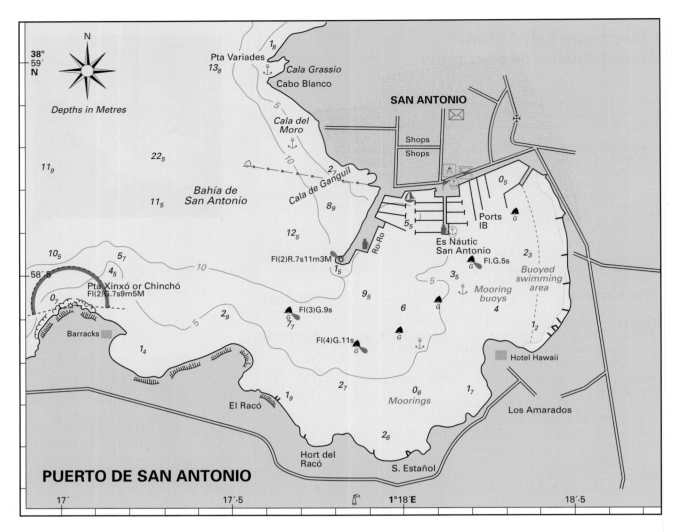

PUERTO DE SAN ANTONIO

From west and south Isla Conejera with its conspicuous lighthouse is easily seen (*see plan on page 48*). In bad weather it is advisable to pass outside this island with an offing of at least 200m before setting a southeast course towards the harbour. In calm conditions the passage between Isla Conejera and Isla Bosque can be used with care. If approaching from the Iberian mainland note that the Islas Bledas lie some 2½ miles west of Isla Conejera, only the largest having a lighthouse.

Anchorage in the approach

There are several possible *cala* anchorages on the south side of the Bahía de San Antonio, as detailed in the preceding pages.

Entrance

Underwater obstructions extend a short distance beyond the end of the breakwater, so allow at least 50m. Otherwise the entrance is wide and without hazards, though shoals run out a short way beyond Punta Xinxó (Chinchó) and its equally inconspicuous eastern neighbour: keep at least the first two starboard-hand buoys to starboard.

Berthing

Ports IB (formerly the Port Authority) has restructured its facility in the NE corner of the harbour with the placement of 3 pontoons running N/S replacing the smaller dinghy quay. Transit yachts can use the W side of the first pontoon going bows/stern to the pontoon using tailed lines. The small Ports IB office is opposite the Es Naútic entrance. In high season, as with all Ports IB berths, a place should be booked online 24 hours or more in advance; you need to be registered first. (*See page 20 for further details.*) A maximum of 5 days' stay only is allowed, though this rule seems to depend on who is on duty. In low season, the pontoon is reduced in length and it is not necessary to book in advance. If there is space, even in high season, or if a reserved berth is not taken by 1800, the staff are accommodating. There are between 16 and 20 visitors' berths for 12m yachts. Bookings cannot be made by phone, but calling on VHF Ch 8 on arrival and taking pot luck is another option and probably the most practical outside of the high season.

Es Naútic moorings can be booked as noted in the cream box above. Space is limited in high season, and in August a waiting system operates. Call the marina after 0900 to get on the list, and call back

Puerto de San Antonio viewed from east with Es Naútic pontoons centre and Ports IB visitors' pontoon lower.
Es Naútic 2014

after 1200 to be allocated a space if one is available. Call on VHF Ch 12 for short stop for water/water and electricity up to 2 hours. (Charged at €9 per half hour.)

Anchorage in the bay

Anchor to the south and east of the green buoys marking the access channel in 5m or less, in sand and weed. Holding is poor in patches, with the best holding in the north of the bay.

RoRo ferries which berth near the root of the breakwater and on the widened area must not be impeded, and a channel must also be left for the fishing boats and tourist ferries which berth east of the Ports IB pontoons. As much of the bay is occupied by moorings this leaves limited space for anchoring in the northern part of the bay but even in the height of summer there is usually room to be found further south.

Some boats anchor in the long but open and unattractive bay just outside and to the northwest of the harbour entrance, Cala des Moro. There is a line of swimming buoys and anchoring would be in about 9-10m over mainly weed with a few patches of sand and rock.

Moorings

There are a few private moorings, some of which may be available. However one can never be sure of intended maximum tonnage, state of repair, or when

San Antonio: a view along the promenade
Geoff Williamson

the owner will return. Certainly a yacht on a borrowed mooring should never be left unattended.

Facilities

Water On pontoons for both marinas and is potable.
Electricity On the pontoons.
Fuel Diesel and petrol from pumps on the breakwater. Diesel at Es Naútic.
Provisions A wide range of shops and supermarkets in the town, several on the road leading from opposite Es Naútic. There are Hiper Centro and Eroski supermarkets near Plaza España, again only a few

Puerto de San Antonio. Hundreds of people flock to the W end of the promenade on foot, by boat or by microlight, to honour the sun as it sets across the outer harbour   *Graham Hutt*

minutes walk from the marina. Also two small supermarkets behind the prominent Hotel Hawaii on the southeast shore of the bay. A produce market on the Carrer Vara del Rey.

Ice From Es Naútic bar and supermarkets.

Chandlery Three near the marinas: Accastillage Diffusion ☎ 607 502831, info@nauticshop.es; Nauticacosmar ☎ 971 345477, nauticacosmar@gmail.com; Nautic Milos ☎ 971 345 565, info@nauticamilos.es

Charts The only agent for Spanish charts on the island is Valnautica SL, Ibinave, Travesia del Mar s/n, local 2, San Antonio ☎ 971 34 52 51, ibnave@wanadoo.es.

Repairs A small yard at Es Náutic able to handle routine maintenance, painting, etc. and other craftsmen and engineers are also available – enquire at the club. A 6·5 tonne mobile crane and 25 tonne travel lift.

Yacht club Es Náutic San Antonio welcomes visiting yachtsmen, including those anchored off. It has a pleasant bar and good but rather expensive restaurant, and an excellent view from its terrace. Several of the staff speak English. ☎ 971 34 06 45.

Showers At Es Náutic. The crews of yachts anchored off are charged a small fee.

Laundry At Es Náutic - it has a pick-up and delivery service.

WiFi Good signal in Es Naútic.

Banks In the town, most with credit card facilities.

Hospital/medical services In the town.

Transport

Car hire/taxis In the town, or arrange through Es Náutic.

Buses Regular bus service to Ibiza town and elsewhere.

Ferries Ferry service to the Spanish mainland.

History

The harbour has probably been in use since prehistoric times, and certainly since the Phoenician and Carthaginian eras. In Roman times it was called Portús Magnus, changed by the Ibicenos to Portmany (meaning 'big bay'). It is claimed that Isla Conejera ('rabbit's burrow') was the birthplace of the Carthaginian warrior Hannibal – not impossible, since the island was in the hands of the Carthaginians at the time. Certainly, many of the stone-slingers in his army came from the nearby Islas Bledas.

Ashore

Little is now evident of the original fishing village, which has given way to tourist development and the bay is now lined with high-rise apartment buildings and hotels, mainly for young English tourists. Although the town itself is without much charm, the bay otherwise, looking south from the town or marinas, is still attractive and largely surrounded by rolling, tree-covered hills.

In the NE corner of Cala de Ganguil just W of the mole is a natural aquarium well worth a visit. It is possible to anchor nearby: take a dinghy or walk (less than 10 minutes) from the marinas.

In spite of its reputation as a noisy and crowded holiday resort, San Antonio still makes a good base for exploring the western and northern coasts.

There are cave paintings of disputed date at the cave 'des Vi' near Cabo Nonó, and a subterranean chapel dedicated to Santa Inés (Santa Agnès in Ibicenco) close north of the town. The church of San Antonio de Portmany, parts of which date back to 1305, is also worth a visit.

Local events

Every night several hundred young people stream down to the W end of the harbour opposite the breakwater to observe and applaud as the sun goes down beyond the horizon. Clubbers' tickets are on sale at many bars and restaurants lining the bay. The largest clubs are in the southeast part of the town.

On 17 January a fiesta is held in honour of San Antonio (patron saint), while on 16 July there is the fiesta of Nuestra Senora de Mont Carmel, with a regatta on the following Sunday. 24 August sees the fiesta of San Bartolomé.

Eating out

An enormous range of cafés and restaurants to suit all purses.

4. CALA GRASSIÓ TO PUNTA MOSCARTÉ

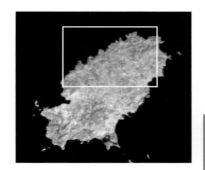

⚓ Cala Grassió (Gració)

38°59'·5N 01°17'·2E

A *cala* just north of Cabo Blanco, surrounded by low cliffs, splitting into two branches near its head, both with small sandy beaches. Open to west and southwest (*see plan on page 52*). Anchor in 4–6m over sand. Swimming buoys are in place. The immediate surroundings are wooded, with houses and apartments set further back. Both beaches are popular with tourist boats and the usual bars and restaurants will be found ashore.

⚓ Cala Salada

39°00'·5N 01°17'·7E

A narrow, largely unspoilt *cala* with steep rocky sides and woods above. The small island of S'Illeta lies close inshore to the north. There are two small beaches. Anchor in 4–8m over mainly weed and the occasional rock, taking care to avoid a more extensive area of unmarked rock carrying some

Cala Grassio N of San Antonio: busy with tourists by day, but peaceful at night *Graham Hutt*

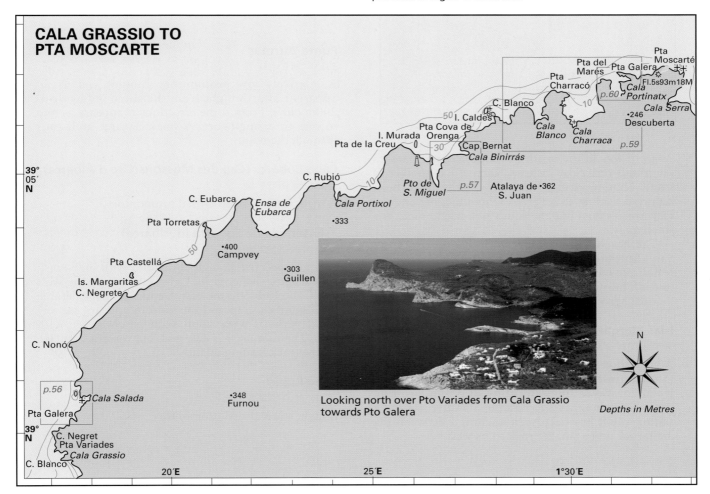

Looking north over Pto Variades from Cala Grassio towards Pto Galera

Cala Salada – unspoilt, but beware shallow, rocky areas *nito 500 / 123RF*

The Islas Margaritas with the prominent arch *Susie Baggaley*

CALA SALADA *Sketch plan*

Sa Foradada

N

S'Illeta

1₅

+ 2₇

14

⚓

2

10

Pta Galera

0   500

Depths in Metres   Metres

Punta Torretas at bottom right with Cabo Eubarca beyond

2·8m or less in the north of the *cala*. Sand patches are found very close inshore. There are a number of small boat moorings. Uneven depths have been reported leading to several yachts dragging anchor. Fishermen's huts line the south side where there is a small quay.

The beaches are popular with day tourists from San Antonio, and there are beach bars and restaurants ashore. Part of the beach, marked by a line of buoys, is marked off for swimmers as a defence against the many water-skiers.

Islas Margaritas (Ses Margalides)

39°03'N 01°19'E (N point)

A horseshoe-shaped group of rocks with a low arch through their centre. They can be left on either side when coastal sailing, an offing of 350m ensuring good water. It appears to be a popular dive site and a sailing yacht has been seen anchored between the main rock and a smaller rock to its west.

Punta Torretas

39°04'·0N 01°20'·7E

A relatively low promontory running out as an apparent afterthought from the surrounding 150-200m cliffs. From some directions it appears as two towers or a small fort. A small natural arch runs through the point.

Cabo Eubarca (Cap des Mossons/Cap d'Albarca)

39°04'·5N 01°21'·5E

A high, (262m) steep-cliffed promontory.

⚓ Ensenada de Eubarca (d'Albarca)

39°03'·9N 01°22'·3E

A large, spectacular, high-cliffed bay with shallowish rocky sides, sheltered by Cabo Eubarca to the west and Cabo Rubió to the east. Depths are considerable until quite close in and the bottom appears entirely rock, perhaps with small sand patches; use with care. The *cala* itself is deserted, but there is a village up the track leading inland.

Cabo Rubió

39°04'·8N 01°23'·8E

A high, steep-cliffed promontory.

Cala Portixol: a bay cut into rugged scenery

⚓ Cala Portixol

39°04'·7N 01°24'·0E

A very small horseshoe *cala* just east of Cabo Rubió, open to north and northeast but otherwise surrounded by high cliffs. Anchor in 4–5m over sand and rock (there is a sand patch near the centre of the *cala*) off the sand and stone beach. It is quiet and unspoiled although a number of smart houses have been built on the ridge high above and to the east.

⚓ Puerto de San Miguel

39°05'·3N 01°26'·5E

Not a true port but a deeply indented *cala*, well protected by Isla Bosch (a rocky peninsula stretching nearly halfway across the inner entrance on the west side) and surrounded by cliffs. It is clear that on the east side near the beach small fishing boats used to be pulled out clear of the water on rails; only a couple seem to have survived but perhaps these are

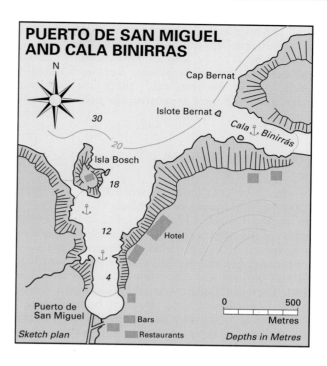

PUERTO DE SAN MIGUEL AND CALA BINIRRAS

Cap Bernat
Islote Bernat
Cala Binirràs
Isla Bosch
18
12
Hotel
4
Puerto de San Miguel
Bars
Restaurants
Sketch plan
Depths in Metres
0   500
Metres

the origin of 'Port'. If approaching from the west and planning to pass inside Isla Murada, watch out for an isolated rock 1·5–2m high which lies in the passage between the island and the shore towards Punta de la Creu.

Anchor in 4–8m over sand behind the peninsula's sand causeway or off the beach clear of the swimming and mooring buoys, open only to north and northeast. There are some permanent moorings the availability and quality of which is unclear and a buoyed-off area is reserved for the water-ski school. At each end of the beaches there are channels to land dinghies, the eastern side of the main beach having a

Puerto de San Miguel: well protected *cala* surrounded by cliffs *Graham Hutt*

small landing dock for a tripper boat whereas the western channel appears rocky and shallow.

At the head of the *cala* are two enormous hotels and various apartment blocks. But alongside the beach, on the western side, there are just two restaurants, one very expensive, the other a simple *chiringuito*. All in all it is a very attractive anchorage.

⚓ Cala Binirrás (Benirrás)
39°05'·4N 01°26'·9E

An attractive *cala* between steep cliffs, less than 1,000m east of Puerto de San Miguel (*see plan p57*). The rocky, pinnacled Islote Bernat (27m) lies in the middle of the entrance. From some angles it is said to look uncannily like the elderly Queen Victoria on her throne, but this needs some imagination. It is without outliers and can safely be passed on either hand. The *cala* is open west to almost north. There are swimming buoys and a few small boat moorings.

Anchor in 5–8m over sand near the head of the *cala* noting that there are rocky shallows (less than 1·8m) in the SE corner. It may be congested here, in which case anchor further out in about 12m over sand with weed patches; the clarity of the water makes it easy to identify sand areas. The area is relatively undeveloped, but the *cala* has restaurants and a lively beach which is crowded in summer. Every Sunday in summer, drummers gather and begin drumming near the time of sunset and continue into the night. Very pleasant and not too noisy from the anchorage.

Punta Cova de Orenga
39°05'·5N 01°26'·9E

A high, cliffed point with a cave at its foot.

Islas Caldes (d'En Calders)
39°06'·2N 01°27'·8E

A group of rocky islands close off Punta Caldes, itself between Punta Cova de Orenga and Cabo Blanco, with offliers up to 350m offshore.

Cabo Blanco
39°06'·3N 01°28'·5E

Note that the rocky spit extends some distance offshore on the NE corner of the cape, so give plenty of offing when heading into or out of Cala Blanco. Keeping N of the 10m contour clears the danger.

⚓ Cala Blanco
39°06'·2N 01°29'E

A small, attractive and peaceful *cala* east of Cabo Blanco, open to the north sector. Anchor at the head of the *cala* in 4–6m over sand in crystal clear water. Note that there are rocky shoals in the NW of the anchorage. Apart from two private houses the *cala* is deserted, and much of the surrounding land is private. Possibly the nicest anchorage in Ibiza.

Punta Charracó (Xarraca)
39°06'·6N 01°29'·3E

A high (73m) cliff-edged headland, covered by trees.

⚓ Cala Charraca (Xarraca)
39°06'·2N 01°30'E

A large, square and attractive bay surrounded by forested cliffs and offering several possible anchorages, open northwest–northeast. There are two small rock-fringed islands near the west side of the *cala* plus a rock awash in the centre of the southwest cove. It is reasonably obvious but nevertheless approach slowly with a lookout on the bow. This southwest corner gives the best anchorage in the *cala*. A rock lies in the southeast corner in approximately 14m, rising to 1·8m. Position: 39°06'·21N 01°30'·43E. Anchor in 5–6m over stones and sand to suit wind direction.

A road runs down to the southwest corner where there are fishermen's huts, a few houses and a restaurant.

Punta del Marés (Punta de Sa Torre)
39°06'·9N 01°30'·7E

A 54m headland crowned by a 9m watchtower. The 'cliffs' are set well back from the present shoreline.

Cala Binirrás. As the sun goes down the profile of the rock Islota Bernat in the middle of the entrance looks remarkably like Queen Victoria   *Graham Hutt*

Cala Binirrás: a very sheltered anchorage though the beach is crowded by day   *Graham Hutt*

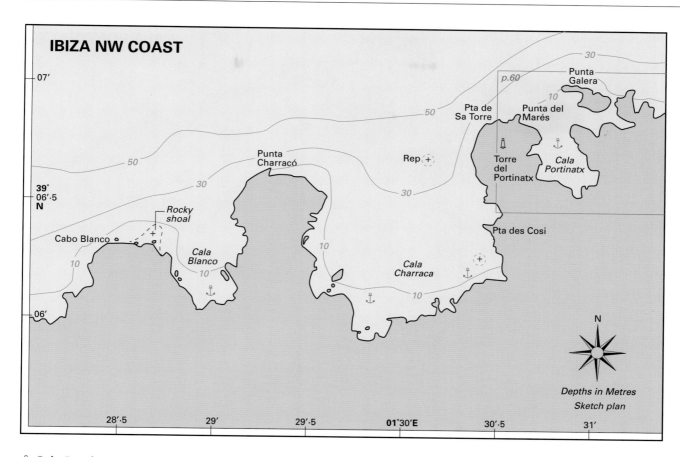

IBIZA NW COAST

Depths in Metres
Sketch plan

⚓ Cala Portinatx

39°06'·8N 01°30'·8E

An attractive multiple *cala* against a backdrop of wooded mountains, Cala Portinatx has seen considerable tourist development over recent years. There are three arms, each with a sandy beach.

There are bars, restaurants; and discos at night (and sometimes during the day).

Anchor in 3–15m over sand and weed as space permits (but note that holding is patchy and very poor in places, particularly in the southern part due to sand that thinly covers rock or is otherwise hard to penetrate); open to northwest and north. There

Cala Portinatx. Looking northeast over Punta Moscarté and its unusual lighthouse. The Torre de Portinatx is visible on the near headland, Punta del Marés.

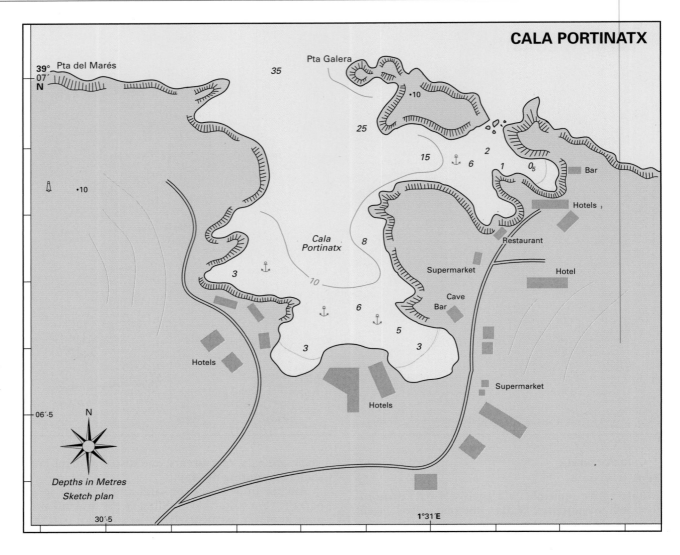

CALA PORTINATX

are some private moorings, mostly in the eastern arm, and each beach has an area roped off for swimmers. There is a small pontoon for dinghies in the SW corner of the SW *cala*.

Amongst the surrounding hotels and apartment blocks are many restaurants, supermarkets and other shops, plus a dive centre on the central beach where scuba bottles can be refilled.

The Torre de Portinatx (or Torre de sa Plana) stands on Punta del Marés to the west of the *cala*. Like most of Ibiza's defensive towers it was built in the second half of the 18th century, but was never fitted with artillery and was later used as a dwelling.

Punta Moscarté (des Moscarter)

39°07'·2N 01°32'·0E

A prominent rocky headland topped by an unusual lighthouse (white round tower with black diagonal stripes, 52m; *see photo*).

Pta Moscarté light E of Portinatx with its distinctive diagonal black stripes *Graham Hutt*

5. PUNTA DEN SERRA TO ISLOTE BOTAFOCH

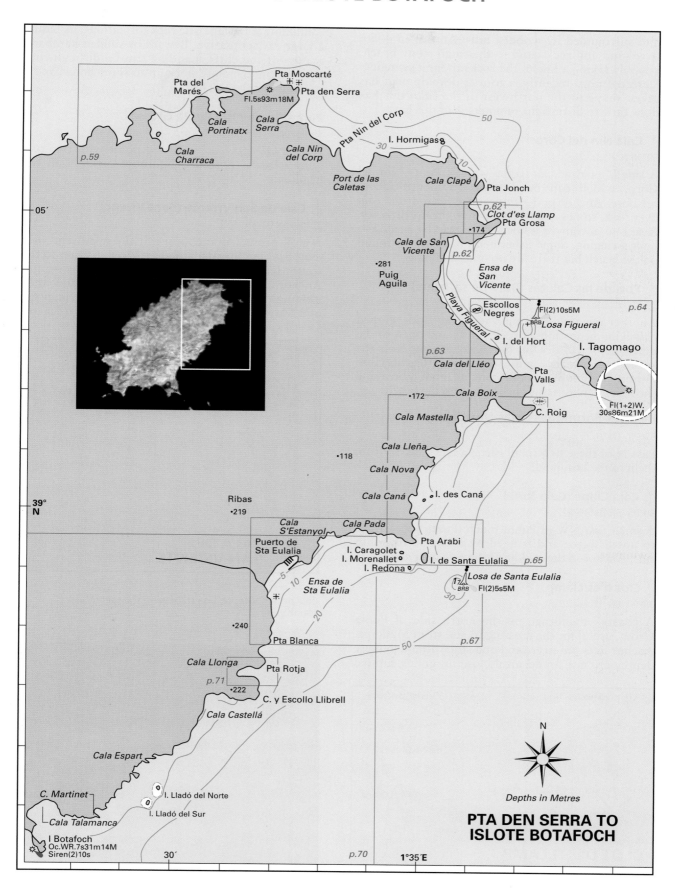

Pta del Marés

Pta Moscarté

Pta den Serra

Fl.5s93m18M

Cala Serra

Cala Portinatx

Cala Nin del Corp

Cala Charraca

Pta Nin del Corp

I. Hormigas

Cala Clapé

Port de las Caletas

50

30

10

Pta Jonch

p.62

Clot d'es Llamp

Pta Grosa

•174

Cala de San Vicente

p.62

•281

Puig Aguila

Ensa de San Vicente

p.64

Escollos Negres

Fl(2)10s5M

BRB

Losa Figueral

Playa Figueral

I. del Hort

I. Tagomago

p.63

Cala del Lléo

Pta Valls

Fl(1+2)W. 30s86m21M

•172

Cala Boix

C. Roig

Cala Mastella

Cala Lleña

Cala Nova

•118

Cala Caná

I. des Caná

Ribas

•219

Cala S'Estanyol

Cala Pada

Pta Arabi

Puerto de Sta Eulalia

I. Caragolet

I. Morenallet

I. Redona

I. de Santa Eulalia

p.65

-5

10

Ensa de Sta Eulalia

BRB

Losa de Santa Eulalia

Fl(2)5s5M

30

•240

20

Pta Blanca

50

p.67

Cala Llonga

Pta Rotja

p.71

•222

C. y Escollo Llibrell

Cala Castellá

Cala Espart

N

Depths in Metres

C. Martinet

I. Lladó del Norte

I. Lladó del Sur

Cala Talamanca

I Botafoch

Oc.WR.7s31m14M

Siren(2)10s

30'

p.70

1°35'E

PTA DEN SERRA TO ISLOTE BOTAFOCH

05'

39° N

⚓ Cala Serra
39°06'·5N 01°32'·4E

An attractive rocky *cala* open to northeast and east and surrounded by wooded hills. Anchor in 4–5m over sand and rock close to the small stony beach, possibly taking a line to the rocks to limit swinging. Deserted until recently, a tourist development has taken shape to the northwest of the *cala*; this has done little to disturb the remoteness of this bay.

⚓ Cala Nin del Corp
39°06'N 01°33'·2E

A small, narrow *cala* to the west of Punta Nin del Corp, which can be difficult to identify from offshore. Anchor in 3–4m near the head of the *cala* over rock, stones and weed; open to the north sector. A second anchor or a line ashore may be needed to limit swinging. Some fishermen's huts will be found on the beach but there are no other buildings.

⚓ Port de las Caletas (Racó de sa Talaia)
39°05'·7N 01°33'·6E

Another misnomer, being a wide but undeveloped *cala* lying beneath high rocky cliffs and open to the north sector. Houses line the zigzag road up from the small beach. Anchor in the west part of the *cala* close inshore in 10m over rock, stone or sand; a breaking shoal lies between this anchorage and the beach.

Illes Ses Formigues (Islas Hormigas)
39°06'·1N 01 35'·4E (N Point)

Pass N of these two small islets; a reef runs SE from them to the headland.

⚓ Cala Clapé (Cala Jone)
39°05'·5N 01°36'·2E

A small *cala* NW of Punta Jonch (Punta Jone), open to north sector and fringed by rocks on its south side. Anchor in the middle of the *cala* over sand.

⚓ Clot d'es Llamp
39°04'·8N 01°36'·2E

A coastal anchorage on the north side of Punta Grosa, useful for the crossing to and from Mallorca. Anchor in 6–9m over sand and stone although these depths are not found until close in, giving limited

swinging room and making this a doubtful overnight anchorage. Open to the north sector and the east, but protected from other directions by high cliffs containing some fantastic rock formations, including a large stalactite cave. Beware of sudden katabatic winds off the cliffs. Landing can be difficult, but once ashore there are steps up to some hotels and a supermarket.

Punta Grosa / Isla Punta Grossa
39°04'·9N 01°36'·7E (NE Point of Isla Punta Grossa)

A high (174m), rocky, cliffed point with two off-lying islands. A ruined lighthouse stands on the headland.

⚓ Cala de San Vicente (Sant Vicenc)
39°04'·5N 01°35'·6E

A well-protected anchorage at the north end of a long bay, the Ensenada de San Vicente, open to the southeast and with some fetch from the south. Anchor close inshore in 3–6m over sand and weed although summer swimming buoys (not in place mid-May 2017) may require anchoring further out

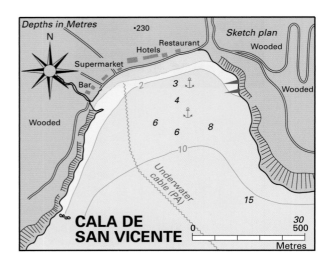

Cala de San Vicente: again showing the spectacular countryside

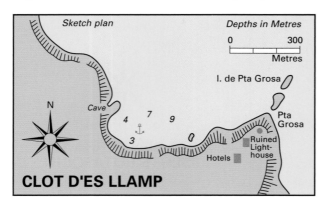

in 6–9m where there is a greater preponderance of weed. A submerged cable noted on some charts seems to have been removed or changed position, as it could not be located by various contributors in recent years (although it could simply be obscured by weed). A few small boat moorings are installed in the northeast corner.

The beach is lined with hotels and tourist apartments against a backdrop of high wooded hills. The beach gets crowded in season and the usual bars and restaurants will be found ashore. Can Gat restaurant on the front is of good reputation and brings customers from afar. Two small supermarkets towards the E of the seafront.

The cave temple of Es Cuyeram, dating back to the 5th century BC and later dedicated to the Carthaginian goddess Tanit, lies in the hills to the north. Excavated in 1907, most of the artefacts have now been moved to the Archaeological Museum of Ibiza.

Aiguas Blancas

39°03'·8N 01°35'·4E

About a quarter of a mile south of Cala Vincente and stretching for perhaps half a mile up to a small holiday development are several small, narrow, mainly sandy, beaches below low cliffs. There are a number of places to anchor off here in sand patches with about 4–5m depth. This area is completely open to the east and can only be regarded as a day anchorage. Care needs to be taken of off-lying rocks.

Playa Figueral

Centred on 39°03'·4N 01°36'E

Playa Figueral follows on from Aiguas Blancas and is the long stony beach occupying the south part of the Ensenada de San Vicente; it has various off-lying dangers. Taken from north to south these are:

- The Escollos Negres, three small, low, black rocky islands lying up to 0·4 miles offshore
- Losa Figueral (39°03'·1N 01°37'·3E), is an awash rock 0·6 miles off the beach. An isolated, lit danger pillar buoy has been laid nearby. Note that dangerous, rocky shoals extend 500m north and south of the Losa itself
- Isla del Hort, 20m in height, lying 200m off the coast inshore of Losa Figueral.

Small inshore rocky islets line much of the playa, in addition to the above.

⚓ Cala del Lléo (Cala San Carlos)

39°02'·2N 01°36'·6E

An open bay anchorage under high cliffs, south of Playa Figueral and northwest of Punta Valls (*see page 64*). There are dangerous rocks on either side of the bay – approach the centre of the sandy beach on a bearing of 220° to anchor in 4–6m over sand and rock. A few fishermen's huts will be found at the head of the *cala* with a café a short walk inland.

Cala San Vicente: a fine and useful anchorage protected from N sector winds *Graham Hutt*

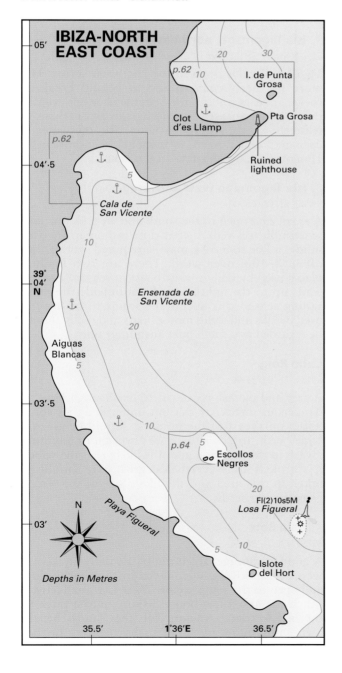

IBIZA-NORTH EAST COAST

I. de Punta Grosa

Clot d'es Llamp
Pta Grosa

Ruined lighthouse

Cala de San Vicente

Ensenada de San Vicente

Aiguas Blancas

Escollos Negres

Fl(2)10s5M
Losa Figueral

Playa Figueral

Islote del Hort

Depths in Metres

I. IBIZA

Punta Valls

39°02'·2N 01°37'·2E

A 67m cliffed promontory with a 9m stone tower.

Isla Tagomago

39°01'·9N 01°39'·0E (lighthouse)

A very conspicuous island nearly one mile long which resembles a huge dolphin heading out to sea. The lighthouse at its southeast tip (white octagonal tower on building, 23m) is obscured from the west by a 114m hill. A large white house occupies the centre of the island.

Pass between Isla Tagomago and Ibiza

A clear pass 0·8M wide and around 40m deep separates Isla Tagomago from Ibiza. However, be aware of the unmarked wreck off Cabo Roig (*see plan*).

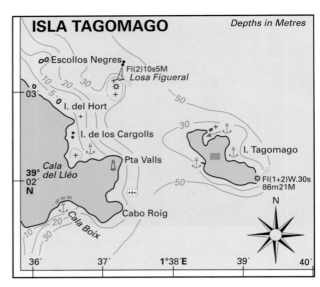

Isla Tagomago: looking east-southeast into the west anchorage

Looking northwest across Isla Tagomago towards Cala de San Vicente

⚓ Isla Tagomago, northeast anchorages

39°02'·4N 01°38'·5E and 39°02'·2N 01°38'·8E

Two small *calas* open to the northeast sector. The more northerly *cala*, tucked in behind breaking rocks, appears to offer the better shelter but even so these are not attractive anchorages except perhaps in westerly winds. Approach with care: the water is deep until very close in, so anchor close inshore in 8–10m over rock with a few sand patches.

⚓ Isla Tagomago west anchorage

39°02'·2N 01°38'·4E

A small *cala* open to the south and west sectors and susceptible to swell. Anchor close inshore in 5m over sand – a line to a rock may be required – or further off in 8–10m over weed. There are two landing places used by daily tourist boats in season. A track leads up to the lighthouse. Even outside the main sailing season this anchorage seems to be heavily used by ribs and small motor boats and really should be regarded as a small boat anchorage only.

Cabo Roig

39°01'·5N 01°36·9E

A grey and reddish rocky cliffed headland (138m). A dangerous wreck, awash but unmarked, lies some 350m northeast of the point. It should be given a wide berth. In 2017 there was no sign of anything awash in this position and it is likely that the wreck has broken up. Nevertheless great care should be taken in this area and the likely site of the wreck given a wide berth.

⚓ Cala Boix

39°01'·6N 01°36'·5E

A good anchorage, albeit not particularly attractive, west of Cabo Roig, surrounded by high rocky cliffs and open to the south sector. There is a small jetty, a beach bar and a few houses ashore, plus a track to the main road. Anchor off the sandy beach. Swimming buoys push the anchoring area further out to 4-8m mainly into areas of weed and rock.

**CABO ROIG TO
ILLA DE STA EULALIA**

N

Depths in Metres
Sketch plan

0   1000
Metres

Cabo Roig

10

25

5   10

Cala Boix

2₁

31

Cala Mastella

2

1₃

Cala Lleña

27

1₁   Cala Nova

5

10

0₈

14

Cala Caná

2   2

5

Islas des Caná

Hotels

Sa Galera

3

10

4

24

Pta Arabi

5

10

I. Morenellet

10

I. de Sta Eulalia

I. Redonda

Cala Boix: the fertile plain highlighted in the sun

Cala Mastella: a tiny *cala* with a development at its head

⚓ Cala Mastella

39°01'·3N 01°35'·8E

A pleasant little *cala* with a beach at its head, surrounded by trees and some houses. Anchor in the centre of the *cala* in 2–4m over sand, weed and occasional rock patches although the only good - sized patch of sand seems to have been commandeered by a private mooring buoy (2017). There is a beach bar and fish restaurant ashore, and the village of Ca'n Jordi about ½ mile away. The restaurant El Bigote has become very popular despite its location and a reservation is needed, especially at weekends, most of the year round. It is famous for its risotto *arroz con bogavante*.

⚓ Cala Lleña (Llenya)

39°00'·9N 01°35'·3E

A wide *cala* with an attractive beach, often crowded, in an outcrop of square white hotels and apartment buildings and with the Club Cala Lleña amongst the pine trees to the south. Swimming buoys have been installed which take up most of the excellent sandy area for anchoring, although there is

Cala Lleña: an attractive beach

still a reasonable space in 7–8m, open to the east–southeast–south.

⚓ Cala Nova

39°00'·5N 01°35'·0E

Another wide *cala* with a long beach and pine trees, but somewhat less built up than Cala Lleña. Even so there are beach bars, etc. to cater for the tourists staying in the nearby resort of Es Caná. The beach is divided into three sections by rocky outcrops and the whole area starts to shallow very quickly about 200m from the shore. Anchor in 3–6m over sand or mixed sand and weed, exposed to the whole eastern sector. If approaching from the south be sure to avoid the Islas des Caná, described below.

Islas des Caná

39°00'·1N 01°35'·3E (E side)

The Islas des Caná comprise Isla de Caná (2·3m) and the smaller Sa Galera, plus some offlying rocks. Shoals run out from the headland north of Cala Caná to about halfway to the islands, and the inside passage should not be attempted without local knowledge.

⚓ Cala Caná (Canar)

39°00'·1N 01°34'·8E

A popular open *cala* with a sandy beach and low rocky sides, surrounded by hotels and apartment blocks. There is a tiny harbour for speedboats and small fishing craft on the south shore. Swim buoys curtail the amount of space for anchoring. Anchor more towards the south side of the beach where the best bottom is found in 2-5m over sand or sand and rock as fringing rocks, covered to a depth of 2m or so, extend from either side. The Islas des Caná lie some 600m offshore due east of the *cala*, but are easily seen on approach.

Cala Caná: surrounded by the usual tourist development, but still a good anchorage

Punta Arabi

38°59'·4N 01°35'·0E

A low (22m) whitish rocky point surmounted by buildings and dark trees.

Isla de Santa Eulalia

38°59'·2N 01°35'·1E (N end)

A peardrop-shaped island, 37m in height and measuring some 350m along its north/south axis.

Passes between Isla de Santa Eulalia and Ibiza

Three small rocky islands which lie to the west of Isla de Santa Eulalia pose a possible hazard. However the passes through should present no problems, being at least 400m wide and with depths of more than 5m throughout (*see plan*). Taken from southeast to northwest these comprise:

- Isla Redona (22m), 400m southwest of Isla de Santa Eulalia and easily seen. Close in it is foul to east and south. It can be left on either side.

- Isla Morenellet, a low, black, rocky islet usually surrounded by breaking seas, some 650m west of Isla de Santa Eulalia and 550m northwest of Isla Redona. Easily seen in daylight but difficult to spot at night. Again, it can be left on either side.

- Isla Caragolet, similar in appearance to Isla Morenaller but 450m to the northwest and about that distance offshore. On no account attempt to pass inside Isla Caragolet, due to shoals.

Losa de Santa Eulalia

38°58'·7N 01°35'·6E (centre of shoal)

This rocky patch 1·7m deep lies less than 1,000m southeast of Isla Santa Eulalia and is often marked by broken water. A buoy has been laid at 110° from the rock at 38°58'·7N 01°35'·5E. This isolated danger buoy has been reported closer inshore.

Other than a few nearby rocks the Losa de Santa Eulalia is surrounded by clear water, and a 32m deep passage separates it from Isla Santa Eulalia.

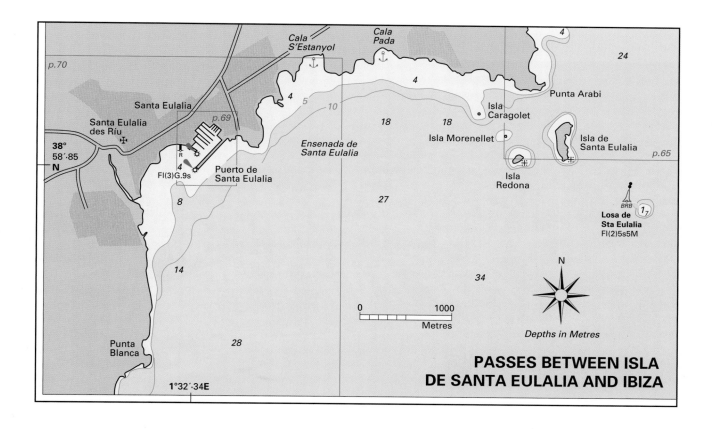

PASSES BETWEEN ISLA DE SANTA EULALIA AND IBIZA

⚓ Cala Pada
38°59'·5N 01°33'·7E

A very small anchorage in a tiny *cala*, surrounded by trees and open southeast–south–southwest. The eastern part of the bay is reserved for boardsailors. Anchor in 3m over sand off the small beach, avoiding the many permanent moorings. A beach restaurant lies directly behind the short wooden jetty.

⚓ Cala S'Estanyol
38°59'·5N 01°33'·2E

A small wooded anchorage near a river mouth, off a sand and stone beach. Anchor in 3m over sand, stones and weed, open to east–southeast–south. Two large white hotel or apartment buildings mark the southern end of the beach.

Puerto de Santa Eulalia del Río (Santa Eulària des Riu)

38°58'·8N 01°32'·5E

A safe and friendly harbour, 50M from Mallorca, easy to enter in most conditions, with berths for 755 vessels up to 25m

Communications
Marina Santa Eulalia VHF Ch 09
 info@marinasantaeulalia.com
 reservas@marinasantaeulalia.com
 www.marinasantaeulalia.com
Club Náutico ☎ 971 336161
 ptostaeulalia@interbook.net

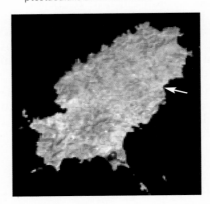

Puerto de Santa Eulalia viewed from southeast

The marina

Santa Eulalia Marina is a large (755-berth) marina, with an easy approach and entrance except in strong winds from southeast and south. The staff are helpful and several speak good English. It has a quiet and pleasant environment.

Pilotage

Approach

From southwest If coming from Puerto de Ibiza or Formentera be sure to identify the two small islands Lladó del Sur (6m), and Lladó del Norte (10m), which lie 0·8M and 1M, respectively, northeast of Cabo Martinet, near the 30m contour (*see plan on page 61*). Once identified, they can safely be passed on either side. Cabo Llibrell can be rounded at 200m, after which the houses and high-rise buildings of Santa Eulalia will be seen. The harbour lies at the northern end of the town, near the middle of the wide bay.

From northeast If approaching the island from the direction of Mallorca and intending to make Puerto de Santa Eulalia the first port of call, Isla Tagomago may be passed on either side. However, if taking the inshore passage give a wide berth to the wreck, awash but unmarked, 350m northeast of Cabo Roig (*see page 61*). The headland itself is steep-to. Off Punta Arabi, either set a course between Isla de Santa Eulalia and Losa de Santa Eulalia, or take one of the passages between Isla de Santa Eulalia and the mainland as described on page 67. The harbour lies at the north end of the town, near the middle of the wide bay.

Anchorage in the approach

There are two small *calas*, Cala Pada and Cala S'Estanyol (*see page 67*), in the north part of the bay. However, the anchorage most convenient for the town is that in the southwest corner of the bay, near the mouth of the Río Santa Eulalia (see *Ensenada de Santa Eulalia* anchorage below). Anchoring immediately outside the marina entrance is forbidden, but most yachts anchor fairly close as it becomes shallower and of variable depth and nature of bottom further away towards the river mouth.

Entrance

At the end of the west mole is situated a round, white, three-storey tower which houses, amongst other things, the marina offices. Approach from anywhere in the bay keeping well clear of the end of the southeast breakwater. The marina entrance is kept dredged to at least 5m.

Berthing

Berth alongside the fuel/reception pontoon, beneath the white tower, to be allocated a berth. There is a 3kn speed limit. The marina can accommodate yachts of up to 25m LOA and 4·5m draught. However, like many marinas in the Islas Baleares, it is usually full to capacity during the high season. It is however well worth trying to book in advance as the berthing fees are about a quarter of those in Puerto de Ibiza (c. €55 per night for a 12m yacht) and it has a quiet, laid-back atmosphere that many yachtsmen will prefer.

Facilities

Water Taps on pontoons and quays. Water drinkable.
Electricity 220v AC points on pontoons and quays.
Fuel Diesel and petrol pumps close beneath the tower on the west mole.
Provisions Shops and supermarkets in Santa Eulalia del Rio nearby, where most requirements can be met. All-day market on Wednesdays in summer. There is also a supermarket at the harbour.
Ice From the marina office.
Chandlery In the marina complex.
Repairs Marina Río boatyard can handle all usual work including GRP repairs ☏ 971 33 04 53. Travel-lift 60 tonnes.
Engineers At Marina Río, Boat Service Germany ☏ 971 33 01 21 is a local service agent for Volvo Penta.
Showers In the 'control tower' building and behind the diving school at the northwest end of the marina.
Launderette In the marina complex.
Banks In the marina complex and in town.
Hospital In the town.

PUERTO DE SANTA EULALIA

Super-market

1₄

1₈

2₃

2₂

3₁

3₃

2₄

3₁

1₁

Fl(3)R.9s4m3M

3₃

3₆

3₃

Fl(3)G.9s11m5M

3₁

5

6₂

N

0   300
Metres

Depths in Metres

Transport

Car hire/taxis Can be arranged via the marina office.
Buses Regular service to Ibiza town (15 minute journey) and elsewhere.
Ferries Tourist ferries berth outside the harbour, near the root of the west mole.
Air Ibiza airport 15 miles.

Ashore

Previously a fishing village and market centre based on the fortified 16th-century church at Puig de Missa, well worth a visit on the hill above the river mouth, Santa Eulalia later became a centre for artists but is now a major tourist resort. The bay has been overwhelmed by hotels and other buildings in recent years, but still offers good, if crowded, sand and rock beaches.

There are many interesting buildings in the old town, plus the remains of a Roman aqueduct across the Río Santa Eulalia. The Ethnological Museum of the Pitiusan Islands is situated in the town.

Local events

Santa Eulalia's day is celebrated on 12 February. There is a Holy Week procession on the afternoon of Good Friday and a Festival of Flowers on the first Sunday in May. The Fiesta de Jesus is held on 8 September.

Eating out

Many, cafés and restaurants of all grades, including several in the marina itself.

Anchorages and features from Puerto Santa Eulalia to Puerto de Ibiza

⚓ Ensenada de Santa Eulalia (Santa Eulària)
38°58′·7N 01°32′·1E

Anchor in the southwest corner of this large bay, southeast of the mouth of Río Santa Eulalia, in 3–5m over sand and mud. A sandy beach runs northeast, with several large hotels a short distance inland. All the facilities of Puerto de Santa Eulalia are available within half a mile. There are rocks awash near the shore south of the river mouth and the whole area of the west side of the Ensenada is shallow with numerous large boulders resulting in rapidly varying depths and care must be taken when finding a useful spot to anchor.

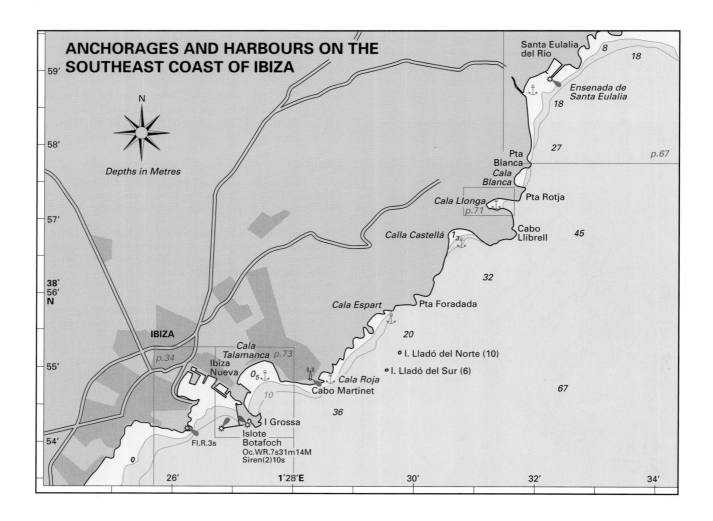

Puerto de Santa Eulalia anchorage SW of the marina entrance
Graham Hutt

Punta Rotja (Roja)

38°57'·4N 01°31'·9E

A high (100m) red and whitish cliffed point with houses on the top.

⚓ Cala Llonga

38°57'·2N 01°31'·6E

A long, high-sided and very attractive *cala* with an excellent but often crowded beach at its head. The entrance can be difficult to spot until almost due east of the *cala*, when the huge blocks of flats and other buildings which line the wooded cliffs will be seen.

Anchor in 4–11m over sand probably about halfway up the *cala* keeping clear of the swimmers' buoys at the west end and the small tripper boat

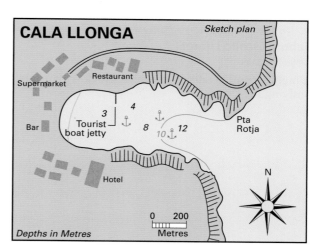

Cala Llonga: a popular anchorage in summer and likely to be more crowded than this

landing. In places it is difficult to get the anchor to set either because there is only a little sand over a rock base or it is a particularly hard sand. Although open only to the east and offering good protection, it can be gusty at times when west winds funnel down the valley. Swell from the east quadrant also works in, rebounding off the sides and setting yachts rolling.

Daily tourist boats visit from Santa Eulalia, causing wash as they weave their way through the anchored yachts, to moor at the jetty in the NW of the *cala*. Bars, restaurants and a supermarket will be found ashore. Buses run to Santa Eulalia. On 15 August Cala Llonga celebrates the anniversary of its patron saint.

Cabo y Escollo Llibrell

38°56'·7N 01°31'·7E

A high (220m) headland of whitish rock with a small outlying islet.

⚓ Cala Castellá (Sól d'En Serra)

38°56'·7N 01°30'·8E

A wide, rather unattractive bay with grey unstable slopes just south of Cabo y Escollo Llibrell, open to east through south to southwest. Anchor in 5m over sand and rock (not much sand) off the long rocky beach.

⚓ Cala Espart (Cala Olivera)

38°55'·9N 01°30'·1E

A small open bay with a track to the main road. Anchor in 5m in the sandy areas off the beach.

Lladó del Norte and Lladó del Sur

38°55'·2N 01°29'·8E (Norte), 38 55'·0N 01 29'·6E (Sur)

Two small islands, 10m and 6m high respectively, 0·5 and 0·7 miles south of Cala Espart, near the 30m contour. They may be left on either side.

Cala Talamanca from Isla Grossa. Punta Sa Tabernera is the rocky spur on the left *David Baggaley*

⚓ Cala northeast of Cabo Martinet (Cala Roja)

38°54'·9N 01°28'·6E

Cala Roja is a small *cala*, not named on some charts, on the northeast side of the cape, to be used with care. Anchor off the small beach in 5m over sand and rock, open to east through south. There is a road at the top of the cliff.

Cabo Martinet

38°54'·8N 01°28'·6E

A low headland of dark rock with trees and houses on the top. An aero radiobeacon, inconspicuous, lies 700m to the west-northwest.

⚓ Cala Talamanca

38°54'·7N 01°27'·5E

A large open *cala*, exposed south and east, with a long sandy beach at its head. It is the closest anchorage to Puerto de Ibiza. The head of the *cala* is shallow and has some reefs; anchor with care north of Punta Sa Tabernera in 3–6m over sand and weed, although with careful sounding, a spot can be found further north in the middle of the *cala*. There are a number of laid buoys, some of which are supporting reasonable sized yachts but their status is not known.

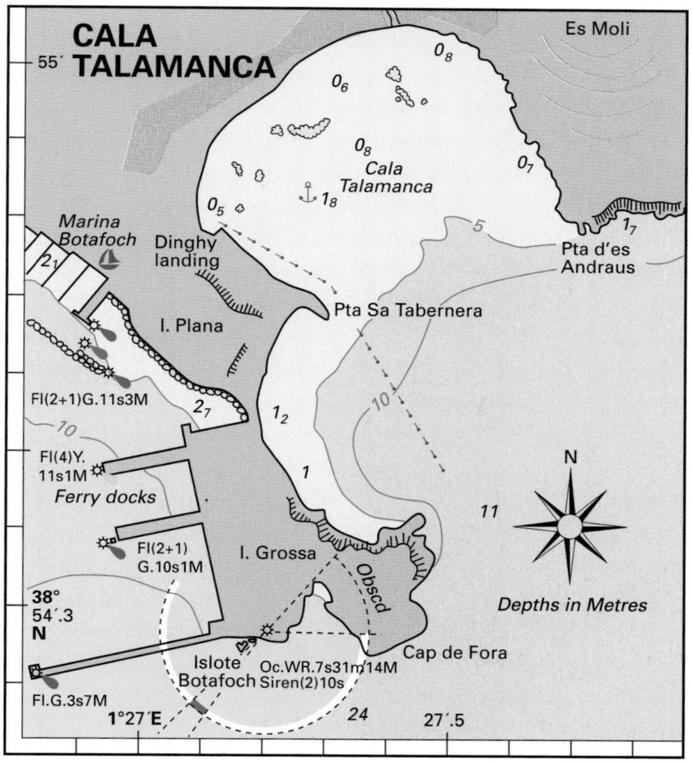

Land in the northwest corner of the bay in front of the Hotel Argos where there is a tiny dock on which a dinghy might be left. From there it is about 20 minutes' walk into Ibiza or a mere 350m to the facilities of Marina Botafoch and the half-hourly ferry across to the centre of town. (*See plan on page 34.*)

The beach is quite pleasant and is backed by a number of simple restaurants in its northwest sector. There are public showers and toilets.

II. FORMENTERA

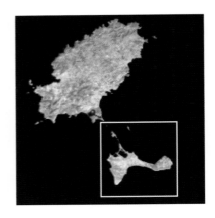

Smaller than Ibiza and without an airport, Formentera is less developed and enjoys a slower pace of life. Nudism is an accepted feature. The low-lying plain in the north, with its associated saltpans and lagoons, is of interest. The only port, Puerto de Sabina, has limited facilities. There are a few pleasant anchorages around the island, and a large bay in which to anchor or pick up a buoy in the adjacent Isla Espalmador, linked to Formentera via a long sandy spit, broken by a rocky passage.

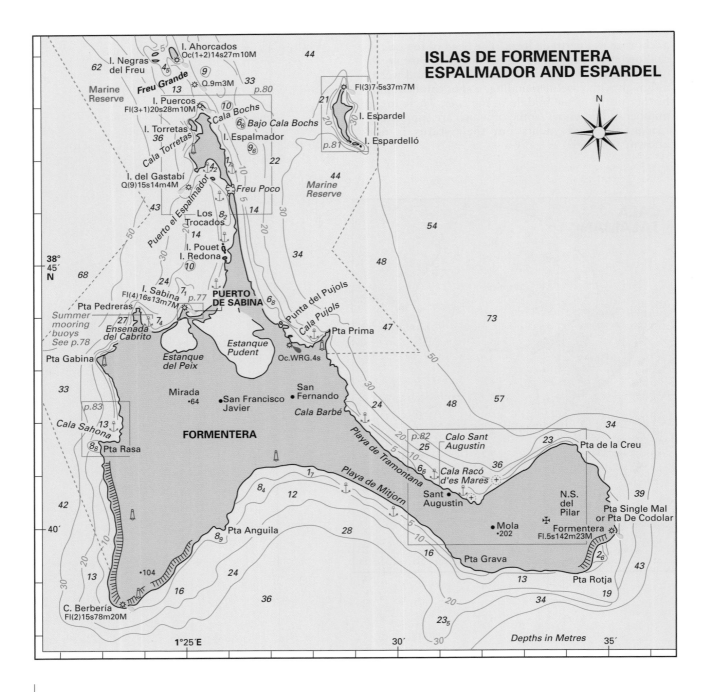

ISLAS DE FORMENTERA
ESPALMADOR AND ESPARDEL

I. Ahorcados
Oc(1+2)14s27m10M

I. Negras
del Freu

Marine
Reserve

Freu Grande

I. Puercos
Fl(3+1)20s28m10M

Cala Bochs

Bajo Cala Bochs

I. Torretas

I. Espalmador

Cala Torretas

Fl(3)7.5s37m7M

I. Espardel

I. Espardelló

I. del Gastabí
Q(9)15s14m4M

Freu Poco

Marine
Reserve

Puerto el Espalmador

Los
Trocados

I. Pouet
I. Redona

I. Sabina
Fl(4)16s13m7M

PUERTO
DE SABINA

Pta Pedreras

Summer
mooring
buoys
See p.78

Punta del Pujols

Cala Pujols

Pta Prima

Ensenada
del Cabrito

Pta Gabina

Estanque
del Peix

Estanque
Pudent

Oc.WRG.4s

Mirada

San Francisco
Javier

San
Fernando

Cala Barbé

FORMENTERA

Cala Sahona

Pta Rasa

Playa de Tramontana

Calo Sant
Augustin

Cala Racó
d'es Mares

Pta de la Creu

Sant
Augustin

N.S.
del
Pilar

Pta Single Mal
or Pta De Codolar

Pta Anguila

Playa de Mitjorn

Mola

Formentera
Fl.5s142m23M

Pta Grava

C. Berbería
Fl(2)15s78m20M

Pta Rotja

Depths in Metres

Navigational information for approaches to Formentera

Coming up from North Africa or the Eastern Mediterranean and heading for Spain, Formentera is a good first landfall in the Balearic Islands if west winds have hindered a westerly passage; in which case, head either for one of the anchorages described on the east side of the island, or for the only port on the island, Puerto de Sabina.

Magnetic variation

Less than 001°E.

Approach and coastal passage charts

Imray	M3, M12, M13
Admiralty	1701, 1702, 2834
Spanish	7A, 478, 479, 479A
French	5505, 7114

Approach lights

Isla Espardel, north point 38°48'·2N 01°28'·6E
Fl(3)7·5s37m7M White truncated conical tower 16m
Formentera (Punta Single Mal or Punta de Codolà)
38°39'·7N 01°35'E Fl.5s142m23M
White tower on white building 22m 150°-vis-050°
Cabo Berbería 38°38'·4N 01°23'·3E Fl(2)15s78m20M
White round tower 19m 234°-vis-170°
Isla Sabina 38°44'·1N 01°24'·9E Fl(4)16s13m7M
White truncated conical tower 11m
Isla del Gastabí 38°46'·5N 01°25'·1E Q(9)15s14m4M
W cardinal tower, 8m

INTRODUCTION

Formentera and the small island of Espalmador to its north, lie two miles south of Punta Portas, the most southerly tip of Ibiza. These islands remain less developed as compared with the rest of the Islas Baleares, with just one harbour serving Formentera. However there are a huge number of ferry boat trips daily between Puerto de Ibiza and Puerto de Sabina, some carrying day trippers and others longer term holidaymakers or commercial traffic.

Espalmador, by far the smaller of the two and virtually deserted, is 1·5 miles long and less than a mile wide, rising to a height of 24m on its west side where there is a conspicuous tower. It is joined to Formentera by a long sandy spit broken by a shallow rocky passage, the Freu Poco (*see page 79*), which separates the two islands.

Formentera is 10 miles long and eight miles wide at its extremes, but being an elongated S-shape, covers an area of only 37 square miles. It comprises two high features: La Mola (192m), an island-like area to the east, and the peninsula running out to Cabo Berbería (107m) to the southwest. These two higher regions are attached by a long, low neck of land. There is a large, low-lying plain in the northern part of the island, the greater part of it occupied by lagoons and salt pans. Salt has long been a major export. Around the two high features the coast is made up of rocky cliffs, but in the north and northeast it is flat and sandy. Much of the island is cultivated and there are pine forests around La Mola.

There is a permanent population of around 12,000 and according to some sources, they are favoured with the longest life expectancy in Spain. Most are involved in some aspect of the tourist industry. Nudism has long been accepted on the beaches of Formentera. Do not be surprised to see sailboarders, waterskiers and yacht crews sailing around naked.

History

The history of Formentera and Espalmador parallels that of Ibiza. The oldest evidence of human occupation is the 2000BC megalithic tomb at Cana Costa. In Roman times they formed part of the Pityusae (Pine Islands): Espalmador was known as Ophioussa and Formentera as Frumentum or Frumentaria (a reference to the large amount of wheat it supplied), since corrupted into Formentera.

During the hundreds of years following the downfall of Rome the island became depopulated as it was frequently raided by Barbarians, Moors, Saracens and even Scandinavians on their way home after taking part in one of the Crusades. It was not until 1697 that the island was repopulated, but even so was still subject to raids by pirates. The local inhabitants even turned to piracy themselves on occasion, and in 1806 captured the British 12-gun brig *Felicity* and sailed her into Ibiza.

Tourist information

Places of interest

San Francisco Javier is an attractive small town with a fortified church, reminiscent of a 'spaghetti western', which once mounted guns on its tower, from which fine views can now be enjoyed. The ravine running down to Cala Sahona on the west coast and the area around La Mola in the east are worth visiting if time permits, with the caves of Xeroni also of interest.

Puerto de Sabina (Port de sa Savina)

38°44'·1N 01°25'·2E

Puerto de Sabina is the only harbour on Formentera. It provides good protection from swell but not so much from the wind as it is a low-lying island. The two marinas within the harbour provide just over 200 yacht berths between them, for yachts up to 22m. Both are always full during the summer.

Distance from Spanish mainland
Javea 60M

Communications
Marina de Formentera VHF Ch 09
Port Authority ☎ 971 32 23 46
 www.marinadeformentera.com
 info@marinadeformentera.com
Marina Formentera Mar ☎ 971 32 3235 / 32 29 63
 info@formenteramar.com
 www.formenteramar.com

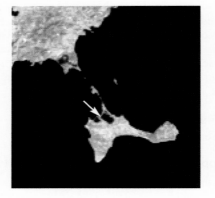

The port

Puerto de Sabina is the only harbour on Isla de Formentera and is in constant use by ferries, commercial shipping and fishing craft. Even so, it has maintained an attractive and laid back atmosphere even though in summer it is overrun with tourists. Evidence of this is the hundreds of motor scooters lined up for hire in Puerto de Sabina.

It is likely that no room will be found for visiting yachts during the summer season and if it is the expense will be great - around € 300 per night for a 12m vessel. The harbour is easy to approach and enter, well sheltered once inside, though the breakwaters offer little protection from the wind. As with many harbours in the islands, more than one marina operates within the same basin.

Formentera viewed from northwest across Puerto de Sabina - note the red salt pans beyond

Pilotage

Approach

From east and northeast Approach to the marina can be made either through the Freu Grande between Ibiza and Espalmador (see *page 39*) or around the south side of the island.

From west Approach from the Spanish mainland is straightforward with no offlying dangers.

From west, northwest and north There are no hazards in the approach to Puerto de Sabina over an arc between Punta Pedreras (unlit) to the west and Isla Gastabí (lit) to the north (*see plan on page 74*). The white buildings behind the harbour show up well, as does the white tower of Isla Sabina lighthouse. Note that this lighthouse is situated near the end of a projecting rocky spur with shallow water to either side.

Entrance

Entrance to the main harbour is generally straightforward, though it can become dangerous in strong northerly or northwesterly winds due to shoaling depths. This has been alleviated with the aid of the four laid buoys (three red, one green), three of which are shown on the plan below, but care is still needed in the entrance in rough weather. Normally the greatest hazard is posed by the many ferries which enter and leave at speed. Both Marina de Formentera in the southwest corner of the basin and Marina Formentera Mar to the east are reached through relatively narrow inner entrances.

Berthing

1. Marina de Formentera

At the southwest end of the harbour.
108 berths up to 20m.
VHF Ch 09
☏ 971 32 31 32
reservas@marinadeformentera.com
www.marinadeformentera.com

2. Marina Formentera Mar

To the east has 90 berths. Contact the marina office on approach or occupy any convenient vacant berth until allocated a spot by marina staff. In summer it is likely that you will be turned away if you have not booked in advance.

☏ 971 32 32 35/32 29 63
info@formenteramar.com
www.formenteramar.com

Facilities

Water Metered taps on pontoons and quays.
Electricity 220v AC points on pontoons and quays, charged by the day.
Fuel The main fuel dock is on the central mole between the two marinas. There is a single diesel pump on the ferry/tripper boat mole opposite, to starboard on entry to Marina de Formentera, which appears to be for the use of the tripper boats and fishermen only.
Repairs A small boatyard centred around the travel-lift and slipway. Boat repairs and engineering services can be arranged via the Formentera Mar marina office. A 35-tonne travel-lift and slipway near the office. Oil collection facility.
Chandlery Motonautica Helix in Marina de Formentera ☏ 971 322373, comercial@nauticahelix.com and

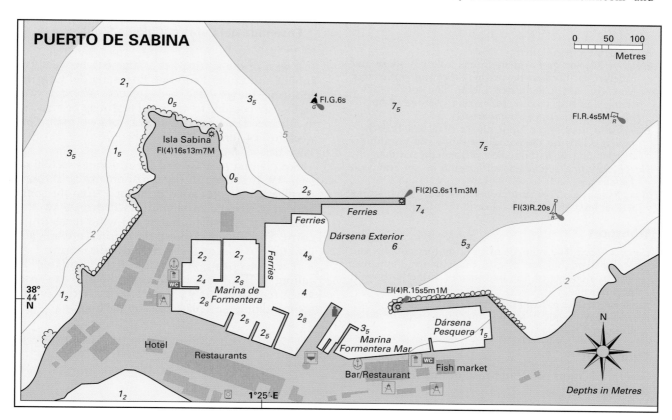

Puerto de Sabina. Good protection from the seas, but the low-lying surroundings give little shelter from the wind

Nautica Pins in Avenida Mediterranea, one street back from the front. ☏ 971 322651, info@nauticapins.com

Provisions Two supermarkets near the harbour in Avenida Mediterranea, plus more in San Francisco Javier a couple of miles inland. A fish market near the east basin.

Ice From the supermarket.

Showers Marina de Formentera has a very modern and excellent facility near the marina office and Formentera Mar also has a dedicated block. The former has a notice limiting its use to marina customers but in practice is open to passing tourists!

Banks and post office None closer than San Francisco Javier; ATMs on the parade of shops and restaurants overlooking the harbour. Post office in the marina.

Hospital/medical services Small hospital in San Francisco Javier.

WiFi Marina de Formentera has a system which works well at least on the berths close to the office.

Transport

Car hire/taxis The number of cars, motor scooters and cycles available for hire through many companies within a couple of hundred metres of the harbour is phenomenal!

Buses Bus service to San Francisco Javier.

Ferries Very frequent ferries (including hydrofoils) to Ibiza.

Eating out

Several pleasant cafés and restaurants overlooking the harbour.

Anchorages and features around Formentera

⚓ Ensenada del Cabrito (Caló de S'oli)

38°43'·8N 01°24'·2E

Just west of the marina lies a large bay between Isla Sabina and Punta Pedreras: Ensenada del Cabrito. Mooring buoys have been placed where it was previously possible to anchor. These may be reserved in advance for a maximum stay of two nights per week from 1 June to 30 September www.balearslifeposidonia.eu.

See plan on *page 74* and the *Moorings* section on *page 19*. It is open to the north-northwest through northeast, but gives good protection from the south and west. Tucked in behind Pta Pedreras, swell is usually not a problem unless the wind turns to the north. This is a good spot if the marinas are full, and if waiting to take on fuel or water in the marina.

The Anchoring Assistance RIB, available by calling VHF Ch 68, is especially helpful at sunset when tens of (mostly charter) yachts arrive on the scene looking for a place to drop the hook.

Cala Sabina, looking west. Ensenada del Cabrito at top of photo *Geoff Williamson*

⚓ Estanque del Peix (Estany des Peix)

38°43'·9N 01°24'·6E (entrance)

At the eastern side of Ensenada del Cabrito there is a shallow (1m), narrow entrance into a large saltwater lagoon, the Estanque del Peix. Once inside, depths are reported to increase and many dinghies and other small pleasure and fishing craft are moored there. The larger Estanque (Estany) Pudent further east has no outlet to the sea.

⚓ Cala Sabina and the long beach areas out to Los Trocados

38°44'·2N 01°25'·4E

Along almost the entire coastal stretch of two or more miles from the port to Los Trocados, a line of yellow buoys has been laid to define an exclusion zone for vessels (to protect swimmers). There are however a number of channels marked for dinghy access to the beach areas (or other small tourist vessels launched from the beach). Outside this line there is again an almost continuous area of sand with good holding qualities for vessels to anchor in 6-9m. The relatively shallow lagoon inside Islas Redona and Pouet (Ses Illetas) and their satellites is almost cut off by the line of exclusion buoys. There is an area unaffected by such exclusion close to the port entrance and to landward of the line of port-hand buoys, which gives a convenient anchorage for access to the port. The whole is open to the west and north and, at the Trocados end, to the southwest also.

There is a restaurant in the ruined windmill at the northern end of the first stretch of beach, Playa de Cabali Borras. The whole anchorage area on this stretch of coast is carefully controlled by Posidonia. It is usually full during July, August and into September.

At the extreme north end of this beach (Playa Trocados) a nature reserve has been created.

Freu Poco (Pas de Trocados)

38°46'·4N 01°26'E

A very shallow channel separating Espalmador from Formentera, Freu Poco lies at the north end of the Playa Trocados, east of Isla Gastabí. (*See plans on pages 39 and 74.*)

The channel can only be transited by dinghy and sometimes it is possible to wade between the islands, though either of these would be unwise if any swell is breaking.

Espalmador looking northeast. The shallow Freu Poco passage is on the right and Freu Grande on the upper left of the picture above. Isla del Gastabí is middle left

Espalmador: looking north-northeast. Puerto El Espalmador centre, Ibiza top.
Note anchorage on east side opposite Puerto El Espalmador

ISLA ESPALMADOR

⚓ Puerto el Espalmador

38°46'·8N 01°25'·7E

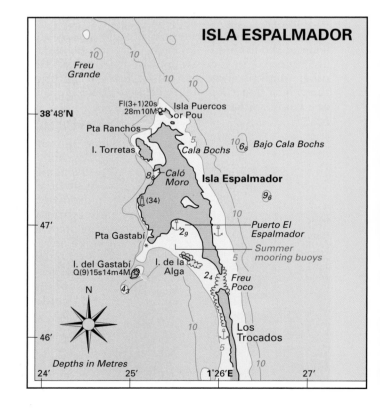

Puerto and *marina* in Spanish can mean any place to accommodate a vessel, even, sometimes, an anchorage off a beach. This bay is by no means a port, but it does give excellent shelter from the north and east, though it is open to the southwest.

From the south, enter between Isla del Gastabí and Isla de la Alga. Two small white buoys between Pta Gastabí and Isla de la Alga mark the entrance, and keep you clear of the shallow patch. Do not attempt to cut between Isla de la Alga and Espalmador itself. From north or west, enter between Punta Gastabí and Isla del Gastabí, keeping at least 200m off Punta Gastabí to avoid shoals. Mooring buoys have been placed in the bay north of Isla de la Alga. These may be reserved in advance from the 1 June to 30 September but are no longer free; the latest report was €29 per night for a 12m yacht and this is consistent with other areas controlled by Posidonia. See the *Moorings* section on page 19 for further details. Away from the buoyed areas there is still reasonable room to anchor, at least outside the main season, but care should be taken to anchor on sand and to avoid chain dragging over sea grass areas which in theory could give rise to a fine.

It remains a tranquil and sheltered spot, probably because the island is privately owned. There appears to be no serious attempt to prevent visitors using the beaches, though the owners' privacy should be respected. In 2016/7 the island was for sale (reputedly for 25 million euros, but offered to the Formentera government for 18 million euros). More recently it has been reported that it has been sold to a private owner. It is possible that this change in ownership may affect beach access.

Sa Gordiola Tower (Torre Espalmador)

38°47'·1N 01°25'·1E

A large (9·6m) and very conspicuous stone tower standing near the cliff edge (at a total elevation of 34m) on the west coast of Espalmador.

⚓ Caló Moro (Cala Morros)

38°47'·5N 01°25'·2E

A tiny anchorage capable of taking one yacht in fair weather. Open to the south through to west. Anchor in 4m over rock and sand with a line ashore.

⚓ Cala Bochs (Cala Boc or Cala Roja)

38°47'·7N 01°25'·6E

A small and shallow anchorage near the northern end of Espalmador. Anchor in 1·5m over sand off the small beach; otherwise, the shore is mostly rock.

⚓ Isla Espalmador east side

In southwest or west winds boats often anchor on the east side of Espalmador directly across the peninsula from Puerto de Espalmador (*see photo on Page 80*). Anchor over sand or sand and weed in 3-6m avoiding rocky areas, the most extensive sand being relatively close in. This anchorage is exposed to all directions apart from southwest to west northwest and should really be regarded as a day anchorage only.

Isla Espardel

38 48'·3N 01 28'·7E (Light on N point)

The island, which lies 2M east of Espalmador, is a mile long with an elevation of 29m. It is low to the west and cliffed to the east, with outlying rocks and islets extending 300m northwards (Piedra Espardelló Tramontana awash) and 500m southeast from Punta Mitjorn to Islote Espardelló. There is no navigable passage between the latter. This island is now a nature reserve and marked by four yellow conical buoys Fl.Y.5s5M with x topmark. No swimming or fishing is allowed and the passage of any pleasure craft is prohibited inside the buoys.

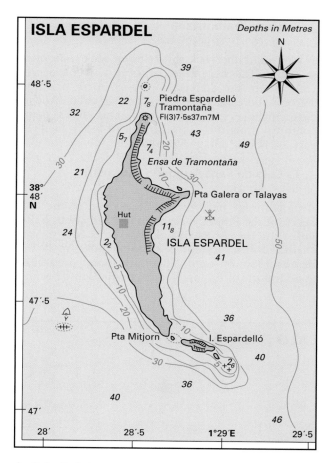

⚓ Cala Pujols

38°43'·5N 01°27'·8E

A rocky-sided *cala* on the northeast coast of Formentera, tucked between the Punta and Islas del Pujols, and Punta Prima (*see plan on Page 74*), littered with shallows, and with rocks on its northwest side. Approach with care and anchor in the southeast corner in 8m over sand, northwest of the old watchtower. There is a large holiday village nearby, complete with supermarkets and restaurants and it is feasible to anchor nearer here taking care to be clear of the rocky islets. There are leading marks for the fishing boat slipway northwest of the anchorage. These are not relevant for deep keeled vessels but may be useful for a dinghy approach to access the village.

Cala Pujols *Susie Baggaley*

II. FORMENTERA AND ESPALMADOR

⚓ Playa de Tramontana

Centred on 38°41'·7N 01°30'·4E

A long sand and rock shore (more rock than sand) stretching for three miles between Cala Barbé and Cala Racó d'es Mares. Open to north and east sectors. There are some interesting sea caves. Anchor close inshore in 5–10m over sand. Even depth contours along this entire stretch of beach facilitate easy anchoring and good holding.

⚓ Es Calo de Sant Augustin (Augusti)

38°40'·7N 001°31'·0E

An anchorage near the southeast end of the long beach of the Playa de Tramontana and about half a mile from the corner of Cala Raco d'es Mares. Very sheltered in all except N sector winds. Anchor in depths 3–6m on sand. There are some particularly good reports of this anchorage, perhaps also because

of the small attractive village where there is a tiny fishermens' harbour giving easy access by dinghy to the cafe and restaurant ashore, together with two small supermarkets, a pharmacy, and a couple of other shops.

⚓ Cala Racó d'es Mares (Reco del Caló)

38°40'·5N 01°31'·8E

Tucked into the southeast corner of Playa de Tramontana is a steep sided cala with good protection from W-SE. There are some rocks in the northwest of the bay, so favour the eastern shore and approach from the NNE. Anchor in crystal clear turquoise water over sand.

Punta Single Mal (Punta de Codolar / Punta de sa Ruda / Punta des Far)

38°39'·8N 01°35'·0E

The headland is 120m high with a tall white lighthouse (Fl.5s142m23M, white tower on white building 22m). It has steep rocky cliffs, as do Punta de la Creu to the north and Punta Rotja to the south. The light is obscured when bearing between 50° and 150°.

⚓ Playa de Mitjorn (Migjorn)

Centred on 38°40'·6N 01°29'E

A 4M long sandy beach which is open to the south sector (*see plan on page 74*). Anchor in 5m over sand and rock in settled weather only. Even a relatively slight breeze from the southern sector renders this area virtually untenable. The ubiquitous line of yellow exclusion buoys runs virtually along the entire length but in the right conditions there is room to anchor outside. Unsuitable for an overnight stay.

CALO SANT AUGUSTIN

N

Depths in Metres

38

63

42'

12

45

5

4 10

8

Playa de Tramontana

38°41'N Calo Sant Augustin

Cala Raco d'es Mares

20

Punta de sa Creu

Punta de sa Palmera

12

Playa de Mitjorn

12 5

10 2

8 2

40'

23

30' 20 31' 1°32'E 33' 34'

Es Calo de Sant Augustin, looking NW across the entrance to the fishing harbour *Susie Baggaley*

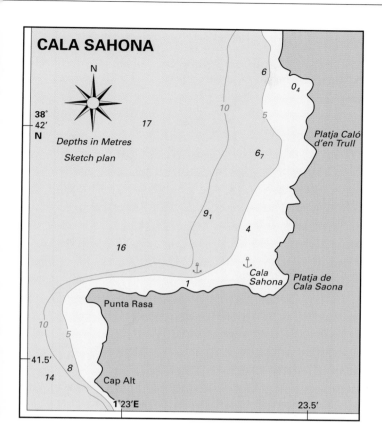

Cabo Berbería

38°38'·4N 01°23'·3E

A steep-to, rocky cliffed headland (55m) in the southwest corner of the island with a lighthouse (Fl(2)15s78m18M, round white tower 19m) and a watchtower 650m to the northeast. The light is obscured when bearing between 170° and 234°.

⚓ Cala Sahona (Saona)

38°41'·7N 01°23'·2E

An excellent anchorage on the west coast off a sandy beach with rocky sides, somewhat spoilt by a large hotel and other buildings ashore. Open to west–northwest–north but in fresh to strong southerly breezes the swell curves round Punta Rassa and the anchorage becomes uncomfortable or untenable. Anchor off the beach outside the considerable exclusion area where there is still much space in 5m+. There is a beach bar and restaurant ashore, and fishermen's huts to the south.

Punta Gabina (Gavina)

38°43'·1N 01°22'·8E

A 14m cliffed headland topped by a 9m tower.

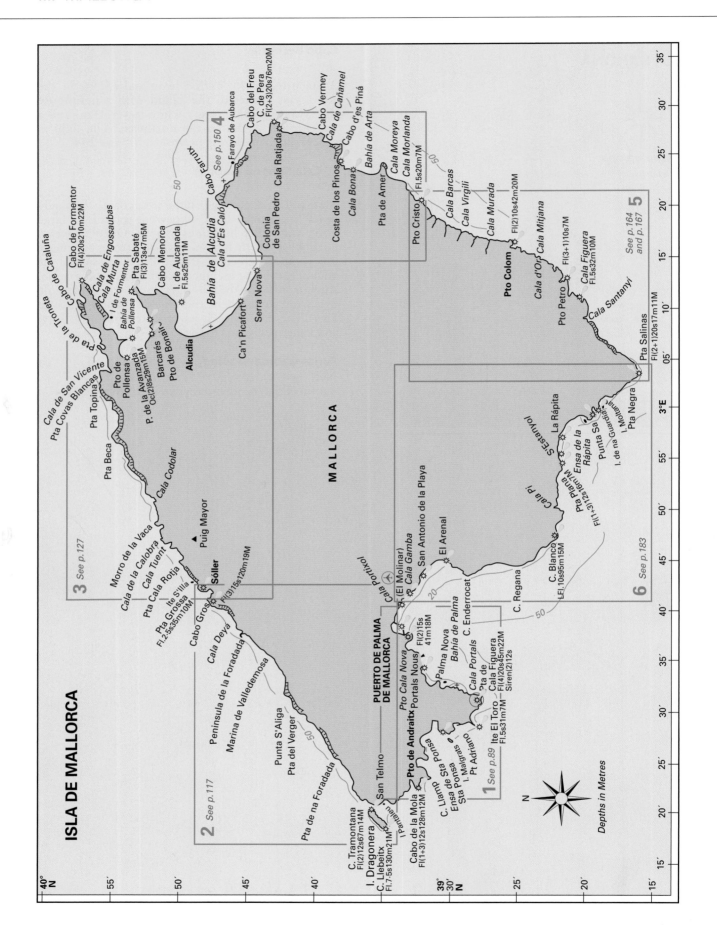

ISLA DE MALLORCA

MALLORCA

III. MALLORCA

Mallorca is the largest and most cosmopolitan of the Islas Baleares and contains the capital, Palma de Mallorca. There are many historical sites to visit, including the old town of Palma whose port provides excellent berthing and every nautical requirement, including the necessary permits for the neighbouring island of Cabrera. There are many superb ports and anchorages around its coasts. Puerto de Sóller is of particular interest with its vintage tramway and Victorian train linking the port with Palma. Inland there are orange and olive groves, vineyards and pine forests. The numerous restored windmills are a unique feature of the interior of the island. The rugged cliffs and mountains of the northwest coast give a magnificently dramatic coastline.

The coastline of Mallorca is covered in six sections in a clockwise direction around the island beginning at Palma.

1. Puerto de Palma to Puerto de Andraitx *p.89*

2. Cala Egos to Sóller *p.117*

3. Punta Grossa to Puerto de Ca'n Picafort *p.127*

4. Puerto de Colonia de San Pedro to Porto Cristo *p.150*

5. Cala Murta to Cala Marmols *p.164*

6. Punta Salinas to Bahiá de Palma *p.183*

Note: Cabrera is covered in Chapter IV

Navigational information on approaches to Mallorca

Coming from the south from North Africa or from the eastern Mediterranean and heading for peninsular Spain or France, or for a crew change, Mallorca may be an appropriate landfall because of its size, international airport and the safe port of Palma. With many ports and anchorages to choose from and the huge Bahía de Palma, calmer waters in any weather conditions are assured.

Magnetic variation

Less than 001°E.

Approach and coastal passage charts

Imray	M3
Admiralty	1702, 1703, 2831, 2832
Spanish	48E, 900, 965, 970, 421, 422, 423, 424, 425, 426, 427
French	5505, 7115, 7116, 7118

Approach lights

Puerto de Palma 39°33'N 02°37'·5E Fl(2)15s41m18M
Square brown stone tower, visible outside Bahía de Palma 327°-040°

Punta de Cala Figuera 39°27'·5N 02°31'·4E Fl(4)20s45m22M
Siren(2)12s White round tower, black diagonal stripes, on building 24m

Cabo de la Mola 39°32'N 02°21'·9 Fl(1+3)12s128m12M
White column, black bands, on white square tower 10m

Cabo Llebeitx 39°34'·5N 02°18'·3E Fl.7·5s130m21M Masonry tower on stone building with red roof 15m 313°-vis-150°

Cabo Tramontana 39°36'N 02°20'·4E Fl(2)12s67m14M
Round masonry tower on stone building with red roof 15m 095°-vis-230° and 346°-vis-027°

Cabo Gros 39°47'·9N 02°41'E Fl(3)15s120m19M
White tower and house, red roof 22m 054°-vis-232°

Cabo Formentor 39°57'·7N 03°12'·8E Fl(4)20s210m22M
White tower and house 22m
Note The characteristics of Cabo Formentor are almost identical to those of Cabo Nati, Menorca

Punta Sabaté (Cabo del Pina) 39°53'·6N 03°11'·8E
Fl(3)13s47m5M White triangular tower, black band 12m

Cabo de Pera 39°43'N 03°28'·7E Fl(2+3)20s76m20M
White tower on white building with dark corners and red roof 21m 148°-vis-010°

Punta de ses Crestas/Punta de la Farola (Puerto Colom)
39°24'·9N 03°16'·3E Fl(2)10s42m20M White round tower, three black bands, on white building with red roof 25m 207°-vis-006°

Torre d'en Beu (Cala Figuera) 39°19'·8N 03°10'·7E
Fl.3s32m10M
White octagonal tower, vertical black stripes 6m

Punta Salinas 39°16'N 03°03'·3E Fl(2+1)20s17m11M
White tower and building 17m 265°-vis-116°

Cabo Blanco 39°21'·9N 02°47'·3E LFl.10s95m15M
White tower and building 12m 336°-vis-115°

INTRODUCTION

Isla de Mallorca (pronounced as Myorca and sometimes spelt Majorca) is the largest island of the Baleares group, being some 62 miles long and 47 miles wide. The northwest and northeast coasts are mountainous with numerous coves (*calas*), whilst the south coast has rolling hills and sandy beaches. The central plain is flat with huge expanses of fertile agricultural terrain. Mallorca has a very large port, several other harbours and many anchorages in *calas*. There is one large offlying island to the south (Cabrera), described in the next chapter.

The mountain range that fringes the northwest-facing coast is high, culminating in the 1,445m peak of Puig Mayor. This stretch of coast is very rugged, with steep rocky cliffs broken by a number of indentations, nearly all located in the northern section and providing some spectacular anchorages for use in settled weather. Puerto de Sóller offers the only harbour on the northwest coast and a refuge in the event of a northwest *tramontana* or *mestral*, which turns the entire coastline into one long and potentially dangerous lee shore.

The northwest coast of Mallorca is truly spectacular throughout its length.
Centre left is Islote Colomer and to the right Punta de la Troneta *Susie Baggaley*

The coast that faces northeast towards Menorca consists of two large sandy bays, each with a major harbour and a number of anchorages and smaller harbours. While not as dramatic as the northwest coast, parts are attractive and safe harbours and anchorages can be found in most conditions.

The eastern coastline comprises the 'Coast of the *calas*'. In general this 35 mile section has low rocky cliffs with ranges of low hills inland. The relatively straight run of the coast is broken by numerous inlets in which lie small harbours and anchorages, the majority very attractive. Notable on this coast is the large but relatively shallow inlet of Porto Colom, the best natural harbour in Mallorca. It was also the cheapest until recently.

The remaining coast, facing the southwest, is centred around the large Bahía de Palma, where the majority of the industry and population of the island is situated. Palma de Mallorca, the capital and a major port, can supply most material, cultural and holiday requirements but, like all cities, it is busy, crowded and noisy. On the southeast side of this bay are high, white cliffs and on the opposite side high, rocky cliffs broken by a number of small bays and *calas*.

With the exception of the heads of the large sandy bays, deep water can generally be carried very close to the shore. Other than Isla de Cabrera and Isla Dragonera there are no offshore dangers, and the few smaller islands and rocks that exist are generally very close in.

Inland, Mallorca is stunningly beautiful, with large areas of fruit orchards, in addition to olive groves and fields of wheat and vegetables. In the more hilly areas Moorish methods of terraced cultivation are still in evidence. The mountains of the northwest provide dramatic views and some challenging hill walks. Away from the coast – and particularly in the eastern half of the island – many of the smaller walled towns remain relatively unspoilt. One feels saddened, and at the same time relieved, that so few tourists appear to venture far beyond the nearest beach and their package holiday hotel. The western side of the island is particularly popular with racing cyclists because of the steep roads, and the presence of 23 golf courses in the island makes it a paradise for golfers.

Two factors have tended to make the Mallorcans more cosmopolitan and subtly different from the inhabitants of the other islands in the group – firstly, wide intermarriage with the Moors, who remained in greater numbers than on the other islands; and secondly, the rise in power and prosperity of Palma in the 14th and 15th centuries, which brought a flow of riches and contact with the outside world which the other islands lacked. Palma is still the seat of the government and parliament of the Autonomous Community of the Islas Baleares, and home to about half of the island's population of around 850,000 people.

Cala de la Calobra (Torrente de Pareis) from southeast

History

Mallorca appears to have been inhabited for at least 6,000 years, with some of the earliest human traces found in a cave near Sóller on the north coast. Later, from around 1200BC, the bronze age *talayot* (tower) culture flourished in both Mallorca and Menorca. Although Menorca has the greater preponderance of sites from this era, Mallorca has some near Artá on the east coast and Lluchmayor further south. Little is known about these early peoples, though successive invasions by Phoenicians, Carthaginians and Greeks have left some traces. According to the 1st century BC Greek writer Diodorus, the inhabitants of both Mallorca and Menorca wore few clothes and were called *gymnetes* (naked men), their islands being collectively known as Gymnesia.

The Romans conquered Mallorca in 123BC and remained until the 5th century. It was known to them as Major, as opposed to Menorca, which was called Minor, and these two formed, together with Cabrera, the Insulae Baleares. The city of Pollentia, now called Alcudia, became their capital, and they also founded the harbours of Palma and Pollensa. However, the Romans used the island more as a staging post than as a permanent settlement and there are few remains of buildings to be found. A notable exception is the Roman theatre at Alcudia, easily reached from the yacht harbour. After the departure of the Romans the island entered the dark ages, overrun by the Vandals and later becoming a favoured base for pirates and Corsairs.

Restored windmills: once used for pumping water and generating electicity, rather than as mills, are a common sight in central Mallorca *Graham Hutt*

Mallorca's next taste of prosperity was under the Moors, who arrived early in the 10th century. Roman Palma was renamed Medina Mayurqa and grew into a bustling city of some 25,000 inhabitants, while throughout the island agriculture was improved and irrigation canals built. However, almost equally little remains of this period, other than the delightful Arabian Baths and the Almudaina arch in Palma.

The destruction of Moorish Palma can fairly be laid at the door of King Jaime I (Rey Jaime Conquistador), who drove the Moors out in 1229, backed by the combined armies of Catalonia and Aragon. A monument to their landing stands on the headland overlooking Puerto de Santa Ponsa on the southwest coast. With them the conquering army brought the Catalan language, which gradually evolved into the Mallorquín dialect spoken by most islanders today.

The 13th to 15th centuries were a golden age, with a vast increase in population and wealth. Palma, with its imposing Gothic cathedral, new castle and growing dock system, became a centre for trade inside the Mediterranean. However, as Spain gradually turned her attention westward towards the New World, her Mediterranean possessions became something of a backwater. Frequent attacks by pirates resulted in coastal villages and towns being rebuilt several miles inland, with only a few huts on the shore or at the harbour. In this way the damage and loss caused by surprise raids were minimised. During the next few centuries little of historical importance took place in Mallorca, other than the building of many churches and of houses for the nobility.

Inland, the north of Mallorca has lush green pine forests and olive orchards *Graham Hutt*

Victorian mahogany train, still in daily service between Palma and Sóller *Patricia Chung*

Palma Mallorca. The ancient cathedral, La Seu, still dominates the skyline after hundreds of years
Mari Kanayama

Gaudi's canopy inside La Seu, with the magnificent 14m eastern rose window, known as the Gothic Eye, above
Jane Russell

Recent history

During the Spanish Civil War the island supported the Nationalists and suffered little damage. Greater changes have come about with the post-war advent of mass tourism. Not only are there now areas in which the ground can barely be seen for high-rise hotels or the beach for sunbeds; but the many support services, from tourist shops to smart restaurants, have revived Mallorca's fortunes and changed its former agricultural-based economy for ever. Some areas have become notorious for excess but the authorities are now attempting to rein in the seedier side of areas such as Magaluf, Palma Nova, and Arenal.

Tourist information

Places of interest

In addition to places of interest described in the harbour sections, there are many other sites further inland which can be visited by taxi, bus or in some cases rail, from almost any port. Mallorca is one place where it is well worth hiring a car. Car rental in the town centres is considerably cheaper than at the airports. There are spectacular mountain ranges and old *pueblos* (villages) to visit, along with a very few ancient remains of Moorish and Roman architecture.

High in the mountains near the northwest coast is the Carthusian monastery at Valldemosa, which was once the palace of the Kings of Mallorca and has fine views. The road running east towards Sóller passes the Peninsula de la Foradada and the Son Marroig estate (once owned by Archduke Luis Salvador of Austria), before winding through the beautiful village of Deya, famous for its associations with the writer Robert Graves. Further northeast, Lluch boasts a monastery built in the 14th century; it is situated at a height of over 300m and provides excellent views. Further north still, a long but worthwhile hike from near Pollensa enables a visit to the Castillo del Rey on a high rocky outcrop with stupendous views of the northwest coast.

In the southern part of the island, Campos has Roman baths and a 15th-century church, while nearby Lluchmayor has prehistoric and Roman remains and is also the site of the battle where Mallorca lost her independence.

Look up the tourist information offices, where a wealth of information will be found on all the sites and events of interest. These are listed in the *General introduction* and at www.illesbalears.es. See also www.infomallorca.net for current events. Many books have been published on the sites of the island, a number of which are available at airports throughout Europe.

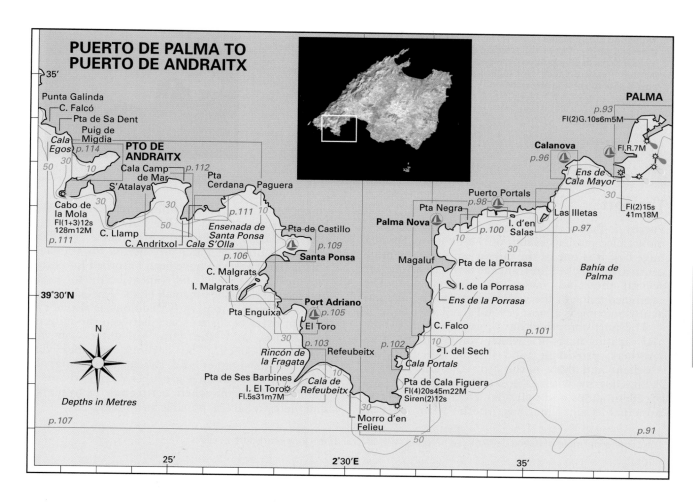

PUERTO DE PALMA TO PUERTO DE ANDRAITX

35'

Punta Galinda
C. Falcó
Pta de Sa Dent
Puig de Migdia
Cala Egos *p.114*
50 30 10

PTO DE ANDRAITX

Cala Camp de Mar *p.112*
S'Atalaya
Pta Cerdana   Paguera
Cabo de la Mola
Fl(1+3)12s 128m12M
30
C. Llamp
C. Andritxol
30
50
p.111

Ensenada de Santa Ponsa
Cala S'Olla
p.111 10
Pta de Castillo
p.109
p.106
Santa Ponsa

C. Malgrats
I. Malgrats

Port Adriano *p.105*
Pta Enguixa
El Toro
p.103
Rincón de la Fragata
Refeubeitx
Pta de Ses Barbines
I. El Toro
Fl.5s31m7M
Cala de Refeubeitx
10

N

Depths in Metres

p.107

Morro d'en Felieu
p.102
30

PALMA
p.93
Fl(2)G.10s6m5M
Fl.R.7M

Calanova
p.96
Ens de Cala Mayor
30

Puerto Portals *p.98*
Pta Negra
Palma Nova
Las Illetas
I. d'en Salas
p.97
p.100
10
30

Magaluf
Pta de la Porrasa
I. de la Porrasa
Ens de la Porrasa
C. Falco
p.101
10
I. del Sech
p.102
Cala Portals
Pta de Cala Figuera
Fl(4)20s45m22M
Siren(2)12s

Bahía de Palma

Fl(2)15s 41m18M

p.91
50

39°30'N

25'   2°30'E   35'

III. MALLORCA

The coastline of ancient and modern construction is a welcoming sight on approach to Palma. Castillo de Bellver is in the background   *Graham Hutt*

Puerto de Palma de Mallorca

39°33'·5N 02°38'E

Within this major commercial port lie several marinas with facilities for several thousand yachts of any size, including super-yachts. However, it is difficult to find a place to berth during July and August and advance booking for any of the marinas is essential then - and indeed preferable even outside that period. The port is safe to enter in any weather.

Distances
Ibiza 60M
Barcelona 120M

Communications
See text

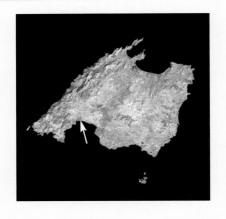

The port

Puerto de Palma shelters several yachting facilities, most called marinas even if only a pontoon. Set in a huge bay, it is one of the largest collective yachting centres in the Mediterranean, with berthing for several thousand yachts and superyachts. The combined value of the vessels sitting in the marinas at any one time is almost beyond comprehension.

The port comprises naval, commercial, fishing and yachting harbours, which can be entered in all weathers, providing good shelter. Amenities are excellent and there is the attractive old town of Palma nearby with extensive fine buildings and excellent shops and markets. There are two large principal yacht marinas, both with palatial clubhouses and all facilities and several other berthing options on a smaller scale but with a bias towards larger and indeed super yachts. The Port Authority no longer has any berths for transient yachts (most seem to have been absorbed into other facilities) and only has permanent berths for locals and these seem to be for small boats. The Dársena de Porto Pi, referred to in earlier editions, is also not an option, there being no space between the military installation and the large freighters on the commercial dock. The harbour becomes very crowded in summer and vacant berths may be difficult to find but there are other yacht harbours in the Bahía de Palma where berths may be available, and there are several possible anchorages.

The commercial mole of Palma de Mallorca harbour, with several of the inner harbours visible

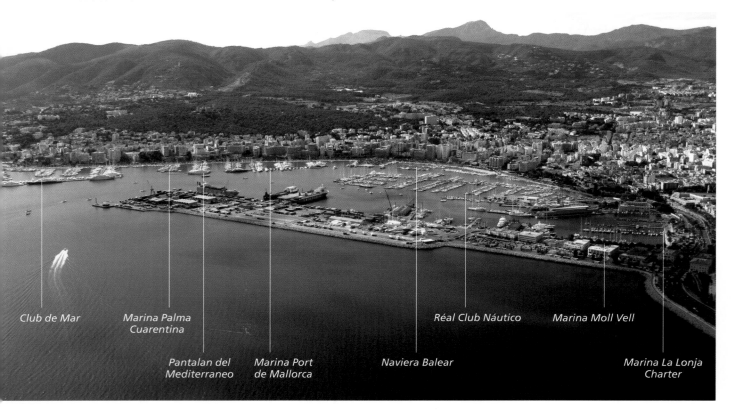

Club de Mar
Marina Palma Cuarentina
Pantalan del Mediterraneo
Marina Port de Mallorca
Naviera Balear
Réal Club Náutico
Marina Moll Vell
Marina La Lonja Charter

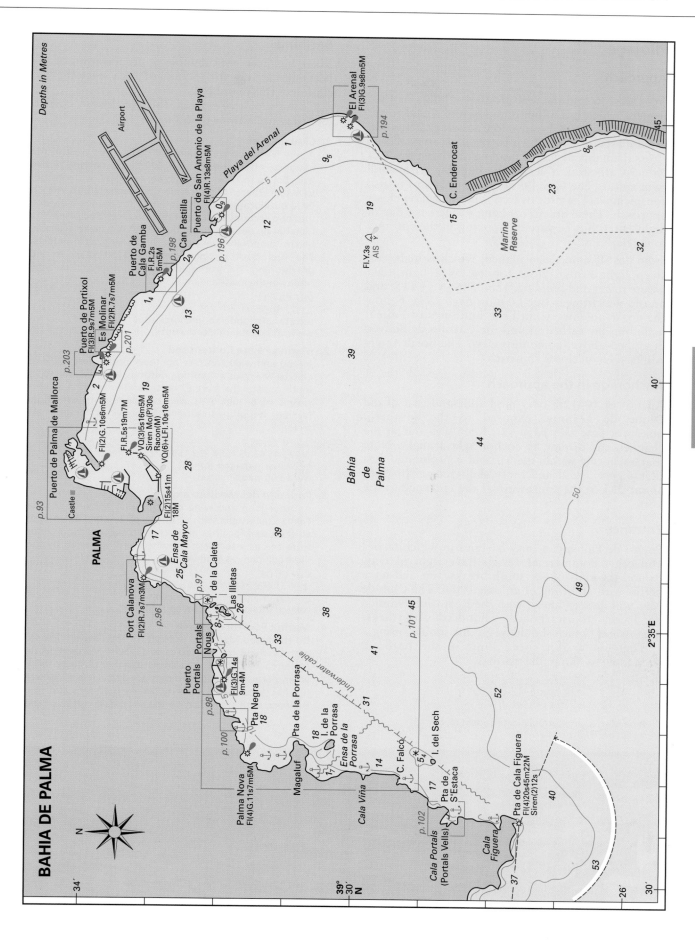

Depths in Metres

BAHIA DE PALMA

N

34´

Airport

Puerto de San Antonio de la Playa
Fl(4)R.13s8m5M

Playa del Arenal

El Arenal
Fl(3)G.9s8m5M

p.194

1

Can Pastilla

Puerto de Cala Gamba
Fl.R.2s 5m5M

Fl.R.7s7m5M

p.198

0.9

p.196

9.5

C. Enderrocat

8.6

45

Es Molinar
Fl(2)R.7s7m5M

Puerto de Portixol
Fl(3)R.9s7m5M

p.201

p.203

1.4

2.9

13

26

19

15

Marine
Reserve

23

32

5

10

12

33

PALMA

Puerto de Palma de Mallorca

p.93

Castle

2

Fl(2)G.10s6m5M

Fl.R.5s19m7M

VQ(3)5s16m5M
Siren Mo(P)30s
Racon(M)

VQ(6)+LFl.10s16m5M

Fl(2)15s41m
18M

19

28

39

Bahía
de
Palma

44

50

Port Calanova
Fl(2)R.7s7m3M

p.96

Ensa de
Cala Mayor

17

25

p.97

I. de la Caleta

Las Illetas

8.1

26

38

45

p.101

49

39

52

Portals
Nous

33

41

Puerto
Portals

Fl(3)G.14s
9m4M

p.98

5

Pta Negra

18

31

Underwater cable

Magaluf

18

I. de la
Porrasa

Ensa de la
Porrasa

14

Pta de la Porrasa

I. del Sech

C. Falcó

5.4

Palma Nova
Fl(4)G.11s7m5M

p.100

17

Cala Viña

17

Pta de
S'Estaca

p.102

Cala Portals
(Portals Vells)

Cala
Figuera

Pta de Cala Figuera
Fl(4)20s45m22M
Siren(2)12s

40

37

53

30

Fl.Y.3s
AIS

39°
30´
N

2°35 E

III. MALLORCA

34´

39°
30´
N

26´

30´

40´

Pilotage

Approach

From west Round the very prominent Punta de Cala Figuera which has a lighthouse (white round tower with black diagonal stripes on building, 24m) and radio masts on its steep cliffs (*see plan on page 91*). Cross the Bahía de Palma heading northeast towards Palma Cathedral, a very large building with small twin spires. The Castillo de Bellver (140m) is also conspicuous. The breakwaters will be seen on closer approach. There are no off-lying dangers for day or night entry, but beware of shipping in the entrance to the harbour.

From east Round Cabo Blanco, which is high with steep light brown cliffs topped by a lighthouse (white tower and building, 12m, 336 - vis - 115) and an old watchtower (*see plan on page 183*). Follow the coast northwest until the buildings of Palma, including the cathedral and the Castillo de Bellver, described above, come into view. The breakwaters will be seen on closer approach.

Anchorage in the approach

Anchor in 10–12m over mud and sand east of the Dique de Levante, exposed to the southerly quadrant *(see plan page 91)*. Keep well out of the channel, and display an anchor light at night. Note that anchoring within the harbour is prohibited. Las Illetas give useful and more sheltered anchorages about 2M to the southwest of the entrance to the port.

Entrance

Puerto de Palma is a busy harbour in which ferries and other commercial vessels have right of way. Round the ends of the south breakwater and ferry berths with an offing of at least 100m. The Club de Mar will be seen ahead with the Réal Club Náutico de Palma to starboard behind the northeast breakwater (which should be given a similar offing).

There is a 5kn speed limit in the harbour, decreasing to 3kn in the marinas.

Berthing

There has been considerable re-organisation of the berthing facilities for yachts in Palma since the last edition of this pilot book.

Going clockwise from the southwest corner, moorings are now as follows:

1. **Club de Mar**
   A very large and well equipped marina due west of the entrance, offering more than 600 berths ranging in size from 8m up to 120m. Facilities are excellent, with charges to match. There is no reception pontoon; call on VHF Ch 09 to be allocated a berth. Note that the marina is divided into two sections with separate entrances (*see plan*). The Club has no defined visitor berths but will make available berths temporarily vacated by permanent berth-holders. The fuel dock is open 0900–2000 all year. To aid provisioning, El Corte Inglés have an order and delivery facility in the marina.
   VHF Ch 09
   ✆ 971 40 36 11
   secretaria@clubdemar-mallorca.com
   www.clubdemar-mallorca.com

2. **Marina Palma Cuarentena**
   A long and wide concrete pontoon located just north of Club de Mar plus a floating pontoon along the wall to its south. In total there are 67 berths and the marina accepts vessels of 8–40m. It is well equipped with the usual facilities. It is prone to surging during winds from the east sector.
   ✆ VHF Ch 09
   ✆ 971 45 43 95 / 654 369 153
   info@marinapalma.com
   www.marinapalma.com

3. **Pantalán del Mediterraneo**
   Another long and wide pontoon just north of Marina Palma Cuarentena with 61 berths of 20–60m, again with all the usual facilities and prone to surge during winds from the east sector. It is owned and managed by the same company as Moll Vell.
   VHF Ch 08
   ✆ 9971 458 211 / 971 220 536
   info@pantalanmediterraneo.com
   www.pantalanmediterraneo.com

4. **Marina Port de Mallorca**
   On the Paseo Marítimo, in front of Hotel Melia Victoria, with berthing for 200 yachts of 12–50m, Marina Port de Mallorca has about 20 visitors' berths, perhaps more when permanent berth-holders are away. It is expensive but has water and electricity on the pontoons and free showers, with the office on the southeast corner of the

Club de Mar; a large, sophisticated yacht club
Nico Martinez/Club de Mar

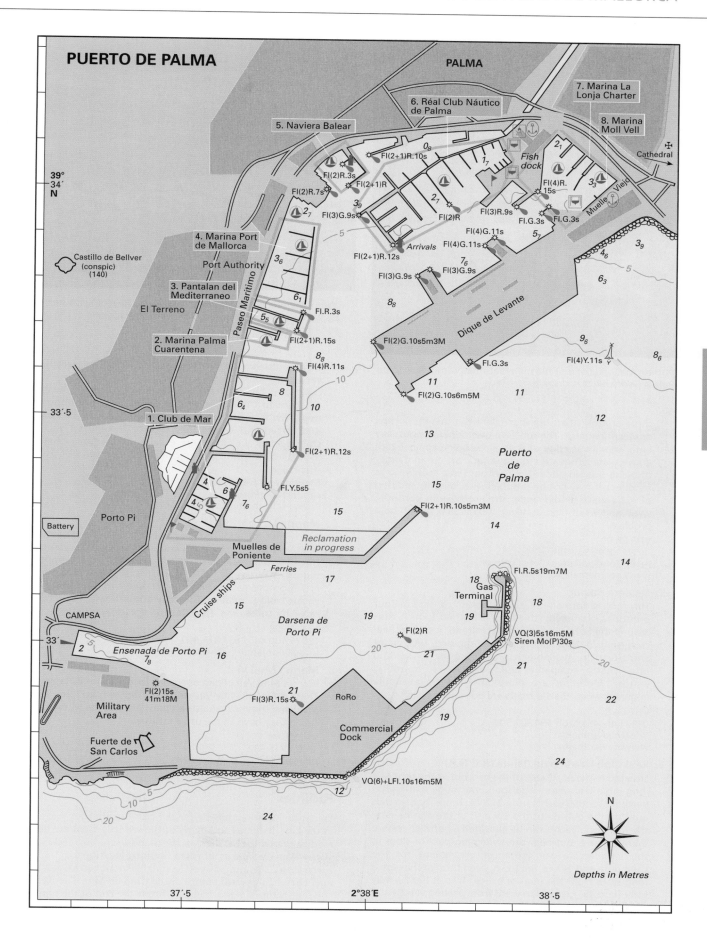

PUERTO DE PALMA

PALMA

5. Naviera Balear

6. Réal Club Náutico de Palma

7. Marina La Lonja Charter

8. Marina Moll Vell

Cathedral

Fl(2+1)R.10s

0₈

1₇

2₁

Fish dock

Fl(2)R.3s

Fl(2+1)R

3₃

Fl(4)R. 15s

Fl(2)R.7s

2₇

2₇

Muelle Viejo

39° 34′ N

Fl(3)G.9s

3₉

Fl(2)R

Fl(3)R.9s

Fl.G.3s

Fl.G.3s

4. Marina Port de Mallorca

3₆

Fl(2+1)R.12s

Arrivals

Fl(4)G.11s

5₇

3₉

Port Authority

Fl(4)G.11s

4₆

Castillo de Bellver (conspic) (140)

3. Pantalan del Mediterraneo

6₁

7₆

Fl(3)G.9s

6₃

5

El Terreno

5₅

Fl.R.3s

Fl(3)G.9s

8₈

9₆

8₆

Paseo Marítimo

Fl(2+1)R.15s

Dique de Levante

Fl(4)Y.11s Y

2. Marina Palma Cuarentena

33′·5

8₈

Fl(4)R.11s

Fl(2)G.10s5m3M

11

8

10

11

11

1. Club de Mar

6₄

8

Fl.G.3s

Fl(2)G.10s6m5M

12

10

13

Puerto de Palma

Fl(2+1)R.12s

15

15

Battery

Porto Pi

4

6

4

5

7₆

Fl.Y.5s5

Fl(2+1)R.10s5m3M

14

14

Muelles de Poniente

Reclamation in progress

Fl.R.5s19m7M

CAMPSA

Ferries

17

18 Gas Terminal

18

Cruise ships

15

19

19

VQ(3)5s16m5M Siren Mo(P)30s

33′

2

Ensenada de Porto Pi

16

Darsena de Porto Pi

19

Fl(2)R

21

21

20

7₈

20

21

Fl(2)15s 41m18M

Fl(3)R.15s

RoRo

22

Military Area

Commercial Dock

19

24

Fuerte de San Carlos

VQ(6)+LFl.10s16m5M

12

5

24

10

20

N

Depths in Metres

37′·5

2°38′E

38′·5

III. MALLORCA

Palma: Overlooking Castillo de Bellver into Réal Club Náutico de Palma, with La Lonja and Moll Vell at the top end of the commercial quay *Geoff Williamson*

Port de Mallorca: one of the many facilities within Puerto de Palma *Geoff Williamson*

shore pontoon. Security is excellent but there is no fuel or reception dock. The concrete pontoons are unusually high, the lower edge of their sides being some 1·25m above water. Thus even quite large craft are in danger of being pushed under the pontoons in a crosswind as fending off may not be possible. Also, despite addition of extra wave breaks under the north/south pontoon, swell and wash from passing craft is said to still be a problem.

VHF Ch 09
① 971 28 96 93 / 98
recepcion@portdemallorca.com or
www.portdemallorca.com

5. Naviera Balear

This facility, formerly Marina Alboran, consists of four pontoons on the north Paseo Maritimo (which runs around the port), opposite Hotel Mirador just W of Real Club Náutico. There are toilets and showers, fuel, water and electricity available. It is the base for Sunsail and other charter companies and is available to transiting visitors. Moorings are more likely to be available midweek when charter boats are out sailing.

VHF Ch 8
① 971 454455 Mob 664 301 300
info@navierabalear
www.navierabalear.com

6. Réal Club Náutico de Palma (R.C.N.P.)

Situated in the northeast of the harbour at the root of a long mole with many side spurs, this huge marina has berthing for 850 yachts from 8–20m. There is an arrivals quay on the outside of the SW arm of the marina near the fuel dock. Yachts can be allocated a berth anywhere there is space, but near the swimming pool or close to the launderette are the most convenient for the clubhouse and exit to the town, even though they are a long walk from the marina office. Transit berths may sometimes be exposed to wash from passing vessels and to significant cross winds. A splendid backdrop is the ancient cathedral a short distance away, though the town centre is a ten to fifteen minute walk. This really is a very good marina and good value – probably the only complaint can be that the WiFi is poor even in berths adjacent to the clubhouse, and even in the clubhouse itself. The staff are friendly and helpful and the club bar and restaurant, where members of recognized yacht clubs appear welcome, are excellent. A stopover here should be a pleasant and enjoyable experience.

VHF Ch 09
Marina ① 971 72 68 48
capitania@rcnp.es
www.realclubnáuticopalma.com

7. Marina La Lonja Charter

his marina for about 50 yachts exists primarily to serve relatively large skippered and crewed charter yachts. However, a substantial number of berths will be empty during the week with turnaround usually being Friday/Saturday. The marina are keen to find visiting yachts from Sunday to Thursday and promise 'economic rates' for those days. They have all the usual facilities.

VHF Ch 08
① 971 100 446 / 634 279 800
info@lalonjamarinacharter.com

8. Marina Moll Vell

Marina Moll Vell began operating in 2014 with 27 berths. These cover 20–40m yachts except for two at 15m. It is probably the most sheltered and safe marina in Palma. Again they have all the usual facilities.

VHF Ch 08
① 971 716 332
palma@mollvell.com
www.mollvell.com

Facilities

Palma de Mallorca has by far the best facilities for yachts in the Islas Baleares and many of the services listed are not readily available elsewhere in the islands.

Water Water points at all yacht berthing locations.

Electricity 220v and 380v AC available at all berths.

Fuel Diesel and petrol pumps at the Club de Mar. The Réal Club Náutico has a fuel berth near the end of the main northwest-going pontoon. Naviera Balear also has a fuel dock.

Bottled gas It is understood that CAMPSA will not now fill any gas bottles, even with a current test certificate. Camping Gaz is, however, widely available.

Repairs See *Appendix* for list of chandleries and repair facilities.

Chandlery Located at entrance to Real Club Náutico is the well-stocked Yacht Centre Palma. ☎ 34 971 715 612, peter@ycp.com.es or info@ycp.com.es
There are several other chandleries in the town

Provisions A massive Carrefour hypermarket in the Porto Pí shopping centre five minutes' walk from the Club de Mar, with another of similar size on the road to the airport. Small supermarket at Club de Mar. A wide variety of other shops, as one would expect of a major city. A produce market at Santa Catalina, ten minutes from the Réal Club Náutico. El Corte Inglés, the Spanish equivalent of John Lewis/Waitrose, has a large store with a food hall in Avenida Jaime 111, about 10 minutes' walk from Real Club Náutico.

Ice Cube ice from the Réal Club Náutico, the fuel berth at the Club de Mar and many supermarkets. Block ice (not for use in drinks) from *La Lonja Charter*.

Yacht clubs Réal Club Náutico de Palma (RCNP) was founded nearly fifty years ago and has bars, a restaurant, bedrooms, a swimming pool, showers, repair workshops, etc. The Club de Mar is a much newer 'marina' yacht club with similar facilities. Apply to the secretary before using either club but members of similar yacht clubs are likely to be welcomed.

Showers At all marinas.

Banks One in the Club de Mar complex, with many more throughout the city. Most (including the Club de Mar unit) have ATMs.

Launderettes Facilities at both marinas and others in the city.

Hospital/medical services Medical Office in Club de Mar and several in the city.

WiFi All the marinas claim to have WiFi coverage for all their berths but most will admit that the quality of coverage is at best variable.

Transport

Car hire A wide choice, with the cheapest rates to be found around the Paseo Marítimo.

Taxis Can be found everywhere.

Buses and trains Bus service throughout the island plus trains to Sóller (recommended) and Inca. Timetables available from tourist offices.

Ferries Car ferries to mainland Spain, Ibiza and Menorca. (See *General Introduction*.)

Air services Busy international airport four miles east of the city and the hub for Air Berlin. (A bus links Plaza de España in the city centre to the airport four times an hour. Times from the airport are between 0610–0215.)

History

The city of Palma is thought to have been founded by the Romans, who knew it as Palmaria and built its first city walls during the 4th century. It flourished under the Moors, who renamed it Medina Mayurqa and whose legacy includes the Arabian Baths and the Almudaina arch. Subsequently it became the Spanish capital of the islands and the centre of a Mediterranean trading empire, giving rise to the first proper harbour works some time in the 14th century.

Ashore

First amongst Palma's treasures must be its soaring Gothic cathedral, begun in 1230 and still able to dominate the eastern part of the city at the north end of the port. Opposite is the Almudaina palace, built by the Moors but swiftly taken over by their Christian conquerors. Behind and slightly inland lies the oldest and most fascinating part of the city, where narrow flagged alleyways lined by shops, bars and restaurants can only be explored on foot. All are within comfortable walking distance of the harbour. Further out of the city on a hillside to the northwest stands the Castillo de Bellver, also built in the 13th century and entered by a drawbridge across the moat. As with any major city there are museums, churches and historic buildings by the score. Do refer to the list of guide books (see *Appendix*) or visit the tourist office to fully enjoy the sights.

Local events

Fiestas are held on 5 January with the Procession of the Three Kings and on 17 January to celebrate the Blessing of St Anthony. Two days later are the Revels of St Sebastian. February sees Carnival Week and March or April the Fair of Ramos. Religious processions are held during Easter Week, with the Fiesta of the Angel on the first Sunday after Easter. The Fiesta de Santa Catalina Tomás, the island's own saint, is held on the first Sunday after 28 July, with the Procession of Sta Beateta on 28 October. On 31 December the old year is rounded off with the Fiesta of the Standard.

Many of the elegant courtyards, which are a feature of the Old Town, are open to the public over the summer and some host musical events.

Eating out

Bars, cafés and restaurants abound all around the harbour and in the city. Of the latter, some of the most intriguing are in the old part of the city behind the cathedral. Many specialist high class Indian, Sushi, Chinese, Malaysian, Thai and French restaurants can be found. Both main marinas have their own restaurants and indoor/outdoor bars.

Anchorage West of Puerto de Palma

⚓ Ensenada de Cala Mayor
39°33'·0N 02°36'·23E

An open bay close to and west of Puerto de Palma, with Port Calanova yacht harbour tucked in on its western side. Anchor in 5m+ over sand and stone about 200m northeast of the Calanova harbour entrance and well clear of the approach, open to southeast through southwest. Five underwater cables run in a south–southeast direction from a point near the centre of the bay, where anchoring is prohibited. The anchorage is backed by large apartment blocks, houses and shops. (*See plans on pages 91 and 96*.)

Port Calanova

39°33'N 02°36'E

Previously known as Puerto de Cala Nova, this is a small friendly harbour a short distance W of Palma but with doubtful space for visitors. It has berths for 215 yachts, most of which are taken up by locals all year round.

Communications
Port Calanova VHF Ch 09
☎ 971 40 25 12
info@portcalanova.com

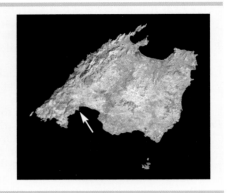

The harbour

A small and rather shallow artificial harbour, built by the Balearic authorities as a base for the national sailing school, the Escola Nacional de Vela, where children and adults learn windsurfing, dinghy and keelboat sailing. Although technically a private harbour, visitors' berths are occasionally available.

Port Calanova is pleasant with good facilities. It is easy to enter with good protection once inside, though a swell works in with strong east or southeast winds.

Pilotage

Approach

For outer approaches see *Puerto de Palma*.

From west (*See plan on page 91.*) After rounding Punta de Cala Figuera cross the Bahía de Palma heading northeast, leaving the low-lying Isla del Sech to port. When past Las Illetas follow the coast at 200m for one mile when Port Calanova will easily be seen.

From east (*See plan on page 91.*) Leave Puerto de Palma's long south breakwater to starboard to enter the Ensenada de Cala Mayor. Port Calanova will be seen in the northwest corner.

Anchorage in the approach

In the Ensenada de Cala Mayor (*see text on page 95 and plan below*).

Entrance

Keep to the middle of the 55m-wide entrance maintaining a careful watch for sailing school craft (novices) entering or leaving. There is a 2kn speed limit inside the harbour.

Berthing

Secure to the inside of the south breakwater unless a berth has already been allocated.

Facilities

Water Taps on quays and pontoons.
Electricity 220v AC points on the quays and pontoons.
Fuel For the sailing school's use only, and not on public sale.
Provisions All normal supplies are available from supermarkets and shops in Cala Nova and nearby San Augustin.
Ice From the Port Calanova bar.
Chandlery By the harbour.
Repairs A 35-tonne travel-lift at the west end of the harbour and a 2·5 tonne crane. A wide but shallow dinghy slipway backed by an area of hard standing.

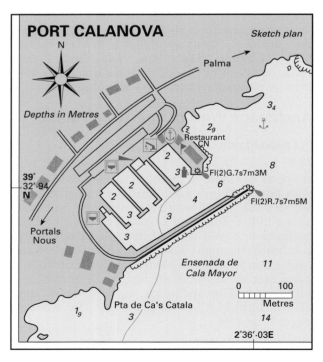

Port Calanova from south

Engineers Enquire at the harbour office.

Yacht club Port Calanova has a pleasant clubhouse on the north mole with a restaurant, bar, terrace, swimming pool, showers, etc.

Showers At the clubhouse.

Launderette Near the harbour.

Hospital/medical services In Palma.

Transport

Car hire/taxis ☎ 971 75 54 40 or from Palma.

Buses To Palma and elsewhere regularly pass the port.

Ashore

As for Palma.

Eating out

Many eating places of all grades, including a restaurant and bar at the Port Calanova clubhouse.

Anchorages West of Calanova

⚓ Las Illetas anchorages

39°31'·5N 02°35'·5E

An attractive group of anchorages best viewed on the chart, surrounded by the exclusive Bendinat holiday development. There are a few dangerous rocks awash between Islote de s'Estenedor (actually a low peninsula) and Illeta, and southwest of Islote de la Caleta. Islote de s'Estenedor is a military area and landing on the beach may not be permitted. Fishing nets supported by lines of floats are sometimes laid in the approaches.

Note From Las Illetas south to Cabo Falcó there may be several fish farms, noted on Spanish charts as obstructions. All are easily seen, if in place.

⚓ **North anchorage (N)** (39°32'·1N 02°35'·6E) Enter heading west or southwest to anchor in 2·5–6m over weed with some sand, open northeast through east to southeast. Holding is suspect. Swimming buoys are in place.

⚓ **Central anchorage (C)** Enter from northeast (inside Islote de la Caleta) or southeast, in which case take care to avoid Bajo Calafat and other rocks southwest of the island. Anchor in 2–3m over sand, open to northeast and southeast, off a small beach.

⚓ **South anchorage (S)** A small, well protected anchorage between Islote de s'Estenedor and Illeta, open only to the east and to swell from northeast and southeast. Anchor in 3–5m over sand.

⚓ **West anchorage (W)** (39°31'·8N 02°35'E) The largest, and the best in terms of space and holding, off a good beach (the property of the holiday complex and technically private). Enter heading northeast to anchor in 4-9m over sand, open to southwest and west. Swimming buoys are in place.

⚓ Portals Nous

39°31'9·N 02°34'·6E

A deeply indented *cala*, close east of Islote d'en Salas. Anchor in 5m over sand, open to south and southwest. There are shops, restaurants, etc. ashore. Close to Las Illetas but a less attractive anchorage.

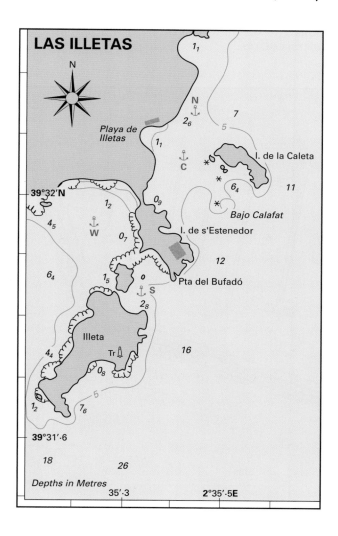

Puerto Portals foreground, looking east over Isla d'En Salas and Las Illetas to Cala Major and the Bay of Palma
Geoff Williamson

III. MALLORCA

Puerto Portals

39°31'·46N 02°35'50E

One of the most luxurious and expensive marinas in the Mediterranean with facilities for 670 yachts from 8–80m

Communications
VHF Ch 09
Puerto Portals ☏ 971 17 11 00
marina@puertoportals.com
www.puertoportals.com

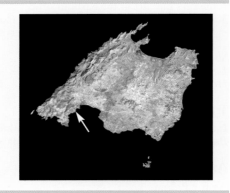

The marina

Opened in 1986 Puerto Portals is, in the words of its brochure 'modern and sophisticated' – as are many of the 670 yachts berthed there. Like Puerto de Palma four miles to the northwest, it is capable of taking superyachts up to 80m overall, and claims to have minimum depths of 4–5m throughout. Staff here have been reported to be quite indifferent to visitors, though they may be more accommodating to a superyacht arrival.

The immediate surroundings include restaurants, cafés, boutiques and various marine-related businesses, against a backdrop of bare sandy cliffs topped by white apartment blocks and hotels. Approach and entrance are straightforward except with a southeasterly gale when care must be taken.

Pilotage

Approach

For details of the outer approaches see Puerto de Palma Approach page 92.

From west After rounding Punta de Cala Figuera follow the coast north–northeast, leaving the low-lying Isla del Sech on either side but then maintaining an offing of about ½ mile. Isla and Punta de la Porrasa are unmistakeable, while Portals Nous's orange cliffs surmounted by white buildings can be seen from afar. In the close approach the long south breakwater will be seen, as will the distinctive square tower on the north mole, which houses the marina offices.

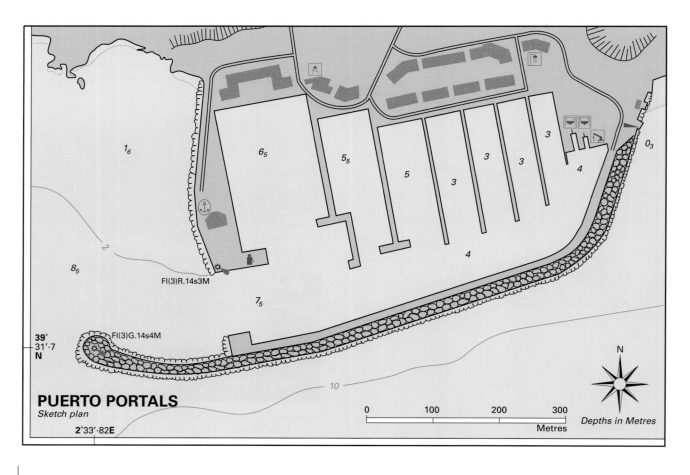

PUERTO PORTALS
Sketch plan

Fl(3)R.14s3M

Fl(3)G.14s4M

**39°
31'·7
N**

2°33'·82E

| 0 | 100 | 200 | 300 |

Metres

Depths in Metres

From east Round Cabo Blanco (*see page 183*) onto a northwest course across the Bahía de Palma.

Anchorage in the approach

Anchor 200m west of the tower in 5m over sand and weed, taking care not to impede the entrance channel. Watch for buoys off the beach.

Entrance

Swing wide around the head of the south breakwater onto an easterly heading, ready to berth alongside the reception quay at the south end of the north mole. There is a 3kn speed limit in the harbour.

Berthing

The harbour is frequently full to capacity in summer, and it is wise to book well in advance or at least call before arrival (telephone or VHF) to ascertain that a berth will be available.

Facilities

Water Taps on all quays and pontoons. Check for quality before filling tanks.

Electricity 220v and 380v AC points on all quays and pontoons.

Fuel Diesel and petrol from pumps at the head of the north mole. Open 0900–1800 all year. Direct supply available to yachts over 18m requiring more than 1,000 litres.

Provisions The shops on the north side of the harbour include a small supermarket. More shops in Portals Nous a short distance inland.

Ice At the fuel berth.

Chandlery Multi-Marine ✆ 971 67 56 62, shop@multimarine.es and Nauti Parts ✆ 971 67 77 30, nautiparts@yahoo.com

Repairs Mundimar Boatyard: Portals SA ✆ 971 676369 at the northeast end of the harbour can handle most jobs on yachts up to 80 tonnes. It has two travel-lifts 80 and 30 tonnes, with 2- and 10-tonne cranes near the travel-lifts. A dinghy slip at the root of the south breakwater.

Engineers Danbrit ✆ 971 67 72 01. Official service agents include: Danbrit – Lugger; Motornautica Portals Nous ✆ 971 67 77 95 – Mercury/MerCruiser, Quicksilver, Volvo Penta; Mundimar Portals SA (see *Repairs*) – Volvo Penta.

Electronic & radio repairs Danbrit ✆ 971 72 39 77.

Showers Two shower blocks in the marina complex, for which a key is required.

Launderette In Portals Nous.

Banks Bank with ATM in the marina complex.

Hospital/medical services In Portals Nous and Palma.

Transport

Car hire Four car hire firms around the harbour.

Taxis Via the marina office or ✆ 971 68 09 70.

Buses Bus service along the coast.

Puerto Portals: one of the most expensive marinas in the Mediterranean

III. MALLORCA

Ashore

As for Palma.

Eating out

Many restaurants and a few cheaper eating houses in the vicinity. There are more than twenty restaurants, cafés, bars and ice cream parlours around the harbour alone. Some of the most expensive restaurants in Mallorca are in this harbour.

Anchorage southwest of Puerto Portals

⚓ Punta Negra

39°31′·5N 02°33′·3E & 02°33′·2E

Halfway between Puerto Portals and Palma Nova, this is a delightful and quiet spot during the week and at weekends after the day trippers have left. A good escape from the jet skis and noise of Palma Nova. Anchor on either side of the headland in 4-5m (W) or 5-6m (E) over sand and weed. The west side is a little prettier. Punta Negra is relatively unspoiled; although the headland is occupied by a low-rise hotel, the buildings are well concealed in the trees. Following the cliff footpath and the paved continuation leads to a well-stocked Mercadona supermarket, as well as bars and restaurants.

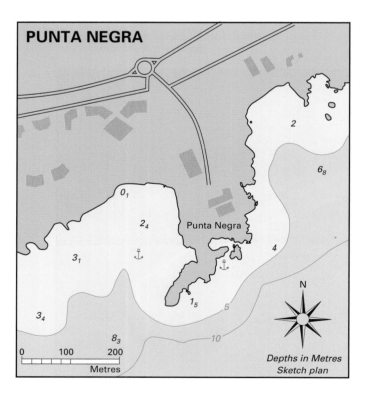

PUNTA NEGRA

Punta Negra

N

Depths in Metres
Sketch plan

0   100   200
Metres

Puerto de Palma Nova

39°31′·5N 02°32′·6E

A small harbour with 82 berths and a restricted entrance due to silting. Hardly worth a mention, but it may spring to life if dredged

Communications
Club Náutico Palma Nova ☎ 971 68 10 55

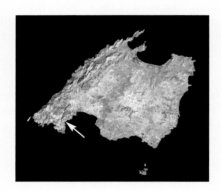

The harbour

This small harbour has been silted up for several years and is only suitable for relatively small motor boats. The depth is generally 1m or less and officially no berths are available for visitors.

Pilotage

Approach

Details of the outer approaches as for Puerto de Palma.

From west (*See plan on page 91.*) After rounding Punta de Cala Figuera follow the coast north–northeast, leaving the low-lying Isla del Sech on either side. Round Isla and then Punta de la Porrasa, after which Puerto de Palma Nova will been seen at the north end of the long beach, Playa de Palma Nova.

From east (*See plans on pages 183 and 89.*) Round Cabo Blanco onto a northwesterly course across the Bahía de Palma. Puerto de Palma Nova will be seen at the north end of the long beach.

Anchorage in the approach

Anchor in 3–5m over sand south of the harbour, open to southeast.

Entrance

Due to the silting problem (sand rather than mud) it would be unwise to enter the harbour in any boat drawing more than 1m without first consulting the Club Náutico by telephone or making a recce by dinghy. The water is generally too cloudy to read depths visually and so a hand-held depth sounder would be needed. There is a 2kn speed limit.

Berthing

Secure in an empty berth and report to the harbour office by the slipway (closed Thursday and Saturday, otherwise open 0930–1300 daily).

Facilities

Water Taps around the harbour.
Electricity A few 220v AC points.
Fuel By can from a filling station on the road to Palma.
Provisions Supermarket and other shops nearby.
Repairs A 6-tonne crane beside the slipway at the north of the harbour, which has 1m depth.
Yacht club Club Náutico Palma Nova ① 971 68 10 55 has a small clubhouse and bar near the slipway.
Banks In Palma Nova.
Hospital/medical services In Palma Nova and Palma itself.

Transport

Car hire/taxis In Palma Nova or taxi ① 971 68 07 80
Buses Bus service along the coast.

Eating out

A vast number of restaurants and cafés (Palma Nova is at the northern end of the Magaluf holiday area).

Anchorages between Palma Nova and Port Adriano

⚓ Playa de Palma Nova

39°31'·0N 02°32'·4E

A long and often crowded sandy beach, broken into three by a pair of low rocky promontories, each occupied by a large hotel. Anchor in 2–5m over sand, open to the eastern quadrant. Behind the beaches are many hotels, restaurants and shops. The north side of the Magaluf peninsular is well-sheltered from S and SW.

⚓ Playa de Magaluf

39°30'·3N 02°32'·3E

An anchorage off a long beach with swimming buoys in the northern part of the Ensenada de la Porrasa, tucked in behind Isla de la Porrasa. The beach is lined with apartment blocks, hotels, beach cafés, shops, etc. but the island is deserted and landing there is possible on the southwest coast. Anchor in 2·5–5m over sand and weed with some rocks. Holding is poor in places.

The island (which is unlit) can be left on either side on entry, though 2·5m shoals extend northwest for 200m. A submarine cable runs southeast from a point just south of the centre of the bay.

Long fishing nets supported by small white or pink floats are sometimes laid near the island.

⚓ Cala Viña

39°29'·7N 02°32'·2E

A small, narrow *cala* surrounded by high-rise buildings, with a small sandy beach. The inner half of the bay is buoyed-off for swimmers. Anchor in

View over Torre Nova and Playa de Palma Nova, with Magaluf behind *Geoff Williamson*

4–5m over sand, open to the east. Not a great deal of swinging room.

⚓ South of Cabo Falcó

39°29'·1N 02°32'·1E

Two very small *calas* lie south of Cabo Falcó (note the 0·4m shoal 100m southeast of the headland). Both anchorages are in 3m over sand, open to the eastern quadrant, with small sandy beaches and a few houses.

III. MALLORCA

Isla del Sech

Bisected by 39°28·8'N 02°32'·5E

A low (10m) flat black rocky islet with 4m shoals extending 500m to the northeast, but with a 0·5M wide passage with depths of more than 10m between it and the shore. (*See plan on page 91.*)

Unlit buoys are laid in February 150m west and north of the island, marking the dive area used by the tourist submarine Nemo I (based in Puerto Portals). These are removed during the winter months.

⚓ Cala Portals (Portals Vells)

39°28'·4N 02°31'·5E

An attractive quadruple *cala* a mile south of Cabo Falco, approached between steep-to cliffs and popular with the tourist operators who visit by ferry (road access is poor). The tiny private harbour is lit but is shallow and can only take craft of less than 9m overall. There are water taps on the quay.

Anchor as space permits in 2–8m over sand and weed. Some rocks are in evidence and a tripline is desirable. All four beaches are buoyed for swimmers. Open to east.

There are tombs dating back to Phoenician times cut into the caves in the southern cliffs, one of which has been turned into a small shrine (take a torch). There is a tower on Pta. de S'Estaca, the northern point.

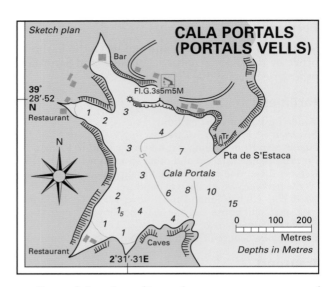

Several beach cafés and restaurants, some of which close for the evening after the tourists depart, overlook the bay. Parts of the beach are designated nudist areas.

Harbour ☎ 971 68 05 56.

⚓ Cala Figuera

39°27'·7N 02°31'·4E

A small *cala* close north of Punta de Cala Figuera. Its steep sides are wooded, with few houses. Anchor in 9m+ over sand and rock, open to northeast and east. (*See plan on page 91.*)

Cala Portals (Portals Vells)

Punta de Cala Figuera
39°27'·4N 02°31'·2E

A very prominent headland with a lighthouse (white round tower with black diagonal stripes on building, 24m) and radio masts on its steep cliffs. The light is only visible when bearing between 293° and 094° – not from within the Bahía de Palma.

Pass between Islote El Toro and Punta de Ses Barbines

39°27'·9N 02°28'·4E

A pass 200m wide and carrying 3m+ depths, leads on a northwest–southeast axis between a small rock just northeast of Islote El Toro (white round tower, 7m) and the double-humped Islote Banco de Ibiza off Punta de Ses Barbines. This latter promontory is very low and difficult to see from a distance, which

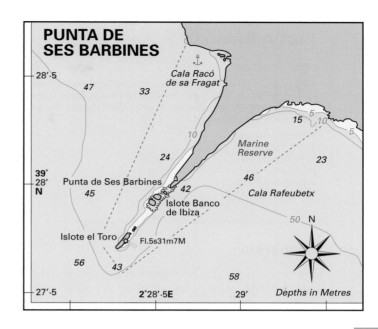

can be confusing on the approach. Best depths (±4m) are reported about two-thirds of the way from Islote Banco de Ibiza out towards the rock. (*See plans on this page and page 107.*)

⚓ Calo Racó de Sa Fragat
39°28'·5N 02°28'·7E

An attractive but deep anchorage close inshore at the root of the long promontory leading to Punta de Ses Barbines, exposed to west and south sectors. The cliffs are steep-to. Anchor in 10–15m over sand and rock, open from southwest to northwest. A trip line is advisable.

View over Punta de Cala Figuera looking northeast into the Bay of Palma *Geoff Williamson*

Islote El Toro and Punta de Ses Barbines showing clearly the bar. Port Adriano is tucked inside the bay on the far side of the peninsula

III. MALLORCA

Port Adriano

39°29'·5N 02°28'·7E

A large yet quiet and pleasant marina with berthing for over 400 yachts up to 18m. Set in the E side of the Cala de Peñas Rojas, it is easy to enter in most conditions and safe inside since the height of the outer breakwater was increased.

Communications
VHF Ch 09
☎ 971 23 24 94
info@portadriano.com
www.portadriano.com

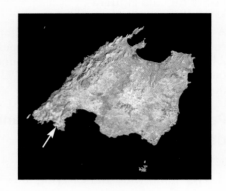

The marina

First impressions on the approach are unattractive, with the enormous grey slab of the new outer breakwater for the marina on one side and on-going development on the point on the other side. Ahead is the huge holiday development of El Toro and the large 5-star Port Adriano Hotel. However, once inside it is a large and pleasant marina with the addition of a commercial zone, gardens, parking areas and berthing for 82 superyachts (bringing the total to nearly 500 berths overall). The original breakwater has been converted into an inner quay with luxury shops and facilities along its length. The new outer breakwater has been built to give greater protection from the seas that came over the original structure and to provide additional moorings for superyachts.

The marina is often very full especially in summer and it is essential to book in advance.

The diving school, Escuela Buceo, in the marina complex covers all aspects of the sport including beginners' tuition. It stocks diving equipment, and has full decompression facilities.

Port Adriano looking towards Isla Malgrats, just right of top centre.
Note buoys marking entry channel; there is room to anchor between these and the red cliff

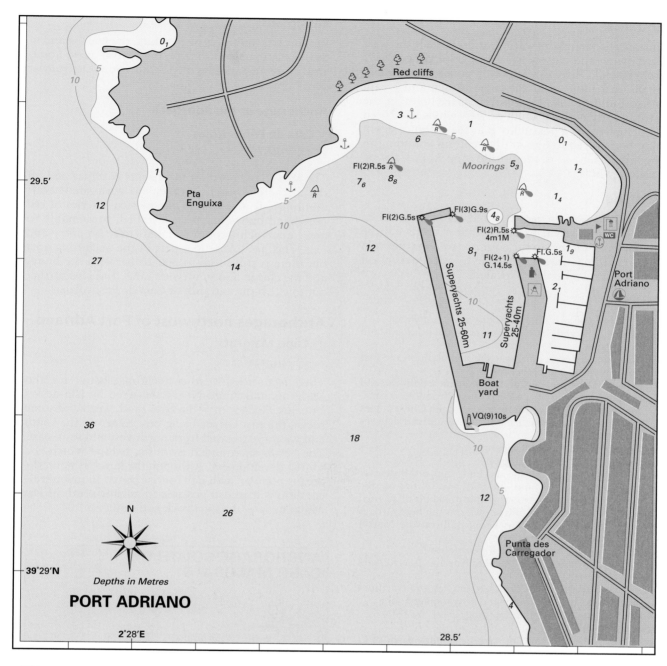

III. MALLORCA

Pilotage

Approach

Port Adriano is simple to approach and enter with reasonable protection once inside:

From the northwest Round Cabo de la Mola, a high headland terminating in sheer cliffs topped by a lighthouse (white column with black bands on a square white tower, 10m) and Cabo Llamp (unlit) (*See plan on page 107*.) Then steer southeast across the wide mouth of Ensenada de Santa Ponsa towards Islote El Toro leaving Isla Malgrats to port. Port Adriano will open up in Cala de Penas Rojas on rounding Punta Enguixa.

From the southeast Round the very prominent Punta de Cala Figuera (*see plan on page 107*) which has a lighthouse (white round tower with black diagonal stripes on building, 24m) and radio masts on its steep cliffs, continuing west to leave Islote El Toro (white round tower) to starboard, or see *page 103* for details of the passage between Islote El Toro and the peninsula. Port Adriano will then be visible just under two miles north, tucked well into the aptly named Cala de Peñas Rojas, 'the bay with red cliffs'. (*See photograph of Punta de Ses Barbines on page 103.*)

Entrance

Entrance is straightforward, but do not cut the west breakwater too closely as stones slope downwards from its end. There is a reception pontoon at the end of the east mole, near the large brown and cream office building. There is a 2kn speed limit in the harbour. After strong south or west winds have been blowing there is a possibility that the entrance depth may be reduced due to silting; careful sounding in the approach is needed following these strong onshore winds.

Berthing

The marina is often very full and contact should be made before arrival to check that a berth will be available. If not met in the entrance by a marinero to assist berthing, secure port side-to at the reception pontoon until a berth is allocated.

Facilities

Water Water points on the pontoons and breakwater.
Electricity 220v and 380v AC points on the pontoons and breakwater.
Fuel Diesel and petrol pumps at the fuel berth on the east mole (by the reception pontoon).
Provisions Supermarket in the marina complex and another at the top of the steep hill up from the marina, but otherwise mainly tourist shops. El Corte Ingles have a facility in the marina for the order and delivery of provisions.
Ice Cube ice from bars and supermarkets.
Chandlery In the marina complex.
Repairs Go to marina website and find 'Shipyard Business'. Boatyard Mar Adriano (℡ 971 10 26 65) at the southern end of the harbour is able to handle all normal work. A 50-tonne lift and slipway in the boatyard. A new commercial zone has being built on the central quay. www.portadriano.com
Engineers At Mar Adriano (see *Repairs* above).
Electronic & radio repairs At Mar Adriano (see *Repairs* above).
Yacht club Club Náutico Porto Adriano has good facilities including a large restaurant and a swimming pool.
Showers In the marina office building.
Launderette In El Toro.
Bank/bureau de change In the nearby holiday town of El Toro.
Hospital/medical services In El Toro and Palma (the latter about eight miles by road).
WiFi is said to be effective.

Transport

Car hire/taxis Arrange via the marina office or taxi ℡ 68 09 70
Buses Bus service to Santa Ponsa and Palma from a stop near the top of the marina access road.

Ashore

Spectacular countryside with huge expanses of pine forests, especially to the northeast. See *Palma* for attractions.

Eating out

Restaurants and cafés overlooking the marina and in the new commercial zone on the central quay; hotels and more restaurants in the surrounding tourist development.

Anchorage in the approach

⚓ Cala de Peñas Rojas
39°29'·6N 02°28'·5E

The area to the north of the marina entrance and off the attractive beach is taken up with small craft moorings. To the west of the marina a series of red port-hand buoys has been installed, presumably to give superyachts room to manoeuvre on entry and exit. This has taken up a part of the anchoring area but there is still room to anchor between the buoys and the cliff in about 5m over sand, and also further out towards the entrance of Cala de Penas Rojas.

Anchorages northwest of Port Adriano

⚓ Cabo Malgrats
39°30'·1N 02°27'·5E

There is a settled-weather anchorage between Cabo Malgrats and Punta Negra sheltered by Isla de los Conejos. Anchor in 5–8m over sand, weed and some rocks, the east corner being best. Open to the south and west and to swell from northwest and southeast. The bay is surrounded by cliffs, behind which is a tourist development. Although the beach is poor, the area is popular with day tourist boats. In favourable conditions it is also possible to anchor south of Isla Malgrats in ±10m over rock and sand.

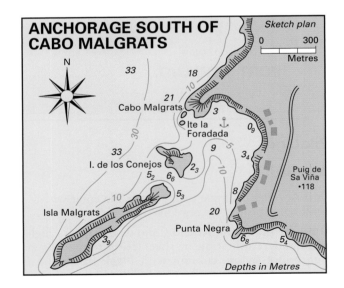

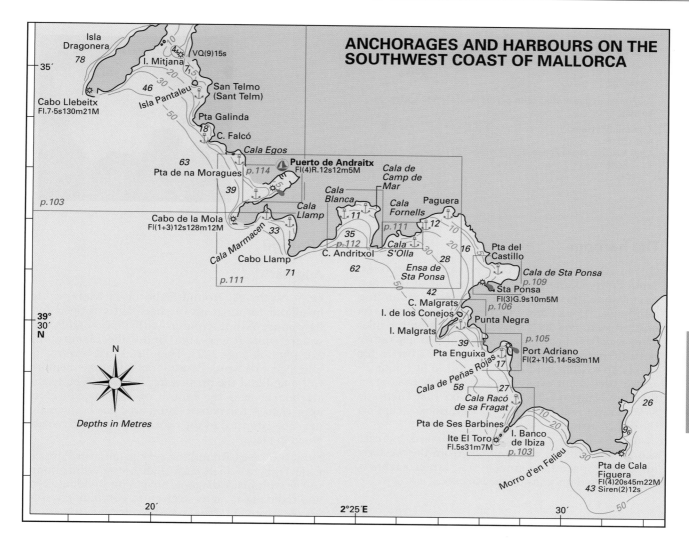

ANCHORAGES AND HARBOURS ON THE SOUTHWEST COAST OF MALLORCA

Passes either side of Isla de los Conejos

Spectacular passes 100m wide exist either side of Isla de los Conejos. The southern pass has a minimum of 8m in the centre and should be taken on a northwest–southeast axis keeping to the centre of the channel. For the northern pass, less than 5m deep, and approaching from the south, leave Punta Negra some 100m to starboard and steer north for Cabo Malgrats. When the northeast point of the island is about 100m on the port beam, steer to follow the island's coast keeping 100m off until a course of northwest is attained and then depart on that course. Coming from the north use the reciprocal.

Puerto de Santa Ponsa

39°30'·8N 02°28'E

A very attractive marina with berths for over 500 yachts up to 20m.

Communications
VHF Ch 09
Club Náutico Santa Ponsa ① 971 69 49 50
cnsp@cnsp.es
www.cnsp.es

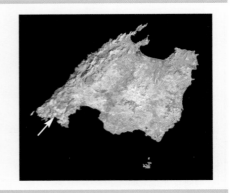

The harbour

On an island with so many attractive harbours, Santa Ponsa (Santa Ponça) must be one of the most picturesque, in spite of the many surrounding buildings. Long and narrow, guarded at its northwestern end by a curved breakwater, the inlet gives excellent protection, though it can get rather hot and airless in summer. There are 522 berths for yachts up to 20m, and there are said to be about 20 visitor berths but even so it is necessary to contact the Club Náutico before arrival. Note that Puerto de Santa Ponsa will not accept reservations except on the day of arrival.

Approach and entry are straightforward, but care should be taken in strong winds from the westerly quadrant. Space for manoeuvring larger yachts is very restricted once inside the harbour.

Pilotage

Approach

From northwest Round Cabo de la Mola, a high headland terminating in sheer cliffs topped by a lighthouse (white column with black bands on a square white tower, 10m) and Cabo Llamp (unlit) (*see plan on page 107*). Then head east towards the long Playa de Santa Ponsa – the tall stone memorial to Jaime I and the breakwater below will be seen to starboard, near the mouth of the bay, on closer approach. A fish conservation area has been created near the entrance to the *cala* which is clearly visible when in place.

From southeast Round the very prominent Punta de Cala Figuera which has a lighthouse (white round tower with black diagonal stripes on building, 24m) and radio masts on its steep cliffs, continuing west to leave Islote El Toro (white round tower) to starboard. Settle onto a northwest course to round Isla Malgrats (or in good weather use the inshore

Santa Ponsa Marina, with the memorial to Jaime I at the entrance, looking southeast: a well-sheltered harbour in pleasant surroundings *Geoff Williamson*

Cala de Santa Ponsa looking across the harbour entrance.
Note shoal patch markers just visible centre of *cala*
Geoff Williamson

passage as previously described), then follow the coast northeast. Soon after rounding Morro d'en Grosser, the tall stone memorial to Jaime I and the breakwater below will be seen to starboard.

Entrance

Approach the head of the northwest breakwater on a south or southeast course. Enter keeping to the starboard side of the channel, ready to berth starboardside-to on the reception quay at the root of the breakwater. There is a 2kn speed limit.

Berthing

It is advisable to contact the Club Náutico before, but on the day of, arrival as most of the berths are permanently occupied and there is often no room for visitors.

A berth will be allocated (if available). The marina office can be contacted on VHF Ch 09, or by dialling 9 at one of the four telephone booths around the inlet (the nearest one to the reception pontoon is situated by the sailing school). Dinghies can be left ashore by arrangement with the marina office in a

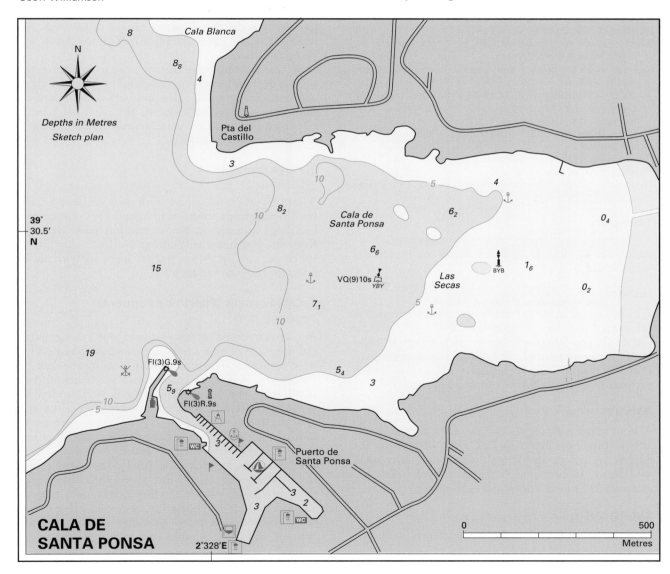

CALA DE SANTA PONSA

designated spot. A security camera scans the area, so better not to leave it without informing the office.

Facilities

Water Taps on quays and pontoons.

Electricity 220v AC points on quays and pontoons. 380v AC available in the boatyard.

Fuel Pumps on the reception quay at the root of the breakwater and on one of the inner pontoons. In summer the fuel dock is open 0930–2000, but mornings only on Mondays, and in winter 0930–1500 but closed on Monday. On Sundays all year the hours are 1000–1400.

Provisioning Small supermarket near the Club Náutico and many shops in Santa Ponsa less than a mile away.

Ice At the fuel berth.

Chandlery In the block containing the Club Náutico and marina office. Also Marine superstore with huge stocks located at 49 Carrer Ill Baleares, Bucatellas poligono industrial, SN07180 Santa Ponsa. ☏ +34 971 690684. (€6 by taxi from town centre).

Repairs Boatyard at the head of the southwest arm with a 50-tonne lift. A 2·5-tonne crane at the sailing school. Three slipways, one in each of the southern arms of the harbour and one at the sailing school.

Engineers At the boatyard and Port Fairline Santa Ponsa ☏ 971 69 07 17 (official service agents for Volvo Penta).

Metalwork Metalnox SL ☏ 971 69 40 11.

Electronic & radio repairs Can be organised via the boatyard or Club Náutico.

Sail repairs In the block containing the Club Náutico and marina office.

Yacht club Club Náutico de Santa Ponsa has a palatial clubhouse on the northeast side of the harbour with lounge, terrace, restaurant, bar, etc.

Showers Below the Club Náutico and at the heads of both the southern arms.

Launderette At the Club Náutico.

Banks Several in Santa Ponsa.

Hospital/medical services In Santa Ponsa and Palma (about 7M by road).

Transport

Car hire/taxis At the marina office or in Santa Ponsa.

Buses Bus services from Santa Ponsa to Palma and elsewhere.

History

This is a place of great historical interest. The area is celebrated for the fact that the combined fleets of Catalonia and Aragon dropped anchor here in 1229 under the command of King Jaime I of Aragon (Rey Jaime Conquistador), landing an army which eventually drove the Moors from Mallorca.

Ashore

A stone cross with scenes commemorating the events above stands on Punta de la Caleta, just inside the harbour entrance and is well worth the short stroll for closer inspection. A fiesta to celebrate the anniversary is held from 9–16 September.

Eating out

Many eating establishments of all grades, including a restaurant at the Club Náutico.

Anchorages around Ensenada de Santa Ponsa

⚓ Cala de Santa Ponsa
39°31′N 02°28′·1E

There are several good anchorages in Cala de Santa Ponsa, a wide bay to the northeast of the harbour surrounded by apartments, houses and hotels (*see plan on page 109*). It is shallow around the sides and near the head – where there is a long but often crowded beach – with two 0·5m shoal patches (Las Secas) near the centre, marked by a west cardinal light buoy at its seaward end and an east cardinal beacon 250m to the east.

An underwater cable runs from the southern end of the beach towards Las Secas before continuing westward. The south side of the *cala* makes a more attractive anchorage as it is clear of the long strip of hotels on the north and gives easy shore access through the marina. Anchor almost anywhere along the southern shore or to the west of Las Secas in 2–6m over sand or sand and weed, open to west and northwest, or in the northeast corner in 4–6m over sand, open to west and southwest. Shallow-draught yachts may be able to work closer in towards the head of the bay but a careful watch on the depth will be necessary.

Routine shopping requirements can be met in the tourist developments surrounding the bay, and there are many restaurants, cafés and bars. If anchored on the north side, a walk out to the fortified Gothic tower and the smaller watchtower on the northern headland might be enjoyed.

⚓ Playa de Paguera
39°32′·2N 02°27′·1E

A large semicircular bay with an excellent beach, with swimming buoys, backed by apartment buildings and hotels. Rocks run out some distance from the southeast side of the entrance. Anchor as space permits in 3–5m over a large area of sand, open to south and southwest.

⚓ Cala Fornells (Puerto de Paguera)
39°32′N 02°26′·4E

An attractive anchorage just north of Pta Cerdana, but not in any sense a port; the most sheltered part is now occupied by mooring buoys administered by Posidonia. It is open to east and southeast and to swell from the south. The *cala* is surrounded by wooded cliffs and a growing number of low-rise apartment buildings plus a few shops. The small sandy beach at the head of the *cala* is often crowded. A fish conservation farm is usually laid just off Pta Cerdana running southeast. Anchor as space allows in 5–10m over sand and weed, the best area probably being off the northern cove. A tripline is advised as there is reported to be considerable debris on the bottom. A buoy has been laid on the 5m contour and yachts should anchor E of this buoy.

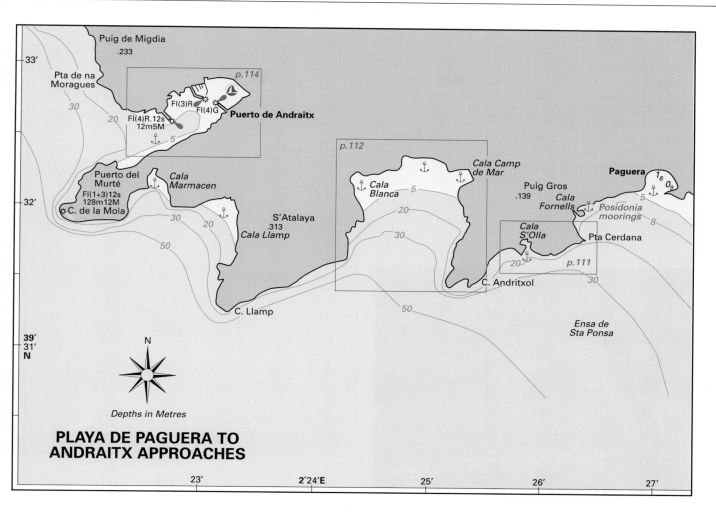

PLAYA DE PAGUERA TO
ANDRAITX APPROACHES

⚓ Cala S'Olla (Cala d'En Monjo)

39°31'·6N 02°25'·9E

A fascinating small *cala* between rocky cliffs, surrounded by unspoilt woodland. Approach with a lookout on the bow to anchor near the entrance in 8–12m over sand, weed and rock as there are several isolated rocks further in. Space is very restricted and two anchors or a line ashore will probably be required. Although open only to the south, the *cala* would quickly become dangerous in any wind from this direction and should be vacated immediately.

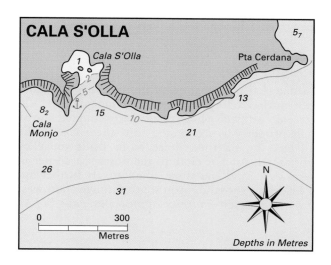

Cala S'Olla from the south. Submerged rocks further in can be clearly seen

⚓ Cala Camp de Mar

39°32'·2N 02°25'·3E

A pleasant bay which has become a popular tourist resort, partly due to a small island in its centre reached by a narrow wooden bridge and housing an outdoor bar/restaurant. A tourist ferry is often moored stern-to the restaurant island. There are several high-rise hotels behind the beach and more close northwest, plus a few tourist shops.

Swimming buoys are in place so anchor southeast of the island in about 5m over sand and rock (shoals extend northwards from the heel of the island towards the white hotel); open to south and southwest.

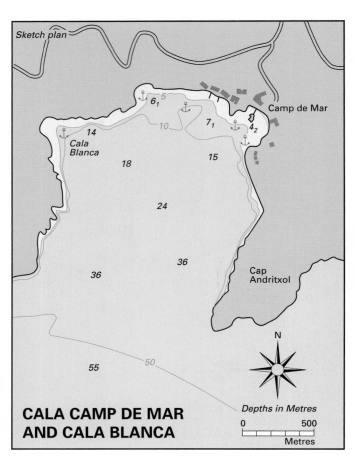

CALA CAMP DE MAR AND CALA BLANCA

Depths in Metres

Cala Camp de Mar island and restaurant *Geoff Williamson*

Note that there is a sandy bottom of 5–10m right across the bay to a small cove with a large detached rock a short distance east northeast of Cala Blanca and anchoring is good anywhere in this area.

⚓ Cala Blanca

39°32'·1N 02°24'·5E

A small *cala* enclosed by cliffs and with a sand and stone beach. Alas, it is no longer undeveloped with houses built and under construction on the northern side. Anchor in 2–3·5m over sand off the beach, open to east through south. Very clear water.

⚓ Cala Llamp

39°31'8N 02°23'·2E

A somewhat unappealing anchorage, very open and with much development despite having no beach. On a recent visit twelve huge cranes were counted and as each property is excavated into the rock of the hillside, the daytime noise from drills must be substantial. Anchor close to the northeast corner in 6–7m over sand and stone, alternatively further out in 11–14m over sand, open south through southwest to west. (See plan *Andraitx Approaches, page 111*.)

Cala Camp de Mar viewed from west. Note island and restaurant left *Graham Hutt*

View over Cala Marmacen and Cabo de la Mola to Andraitx harbour

Cala Blanca: a pleasant but very busy bay in the high season. There is now some development on the northern point of the cala *Geoff Williamson*

⚓ Cala Marmacen
39°32'·1N 02°22'·6E

A spectacular anchorage surrounded by cliffs in the approach and narrow at its head. There are many detached boulders round the edge. Anchor in 5m over mainly weed and some sand near the head of the *cala*, open to the southern quadrant. Much new development surrounds the *cala*.

Cabo de la Mola
39°32'N 02°21'·9E

A high headland terminating in sheer cliffs topped by a rather inconspicuous lighthouse (white column with black bands on a square white tower, 10m). The light is only visible when bearing between 304·4° and 158·2° and is obscured during the final approach to Puerto de Andraitx.

Puerto de Andraitx

39°32'·5N 02°22'·6E

One of the oldest yachting marinas in Mallorca, Puerto de Andraitx offers nearly 500 berths for yachts up to 25m, with easy access through a buoyed channel. The harbour is often full and in summer advance booking for both marina berths and mooring buoys is essential.

Communications

Ports IB ☎ +34 971 674216
   VHF Ch 08
   port.andraitx@portsib.es

Club de Vela Puerto de Andraitx ☎ 971 67 17 21
   VHF Ch 09
   info@cvpa.es
   www.cvpa.es

The harbour

A large yachting and fishing harbour in dramatic surroundings, with a pleasant village on the harbour and a larger (and much more atmospheric) town some two miles inland.

The harbour is easy to approach and enter and offers good protection, though strong gusts of wind can flow down from the surrounding hills. A heavy swell sets in with strong winds from west and southwest. Very occasionally the phenomenon known as resaca or seiche occurs (see *Tides* section in the *General Introduction on page 9*), particularly dangerous to yachts berthed on the quays.

Pilotage

Approach

From north Pass either side of Isla Dragonera (*see separate plan of island on page 118*) towards Cabo de la Mola, a high headland terminating in sheer cliffs topped by a lighthouse, white column with black bands on a square white tower, 10m. The entrance to Puerto de Andraitx lies to the north of the headland and will come into view on rounding Punta de na Moragues, which has a massive housing development on its sloping face (*see plan on page 111*).

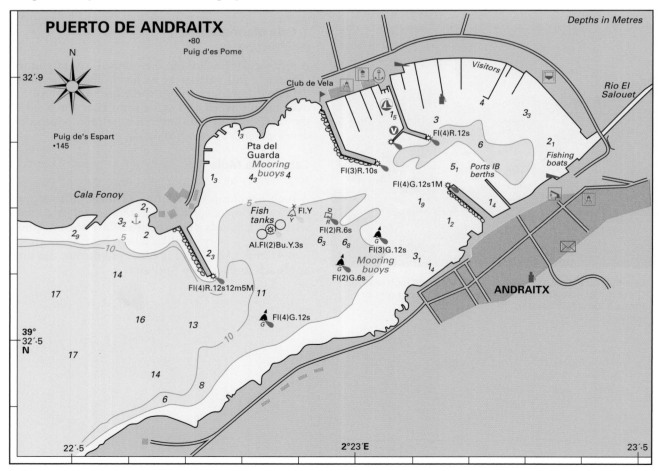

Andraitx Harbour viewed from southeast. Club de Vela on far side and Ports IB moorings bottom of picture.

From southeast Cross the wide mouth of Ensenada de Santa Ponsa towards Cabo Llamp (high and pine-covered) and Cabo de la Mola (*see page 111*). The entrance to Puerto de Andraitx will open up on rounding the latter.

Anchorage in the approach

Most of the outer harbour is laid to buoys managed by Club de Vela on the N and S side of the *cala*, on either side of the channel. Even if a reservation has been made, the Club should be contacted on Ch.9 before picking up a mooring and a marinero will be despatched to allocate a mooring. In northerly winds, anchoring is possible in Cala Fonoy on the north side of the entrance in 2m+ over sand. In southerly winds, tuck in southeast of Punta del Murté in 3m over sand and stone. Named as Cala Racó on some charts, 39°32'·3N 02°22'·4E, this is a small anchorage under steep cliffs, only suitable for use in settled weather. These anchorages should only be used in good conditions and neither gives much protection. Anchoring in the outer harbour is discouraged by the authorities, but some yachts do so on the starboard (south) side of the outer harbour (keep out of the buoyed channel and well clear of laid moorings). Anchoring in the inner harbour is prohibited.

Entrance

Approach down the centre of the bay leaving the head of the outer breakwater some 50m to port. Keep to the buoyed channel, taking care to avoid the shoal area close southwest of the south mole. There is a speed limit of 4kn in the outer harbour decreasing to 3kn in the inner harbour.

The fish keeps (in place 2017) may be marked by one or more yellow lights (Fl.Y.4s) and several unlit reflectors, but are out of the channel to the north.

Note

Where 4m depths at the northeast end of the harbour are shown on some charts, information indicates that it is now reduced to 2·3m.

Berthing

If intending to stay in the yacht harbour run by the Club de Vela Puerto de Andraitx, secure to the inner side of the head of the north mole until a berth is allocated (assuming one is available – the Club de Vela has 475 berths for yachts up to 25m, but is often full, and even outside the peak season advance booking may be essential). Visitors are often allocated berths on the quay in the northeast of the harbour, between the pontoons and the travel-lift (which is near the end of the stone wall) or on the pontoon running out from the travel-lift. Yachts lie bow or stern-to, and a mooring line is provided tailed to the quay.

Ports IB has the concession for the long floating pontoon and the concrete dique in the SE of the harbour. Bookings must be made online at www.portsib.es. The outer end of the NE side of the dique is for larger vessels who will need to lay an anchor and go stern-to the quay. Note that there are underwater rocks protruding from the dique which are not always obvious and it is necessary to berth well off and use a long pasarelle. The Ports IB visitors' berths for vessels up to 12m are on the floating pontoon running parallel to the dique on the

III. MALLORCA

SE side of the harbour, with berthing bows or stern-to the pontoon. Ports IB may not have WiFi but reception from public networks is good and many bars and restaurants have WiFi.

Note that depths towards the outer end of the floating pontoon are 4m, but it gets shallower towards the shore. The SW side is taken up with local vessels - mostly fishing boats - as is the NE side near to the shore.

Moorings

The area between the outer breakwater and the N mole is now filled with buoys administered by Club de Vela, contact details above. In high season these are often all booked, so do call in advance. These are very pleasant moorings and the outer mole gives good protection against strong southwest to northwest winds, albeit an uncomfortable swell sometimes curves round the end of the mole. A Club de Vela marinero efficiently assists pick-up of the mooring. There is easy access to the bars and restaurants. An area on the W side of the main quay near the hotel is suitable for dinghies.

Facilities

Water On the Club de Vela pontoons and at the fuel berth and at Ports IB berths. The quality has been reported to be poor – brackish and over-chlorinated.

Electricity 220v AC points at the Club de Vela and on the south mole and adjacent pontoon, also Ports IB berths.

Diesel and petrol At the fuel berth on the furthest but one pontoon at the Club de Vela. There is a diesel pump on the fish quay but it is for fishing vessels only.

Provisions El Corte Ingles have a facility at the Club de Vela for the order and delivery of provisions. There is a fish market by the trawler dock in the same building complex as the Ports IB office and a good supermarket in the next block (Eroski) with other food shops nearby, plus many tourist shops. Two small supermarkets north of the harbour. The town of Andraitx two miles inland has many more shops and a good regular market on Wednesdays.

Ice From Tim's Bar close southwest of the south mole and from most supermarkets.

Chandlery One at the Club de Vela plus a chandlery/fishing tackle shop behind the Ports IB office.

Repairs Can be carried out at the yacht harbour boatyard – enquire at the Club de Vela office. A 50-tonne capacity lift and a 3-tonne crane in the yacht harbour. A large slipway at the yacht harbour and another at the southeast corner of the inner harbour.

Engineers Phoenix Marine ☎ 971 67 20 12 are official service agents for Mercury/MerCruiser and Volvo Penta. Taller Náutico Toni Mas ☎ 971 13 79 61, *mobile* 636 585 963, www.tallernáuticotonimas.com, are official service agents for Mercury/MerCruiser and Yanmar.

Electronic & radio repairs Enquire at the Club de Vela office.

Yacht club The Club de Vela Puerto de Andraitx ☎ 971 67 23 37 occupies an impressive building north of the yacht harbour with lounge, bar, restaurant, swimming pool and showers.

Showers At the Club de Vela, free to those staying in their marina but with restricted hours. Also attached to the

Yachts at anchor and on mooring buoys, to starboard on entering Andraitx harbour *Graham Hutt*

Ports IB office (but open to fishermen and general public).

Laundry/launderette In the town.

Banks In the town south of the harbour.

Hospital/medical services In Andraitx and Palma (the latter about 15 miles by road).

Transport

Car hire/taxis In the town or arranged through the Club de Vela.

Buses Frequent buses to Andraitx 2½ miles inland and several each day to Palma.

Ferries A tourist ferry makes the trip to Isla Dragonera via San Telmo.

Ashore

In addition to the old town, where there is an interesting church, a walk along the upper roads and tracks on either side of the harbour is rewarded with excellent views. The two marinas are on opposite sides of the huge *cala*. The Ports IB moorings are on the SE side, close to the old town and many tourist facilities including restaurants and bars. There is a small supermarket and a larger Eroski Supermarket and a laundry close to the Ports IB office.

The newer Club de Vela moorings are on the N side, and a short (10 minute) walk from the town. The club is in more of a residential area with some restaurants. The club has several excellent facilities for its berth holders including a swimming pool and club restaurant.

Local events

Fiestas are held on or about 29 June (a public holiday), in honour of San Pedro, with waterborne processions; 15–16 July, Fiesta de la Virgen del Carmen, again with waterborne processions, and the two weekends around 19–20 and 26–28 August, S'Arracó El Santo Cristo (also a public holiday).

Eating out

Many eating places around the harbour, with the southern waterfront seemingly wall-to-wall with cafés and restaurants.

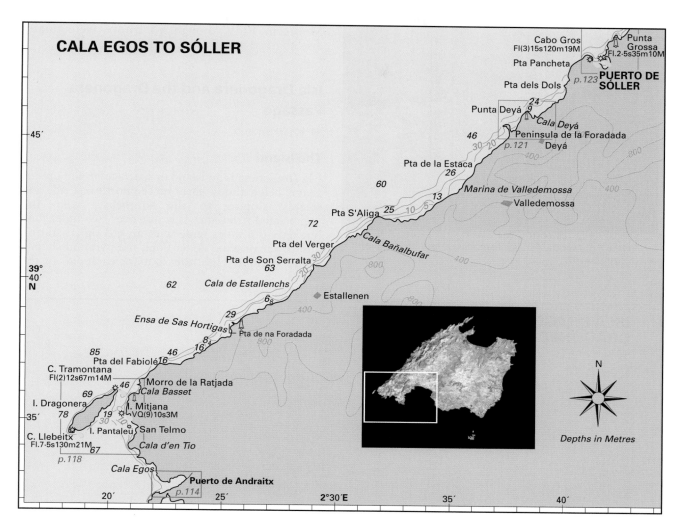

CALA EGOS TO SÓLLER

Depths in Metres

⚓ Cala Egos
39°33'·2N 02°21'·9E

A pleasant anchorage in a small, unspoilt *cala* with a pebble beach surrounded by rocky cliffs southeast of Pta de sa Dent. Anchor in 4m over sand and rocks off the beach, open to south through west. Popular due to its proximity to Puerto Andraitx, it gets very crowded.

⚓ Cala d'en Tio
39°33'·77N 02°21'·18E

An even smaller version of Cala Egos, a few hundred yards to the northwest. Yachts anchor in the northwest corner.

⚓ Playa de San Telmo (Sant Telm or San Elm)
39°34'·5N 02°21'·1E

A pleasant bay with sandy beaches and a small tourist resort. Isla Pantaleu (29m) 220m long by 200m wide in the mouth of the bay gives some protection from the west, as does Isla Dragonera

further offshore. Parts of the beach are buoyed off for swimmers.

Mooring buoys have now been laid here, administered by Posidonia, which can be booked in advance, for 1 June to 30 September at www.balearslifeposidonia.eu. See the plan on *page 118* and the *Moorings* section on *page 19* for details. Enter the bay from the southwest to pick up your mooring. In October 2016 some of the buoys lacked their pick up tails. There is still plenty of space to anchor in 5–8m over sand. Good public WiFi signal.

Be aware that the bay is open to the southwest with a mile or more's fetch to the northwest. The winds can also funnel down from the mountains, causing disturbances on the water and heavy swell.

The approach from the northwest, that is to the north of Isla Pantaleu, is shallow, and may be obstructed by the stern anchors of tourist ferries lying bows-on at the quay as well as moored small craft. Several years ago plans were drawn up to construct a large yacht harbour in the bay north of Isla Pantaleu but these appear to have been dropped,

III. MALLORCA

San Telmo from southwest. Isla Pantaleu centre, north tip of Isla Dragonera left

along with many other marine expansion plans for the island, due to environmental considerations.

Isla Pantaleu was the first landfall of King Jaime I of Aragon on his way to liberate Mallorca from the Moors in 1229, though his troops were finally disembarked near Santa Ponsa.

Isla Dragonera and the Dragonera Passage

39°35'·3N 02°20'·2E

The Island

Isla Dragonera is an island of spectacular and unique shape, being almost sheer on the northwest side and steeply sloping to the southeast, seen and appreciated from afar. It is just over two miles long but only 0·6 miles wide with an old signal station and tower on Puig de Sa Popi, the pyramid-shaped 360m summit. Lighthouses mark each end of the island.

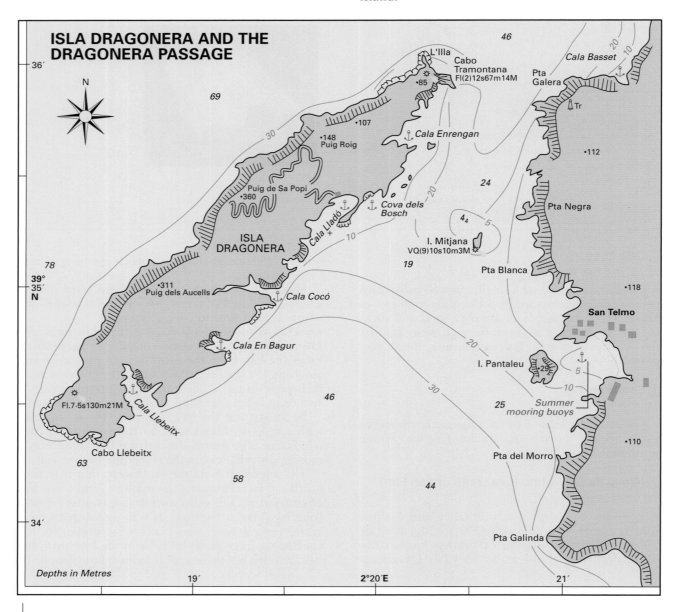

The passages

The passage between Isla Dragonera and Mallorca should present no problems to yachtsmen: the height of the surrounding hills make it appear much more alarming than it really is. The passage is funnel-shaped, opening to the south, with shoals and small rocky islets on either side of the narrows at the northern end. There are effectively two passages, either side of the 8m Isla Mitjana. The main channel is that to the west, which although wider has unmarked foul ground on both sides stretching some 200m from both Isla Mitjana and Isla Dragonera, leaving a passage 350m wide and 19m deep. The eastern channel, though much narrower at less than 200m, has a good depth of water (10m+) close to both Isla Mitjana and Mallorca.

Heavy gusts can descend from the high land around the passage without warning. Strong currents may flow through it in either direction after a gale; the direction dictated by the wind. Fishing nets supported by small white or pink buoys may be laid from either shore of the passage. The area between the island and mainland is marked on Spanish charts as a naval exercise ground, though no prohibitions are apparent.

Pilotage

Approach and passages

From northeast Following the coast southwest from Puerto de Sóller or beyond; Isla Dragonera will be seen from afar and its dramatic shape best appreciated. Cabo Tramontana, round masonry tower on stone building with red roof, 15m. (*See plans on pages 117-18*.) The Mallorcan coast is steep-to and can be followed close inshore past Punta Galera, with its prominent watchtower, into the northern entrance to the passage. Then work 200m offshore to take the eastern passage between Isla Mitjana and Mallorca in a north–south direction, approximately down the centre. There are no further hazards once the island has been passed.

Dragonera southern island light with San Telmo behind
Geoff Williamson

Alternatively the western passage can be used, passing equidistant between Isla Mitjana and the coast of Isla Dragonera (note the offlying rocky islands) on a south–southwest heading.

From southeast Round Punta Galinda and then Isla Pantaleu, leaving the latter 300m to starboard (*See plan opposite*). To take the east channel pass halfway between Isla Mitjana and the Mallorcan coast, then follow this coast past Punta Galera with its prominent watchtower, into the open sea.

The west channel can be used by standing out into the centre of the passage to pass equidistant between Isla Mitjana and the coast of Isla Dragonera (note the offlying rocky islands) on a north-northeast bearing before heading northeast to round Punta Galera.

At night Transiting either passage after dark is not recommended unless the area is already familiar. It would be safer to sail the extra few miles around Cabo Llebeitx at the southwest end of Isla Dragonera.

Ashore

There is very little ashore on the island, but tracks link Cala Lladó to the lighthouses and the northwest coast and offer some memorable walks.

Anchorages around Isla Dragonera

There are several possible daytime anchorages on the southeast coast of Isla Dragonera, all framed by spectacular cliffs. Without exception they are very small with sand and rock bottoms, and tenable only in settled conditions. Swell from either direction would probably render them untenable and they should really be regarded as being daytime anchorages for small boats (if anchorages at all). There are frequent small ferries to Cala Llado from San Telmo and these could give a sensible access to the island.

Taken from northeast to southwest the anchorages are as follows (*see plan on page 118*):

⚓ Cala Enrengan
39°35'·6N 02°20'·1E

Reasonable space for only one yacht, open to north and northeast but vulnerable to any swell. Very deep until close to shore, a shoreline would probably be necessary. The bottom is rock with little sand and the anchor will need to be dropped in about 15m. A small island lies off the southeastern promontory.

⚓ Cova dels Bosch
39°35'·3N 02°20'·0E

A wide open, cliffed *cala*, open from east round to south and to swell from southwest. Careful eyeball pilotage is called for. There is a low, isolated rock to the east.

III. MALLORCA

⚓ Cala Lladó
39°35'·2N 02°19'·7E

A narrow *cala* with a rock with no more than 2m water over it in the centre of the entrance; another lies fairly close to the starboard (east) shore and there is a significant area of shallow rocks on the western side outside the entrance. Swinging room inside the *cala* is probably sufficient for only one vessel, maybe more if small and with lines ashore. A stone watchtower stands on the promontory to the southeast, with a small quay (reserved for lighthouse officials and tourist ferries) opposite. Anchor in 2m+ over sand and rock, open to southeast through south to southwest.

⚓ Cala Cocó
39°34'·9N 02°19'·4E

Anchor close inshore under steep cliffs, open to northeast through east to southeast. Room for only one yacht.

⚓ Cala En Bagur
39°34'·7N 02°19'·2E

Again anchor close inshore under steep cliffs, open to northeast through east to southeast.

⚓ Cala Llebeitx
39°34'·4N 02°18'·5E

Slightly larger than Cala Cocó or Cala En Bagur, but still very small. Anchor under steep cliffs near the head of the *cala*, open east round to south.

Anchorages from Isla Dragonera to Sóller

There are a small number of rocky anchorages on this stretch of the northwest coast of Mallorca, only suitable for use with great care in settled conditions and probably as daytime anchorages only. The nature of the bottom in all of them is such that a trip-line would be desirable. The only shelter is the port of Sóller in the event of sudden weather deterioration. The mountains and sheer cliffs which form much of the Costa Mirador offer spectacular scenery but also a totally unforgiving lee shore in the wrong conditions – in particular the northwest *tramontana*. The mountains and narrow valleys influence the wind in both strength and direction, and a generous offing must be allowed in turbulent conditions. The dramatic coast is generally steep-to so that in settled conditions it can be followed closely. The spectacular views can perhaps be best appreciated from ½ to 1 mile offshore. *See plan on page 117.*

⚓ Cala Basset
39°35'·8N 02°21'·2E

Close north of Punta Galera, which has a tower, a small house and track to the road. Enter with a lookout forward as there are several isolated breaking rocks close in. Open west–north. Bottom is sand and rock, the best sand patches being found on the western side in about 6m. Holding has been reported to be poor.

⚓ Cala de Estallenchs
39°39'·7N 02°28'·3E

A very open *cala* under the village of the same name, totally exposed to the entire west sector. There is a track up to the village. There is a small rock awash about 30m northeast of the small stone jetty to starboard on entry. Anchor over sand and rock in 5–7m.

⚓ Cala Bañalbufar
39°41'·6N 02°31'E

Another open *cala*, exposed to the west sector, with a track up to the village. There is the remains of a rocky mole to starboard on entry and a low concrete quay from which rocks protrude. Behind this quay the cliffs are supported by very substantial man-made columns. The whole scene suggests something post smallscale industrial. The hillsides above the *cala* and for some distance around the village of Banyalbufar are composed of ancient terraces built over hundreds of years and on most of which the Malvasia grape was grown. It is said that each generation of each family was expected to add a terrace. Possibly the wine produced was exported from the *cala*. The bottom is rock and weed with a few sizeable sand patches; anchor in about 6–7m.

Cala Banyalbufar. Note columns supporting the cliff
Veronica Galkina / 123RF

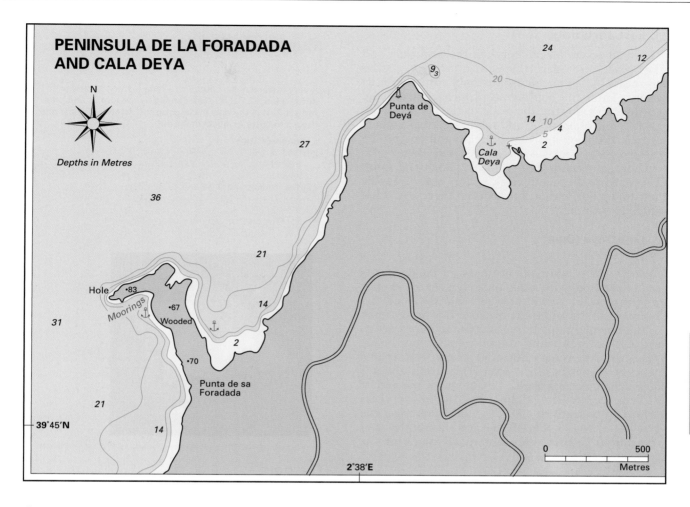

PENINSULA DE LA FORADADA
AND CALA DEYA

N

Depths in Metres

24

12

9
3

20

Punta de
Deyá

14 10
5   4
2

Cala
Deya

27

36

21

Hole •83

Moorings

•67
Wooded

14

31

2

•70

Punta de sa
Foradada

21

14

39°45′N

2°38′E

0   500
Metres

⚓ Cala de Valledemossa

39°43′·2N 02°35′·3E

Very little shelter and exposed to the entire western sector, but there is a tiny quay backed by a small, pretty village, both dwarfed by breathtaking pine-covered mountains. There are restaurants in the village. Worth a detour inshore if time and weather conditions permit. However, the bottom is a chaotic mass of rocks and weed. Anchor, if at all, in 4–6m, picking a spot carefully.

Peninsula de la Foradada

39°45′·4N 02°37′·3E (N tip of peninsula)

This extraordinary promontory, 600m in length, has anchorages on either side, though the more sheltered area is now full of moorings. (Note: no moorings in place in October 2016 and May 2017, but probable that there are some in summer.) It is possible to land at the northwest corner where there is a path up to a white house. A track inland leads to a large and conspicuous house known as Son Marroig, once owned by Archduke Luis Salvador of Austria who kept his steam yacht in the anchorage below (*See plan.*)

⚓ West anchorage

The most sheltered area, in the angle of the 'L', may be occupied by moorings (*see above*); anchor as close in as these permit in 5–10m over rock and weed with a few sand patches, open (depending on position) to southwest–west–northwest. Holding is generally poor. The spectacular hole through the end of the outcrop is best seen from this side.

Peninsula de la Foradada. The hole is best seen from the landward side *Susie Baggaley*

⚓ East anchorage

This anchorage, tucked between the peninsula and the coast, is open through northwest–north–northeast. As an anchorage, its only attraction is as shelter from the southwest. Approach from the northwest, following the coast of the peninsula, to avoid a line of breaking and submerged rocks which extend 100m or so from the mainland coast. The easternmost rock is about 100m from the anchorage. Anchor in 7–10m over rock and sand. The water is deep until close inshore and it may be best to anchor with a line ashore. There is a track uphill to the road.

⚓ Cala Deya (Deia)

39°45'·8N 02°38'·5E

A small, picturesque *cala* northeast of the Peninsula de la Foradada, with a tiny quay at its head. Anchor with care in the very clear water near the middle in 4–6m over sand and some sizeable rock heads, open to the northerly quadrant. Swimming buoys are in place. There is probably room for about four boats. There are fishermen's huts and several restaurants near the water, but little else. Deya itself, about a mile inland, is celebrated as the home of the author Robert Graves (I, Claudius, etc.) for many years prior to his death in 1985. It is also amongst the loveliest of Mallorca's villages and the antithesis of the tourist resorts that abound on much of the coastline.

Cala Deya *Anna Lurye / 123RF*

Puerto de Sóller

39°47'·9N 02°41'·2E

A very attractive harbour with a long history, tucked well inside a large cala. It is surrounded by mountains and pine forests. This is the only harbour on this stretch of coast and is easy to enter in most conditions

Communications
Ports IB ☎ +34 971 186129
   VHF Ch 08
   www.portsib.es
Marina Tramontana ☎ +34 971 632 960
   Mobile +34 671 037 671
   VHF Ch 09
   info@marinatramontana-portdesoller.com
   www.marinatramontana-portdesoller.es

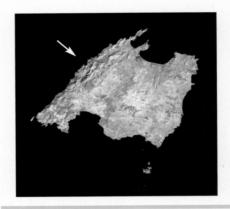

The port

Lying at the northeast end of a beautiful bay, in the midst of spectacular mountainous scenery, Puerto de Sóller is the only significant harbour and foul weather refuge on the rugged and inhospitable northwest coast of Mallorca. It is a fishing port, has numerous ferries taking tourists to beaches and attractions along the coast and has a largely inactive naval base. It is itself a fairly small holiday destination with numerous modest hotels and self-catering apartments and villas, with restaurants and shops to support these. Together with the town of Sóller some two miles inland it is a centre for walking in the dramatic mountains of the Sierra de Tramontana. With the addition of a new pontoon run by Ports IB, and the expansion of the Marina Tramontana on the refurbished town quay, many more yachts are now able to be accommodated in Sóller and to enjoy the surrounding spectacular countryside. The anchorage west of the port has been laid to buoys, but there is still a large area for anchoring outside these.

Pilotage

Approach

The approach and entrance present no problems in normal conditions, but could become difficult and perhaps dangerous in a gale from the northwest, north or northeast.

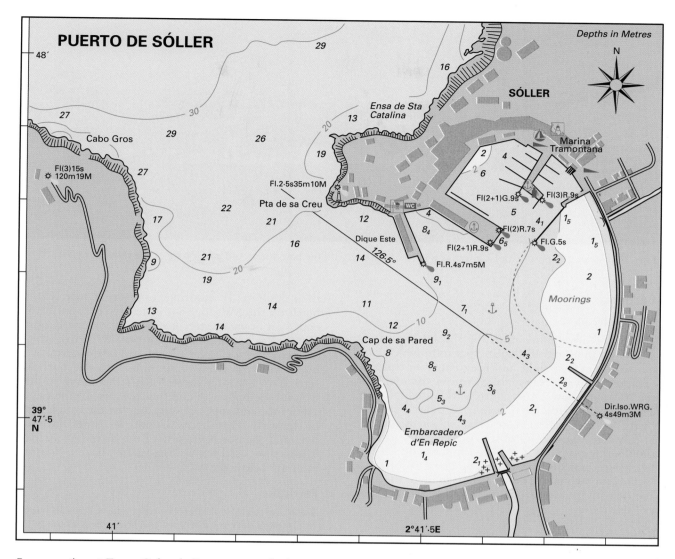

From northeast From Cabo de Formentor, which can be recognised by its lighthouse (white tower and house, 22m), the coast comprises high rocky cliffs, very rugged and broken (*see plan on page 127*). Careful pilotage is necessary because many of the headlands are similar. The following may be recognised: Cala de San Vicente, which has a tourist development at its head, Punta Beca with a long beak-like extension, and Morro de la Vaca, looking like the head of a cow from some directions. In the last three miles two conspicuous watchtowers and the small Islote S'Illa will be seen and, in the close approach, the two lighthouses at the harbour entrance. Puig Mayor (1,445m), the highest point on Mallorca with radio towers (F.R) and two radomes (a military communications base, with entry prohibited, preventing walkers from reaching the absolute summit), is just under five miles east of the entrance.

From southwest From Isla Dragonera, a large, high and conspicuous island with two lighthouses the coast is very high with broken rocky cliffs backed by mountains inland (*see plan on page 117*). The

unmistakable Peninsula de la Foradada will be seen if coasting close inshore, with Cabo Gros and its white lighthouse 3·8 miles beyond. Punta de Sa Creu on the east side of the entrance is considerably lower and will not open until Cabo Gros has been rounded.

Entrance

Enter on a southerly course between Cabo Gros and Punta de sa Creu, swinging southeast and then east to remain near the centre of the channel. There is a 4kn speed limit. Keep well clear of the naval base.

Entrance at night should not present problems in reasonable weather: follow the leading lights into the anchorage.

Anchorage in the approach

Anchor as space permits in 5–10m over mud and sand. There have been some reports of poor holding, presumably in the patches of weed. Moorings extend to the 5m line, but appear too light for all but the smallest yachts. In summer the anchorage may become very full.

III. MALLORCA

Entry into Sóller. The port occupies less than a third of the bay, with the harbour tucked into the NE of the *cala* *Graham Hutt*

Berthing

Ports IB moorings

There are now many more berths for transiting yachts on the Ports IB floating pontoon which runs out to the Fl.G.5s light and is extended in summer. Charges are very reasonable, even in summer. Use the NW side, bows or stern-to the floating pontoon. The SE side is for local fishing craft and smaller boats. It is essential to make a reservation in advance in July and August. Out of season, the end section of the floating pontoon is removed to leave only a few berths for transiting yachts. The Ports IB office is located on the main L mole, a short walk to the N of the floating pontoon. Showers and toilet facilities are also there.

Tramontana Marina

The operating concession for the SE part of the old jetty has been given to Marina Tramontana. This has added considerably to the number of visitors' berths available. It is very much more expensive than the Ports IB moorings opposite. Larger yachts berth on the SW side, with smaller craft on the SE end with bows or stern-to the jetty, which is quite high. It has been reported that the SW berths, which are generally for larger yachts, can be dangerous if a big northwest swell is running into the harbour setting up a strong surge; yachts then have to pull well off the high wall and the crew are unable to get ashore to tend ropes chafing against the rough edge of the wall. Most areas around the inner harbour wall and the northeast side of the main jetty, which is also now used for visiting yachts, have a floating pontoon below the wall.

Facilities

Water Available at all marina berths and at Ports IB berths although perhaps not early and late season as the outer pontoon is dismantled in the winter. Reports regarding quality vary: seek advice before filling tanks.

Electricity 220v and 380v AC points on the commercial mole.

Sóller bay seen from the south *Katie Le Ray*

Puerto de Sóller. The addition of the Ports IB floating
pontoon gives many more visitors' berths than previously
David Evernden

Fuel Diesel and petrol from pumps at the angle of the
central mole. Open 0900–1300 and 1600–1900
(morning only on Saturday and closed on Sunday).

Provisions Shops and supermarkets in the village around
the harbour, with a much greater selection in the town
two miles inland. Produce/fish market every morning
except Sunday in Sóller town.

Ice Marina Tramontana, bars and supermarkets.

Chandlery Small chandlery/fishing tackle/hardware shop
up the hill behind the central mole.

Repairs There is no boatyard of any size, but local
craftsmen are available and should be able to carry out
minor works. However, Marina Sóller, near the tram
terminus, have a 20-ton crane but only a very small
shore area.

Engineers Available, but more accustomed to fishing
boats.

Yacht club There is a small *club náutico*.

Launderette In the village.

Banks In the village and at Sóller town.

Hospital/medical services In Sóller town. Medical emergencies
① 971 63 30 11 or 63 30 50. Other emergency and useful
local numbers on the marina website.

Showers and toilets Portacabins near Marina Tramontana
office, and a good modern facility next to the Ports IB
office, this latter open to the public.

WiFi Good WiFi at Marina Tramontana visitors' berths.

Transport

Car hire/taxis In Sóller town.

Buses Bus service to Sóller and elsewhere.

Trams A quaint old wooden tram provides transport
between the port and the town. The 2-mile journey
takes about 20 minutes and cost €6 each way in 2016.

Trains Rail link from Sóller town to Palma by Victorian
train (1 hour).

Ferries Tourist ferries to several of the *calas* along the coast
to the northeast.

History

Several prehistoric artifacts have been found in the
town indicating its ancient past. When under
Moorish Arab power it was known as Puerto de
Santa Catalina (which perhaps demonstrates the
religious tolerance of the Moors.). Some years later
King Jaime I reconquered the island and the port
was renamed Puerto de Sóller.

Bay of Sóller. Note dredger at work in bay

Ancient tram still in service, linking Sóller town to the port
Patricia Chung

The port has been of crucial importance since the thirteenth century when it was the only stopover on this coast between the islands and the Spanish mainland.

After 1399 it became a trading post, principally for the sale of local agricultural produce and raw materials destined for Spain, South of France, Italy, North Africa, and other closer destinations. Because of its inaccessibility behind the Sierra de Tramontana it was generally easier to move supplies by boat than overland to the port of Palma.

The construction of several towers along this coast, including Torre Picada and the Castillo del Rey, are testimony to the frequent and continous attacks by Arab bandits and pirates since the 13th century. The Es Firo festival celebrates a rebuffed pirate attack.

From the Middle Ages onwards Sóller had a huge fleet of merchant, fishing vessels and passenger ferries.

The port was rebuilt in the 18th century, and the splendid quays were used from 1936–39 by Franco as a major military base. It later became the centre of learning for the submarine service.

After the civil war the shipping trade was in decline but tourism created new oportunities. The whole region has been transformed by the construction of hotels, restaurants, bars and other trades, though the charm and originality of this port remains.

A small naval fleet remained until recently and the port is becoming more accommodating to yachtsmen.

Ashore

The attractive old rural town of Sóller – the name derived from the Arabic Sulliar, meaning 'golden valley' – was set well back from the sea as a first defence against pirate raids. It was long known for its oranges and lemons, which were exported in the famous *balancelles* (small, single-masted vessels). Even with the loss of that trade to Valencia the orange groves surrounding the little town remain. Sóller is linked to its port by a vintage tramway, an excursion highly recommended, as is a trip on the Victorian train which connects Sóller to Palma. Sóller, along with numerous other places in the western Mediterranean, claims to have been the birthplace of Christopher Columbus.

Further information is available from the small tourist office next to the Ports IB office on the central jetty behind the tram terminus. ☏ 971 63 30 42. Open between March and October 1000–1300 and 1500–1830 weekdays, Saturday 1000–1300. A larger tourist office can be found in Sóller town, in an old railway carriage in Plaça de España, just by the railway station.

Tickets for bus excursions may be found at change offices, car rental and tourist agencies in the port.

Local events

The fiesta and pageant of Nuestra Señora de la Victoria is held on the second Sunday in May to commemorate a victory over Moorish pirates in 1561. In practice the festivities go on for three days, starting on the Saturday and culminating on Monday with a battle between *los Moros y Cristianos* involving much alcohol, jollity, blackened faces and firecrackers. 15–16 July sees the Fiesta de la Virgen del Carmen with a waterborne procession; 25 July a fiesta in honour of Sant Iago (St James), and 24 August a fiesta in honour of San Bartolomé. Most fiestas finish with fireworks.

Eating out

A number of hotels and many restaurants, bars and cafés around the harbour.

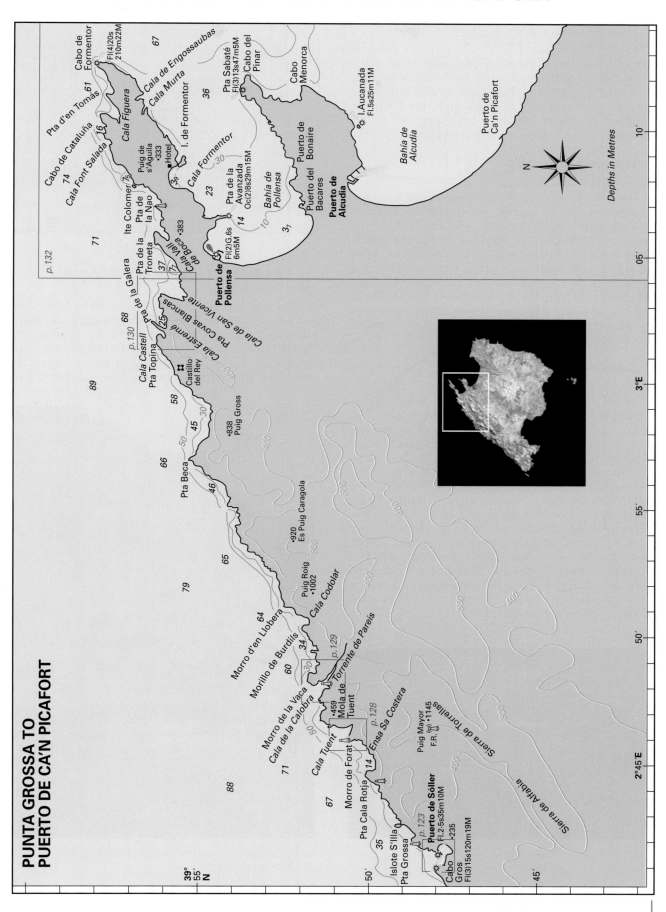

PUNTA GROSSA TO PUERTO DE CA'N PICAFORT

Cabo de Formentor
Fl(4)20s 210m22M
Pta d'en Tomas 61
Cabo de Cataluña
Cala Font Salada 74
Cabo de Cataluña 16
Cala Figuera
Cala de Engossaubas 67
Cala Murta
Cala Murta
I. de Formentor 36
Ite Colomer 75
Pta de la Nao
Puig de s'Aguila •333 ■Hotel
Cala Formentor
39
30
23
Pta Sabaté Fl(3)13s47m5M
Cabo del Pinar
Cabo Menorca
Pta de la Avanzada Oc(2)8s29m15M 14
I.Aucanada Fl.5s25m11M
Puerto de Bonaire
Puerto del Bacares
Puerto de Alcudia
Bahía de Pollensa
10
31
Puerto de Ca'n Picafort
Bahía de Alcudia

Depths in Metres

N

71
Pta de la Galera
Pta de la Troneta 37
17
Cala Vall
•383
Cala de Boca
Fl(2)G.6s 6m5M
Puerto de Pollensa

p.132

III. MALLORCA

Cala Castell
Pta Topina
Cala Estremé
Pta Covas Blancas
Cala de San Vicente 25
68
p.130

Castillo del Rey
Puig Gross •838
89
58
50 45 30
66
Pta Beca
46
65
79

Es Puig Caragola •920
800
Puig Roig •1002
Cala Codolar
400

Morro d'en Llobera
Morillo de Burdils 34
60
30
p.129
Mola de Torrente de Pareis
459•
Tuent
p.128
Morro de la Vaca
Cala de la Calobra
64
Cala Tuent
50
Ensa Sa Costera
Puig Mayor •1145 F.R.
Sierra de Torrellas
Morro de Forat 14
Sierra de Alfabia
Morro Cala Rotja
p.123
Puerto de Soller Fl.2.5s35m10M
67
•235
Islote S'Illa
Pta Grossa 35
Cabo Gros Fl(3)15s120m19M

39°
55'
N
50'
45'

2°45'E
50'
55'
3°E
05'
10'

Anchorages along the northwest coast

⚓ Ensa de Santa Catalina
39°47'·9N 02°41'·5E

Literally just round the northern corner to the north from Puerto Sóller is a small bay with anchoring potential for three or four yachts. The bottom is uneven with patches of sand and weed with a number of rocks. Anchor with care in 5-7m. Probably only of value as a day anchorage.

⚓ Ensenada Sa Costera
39°49'·9N 02°45'E

A wide, deep bay and a pleasant anchorage in settled conditions. Rocks line the shore but the water is usually very clear; approach carefully with a bow lookout, to anchor in 10–15m in the southwest corner, over sand and weed with some rocks, open to north and northeast. Close inshore there is a prominent rock reminiscent of a whale's tail. Puig Mayor (1,445m), the highest point on Mallorca with radio towers (F.R) and two radomes prominent on its summit, lies just over two miles directly inland but is out of view from this anchorage.

⚓ Cala Tuent
39°50'·6N 02°46'·4E

A small *cala* with a wide sand and stone beach, amidst spectacular surroundings, 4·8M northeast of Puerto de Sóller. Morro de Forat, close southwest, has a ruined watchtower and off-lying rocks. Anchor in 7–10m over sand and rock, open to northwest and north. The water is very clear. Swimming buoys are in place and in 2016 there were two mooring buoys for very small motor boats carefully positioned in the middle of the *cala* to limit the anchoring potential for larger vessels! There are a few houses and a restaurant on the slopes overlooking the *cala* and a very winding road. The summit of Puig Mayor can be seen from here; the domes and aerials are a military communications base and access to the ultimate summit of Mallorca's highest peak is not permitted.

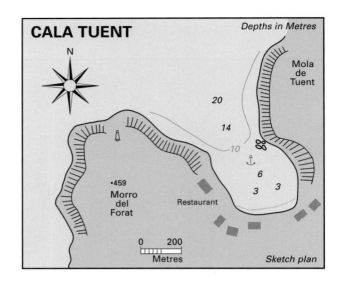

Cala Tuent viewed from northwest

⚓ Cala de la Calobra (Torrente de Pareis)
39°51'·3N 02°48'·2E

A large and spectacular *cala* just south of Morro de la Vaca, with several mini bays and a slit in the high rocky cliffs behind, through which the Torrente de Pareis (more often a gentle stream) enters the sea. Anchor in 9-11m over sand and stones, open to northwest and north. Swimming buoys laid at about

Cala de la Calobra. Looking through the cleft to the barranca *Susie Baggaley*

8m prevent access to the beach. Tourist ferries land their passengers for this major tourist attraction near the hotel overlooking the southwest beach and should not be impeded. From there a track has been carved and tunnelled into the cliff to give access to the Torrente with its lagoon and beach.

The Torrente de Pareis is considered one of the sights of Mallorca and is a popular destination by both road (not for the faint-hearted) and sea, resulting in the usual restaurants and beach cafés.

⚓ Cala Codolar

39°51'·8N 02°50'·6E

A small *cala* surrounded by high cliffs close east of Morillo de Burdils. The water is deep (10m or so) up to the shore and the bottom is very rocky. If anchoring, it is essential to use a tripline.

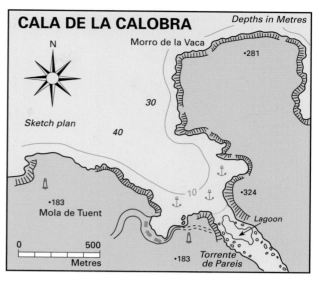

CALA DE LA CALOBRA
Depths in Metres

Cala de la Calobra. Considered the most spectacular *cala* in the Baleares. The towering cliffs either side of the *cala* dwarf any number of yachts entering the anchorage *Graham Hutt*

III. MALLORCA

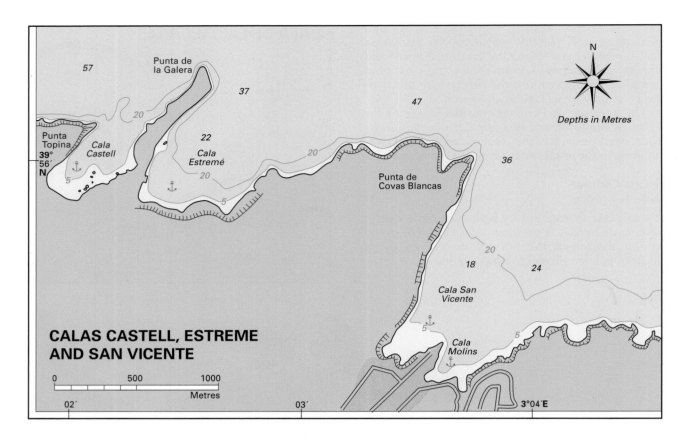

CALAS CASTELL, ESTREME AND SAN VICENTE

0   500   1000

Metres

⚓ Cala Castell

39°56'N 03°02'·1E

A narrow *cala* open to the north and northeast, separated from Cala Estreme by Punta de la Galera, a narrow peninsula which is a rather spectacular jumble of huge boulders. Punta Topina, close west, is a distinctive wedge shape when seen from the northeast. The dramatic rock peak on which is perched the Castillo del Rey can be seen clearly and to best advantage from here. The castle is on private land and officially permission to visit is required from the town hall in Pollensa from where it is a long walk in through the aforesaid private land. There is a relatively short and direct way, rather steep, from Cala Castell. It is thought that the site was originally used for a watchtower by the Romans. Later the Moors built a castle which was expanded by King Jaime I after the *Reconquista* and was manned until 1715. Since then it has fallen into decay but is still impressive, not least for its dramatic position.

Anchor in 5m over rock, weed and small sand patches in the centre of the *cala* or in 3m over sand near the beach. Rocks line the eastern side. There is a small building behind the beach at the head of the *cala*, and a track leading inland which meets the track from Pollensa to the Castillo del Rey.

Cala Estremé

⚓ Cala Estremé

39°56'N 03°02'·8E

Close east of Punta de la Galera and less sheltered than its neighbour, Cala Castell. Anchor over rock and sand in 9–15m near the small beach, open to northeast and east. Not an enticing anchorage.

⚓ Cala de San Vicente

39°55'·4N 03°03'·6E

A large *cala* backed by holiday developments. The dramatic headland of Punta de la Troneta on the east side of the *cala* has an equally dramatic rock ridge which stretches almost to San Vicente. There are two prominent 'windows' formed by rock arches

Cala de San Vicente. A large expanse of sand makes this the most substantial anchorage north of Sóller

below the crenellated crest, the smaller near the point and the other about half way along. At the head of the *cala* there are two sandy beaches separated by a rocky point, which has a reef stretching some 30m beyond it. There are substantial areas in which to anchor off either beach in 4-7m over sand, making this the only large anchorage with good holding on the northwest coast apart from Sóller; it is therefore an important anchorage for planning a voyage round the island. The water is brilliantly clear. There is a very small stone quay in the southwest corner of the western *cala*. The beaches are fringed by hotels and apartments plus the usual cafés and restaurants and a small supermarket. A fiesta in honour of La Virgen del Mar is held on the first Sunday in July. Good public WiFi. All in all a very attractive anchorage.

Cala Vall de Boca. Spectacular view looking from northeast between the cliffs, Punta Troneta on right

⚓ Cala Vall de Boca

39°55'·8N 03°05'·9E

A narrow *cala* with a small stony beach between high rocky cliffs. Anchor in ±5m over rock, open to north and northeast. There is an overland track to Puerto de Pollensa. *See plans on page 127 and 132.*

Punta Troneta looking up the cala towards San Vicente
Susie Baggaley

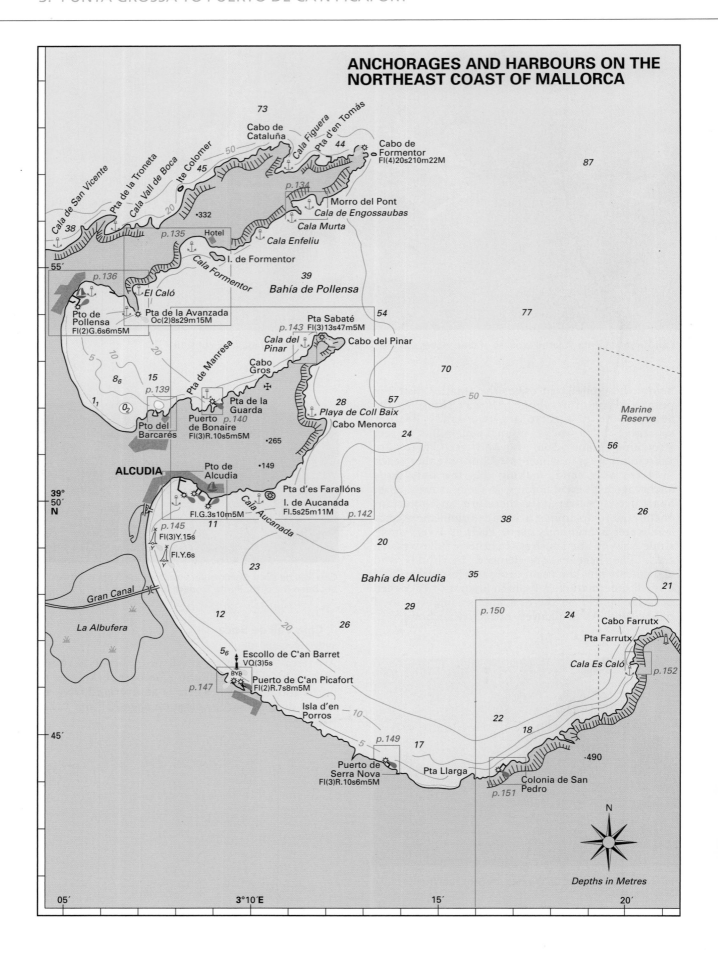

ANCHORAGES AND HARBOURS ON THE NORTHEAST COAST OF MALLORCA

73

Cabo de Cataluña

Cala Figuera

Pta d'en Tomás

44

Cabo de Formentor
Fl(4)20s210m22M

87

Cala de San Vicente

Pta de la Troneta

Cala Vall de Boca

Ite Colomer

45

50

20

•332

p.134

Morro del Pont
Cala de Engossaubas

Cala Murta

38

p.135

Hotel

Cala Enfeliu

55'

p.136

I. de Formentor

Cala Formentor

39

Bahía de Pollensa

El Caló

Pta de la Avanzada
Oc(2)8s29m15M

Pta Sabaté
p.143 Fl(3)13s47m5M

54

Pto de Pollensa
Fl(2)G.6s6m5M

Cala del Pinar

Cabo del Pinar

77

Pta de Manresa

Cabo Gros

20

5

10

15

8 6

p.139

Pta de la Guarda

28

57

Playa de Coll Baix

70

1 1

O 2

Puerto de Bonaire
Fl(3)R.10s5m5M

Cabo Menorca

24

50

Marine Reserve

Pto del Barcarés

•265

56

ALCUDIA

Pto de Alcudia

•149

Pta d'es Farallóns

I. de Aucanada
Fl.5s25m11M

p.142

39° 50' N

Fl.G.3s10m5M

11

Cala Aucanada

38

26

p.145
Fl(3)Y.15s

Fl.Y.6s

20

Gran Canal

23

Bahía de Alcudia

35

21

La Albufera

12

29

p.150

24

Cabo Farrutx

26

Pta Farrutx

5 6

Escollo de C'an Barret
VQ(3)5s

22

18

Cala Es Caló

p.152

BYB

Puerto de C'an Picafort
Fl(2)R.7s8m5M

p.147

Isla d'en Porros

10

22

18

•490

45'

5

p.149

17

Colonia de San Pedro

Puerto de Serra Nova
Fl(3)R.10s6m5M

Pta Llarga

p.151

N

Depths in Metres

05'   3°10'E   15'   20'

Cala Figuera. In spite of the remote location the small beach receives many tourists. A spectacular setting *Veronica Galkina / 123RF*

⚓ Cala Figuera
39°57'·4N 03°10'·8E

A remote and deserted *cala* 1·6M west of Cabo de Formentor, surrounded by rocky hills and cliffs and with a small stone and sand beach at its head. Swimming buoys are in place. A surprising number of tourists do make it to the beach and it is a popular spot for canoe campers. Anchor in 5m over sand and rock, open to north and northeast. There is a rough track leading up to the road from the beach but little else.

This is one of three Cala Figueras around the coast of Mallorca, the others being at the southwest end of the Bahía de Palma and on the southeast coast near Punta Salinas.

Note There have been reports of rock falls in the NE corner of the *cala*, restricting swinging room, but it may be that these date back to the construction of the road to the Cap de Formentor lighthouse which passes directly above.

Cabo de Formentor
39°57'·7N 03°12'·8E

A bold cape of some 200m in height and capped by a prominent lighthouse (Fl(4)20s210m22M white tower and house 22m). This is the most northerly point of Mallorca. There are frequently large numbers of sport fishing boats in the area around the point and wind strength and direction can change suddenly.

Rounding Cabo de Formentor looking southwest. Cala Figuera near to the top right

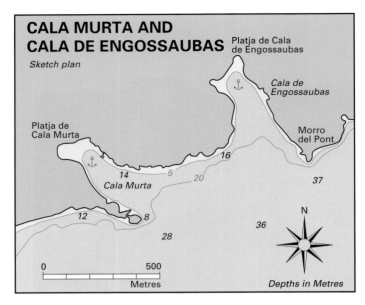

CALA MURTA AND CALA DE ENGOSSAUBAS

Sketch plan

Platja de Cala de Engossaubas

Cala de Engossaubas

Platja de Cala Murta

Morro del Pont

Cala Murta

N

0   500

Metres

Depths in Metres

Cala Engossaubas: crystal clear waters

Cala Formentor looking northwest over Isla de Formentor. Note mooring buoys

⚓ Cala de Engossaubas (Cala en Gossalba)

39°56'·3N 03°11'·5E

A very beautiful and deserted *cala* 1·7M southwest of the tip of Cabo de Formentor, reasonably wide and completely unspoilt; between high steep cliffs. Anchor close to the head in 2·5m over sand, or further out in 6m over sand, weed and rock. Open to southeast round to southwest though an east or even northeast swell may work in. Ashore there is a steep track up to the road.

⚓ Cala Murta

39°56'·2N 03°11'·3E

Another pleasant and unspoilt small *cala* with rocky sides (37m), a stony beach and beautiful rock scenery. There is a house behind the beach and swimming buoys are in place which appear to benefit only its occupiers and which force vessels to anchor further out in weed with some sand patches in 10-11m., with the result that there is probably only room for one vessel to swing at anchor unless lines are taken ashore. Open to east and south. There is a large castle-like rock island (just!) at the entrance and very clear water. Anchor in 3–5m over sand if the swimming buoys are not in place.

⚓ Cala Enfeliu

39°55'·7N 03°09'·9E

A very tiny *cala*, more a gully, with rocky sides and a small stony beach. Enter with care to anchor in 3–5m over rock and sand, open to northeast–southeast–southwest. Probably only suitable for one small boat with lines ashore to prevent swinging.

⚓ Cala Formentor (Cala Pino)

39°55'·6N 03°08'·4E

This used to be a very popular open anchorage northwest of Isla de Formentor (34m).

The whole *cala* has been laid with buoys and it is now forbidden to anchor inside the (approximately) 15m contour. Anchoring is permitted outside the bay but there is little protection in that area from wind and swell from any direction. Note that in a recent October visit there were no buoys and a number of vessels were anchored in 4-7m. The bottom is almost entirely weed and it may take more than one attempt to get the anchor to hold; water clarity is not good. The surroundings are spectacular.

The narrow passage inside Isla de Formentor now has a depth of only 1m.

The beaches are popular with day tourists, and speedboats, jet-skis and water-skiers weave amongst the moored yachts. Some areas may be buoyed off for bathers. As a contrast to the five-star Formentor Hotel there are various beach bars and restaurants. Grace Kelly and Prince Rainier of Monaco famously spent their honeymoon at the Formentor Hotel. The small jetties and quays in the northwest corner are privately owned and there is a small dock for tripper

Cala Formentor. In summer there are many 'Posidonia' buoys and anchoring is forbidden *Susie Baggaley*

Looking across Pta de la Avanzada towards Puerto de Pollensa

Anchorage southwest of Pta de la Avanzada: note seaplane base right and Pollensa anchorage above

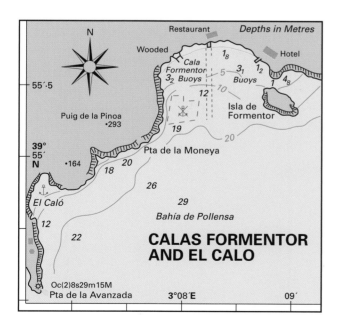

boats. One of the establishments has a raucous clientele and plays loud music late into the night spoiling the tranquility of an otherwise excellent night anchorage.

⚓ El Caló

39°54'·6N 03°06'·7E

A small *cala* close east of the root of Punta de la Avanzada. Anchor in ±5m over sand.

⚓ Behind Punta de la Avanzada

39°54'·1N 03°06'·3E

A well-sheltered anchorage close west of Punta de la Avanzada (octagonal stone tower on building, 18m) and only 1M east of Puerto de Pollensa. Mooring buoys have now been laid here, administered by Posidonia, they can be reserved in advance at www.balearslifeposidonia.eu for 1 June to 30 September (note that in 2017 these buoys were not in place and there was no trace of equipment on the bottom). See plan on *page 136* and the *Moorings* section on *page 19* for further details. Apart from the considerable daytime disturbance from speedboats and jet-skis, the anchorage is calm. Unfortunately the old castle on the promontory, known as La Fortaleza, is privately owned and explorations ashore are said to be unwelcome. This property was used extensively in the television adaptation of John Le Carré's book *The Night Manager*.

Puerto de Base de Hidros (Seaplane Base)

39°54'·5N 03°6'·1E

This small and very shallow harbour belongs to the Spanish Navy and is a seaplane base. For obvious reasons it does not welcome yachts.

III. MALLORCA

Puerto de Pollensa (Pollença)

39°54'·1N 03°05'·1E

A very friendly and sheltered harbour with a total of 648 berths with Club Náutico and Ports IB.

Distances
Barcelona 100M
Menorca 35M

Communications
Ports IB   VHF Ch 08
   ☎ 971 865 914
   ports.pollensa@portsib.es   www.portsib.es

Real Club Náutico de Pollensa   VHF Ch 09
   ☎ 971 864 635
   oficina@rcnpp.net   www.rcnpp.net

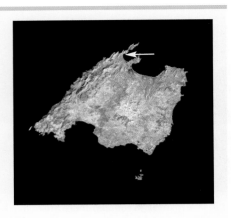

The harbour

A good sized yacht and fishing harbour with 648 berths and 90 designated for visitors. Puerto de Pollensa is at the head of a beautiful wide bay surrounded by spectacular mountains. The approach and harbour are both somewhat shallow, but should present no problems other than in strong east winds. The bay is open to the sea from northeast through east to southeast, and in heavy winds or swell from these directions, the head of the bay is best avoided. The anchorage behind Punta de Avanzada provides a

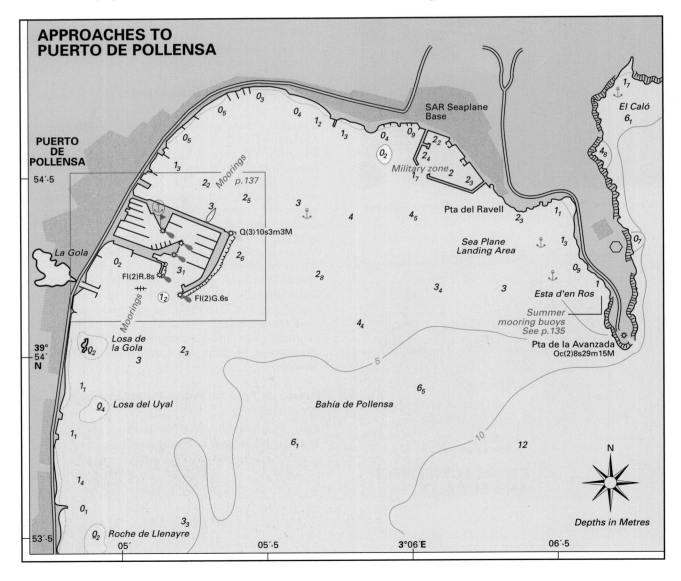

APPROACHES TO PUERTO DE POLLENSA

Puerto de Pollensa from northeast: protected in the bay and in spectacular surroundings. The fuel dock is at the end of the broad central quay   *Geoff Williamson*

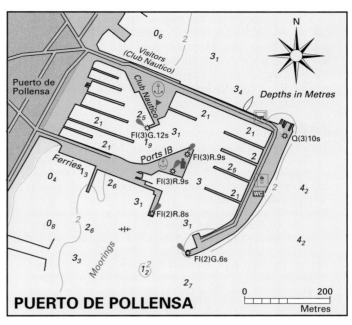

PUERTO DE POLLENSA

sheltered alternative, though during gales from the north quadrant violent gusts may be experienced. (*See plan on page 132 for details.*)

Pilotage

Approach

From south Cross the wide Bahía de Alcudia (*see page 132*) towards Cabo del Pinar and Punta Sabaté (conspicuous), with high rocky cliffs (white triangular tower, black band, 12m). Cabo de Formentor will be seen beyond. Round Punta Negra onto a westerly course towards Punta de la Avanzada (octagonal stone tower on building, 18m), after which Puerto de Pollensa will open up.

From north Round the almost vertical rocky cliffs of Cabo de Formentor (white tower and house, 22m), then follow the coast southwest past the lower Punta de la Avanzada. Puerto de Pollensa will be seen once past this headland.

Anchorage in the approach

See *Anchorage behind Punta de la Avanzada* on *page 135*. Anchoring is now prohibited in the bay N of the harbour, and buoys have been laid, administered by Posidonia. However, some yachts report that they have anchored in the area between buoys without

being challenged. Many yachts anchor further to the east, outside the buoyed area.

Less protection can be had southwest of the harbour towards the two training walls (*see plan*) in 2m+ over sand, mud and weed. There are some moorings in this area. In strong southeast winds the best shelter will be found close west of Puerto de Bonaire, some 3·5M across the bay, in 4–6m over sand.

Entrance

Approach the head of the east breakwater from east or southeast, leaving it 30–40m to starboard on entry. There are shoals close southwest of the entrance (*see plan*) and the wreck of a yacht is noted on some charts, unmarked at 39°54'·1N 03°05'·01E just south of the entrance, apparently covered by only 1m of water.

Berthing

Club Náutico visitors' moorings are on the outside of the north quay, exposed to a short fetch from the N and E. Mooring lines are tailed to the quay and water and electricity is available.

Pollensa bay and Pta de la Avanzada viewed from SE
Graham Hutt

Ports IB moorings are located on the N side of the SW mole, also with mooring lines tailed to the quay and with water and electricity provided for each berth and are much more sheltered. Communicate on VHF Ch 08. Ports IB also control the moorings on the S side of the SW mole, formerly used by visitors, but now designated for tourist boats.

Facilities

Water Taps on quays and pontoons. There is a tap by Hotel Diana's swimming pool – and a place for a dinghy.

Electricity 220v AC points on all quays and pontoons, plus some 380v points.

Fuel Diesel and petrol pumps on the head of the southwest mole. In summer open 0800–2000 every day. In winter open 0800–1300 and 1500–1900 every day except Sundays and holidays when it is 0800–13.00 only.

Provisions Two supermarkets and other specialist food shops able to supply all normal requirements. An open-air market on Wednesday mornings in Puerto de Pollensa and Sunday in Pollensa town nearby, where there are also good shops.

Ice At the fuel berth, the Réal Club Náutico bar and a shop opposite the harbour.

Chandleries In the town. Náutica Brúixola SL ☏ 971 53 11 93, Nautica El Cano ☏ 971 86 63 51, La Nautica ☏ 630 66 36 93 and 971 86 78 80, and others. Maritime International ☏ 971 86 72 99 offer a total boat care and maintenance service as well as selling chandlery from an office/shop close to the marina.

Repairs Astilleros Cabanellas boatyard on the southwest mole can handle all normal work. A 50-tonne lift at the northeast breakwater elbow. A 1-tonne crane on the northeast breakwater and 4-tonne crane at the boatyard. A small slipway in the interior of the harbour and a larger one, with cradle able to take vessels up to 21m, at the boatyard.

Engineers At the boatyard. Motonautica Bonaire ☏ 971 53 04 62/89 23 01 are official service agents for Mercury/MerCruiser, Sole Diesel, Tohatsu, Volvo Penta and Yamaha.

Sailmaking and repairs Wilson Yachts ☏ 971 86 40 67; Plana Velámenes ☏ 971 86 60 61.

Yacht club Club Náutico de Puerto de Pollensa has a smart, modern clubhouse on the northeast breakwater with lounge, terrace, bar, restaurant, swimming pool and showers.

Post-storm seascape looking from Puerto de Pollensa across Pollensa Bay *Geoff Williamson*

Pollensa: a busy Sunday market in the town, a 20 minute bus ride from the marina *Graham Hutt*

Showers At the Club Náutico free to visitors using their berths, otherwise a small fee is charged.

Launderette Next to the Ports IB office on the southwest mole.

Banks In Puerto de Pollensa and Pollensa town.

Hospital/medical services In Puerto de Pollensa and Pollensa town three miles inland.

Transport

Car hire/taxis In Puerto de Pollensa and Pollensa town.

Buses Frequent service to Pollensa town, several times daily to Palma.

Ashore

There are good walks around the harbour, and particularly among the hills to the north with some dramatic views over the north coast of Mallorca. Two recommended hikes are across the Peninsula de Formentera to Cala de San Vicente and further northeast to Cala Vall de Boca.

Pollensa town – built, like Sóller, some distance inland from its harbour – is attractive with good shops and some interesting ancient buildings. Its name comes from the Latin *pollentia* meaning powerful, though it is now agreed that the famous Roman city of Pollentia was actually sited near Alcudia. Nearby at Campanet are spectacular caves, well worth a visit, with 50-million-year-old stalactites and stalagmites. A regular bus service runs from the promenade to Pollensa town. The town centre hosts a regular Sunday market worth the bus ride.

Local events

Fiestas are held on 17 January (San Antonio) and 20 January (San Sebastian) with the usual processions; on Good Friday, in mid-July, with the week-long Fiesta de la Virgen del Carmen; and on 2 August in honour of Nuestra Señora de los Angeles, incorporating a mock battle between Moors and Christians as in Sóller.

Eating out

Many eating establishments – Pollensa is a popular tourist resort. A restaurant and bar at the Club Náutico.

Puerto del Barcarés

39°51'·9N 03°07'·2E

A small shallow harbour of little interest to yachts, but with possibilities for anchoring in the approach

Communications
Puerto del Barcarés ① 971 53 18 67

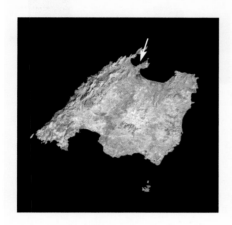

Puerto del Barcarés from northwest: shallows easily seen left of small harbour

The harbour

Puerto del Barcarés is a tiny harbour limited to small fishing boats and yachts drawing less than 1m and is in no way a port, though in the right conditions it would be possible to anchor off and visit by dinghy. The light was removed years ago but the structure is still there and now painted white. There are no facilities other than a single water tap on the quay.

Pilotage

Approach

Punta del Barcarés lies near the southwest corner of the Bahía de Pollensa (*see plan on page 132*), west of Punta de Manresa and some 3M southeast of Puerto de Pollensa. There are shoals in the approach, including the 1·5m Losa del Barcarés 400m northeast of the entrance and an unnamed breaking patch southeast of Islote del Bacarés (itself only a low rocky ledge).

Anchorage in the approach

Anchor north of Islote del Bacarés in 2–5m over sand and weed, open to west–north–northeast.

Entrance

Inadvisable except by dinghy. Swing wide of the unnamed shoal mentioned above to round the north mole at slow speed. The entrance is no more than 2·5m wide and less than 1m deep.

Berthing

There is a dinghy slipway opposite the entrance.

Facilities

Water Tap on the quay.

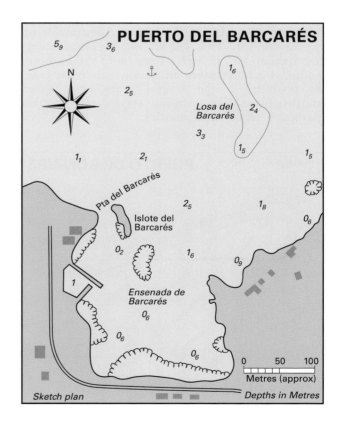

Puerto/Marina de Bonaire (Cocodrilo)

39°52'·1N 03°08'·5E

A well sheltered marina on the S side of Bahía de Pollensa with 352 moorings up to 17m, most occupied by local boats. It is easy to approach and is pleasantly located in a deeply forested region of the bay

Communications
VHF Ch 09
Marina de Bonaire ① 971 54 69 55
info@marinadebonaire.com
www.marinadebonaire.com

The harbour

Formerly known as Port del Cocodrilo, and still called by that name on several road signs locally and some charts, Puerto de Bonaire is an attractive, purpose-built yacht harbour amongst pleasantly wooded surroundings, believed to be on the site of one of the original Phoenician landings. The harbour is simple to approach and enter and offers excellent shelter. Most of the 352 berths for yachts up to 17m are permanently occupied. Unlike many similar harbours in the Islas Baleares there is no commercial or fishing usage.

When winds of over 100kn struck the port some years ago, there was severe damage caused, including the sinking of 22 yachts and destruction of the restaurant. This led to the entrance being reshaped and a 2m high extension to the harbour wall, giving much more protection. There has been no problem in the several years since these improvements. The staff are very friendly and the *marineros* helpful with mooring.

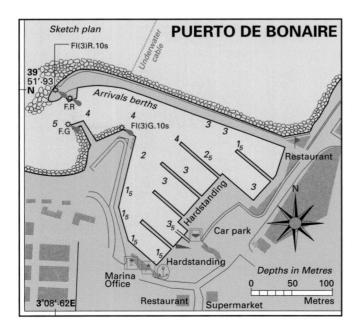

Pilotage

Approach

From south Cross the wide Bahía de Alcudia towards Cabo del Pinar and Punta Sabaté – conspicuous, with high rocky cliffs (white triangular tower, black band, 12m). Round Punta Negra to follow the south coast of the Bahía de Pollensa past Cabo Gros and Punta de la Guarda. Puerto de Bonaire lies 0·5M further west. (*See plan on page 132.*)

From north Round the almost vertical rocky cliffs of Cabo de Formentor (white tower and house, 22m), then steer southwest towards Punta de Manresa, a low, dark rocky point surmounted by a castle. Puerto de Bonaire lies 0·5M east of this headland.

Anchorage in the approach

Anchor in the bay west or east of the harbour entrance in 5m over sand, leaving a clear passage to the marina entrance; open to the northern quadrant.

Entrance

The entrance is relatively narrow with a distinct dogleg. Approach on a southerly course, slowly closing the coast west of the north breakwater until the west mole comes into view. Then swing east and northeast to remain in the centre of the channel. The reception quay is to port immediately inside the entrance. Depth in the entrance is about 3·5m.

If entering at night (quite feasible in settled conditions) note that the light on the north breakwater is some distance from the end of the rubble breakwater. A bow lookout with a strong torch is recommended. In summer there may be F.R and F.G lights on the spurs each side of the entrance.

Berthing

Berth at the reception quay until directed elsewhere by marina staff, preferably having already called on VHF Ch 09.

Puerto de Bonaire: an attractive purpose-built marina

Facilities

Water Taps on quays and pontoons.
Electricity 220v AC points on quays and pontoons.
Fuel Available at Puerto de Pollenca, 3M away.
Provisions Small supermarket just south of the harbour (opposite a restaurant) and many shops in Alcudia a mile southwest.
Ice From the bar/restaurant at the root of the north breakwater.
Chandlery Next to the marina office.
Repairs Workshops near the marina office. Motonautica Bonaire ☎ 971 53 04 62. A 30-tonne lift in the south part of the harbour. Slipway next to the travel-lift.
Engineers Engineering workshop near the marina office and Motonautica Bonaire (*see above*).
Electronic & radio repairs Enquire at the marina office.
Showers Near the marina office.
Launderette By the shower block.
Hospital/medical services In Alcudia.
Banks In Alcudia.

Transport

Car hire/taxis From Alcudia. Enquire at the marina office.

Ashore

There are excellent walks in the area and good views from Punta de Manresa, while the old Roman city of Alcudia is just over a mile away.

Eating out

Bar/restaurant at the root of the north breakwater and another south of the harbour. Others in the vicinity.

Bonaire seen from west on entry. A delightful and friendly marina with visitors' berth immediately to left on entry
Graham Hutt

III. MALLORCA

Looking east over Cala del Pinar to Pta Sabate and Cabo del Pinar

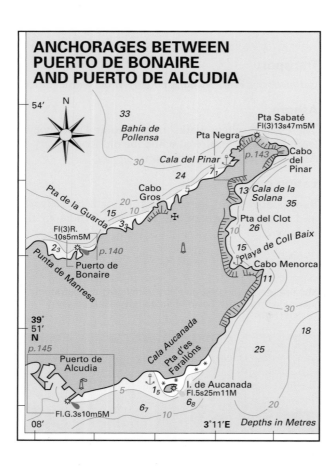

Anchorages on Peninsula Cabo del Pinar

⚓ Cala del Pinar (Ses Caletas)

39°53'·2N 03°11'·2E

An anchorage behind Punta Negra on the north side of the peninsula Cabo del Pinar, consisting of a double *cala* plus a smaller one to the north. Cabo del Pinar is a military area, with landing in the *calas* forbidden and access totally restricted by buoys. It appears to be a recreation facility for the military and the surroundings are really very pleasant. Anchor in 10-15m outside the buoyed areas over sand and weed, although it may be possible for small vessels in stable conditions to anchor closer to the cliffs in the southeast of the anchorage in lesser depths, at least for a daytime stay. It is a popular place for day visitors from Puerto de Pollensa and can become crowded.

⚓ Playa de Coll Baix

39°51'·9N 03°11'·4E

An open anchorage on the south side of the peninsula beneath dramatic cliffs off a small sand and stone beach. It is a beautiful anchorage with exceptionally clear water. Anchor in 6–9m over sand and stones with some large rocks particularly on the east side, open to north–northeast–east and to swell from the southeast. Ashore there is a steep and rough track to the road but nothing else.

⚓ Cala Aucanada

39°50'·0N 03°09'·9E

A wide but shallow bay 600m west-northwest of Isla Aucanada (white tower and house, 15m). The surrounding land is generally flat – quite a contrast if coming from the north.

Playa de Coll Baix with Cabo Menorca looming left

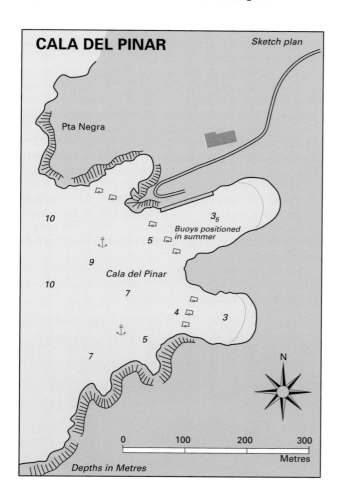

CALA DEL PINAR

Sketch plan

Pta Negra

10

3₅

Buoys positioned in summer

5

9

Cala del Pinar

10

7

4

3

5

7

N

0   100   200   300

Metres

Depths in Metres

Approach from the south or southwest to anchor in 1·5m+ over sand, open to the south quadrant. The beach close northwest of the island is fringed by reefs and the narrow passage between the island and Punta Aucanada is very shallow. There is a road down to the point and there are a few houses.

Isla de Aucanada looking west with anchorage behind

Puerto de Alcudia (Marina Alcúdiamar)

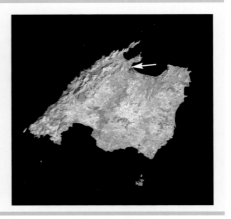

39°50'·0N 03°08'·0E

A very sheltered marina with easy access and berthing for over 700 yachts, but shallow at the N end of the harbour. A commercial and naval port lie just outside the marina.

Communications
Pilots (Alcudia Prácticos) VHF Ch 11, 13, 14, 16
Marina Alcúdiamar VHF Ch 09
☏ 971 54 60 00/04
alcudiamar@alcudiamar.es
www.alcudiamar.es

The marina

Alcúdiamar is a large, well-equipped but rather shallow marina able to accommodate 744 yachts of up to 30m. It lies northwest of a small commercial port handling cargo ships and ferries, with a small naval zone sandwiched between the two. The marina is easy to approach and enter and is well sheltered once inside. It shares its location with an old fishing harbour and access to the local bars and restaurants on the W breakwater means security is low, although access to the pontoons is via key card.

Pilotage

Approach

From south and east The high headland of Cabo de Pera (white tower on white building with dark corners and red roof, 21m) and the even higher (272m) Cabo del Freu, which has a long low rocky projection at its foot, are both unmistakeable. (*See plans on pages 132 and 150.*) Follow the coast northwest towards Cabo Farrutx, passing the islet of Farayó de Aubarca (23m high and about 750m offshore) en route. There is good water on either side of the island.

On rounding Cabo Farrutx (unlit, though there are red lights on Puig Tudosa 1·5M to the south) the Bahía de Alcudia opens up, with Puerto de Alcudia in the northwest corner.

From north Cross the Bahía de Pollensa and round first the steep, reddish cliffs of Cabo del Pinar and then the even higher, but not so prominent, Cabo Menorca. Follow the coast (now becoming low and flat) at 500m to pass outside Isla de Aucanada (white tower and house, 15m) and leave the head of the southeast breakwater at least 50m to starboard. The two tall chimneys near the root of the breakwater are conspicuous.

Note The approach and entrance to the yacht harbour are relatively shallow and can be dangerous in heavy seas from east and southeast. The area is prone to silting up and charted depths should not be relied upon.

Submarines occasionally exercise in the Bahía de Alcudia and its approaches. Commercial ships may be anchored south of the harbour.

Bahía de Alcudia viewed from north, with Isla de Aucanada left

PUERTO DE ALCUDIA

Anchorage in the approach

Anchor southwest of the marina in 2–4m over sand and weed, open to southeast and south, keeping well clear of the entrance. Some moorings have been laid out to about 100m from the breakwater.

Entrance

Leave the head of the southeast (commercial) breakwater a good 50m to starboard. Keep well clear of any commercial ship or ferry movement. Then steer north to pass between the marina breakwater lights and the first starboard hand buoy. Once into the channel, come round to port, leaving the breakwater end 50m or so to port to approach the marina entrance on a westerly heading. Depth at the entrance is dredged to 4m but silting can occur after strong winds, so proceed with caution. There is a 3kn speed limit in the harbour.

Berthing

There is a reception area on the south side of the fuelling quay, but it is preferable to contact the marina office on VHF Ch 09 before arrival so that a berth can be allocated. Anchoring is not allowed inside the yacht harbour. Booking in advance is essential as there are generally few visitor berths available, these depending on the absence of regular berth-holders' yachts.

Facilities

Water Taps on quays and pontoons, and at the fuelling berth.

Electricity 220v AC at all berths plus 380v AC at berths over 14m.

Fuel Diesel and petrol pumps on the inner arm of the southwest breakwater. Available 24 hours on calling the marina *marineros* on Ch 09.

Gas No Calor gas cylinders can be refilled in Mallorca now, but Náutica Mahón stocks Camping Gaz.

Provisions Small supermarket on the southwest breakwater, many more in Puerto de Alcudia and Alcudia town. A produce market Sunday and Tuesday mornings in Alcudia town.

Ice From the fuel berth.

Chandleries Multimar Alcudia ☎ 971 89 71 67, Yacht Centre Palma and others in the marina.

Repairs Construcciones Navales Benassar SA boatyard ☎ 971 54 67 00. All repair work can also be undertaken by Náutica Mahón ☎ 971 54 67 50 which has its offices in the marina complex. A 150-tonne lift and an 80-tonne lift are available on the southwest breakwater. An 8-tonne mobile crane is also available.

Puerto de Alcudia and southwest anchorage looking north into Bahía de Pollensa

Small slipway in shallow (0·7m) water on the north side of the yacht harbour. There is a substantial haul-out and hard standing area in the marina for which major improvements are planned for 2018.

Engineers Náutica Mahón (see *Repairs* above) Multimar Alcudia (*see above*) and Motonáutica Alcudia ① 971 54 61 30. The latter is the official service agent for MerCruiser, Tohatsu, Volvo Penta, Yanmar. Europa Marine Services (Balearics) S.L. ① 971 54 92 15 can service inboard/outboard engines and refrigeration units.

Electronic & radio repairs Náutica Mahón (*see above*) and others.

Sailmaker Plana Velámenes ① 971 86 60 61.

Rigging Yacht-Rigger ① 908 43 59 75.

Showers On the southwest breakwater and near the restaurants.

Laundry In the marina.

Banks In Puerto de Alcudia and Alcudia town.

Hospital/medical services Medical services via marina office, hospital in Alcudia town.

Transport

Car hire/taxis In both Puerto de Alcudia and Alcudia town. A taxi rank at the root of the southwest breakwater.

Buses Bus service to Alcudia town, Palma and elsewhere.

Ferries Regular service to Ciudadela in Menorca, Barcelona and Port Vendres in France.

History

Both the port and the old town a mile inland date back to Phoenician times, the latter a typical settlement site on a hilly peninsula served by two harbours on opposite sides of the isthmus. In due course the Romans took it over, calling the area Pollentia ('powerful') and making it the capital of the island; however, the Vandals occupied the town after the fall of Rome and destroyed most of the Roman buildings. Little evidence is left of the Moorish occupation except the name, Al Kudia, which means 'the hill'. After the Christian re-conquest, walls were built around the town.

Ashore

Sections of the walls can still be seen, together with the remains of the Roman theatre. In addition to the theatre (on the road between the harbour and the town), St Martin's cave, the castle and the museum are worth visiting. The old town as a whole is delightful.

For those who are interested in birds, the Albufera Nature Reserve behind the beach to the southwest is an important site. Follow the coast road south for about three miles, cross the Gran Canal and the entrance to the park is clearly labelled. There is an entry fee, but bird hides, etc. are provided. The Bahía de Alcudia is a popular tourist area, largely due to its excellent beaches.

Local events

Fiestas are held on 29 June in honour of San Pedro, with land and sea processions. On 2 July the Romería a la Virgen de la Victória includes a pilgrimage to the Santuari de la Victória on a peak three miles away, and on 25 July a fiesta in honour of Sant Iago (St James), the patron saint of the town, includes a parade on horseback.

Eating out

Many restaurants and cafés line the marina. There is a 4-star hotel in the northwest corner of the marina, offering special rates for visiting yachtsmen.

Puerto de Ca'n Picafort

39°46'·1N 03°09'·5E

A small harbour with 470 yacht berths, easy to enter and offering excellent protection. It is 4M S of Alcúdimar with superb beaches on either side.

Communications
VHF Ch 09
Club Náutico Ca'n Picafort ☎ 971 85 01 85
pdcanpicafort@futurnet.es

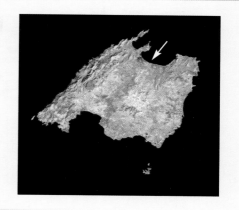

The harbour

Ca'n Picafort is a fairly small yacht harbour able to take 470 boats up to 12m, built onto a small, old fishing harbour. It is backed by a popular tourist resort of fairly recent origin, the first hotel having been built in 1933 when building controls were lifted.

Approach is straightforward, but entrance is dangerous with even moderate seas from the east or northeast quadrant, due to shoaling water around the entrance. This is well marked.

Pilotage

Approach

For outer approaches see plan on page 132.

From southeast Round the high (432m) Cabo Farrutx on to a course just south of west. Puerto de Ca'n Picafort lies nine miles away, near the south end of the hotels which line much of the Bahía de Alcudia. There is a day-mark close to the harbour entrance, but it may be lost against the high-rise buildings behind.

III. MALLORCA

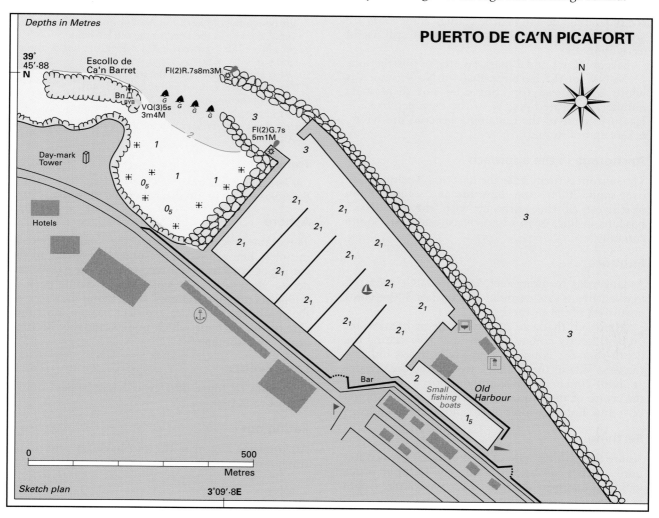

Puerto de Ca'n Picafort. Seas breaking over the Escollo de Ca'n Barret reef

From north After rounding Cabo Menorca head south-southwest across the Bahía de Alcudia, Puerto de Ca'n Picafort lies six miles away, identified as above.

Beacons

Seventeen pairs of tall day-marks, about 1000m apart and numbered from N to S, were erected along the coast from a point just S of the Gran Canal to the NE of Colonia de San Pedro. Though some pairs are now missing, the remaining beacons are still useful navigationally.

Beacon Nos 1 and 2 mark an area of obstructions 1½M NW of the harbour. Beacon No 4 (which is white with a red top, but does not display its number) is located just W of the entrance to Ca'n Picafort. Some of the remaining beacons are white, others natural stone.

Anchorage in the approach

The bottom is rocky near the harbour. Anchor in 5m over sand, 700m from the shore and some 1,000m northwest of the harbour, with the two No.3 beacons in line; open to northeast and east. Sound carefully.

Entrance

A dangerous breaking reef, Escollo de Ca'n Barret, marked by an east cardinal beacon lies 300m west-northwest of the entrance.

Approach the head of the northeast breakwater on a southerly course at slow speed, watching the depth-sounder. A line of four green buoys indicate the west side of the channel. Round the breakwater at about 20m and turn sharply to port to line up for the centre of the entrance, where at least 3m should be found. Entrance after dark is not recommended.

Berthing

Secure to the inner side of the northeast breakwater until a berth can be allocated. The harbour office will be found near the root of the west mole. Depth in the marina is generally around 2·1m.

Facilities

Water Taps on quays and pontoons. Check quality before filling tanks.
Electricity 220v AC points on quays and pontoons, 380v on hardstanding.
Fuel No fuel pumps.
Provisions Many shops and supermarkets in the town. Market on Tuesday afternoons in Calle Cervantes.
Ice Available from bars and the Club Náutico.
Repairs Basic boatyard services near the 20-tonne travel-lift beside the old harbour. An 8-tonne mobile crane. A small slipway at the head of the old harbour.
Yacht club Club Náutico de Ca'n Picafort has a lounge and bar.
Showers Shower block near the travel-lift.
WiFi in the marina office and restaurant only.
Laundry In the town.
Banks In the town.
Hospital/medical services Doctor in the town, otherwise in Alcudia.

Transport

Car hire/taxis In the town.
Buses Bus service to Alcudia, Palma and elsewhere.

Ashore

The name Picafort is from the Spanish words meaning 'hew strongly', presumably referring to the cutting of stone from nearby quarries. The Necropolis de Son Real (a Bronze Age cemetery dating back to 700BC) is only ten minutes' walk along the shore to the southeast. There are excellent beaches on either side of the harbour which understandably become crowded in summer.

Local Events

The fiesta of Mare de Deu d'Agost is held on 15 August each year.

Eating out

An outdoor bar near the old harbour and many restaurants and cafés in the town.

Puerto de Serra Nova

39°44'·4N 03°13'·4E

A tiny harbour with berths mostly for small boats. An exceptionally narrow entrance, with silting in the approach: hardly worth mentioning, except that plans for greater things have been submitted

Communications
Puerto de Serra Nova ② 971 85 40 30

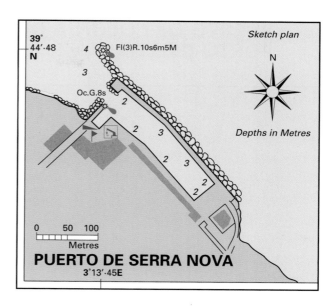

The harbour

Puerto de Serra Nova is another tiny, shallow harbour which hardly rates 'port' status. It was built as the first stage of a large yacht harbour to complement the 'urbanisation' of Son Serra Nova, but there are no signs of further development. Currently the harbour and surroundings are bleak and facilities very limited.

Approach is straightforward but it would be dangerous with heavy seas from the northern quadrant. Entrance is limited to small vessels no more than 9m in length and drawing less than 2m. The entrance is formed by two huge concrete blocks, making it very narrow and intimidating.

Pilotage

Approach

For outer approaches see page 132.

From southeast Round the high (432m) Cabo Farrutx and follow the coast westwards at a distance of 500m once past Colonia de San Pedro. Puerto de Serra Nova lies three miles beyond, at the northern end of an area of scattered houses backed by pine forest.

From north After passing Cabo Menorca, head south across the Bahía de Alcudia to close the coast close northwest of the harbour, which lies at the northern end of the area of scattered houses and pine forest. The surrounding countryside is generally flat.

Anchorage in the approach

Anchor in 5m over sand about 400m from the shore, north of the harbour entrance; open to northwest–north–northeast.

Entrance

Approach the head of the northwest breakwater at slow speed on a southwesterly course. The entrance, which lies a short distance beyond, is narrow – 10m or less – and room to manoeuvre once inside is very restricted. In bad weather the entrance can be closed by a metal barrier.

Berthing

Secure in a vacant slot and await allocation of a berth. The harbour shoals towards its head.

Facilities

Water Taps around the harbour.
Electricity 220v AC points around the harbour.
Fuel No fuel available.
Provisions The nearest shops are in the village of Son Serra 1·25 miles inland.
Repairs A 3-tonne crane and slipway at the Club Náutico.
Yacht club Club Náutico Serra Nova has a small clubhouse with bar near the west mole.

Transport

Car hire/taxis Call a taxi from Ca'n Picafort.
Buses Bus service along the main road a mile inland.

Eating out

Friendly bar at the *club náutico* and a café or two in the 'urbanisation'. No restaurants nearby.

Puerto de Serra Nova: insignificant unless earlier expansion plans are implemented

III. MALLORCA

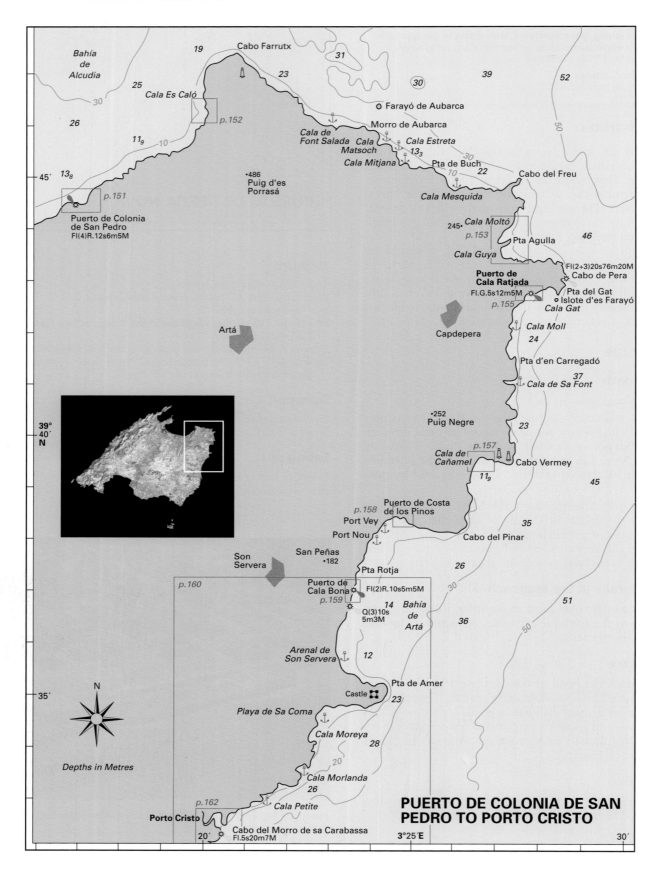

Bahía
de
Alcudia

19 Cabo Farrutx

31

25

39 52

Cala Es Caló

30

p.152

26

Farayó de Aubarca

Morro de Aubarca

11₉ 10

50

Cala de
Font Salada Cala
Matsoch Cala Estreta

30

Cala Mitjana 13₃

45´ 13₈ Pta de Buch

486
Puig d'es
Porrasá

10 22 Cabo del Freu

Cala Mesquida

Puerto de Colonia
de San Pedro
Fl(4)R.12s6m5M

245• Cala Moltó

46

p.153

Pta Agulla

Cala Guya

Fl(2+3)20s76m20M
Cabo de Pera

Puerto de
Cala Ratjada

Pta del Gat

Fl.G.5s12m5M Islote d'es Farayó

Artá p.155 Cala Gat

Capdepera Cala Moll

24

Pta d'en Carregadó

37

Cala de Sa Font

252•
Puig Negre

23

39°
40´
N

p.157

Cala de
Cañamel Cabo Vermey

11₉ 45

Puerto de Costa
de los Pinos

p.158

35

Port Vey

Port Nou Cabo del Pinar

San Peñas
Son •182
Servera

26

p.160 Pta Rotja

Puerto de
Cala Bona Fl(2)R.10s5m5M

p.159 14 Bahía
de
Artá

30

Q(3)10s
5m3M 36

51

35´

N

Arenal de
Son Servera 12

Pta de Amer

Castle 23

Playa de Sa Coma

Depths in Metres

Cala Moreya

28

20

Cala Morlanda

26

p.162

Cala Petite

Porto Cristo

20´ Cabo del Morro de sa Carabassa
Fl.5s20m7M

3°25´E 30´

Puerto de Colonia de San Pedro (Sant Pere)

39°44'·3N 03°16'·2E

A recently completed private marina in the E of Alcudia Bay, located within a nature park; with berths for over 300 yachts from 6 to 15m.

Communications
VHF Ch 09
Club Náutico ☎ 971 589 118
oficinacncsp@gmail.com, oficina@cncoloniasp.com or marineria@cncoloniasp.com
www.cncoloniasp.com

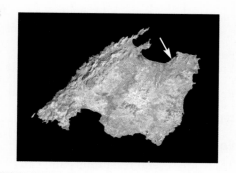

The harbour/marina

A privately funded marina, which was built in 2001. There are berths and services for 308 craft up to 15m. Although privately owned by the local Club Náutico members, visitors are welcome to use any empty berths, same-day advance booking being prudent. It is set in an area of considerable natural beauty, and much of the surrounding countryside is protected. The urbanisation is still developing with a major project by Taylor Wimpey in progress.

Pilotage

Approach

From northeast Round the high (432m) Cabo Farrutx and follow the coast westwards at a distance of 500m for 4M and the port will be clearly seen (*see plan on opposite page*).

From northwest After passing Cabo Menorca, head south across the Bahía de Alcudia to close the coast near to the harbour. The immediate surrounding countryside is flat with mountains as a backdrop (*see plan on page 132*).

Anchorage in the approach

Whilst it is possible to anchor west of the entrance in 6m, the nature of the bottom – rocky ledges with many crevices – gives very poor holding or a fouled anchor so a tripline is essential. There are shallow rocks extending out to 75m from the shore. Anchoring is discouraged but it may be possible to anchor 0·5M further northwest.

Entrance

Approach the head of the north breakwater on a southerly course, rounding and entering when the northeast part of the breakwater is abeam and in transit.

Berthing

Secure in a vacant slot as available and await allocation of a berth. It is essential to call ahead on Ch 09 or better still telephone early in the day - only same day reservations can be made.

III. MALLORCA

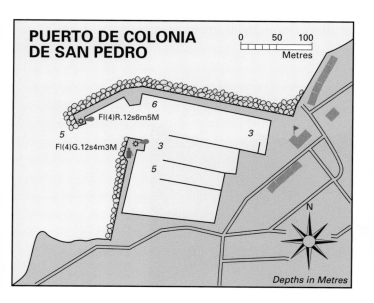

PUERTO DE COLONIA DE SAN PEDRO

0   50   100
Metres

6
Fl(4)R.12s6m5M
5
Fl(4)G.12s4m3M
3
3
5
3

N

Depths in Metres

Puerto de Colonia de San Pedro viewed from northeast. The new fuel dock is immediately to starboard on entry

Facilities

Water Water tap near the slipway at the head of the harbour.
Electricity On each berth
Fuel There is a fuel berth to starboard on entry. Opening hours are 0800–2000 each day in summer, 0800–1700 in winter.
Provisions A few shops in the village.
Yacht club Club Náutico de Colonia de San Pedro across the road from the harbour has a bar and restaurant.
Repairs 35-tonne travel hoist. A slipway at the Club Náutico.
WiFi Reportedly good throughout the marina.

Eating out

There are several restaurants and cafés including the bar and restaurant at the *Club Náutico*.

Anchorages between Puerto de Colonia and Puerto de Cala Ratjada

⚓ Cala es Caló

39°46'·4N 03°20'E

An isolated anchorage 1·2M southwest of Cabo Farrutx (*see plan on page 150*) set against a dramatic rocky backdrop, Cala Es Caló offers a useful anchorage if waiting to round the cape. There is a short mole but no harbour. There was a light on an extension to the mole but this section and the light were destroyed some years ago. Swell can curve round from Punta d'es Calo and the wind escalates on that corner and fairly whistles round. However if you can tuck in close east or southeast of the mole these are largely avoided. Note that to the west of the mole there is an extensive area of relatively shallow rocky ground. There are no facilities and only a track ashore.

Approach from west or northwest to anchor in 5–6m over sand, weed and some large rocks, south or southeast of the molehead; open to west and northwest with some fetch from southwest and south. Holding is poor in places. The short mole has underwater projections near its head and its east (inner) side is sometimes used by fishing vessels, which must not be obstructed. Nets may also be laid in the vicinity.

There are good walks in the surrounding hills, and for the fit the climb to the top of Atalaya de Morey (432m), overlooking Cabo Farrutx, is rewarding. The Cueva (cave) des Vells Marins some 600m south of the anchorage, is also worth visiting.

⚓ Cala de Font Salada

39°45'·9N 03°23'·1E

One of several similar *calas* in a large shallow bay southeast of Cabo Farrutx. Anchor off a white sandy beach in 4–6m over sand, exposed to northwest–north–northeast. A track leads to a road some distance inland.

Farayó de Aubarca

39°46'·2N 03°24'·4E

A small nobbly islet 23m high and some 750m offshore, off the headland of Morro de Aubarca, which is topped by a watchtower. There is good water on either side: the inshore passage has depths of 20m or more and is free of dangers.

CALA ES CALO

N

Punta d'es Caló

0   50   100
Metres

Cala Es Caló

Sketch plan

5   5   3   1
8   6   1

Cala Es Caló viewed from southwest, nestling on south side of Cabo Farrutx

⚓ Calas Matsoch, Estreta and Mitjana
39°45'·6N 03°24'·4E to 39 45'·2N 03 24'·9E

Three small open anchorages off narrow white sand and stone beaches, backed by sand dunes. Anchor in 3–5m over hard sand, open northwest to east. All three can be reached by road and are frequented by tourists. Cala Mitjana has a beach café.

⚓ Cala Mesquida
39°44'·8N 03°26'·1E

An open anchorage off a long white sandy beach, with a growing tourist resort behind. Anchor in 3–5m over sand, open through north, northeast and east and to swell from the northwest. Water and basic provisions are available.

⚓ Calas Moltó and Guya
(Calas Molta and de S'Agulla)
39°43'·8N 03°27'·4E (Moltó) 39 43'·5N 03 27'·4E (Guya)

Two *calas* either side of a narrow rocky promontory terminating in Punta Agulla, Cala Moltó has a very small beach and no facilites whereas Cala Guya has a much longer sandy beach, which is popular with holidaymakers. There is a growing tourist development on its south shore.

Anchor in 3–5m over sand in either cala, taking particular care in Cala Moltó to avoid a pipeline running northeast towards Menorca. Cala Moltó is open to the northeast, Cala Guya to northeast and east. Both would be equally susceptible to swell from the eastern quadrant.

⚓ Cala Gat (Cat)
39°42'·7N 03°28'·2E

Posidonia conservation authorities have advised that it is now prohibited to anchor in Cala Gat. The *cala* is tucked well under the northwest side of Punta del Gat with Islote d'es Farayó to the east and Puerto de Cala Ratjada to the west. Cliffed and wooded slopes

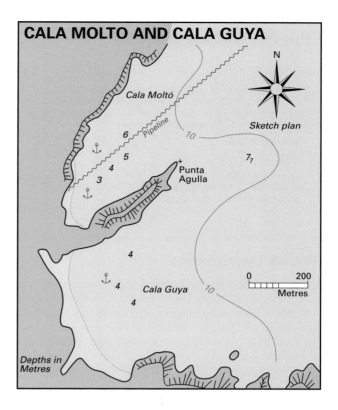

are overlooked by several houses, including the conspicuous Palacio Torre Ciega, on a hill 200m to the west. Patrols in the area are daily and fines can be imposed for contravening the regulation. Although there is a channel carrying 4m between Punta del Gat and Islote d'es Farayó, it is not recommended without local knowledge. Foul ground extends some distance to the south of the island.

View from southeast over Cala Guya. Cala Moltó far side of Punto Agulla

Puerto de Cala Ratjada

39°42'·5N 03°27'·8E

A small and very friendly harbour tucked under Cabo de Pera, offering berthing and facilities for 100 small yachts inside and larger vessels on the sheltered outer mole. The closest harbour to Menorca (23M away)

Communications
Ports IB VHF Ch 08
⏱ 971 56 50 67
www.portsib.es
Club Náutico de Cala Ratjada ⏱ 971 56 40 19
clubnáutico@calaratjada.e.telefonica

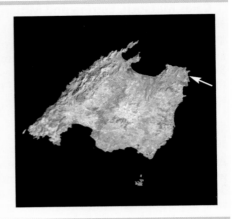

The harbour/marina

Once a little fishing harbour but now a thriving (and rather pleasant) tourist resort with a strong German influence. The vast majority of local boats are small and the Club Náutico pontoons can only take craft up to 12m or so. However, yachts up to 20m can lie alongside or stern/bows to the breakwater outside the harbour proper, which is well sheltered in most conditions. Menorca is only 23M to the east, making Puerto de Cala Ratjada a popular destination or departure point for the inter-island passage.

Approach is straightforward but the entrance to the inner harbour is narrow and the harbour congested with fishing craft. Strong winds from between east and south create a heavy swell in both entrance and harbour, and the outside berths might become untenable.

Puerto de Cala Ratjada harbour. Centre and left: inner harbour and Club Náutico moorings. Right: Ports IB moorings Graham Hutt

Pilotage

Approach

From south The coast is very broken, with high rocky cliffs backed by even higher tree-covered hills (*see plan on page 150*). Cabo Vermey (Vermell) is high (252m sloping down to 185m) and has a rounded profile of reddish rocks with two towers on the top. Puerto de Cala Ratjada lies 4·4M north of this headland and about 0·8M west of Cabo de Pera (Fl(2+3)20s76m16M, white tower on white building with dark corners and red roof 21m).

From north and west Cross the wide Bahía de Alcudia towards Cabo Farrutx, a high sloping promontory (unlit, though there are red lights on Puig Tudosa 1·5M to the south). Follow the coast southeast to Cabo del Freu – a low, narrow, pointed promontory, also unlit – passing en route Farayó de Aubarca islet, 23m high and about 750m offshore. There is good water on either side of the island.

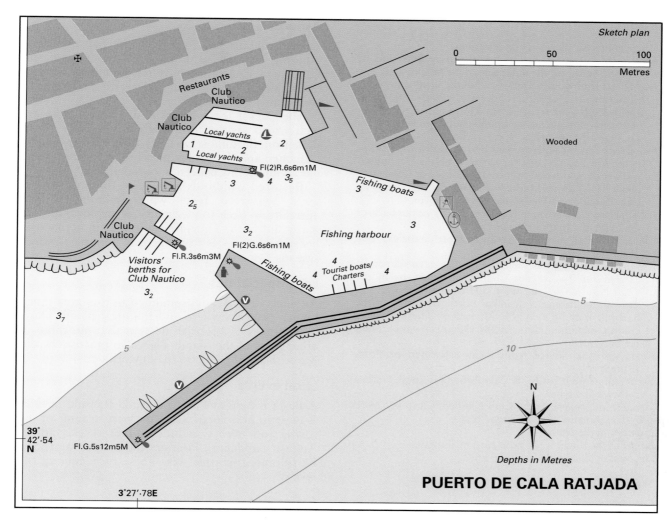

PUERTO DE CALA RATJADA

Cabo de Pera 2·1M south-southeast of Cabo del Freu is easily identified by its lighthouse. Follow its steep rocky cliffs southwest to round Islote d'es Farayó off Punta del Gat, after which the harbour will be seen 0·7M to the west.

Anchorage in the approach

Anchor 500m southwest of the end of the breakwater in 5m over sand, open from northeast through east to south. Closer to the entrance the bottom is of rock, stone and weed and unsuitable for anchoring. There are a few sand patches opposite the breakwater head in 2–5m.

Note that anchoring is strictly prohibited in Cala Gat, just to the E of Cala Ratjada.

Entrance

Round the end of the breakwater at 30–40m to seek a berth on the inner side. There is a 3kn speed limit. A rock carrying less than 3m has been reported 90–100m south-southwest of the breakwater head.

Sea levels

The level of the water increases by about 0·5m with onshore winds and decreases by the same amount with offshore winds.

Berthing

Ports IB moorings

Changes in recent years have increased the visitors' berths considerably (*See plan*). Ports IB now have the concession for the entire N side of the breakwater from the entry light to the NE end of the harbour where small fishing boats lie. The outer harbour may seem somewhat exposed, but even in strong winds it is actually quite comfortable despite some surging. Lines are tailed to the quay and water and electricity are available. As with all Ports IB moorings, electricity and water are included in the mooring fee. There is a café on the quay alongside the visitors' berths which sometimes plays loud music which might be annoying to some.

Club Náutico moorings

On the N side are the Club Náutico moorings, almost entirely given over to small motor boats. The small number of moorings on the N side of the outer harbour are Club Náutico transit/visitor berths.

Facilities

Water Points on all quays and pontoons.

Electricity 220v AC points on the pontoons and at visitors' berths on the inner side of the breakwater.

Fuel Diesel from pumps at the head of the breakwater spur (fishermen's quay). Hours are 0900–1300 and 1600–1900 year round from Monday to Friday, but not open on weekends and public holidays. Petrol from a garage ¾M northwest of the harbour.

Provisions Several supermarkets and specialist food shops in the town and a large supermarket about 15 minutes' walk at the south end of town, with more in Capdepera about 1½M away. Markets are Saturdays in Puerto de Cala Ratjada and Wednesdays in Capdepera.

Ice Supermarkets or there is an ice factory at the back of the town just south of the *plaza*.

Chandlery Small chandlery/hardware store on the east side of the harbour.

Repairs No boatyard as such, though basic repairs can be carried out. Two cranes 10 and 7·5-tonnes are by the Club Náutico on the west side of the harbour. The slipway for fishing craft in the northeast corner of the harbour may be available for yachts. There are two cradles, maximum draught 2m. Other slipways around the harbour.

Engineers Ask advice from local fishermen or Ports IB staff.

Yacht club Club Náutico de Cala Ratjada is small, but has showers and a bar.

Showers and toilets At the Club Náutico. Clean but basic public showers by the visitors' berths.

Laundry In the town.

Banks In the town, with credit card facilities.

Hospital/medical services In the town.

Transport

Car hire/taxis In the town.

Buses Bus service to Capdepera and onward to Palma, etc.

Ferries Tourist ferries make daily trips to a number of popular beaches in the area.

Ashore

Little of the original town has survived the tourist building boom, but both Artá 5M inland and Capdepera 1½M away have retained many of their old buildings, both including interesting castles with particularly good views.

The Cuevas (caves) de Artá at Cabo Vermey are well worth visiting (although this is more easily done from the almost adjacent anchorage at Cala de Cañamel) and the garden museum of Sa Torre Cega has an interesting collection of sculptures.

Restored windmills abound in the area – most were converted from water pumps for the agricultural area to electricity generators, though many did both. They are no longer in active use, because of supplies from the grid and mains water systems.

Local specialities

An enclave of Moors remained in this area much longer than elsewhere and the local people show more traces of Moorish descent than do those in other parts of the island. They also practise the old Moorish art of palmetto (palm work).

Local events

A fiesta is held at Puerto de Cala Ratjada in mid-August in honour of San Roc, patron saint of the town, and events include sailing races. On 24 August Capdepera honours its patron saint, San Bartolomé, this time with horse races among the revelry.

Eating out

Many eating houses of all descriptions, with the harbour surrounded by pleasant cafés and restaurants. Cala Ratjada is a fishing port and there are many restaurants specialising in fish and shellfish.

Ratjada breakwater looking E   *Graham Hutt*

Anchorages between Puerto de Cala Ratjada and Puerto de Costa de los Pinos

⚓ Cala Moll

39°42'·3N 03°27'·5E

A wide bay off a popular sandy beach ¾M southwest of Puerto de Cala Ratjada (*see page 150*), Cala Moll has low rocky sides and is largely surrounded by buildings, a landmark being a large square hotel building which appears to be constructed mainly of glass. Anchor about 150m off the beach in 2·5m over sand, open to the east quadrant. The small Islote Forana lies to the southeast and should be left on the landward side.

⚓ Cala de Sa Font (Cala de San Geroni)

39°40'·9N 03°27'·5E

A sizeable, attractive *cala* with a fine sandy beach and some apartment buildings and huge hotel nearby. Anchor off the beach in 4-6m over sand and stone, open to the east quadrant. Some facilities ashore, otherwise Capdepera is less than two miles by road.

⚓ Cala de Cañamel

39°39'·4N 03°26'·6E

Rather an open anchorage in a bay just south and west of Cabo Vermey (Vermell), a reddish cape with little vegetation, and the famous Cuevas (caves) de Artá (*see Ashore page 156*). The sandy beach at the head of the *cala* is backed by hotels and apartments, but a good deal of greenery has been retained. A river flows through the beach on its northern side. Anchor in 3–5m of very clear water over sand, open to the east, southeast and south. The bottom shelves gradually and in heavy weather waves break some distance offshore. There are some shops in the tourist

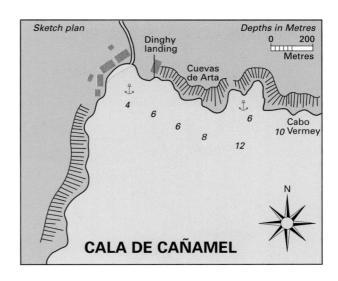

Sketch plan — Depths in Metres — 0 200 Metres — Dinghy landing — Cuevas de Arta — Cabo Vermey — N

CALA DE CAÑAMEL

complex, including a small supermarket. Almost in the northwest corner of the bay there is a good restaurant which has a small dinghy landing jetty marked by a white post; very useful not just for accessing the restaurant but also for provisioning or a visit to the caves. There is much noise from local property development as the hillside is excavated prior to construction, but this would probably not be permitted in the main summer season.

A second anchorage, with less swell but having room for only two boats, will be found in a very small *cala* halfway to Cabo Vermey.

Puerto de Costa de los Pinos

39°38'·1N 03°24'·7E

A jetty rather than a port, but with a pleasant anchorage with easy access ashore nearby.

The jetty and anchorage

A very small, shallow facility that is not much more than a broad quay with a short protective extension. Built as an amenity for guests of the four-star Hotel Golf Punta Rotja, the 'Puerto' offers little shelter and can take only the smallest craft. The bay is often used for water-skiing, etc. but it nevertheless makes a pleasant anchorage.

Pilotage

Approach

The jetty and anchorage lie close west of Cabo d'es Piná (Cabo d'es Ratx), itself some 1·3M south of Cabo Vermey and 3·6M north of Punta de Amer. The square, white hotel overlooking the harbour will be seen for many miles.

Anchorage in the approach

Anchor in 2–4m over sand and weed west of the molehead, open to south and west. The bottom is uneven with some rocks and a careful watch on the depth sounder will be necessary.

Cala de Cañamel looking west, with Cabo Vermey dominating right of picture

III. MALLORCA

PUERTO DE COSTA DE LOS PINOS
Sketch plan

Supermarket

Cafe

Hotel (conspic)

0₅

2

2

2

1

2

1₅

Dique

3

2

N

0   50

Metres

Depths in Metres

Entrance

Approach the northwest corner of the quay, sounding continuously.

Berthing

Secure as space permits. There are a few projecting underwater rocks. Officials may appear, otherwise visit the hotel reception desk.

Facilities

Water Tap on the quay.
Provisions Supermarket behind the hotel.
Repairs Two small dinghy slipways.

Eating out

A choice of restaurants and cafés.

Anchorages off Puerto de Costa de los Pinos

The long stretch of sandy beaches and small *calas* between Puerto de Costa de los Pinos and Puerto de Cala Bona make good anchorages in settled weather. Port Vey (Vell) and Port Nou are marked on the plan at the beginning of this section on page 150. Far from being ports, these are pleasant anchorages off the open beach. Anchor in 3–4m over sand and weed. A few houses, hotels, shops and cafés line the road behind the beach.

Puerto de Cala Bona

39°36'·9N 03°23'·7E

A rather pleasant small but safe harbour with the recent addition of diesel and petrol pumps, and 20 berths allocated for visitors, with maximum boat length of 12m.

Communications
VHF Ch 08
Puerto de Cala Bona ① 971 58 62 56 / 629 475 789
port.calabona@portsib.es
www. portsib.es

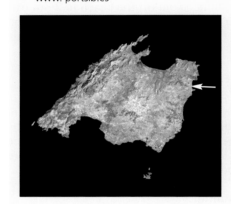

The harbour

Originally a small fishing harbour with an even tinier inner harbour, Puerto de Cala Bona has been improved by the construction of two outer breakwaters. Even so it is not large, with a total of 192 berths. The approach is straightforward but should not be attempted in strong onshore winds. The harbour is home to a number of glass-bottomed and other tourist excursion boats.

Pilotage

Approach

From south Punta de Amer is a low, rocky-cliffed promontory with a small castle on its summit. The wide Bahía de Artá stretches northwards from it as far as Cabo d'es Piná and the harbour is located near its centre, at the northern end of the heavily built up area.

From north The high, rounded profile of Cabo Vermey, which has reddish rocks, is recognisable as is the dark-cliffed Cabo d'es Piná. South of Cabo d'es Piná lies the wide Bahía de Artá, with Puerto de Cala Bona near its centre, at the northern end of the heavily built up area. *See plan on page 150.*

Anchorage in the approach

There are sand patches off the harbour entrance in 5m+, but it would be distinctly exposed.

Entrance

There are a number of rocky breakwaters close south of the harbour, established to retain sand on

Puerto de Cala Bona: still a small harbour, despite the extensions and rather shallow, especially near fuel dock

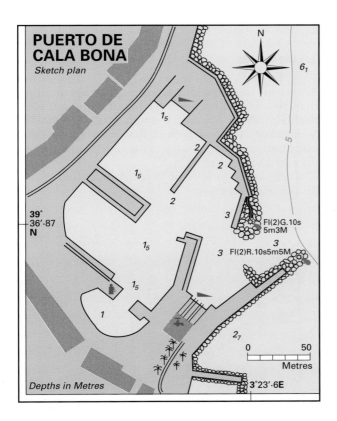

Berthing

Secure bow or stern-to on the inside of the south breakwater. This position is exposed to wind or swell from east or northeast but well protected from the southeast quadrant.

Facilities

Water In containers from the fishermen's co-operative near the old inner harbour, or from one of the bars or restaurants.

Electricity A few 220v AC points around the harbour.

Fuel Diesel and petrol are available but depth at the fuel dock is only 1·5m. Open 0900–1300 and 1430–1630 each day in summer but only Wednesdays and Saturdays in winter. ☎ 650 634451.

Provisions Shops and supermarkets to the south of the harbour, more in Son Servera, two miles inland. Friday market in Son Servera.

Ice From the fishermen's co-operative or from one of the bars or restaurants.

Repairs Three slipways around the harbour, but little more than dinghy size.

WiFi In summer only.

Banks To the south of the harbour and in Son Servera.

Hospital/medical services In Son Servera.

Transport

Car hire/taxis In the town.

Buses Bus service to Son Servera and beyond.

Eating out

Many eating places around the harbour.

the beaches, so ensure that the harbour entrance is identified beyond all doubt. Enter at slow speed on a southwesterly course. Once inside there is little room to manoeuvre and parts are shallow. Depths are generally about 1·9m, but the inner parts are even more shallow.

III. MALLORCA

Cala Morlanda viewed from northeast across
Punta de Sa Roca

Anchorages from Puerto de Cala Bona to Porto Cristo

Cala Millor

39°36'·3N 03°23'·4E

The large holiday development of Cala Millor lies half a mile south of Cala Bona, marked by a small lit pier. It is not recommended to moor there but is included here in case the light confuses passing yachtsmen.

⚓ Arenal de Son Servera

39°35'·6N 03°23'·3E

A long sand and stone beach immediately north of Punta de Amer. Anchor in 5m over sand and rock near the southern end of the Cala Millor holiday development. There are numerous restaurants and cafés ashore plus a few shops.

⚓ Playa de Sa Coma

39°34'·4N 03°22'·8E

A wide and often crowded sandy beach close south of Punta de Amer. Anchor in 2–4m over sand and some weed, with some rock and weed further out, open to southwest–south–east.

⚓ Cala Moreya

39°34'·1N 03°22'·6E

A sandy bay close south of Playa de Sa Coma but surrounded by the much denser development of the S'Illot holiday town. Anchor in 2–4m over sand. Open to the east sector with best protection in the lee of a small island.

⚓ Cala Morlanda

39°33'·3N 03°22'·3E

A double *cala* at the south end of the S'Illot holiday development, with rocky sides and two small stony beaches. Anchor in 4–5m over sand and weed. Open to the east. Rather bleak and unattractive.

⚓ Cala Petite

39°32'·8N 03°21'·4E

A narrow, dog-legged *cala* with space for no more than two boats, enclosed by rocky cliffs and with nothing ashore beyond a rough track. Anchor in 3–6m over sand and rock in the centre of the *cala*, using two anchors to restrict swinging room; open to the east and southeast.

There are a number of isolated rocks awash just off the small beach.

Cala Petite, bottom right-hand, looking southwest to Porto Cristo

Porto Cristo
(Port de Manacor)

39°32'·1N 03°20'·4E

A very sheltered harbour with a total of 500 berths up to 16m, tucked well into the Cap de Estoy river

Communications
Ports IB Porto Cristo VHF Ch 08
  ☎ 971 82 04 19
  www.portsib.es
Club Náutico de Porto Cristo VHF Ch 09
  ☎ 971 82 12 53
  info@cnportocristo.com
  www.cnportocristo.com

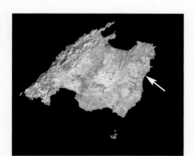

The harbour

A long and well-sheltered inlet with several doglegs, which has managed to retain a good deal of its charm despite the growth of the town. Approach and entrance present no problems other than in strong onshore winds. There are 497 berths, with facilities on both banks of the river at a *club náutico* on the southeast side, and the public quays on the northwest side, which are now managed by Ports IB. The harbour is often full in summer and bookings must be made in advance at www.portsib.es. or with the Club Náutico who generally accept bookings for the same day only.

Pilotage

Approach

From south The coast from Porto Colom is of low rocky cliffs which are broken by many *calas*, all very similar and difficult to identify. However, at Porto Cristo the conspicuous lighthouse tower on Cabo del Morro, with black and white vertical stripes is easily seen (*see plan on page 162*).

From north Cross the wide Bahía de Artá which terminates on its south side at Punta de Amer, which is relatively low but prominent. Porto Cristo lies 4M to the southwest and can be identified as above.

III. MALLORCA

Porto Cristo: a very safe and sheltered harbour. Fuel dock at lower right

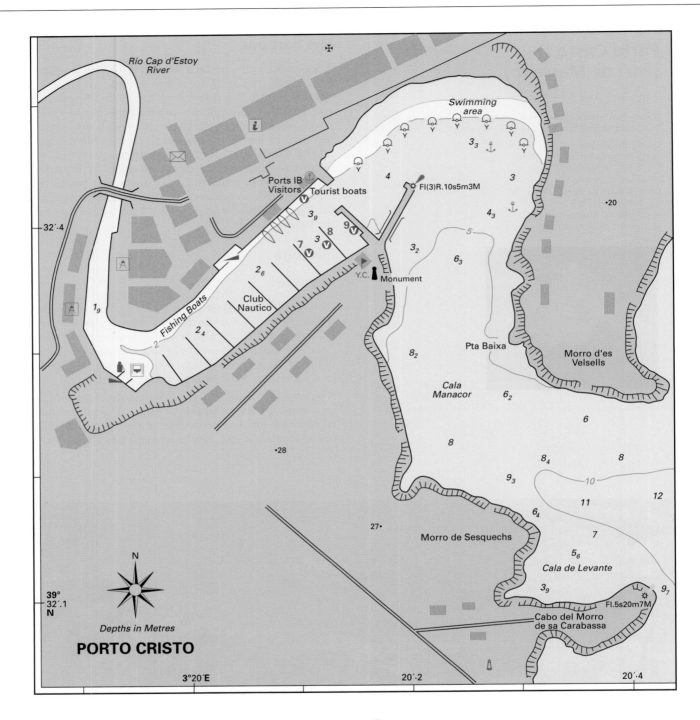

PORTO CRISTO

Depths in Metres

39°
32'.1
N

Anchorage in the approach

It is possible to anchor under the cliffs on the east side of the channel opposite the monument, or further north outside a line of yellow buoys marking the bathing area, in 3–5m over sand, mud and weed. Both spots can be rolly, due either to swell or to wash from passing tourist or other power boats, and may be affected by a circular current in low pressure weather. Anchoring in the harbour itself is not permitted.

Entrance

The entrance channel is both wide and deep. Keep to the centre or slightly to starboard before rounding the northeast mole into the yacht harbour (this mole is not completely solid but includes a bridge near the shore). Strong currents can occur when the river Cap d'Estoy is in spate (which is not often) and in heavy weather a strong surge may build up. In pleasant conditions it is not unusual to find swimmers and snorkellers virtually under the bow. A series of yellow buoys with a connecting line lies some way off the bathing beach. There is a 3kn speed limit.

Porto Cristo distinctive entry light on Cabo del Morro
Graham Hutt

Berthing

The Club Náutico has several pontoons which provide the berthing on the SE side of the river, whilst Ports IB has the concession for the NW side. The first 50m from the short mole at the entrance on the NW side is given over to the large tourist catamarans. These make a fast entry and turn quickly, so a good lookout is needed on entry and departure. Fishing boats occupy the moorings from about half way down the public quay, on the NW side. The space between is for Ports IB transit visitors. The usual lazy lines run out from the quay. These should be booked on the Ports IB website in advance during summer www.portsib.es. Note that big swells from the easterly quadrant do find their way round the dog-legs of the harbour making the berths somewhat rolly.

The Ports IB office is manned from 8am to 9pm and very helpful staff will assist in identifying your berth and take lines.

The Club Náutico reserves the three pontoons furthest to the northeast (numbered 7, 8, 9) for visiting yachts. Moorings with lazy lines are provided and a berthing master is usually on duty. However, the marina is often full in summer, so it is advisable to call on VHF Ch 09 to check whether a berth will be available, even though they cannot be reserved before the day of arrival. The visitors' pontoons have 3m or more at the outer ends, shoaling towards the quay.

Note The Club Náutico moorings are on the opposite side of the river to the town, making for a long walk around and across a low bridge. Ports IB moorings are located within minutes of the town centre and are half the price.

Facilities

Water Water points on the quay and pontoons and at the Club Náutico.

Electricity 220v AC points on quays and pontoons.

Fuel Diesel and petrol from pumps next to the travel-lift.

Provisions Shops of all types in the town including several small supermarkets, but a long walk round from the Club Náutico yacht pontoons (alternatively use the dinghy). A fairly large and well-stocked Hiper Centro supermarket is about 10 minutes' walk up the hill from the Ports IB dock. There are produce and fish markets on Sundays in Porto Cristo and Mondays in Manacor six miles inland.

Ice From the Club Náutico bar and supermarkets.

Chandlery Two well-stocked chandleries either side of the channel north of the boatyard.

Repairs A 50-tonne travel-lift and 12·5-tonne crane in the boatyard. Small slipways on both sides of the harbour. Jaume Vermell Náutica boatyard ☎ 971 82 20 22 at the southwest end of the harbour has most facilities including a small but very protected winter lay-up area.

Engineers At the boatyard. Marina Marbella Balear SA ☎ 971 82 05 90 is official service agent for Mercury/MerCruiser and Volvo Penta.

Yacht club Club Náutico de Porto Cristo has a smart clubhouse with bar, restaurant, swimming pool, terrace, showers, etc.

Showers Showers for Club Náutico visitors at the clubhouse. Showers and toilet facilities for Ports IB moorings are close to the Ports IB office below the terrace restaurants.

Launderettes In the town.

Banks Several in the town, mostly with credit card facilities.

Hospital/medical services Medical services in Porto Cristo, hospital in Manacor six miles inland.

Transport

Car hire/taxis In the town.

Buses Regular service to Manacor, Palma, etc.

Ashore

The area is famous for the caves discovered by MEA Martel in 1896, and for an unsuccessful landing by Communist forces during the civil war. There are two monuments to this landing, one near the root of the northeast mole and another at the northwest end of the town. In earlier times it was also favoured by the kings of Mallorca for their summer holidays.

The spectacular Cuevas del Drach (Caves of the Dragon) and Cuevas del Hams south of the town should not be missed (open 1000 to 1700). There is also a wildlife park nearby. Spectacular views of the coast can be seen from the tower southwest of the lighthouse.

Local event

The Fiesta de la Virgen del Carmen, with waterborne processions, is held on 16 July.

Eating out

A large number of restaurants, cafés and bars.

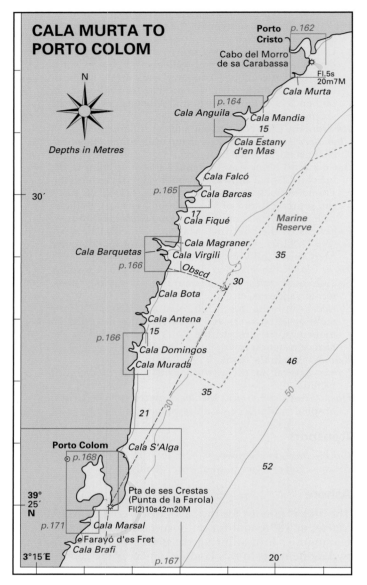

CALA MURTA TO PORTO COLOM

N

Depths in Metres

Porto Cristo *p. 162*
Cabo del Morro de sa Carabassa
Fl.5s 20m7M
Cala Murta

p. 164
Cala Anguila   Cala Mandia
15
Cala Estany d'en Mas

Cala Falcó
p. 165   Cala Barcas
17
Cala Fiqué

Cala Magraner
Cala Barquetas   Cala Virgili
p. 166   Obscd
30

Marine Reserve
35

Cala Bota

Cala Antena
15
p. 166
Cala Domingos
Cala Murada
46
35
21

Porto Colom   *p. 168*
Cala S'Alga
52

39° 25' N

Pta de ses Crestas (Punta de la Farola)
Fl(2)10s42m20M

p. 171   Cala Marsal
Farayó d'es Fret
Cala Brafi

3°15'E   *p. 167*   20'

30'

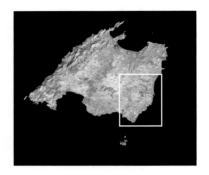

Anchorages between Porto Cristo and Porto Colom

⚓ Cala Murta
39°31'·9N 03°20'·1E

A narrow *cala* between steep rocky sides, with some new buildings to the north. Anchor in 3–5m over sand, open to the east and southeast.

⚓ Calas Anguila and Mandia
39°31'·2N 03°19'·2E

A small double *cala* with sandy beaches. A holiday development, Porto Cristo Nova, lies on the north side but is not intrusive, and there are others to the south. Anchor off either beach in 3–5m over sand, open to the east and swell from the entire east semicircle. Nice beaches and several nearby restaurants and cafés. A sea cave at the northern point of the entrance exhibits stalactites.

Calas Mandia (right), Anguila (centre), and Cala Estany d'en Mas (left)

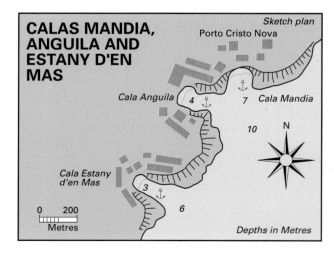

CALAS MANDIA, ANGUILA AND ESTANY D'EN MAS

Sketch plan

Porto Cristo Nova

Cala Anguila   4   7   Cala Mandia
10   N

Cala Estany d'en Mas
3
6

0   200
Metres

Depths in Metres

⚓ Cala Estany d'en Mas
39°30'·9N 03°18'·9E

A small *cala* with rocky sides, the northern one almost completely covered with low-rise buildings. Anchor in 2–4m over sand off the crowded beach, open to the east and southeast. Beach bars and *chiringuito* (summer beach restaurant). A nice anchorage, but of course affected by swell from anywhere east.

⚓ Cala Falcó
39°30'·2N 03°18'·1E

A very open, totally deserted *cala*, with a track to the Cuevas del Pirata about a mile inland. Anchor in 2–5m over sand off the small stony beach, open to the eastern quadrant.

⚓ Cala Barcas
39°29'·9N 03°18'·1E

A wide, square, undeveloped *cala*, the two sandy beaches at its head separated by a stretch of dark rocks. There is a shallow rocky outcrop projecting from the cliffs to the north, which have many sea caves. One cave on the north side has some sizeable stalactites. Keep to the centre of the entrance to anchor off either beach in 3–5m over sand, open to the northeast and east. There is only a very rough track ashore, but the *cala* is popular with tourist boats and can become crowded in summer. Nevertheless it is one of the best anchorages on the east coast.

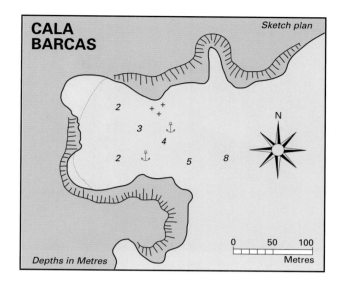

⚓ Cala Fiqué (Cala Serrat)
39°29'·6N 03°17'·7E

More accurately three very small, deserted *calas*, perhaps better described as indentations, with rocky headlands between. Anchor in 3–5m over sand, open to the eastern quadrant.

III. MALLORCA

Cala Barcas: there are several nearby *calas* with good anchoring

Calas Magraner (right), Barquetas and Virgili, (left) viewed from southeast

⚓ Cala Bota

39°28'·4N 03°17'·3E

A small undeveloped *cala*, its mouth partially obstructed by a breaking rocky shoal running out from the southern cliffs, Cala Bota should be approached with extreme care. Enter from the northeast with a lookout on the bow, to anchor in 4–5m over sand and weed, open to the east and southeast.

⚓ Cala Antena

39°28'N 03°17'E

A small *cala* between high rocky sides, with some sizeable sea caves and overlooked by a high-rise tourist complex to the south. Anchor off the beach in 3–5m over sand, open to the eastern quadrant.

⚓ Calas Magraner, Barquetas and Virgili

39°29'N 03°17'·6E

A triple *cala*, with sandy beaches, offering good protection near their heads, although an easterly swell reaches all parts. Anchor in 2–4m over sand or just south of the projecting headland in Cala Virgili, in 3·5m. Other than a small grey hut on the northern headland there are no buildings, and the development shown behind the *calas* on several local maps does not appear to have taken place. Consequently Magraner and Barquetas are deserted and rather lovely. In contrast Virgili appears rather barren. Tracks ashore lead inland which is deserted apart from goats foraging, and cormorants can be seen roosting. No facilities.

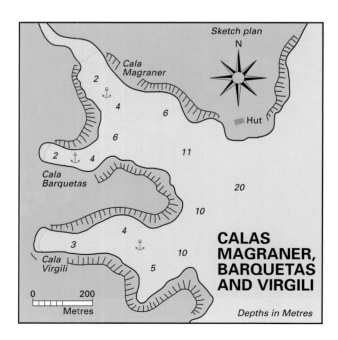

CALAS MAGRANER, BARQUETAS AND VIRGILI

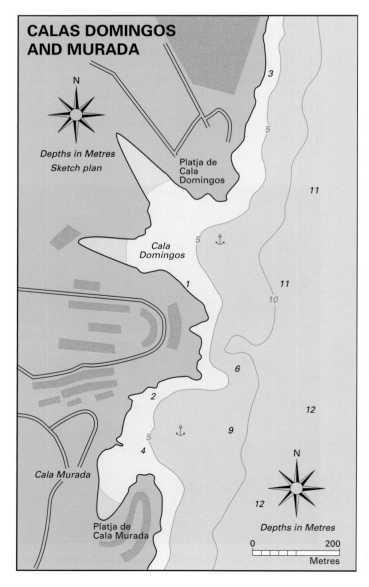

CALAS DOMINGOS AND MURADA

⚓ Cala Domingos

39°27'·4N 03°16'·8E

A pleasant, double *cala* with two fine (and frequently crowded) sandy beaches, inevitably surrounded by tourist development. Anchor in 3–5m over sand, open through northeast–east–southeast. There are several large hotels close north, and the southern arm is backed by a restaurant with a distinctive conical roof.

⚓ Cala Murada

39°27'·2N 03°16'·8E

A small, curved *cala* with a sandy beach at its southern end and dense housing on the point: once again, the beach is often crowded. Anchor off the beach in 3–5m over sand and weed, open to the northeast and east. Swell tends to follow the curve of the *cala*. Protection is best close to the beach, where there is a bar/restaurant.

⚓ Cala S'Alga

39°25'·7N 03°16'·7E

A large, and rather bleak open *cala* with rocky sides and a very small stony beach, one mile north of the entrance to Porto Colom. The best spot to anchor is tucked in behind the point to port on entry, in 3–5m over sand and weed, open to northeast and east. There is a road across the headland to Porto Colom where supplies are available.

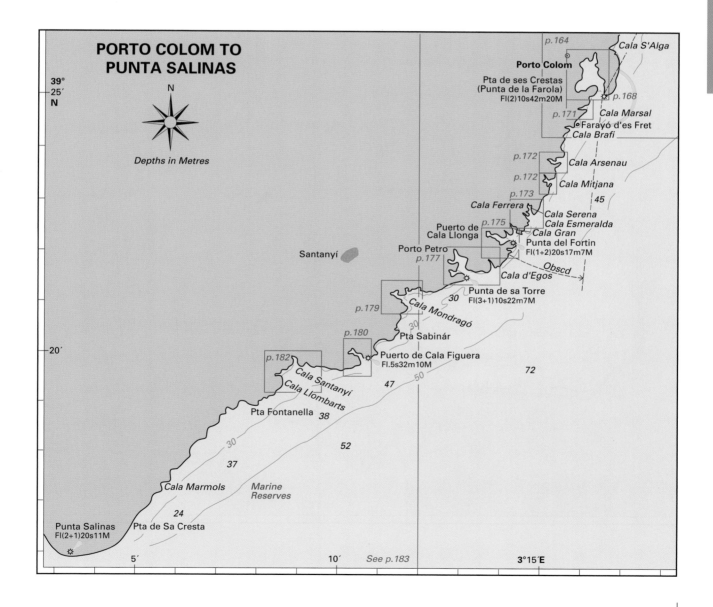

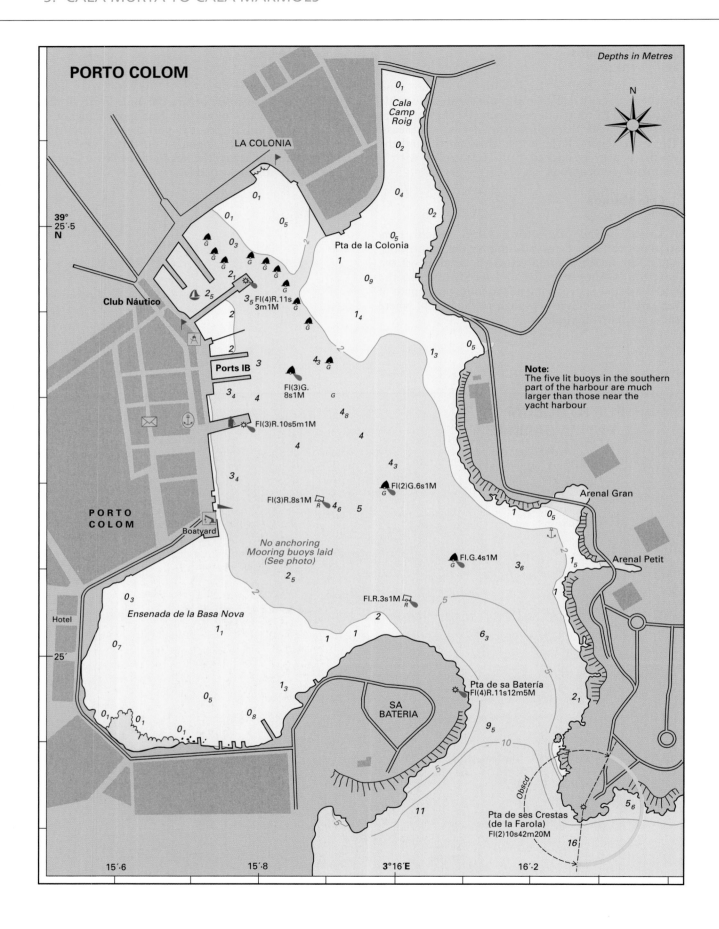

PORTO COLOM

Depths in Metres

Cala Camp Roig

LA COLONIA

39° 25′·5 N

Club Náutico

Pta de la Colonia

Ports IB

Fl(4)R.11s 3m1M

Fl(3)G. 8s1M

Fl(3)R.10s5m1M

Note:
The five lit buoys in the southern part of the harbour are much larger than those near the yacht harbour

Fl(2)G.6s1M

Arenal Gran

Fl(3)R.8s1M

Boatyard

PORTO COLOM

Arenal Petit

Fl.G.4s1M

No anchoring Mooring buoys laid (See photo)

Fl.R.3s1M

Hotel

25′

Ensenada de la Basa Nova

SA BATERIA

Pta de sa Batería
Fl(4)R.11s12m5M

Obscd

Pta de ses Crestas
(de la Farola)
Fl(2)10s42m20M

15′·6   15′·8   3°16′E   16′·2

Porto Colom

39°24'·8N 03°16'·1E

A large natural and well protected harbour with berthing for 250 yachts and many mooring buoys. One of the most pleasant places to visit in Mallorca

Communications
Ports IB VHF Ch 08
  www.portsib.es
Club Náutico de Porto Colom VHF Ch 09 for both marina berths and mooring buoys
  ☏ 971 82 46 58 Mobile 681 60 79 21
  administracio@cnportocolom.com
  www.cnportocolom.com

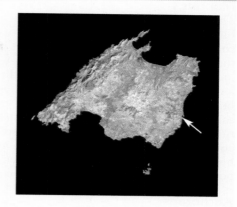

The harbour and anchorage

A large natural harbour with moorings for over 200 vessels in the Club Náutico de Porto Colom, operating in the northwest corner of the harbour. With many more mooring buoys laid south of the port, anchoring is now technically prohibited, though many yachts do still anchor away from the port as described below. The port is well protected with a deep and narrow entrance, though much of the interior is relatively shallow, under 2·5m. Although there is a low-rise housing development around the harbour, the area is surprisingly undeveloped.

Ports IB has the concession for the floating pontoon moorings south of Club Náutico de Porto Colom, whilst the Club Náutico, as well as the marina, now has control of all the buoys in the harbour. Their RIB is always around to collect payment, and bookings should be made for buoys in advance in high season. Contact the office on VHF Ch 09 on entry or via the communications info above. *See page 20 for Ports IB booking information.*

Pilotage

Approach

From south The coast from Porto Petro and beyond is of low rocky cliffs broken by many *calas*. The distinctive lighthouse on Punta de ses Crestas (white round tower with three black bands on white building with red roof 25m) on the east side of the entrance can be seen from many miles off, though if sailing close inshore the light itself will be obscured when bearing more than 006°. There is a small islet, Farayó d'es Fret (11m), 0·8M southwest of the entrance.

From north The coast from Porto Cristo also consists of low rocky cliffs broken by many *calas*. When very close inshore the lighthouse on Punta de ses Crestas (*see opposite*) is obscured when bearing less than 207° but is otherwise clearly seen from many miles. The entrance itself does not open until around this headland.

Entrance and buoyed channel

The entrance is deep and unobstructed, other than a small rocky islet against the eastern shore. As the harbour widens, follow the buoyed channel to remain in depths of 4–5m. Unlit fish cages used to be anchored to the east of the channel, but have not been in place for some years.

Much of the harbour is shallow and all manoeuvring outside the buoyed channel should be done with one eye on the depth-sounder, particularly since some of the banks appear to be unusually steep-sided.

Berthing

Secure bow or stern-to the south side of the yacht marina south mole, or to one of the two Ports IB pontoons close south. The former has no more than 2·2m at its outer end and all three shoal towards the shore. Lazy lines are tailed to both mole and pontoons. None of these berths are tenable in very strong southeast winds. Even in light east or southeast winds, with a moderate swell at sea, the outside marina berth is subject to considerable surge and noise from the swell hitting the mole. Another option is on the fuel jetty, which is close to the harbour office. The Club Náutico marina is expensive; a 13m yacht was charged €70 per night in early November 2016. The Ports IB facility is very much cheaper.

Porto Colom entrance with distinctive lighthouse on Punta de ses Crestas *Graham Hutt*

III. MALLORCA

Moorings

The area south of the fuel jetty is now completely full with moorings leaving no space to anchor. The concession for all moorings in the port was given to the Club Náutico in 2013. Charges for their use include showers and water from the jetty tap, located close to the Ports IB office. Water is reported brackish in summer. A RIB patrols the moorings and can be contacted on VHF Ch 09. Usually the RIB turns up to collect payment even before mooring is completed. Prior booking for both marina and buoys is usually essential in summer. A floating pontoon just S of the fuel quay has been installed.

Anchorages

It is now almost impossible to anchor anywhere in the harbour as it is laid to buoys – with a long waiting list of local residents hoping for a private buoy. One remaining possibility is Arenal Gran and Arenal Petit, on the E side of the entrance. These areas are affected by the S sector winds and fast moving fishing boats. Some yachts have been observed anchoring on the E side of the harbour opposite the Ports IB pontoon, but are usually quickly informed that it is illegal to anchor there. Out of season, yachts have been observed at anchor immediately to port on entering Porto Colom, between the first red port-hand buoy and the mooring buoys controlled by the Club Náutico.

Facilities

Water At Club Náutico moorings on pontoons. Ports IB moorings have access to water on the pontoon and at the fuel berth (charged for). The quality is very poor in summer and not considered potable.

Electricity 220v AC points on yacht harbour mole and pontoons, and on the public pontoons.

Fuel Diesel from pumps on the south side of the west mole (claimed to have 4m alongside). Petrol from a garage near the root of the mole.

Provisions Many shops in town, including an Eroski supermarket and a recently opened delicatessen with a range of prepared meals, on the sea front. Two supermarkets near Ensenada de la Basa Nova, S of the yacht pontoons.

WiFi Club Náutico marina claims to have WiFi but it seems as unreliable as most other marinas.

Ice From the Club Náutico and the filling station above.

Chandlery Near the Club Náutico.

Repairs A boatyard on the corner north of the Ensenada de la Basa Nova capable of straightforward work in wood or GRP. Also engine repairs. 10-tonne and 5-tonne mobile cranes at the boatyard. A 1·5m slipway at the boatyard and several others around the harbour.

Yacht clubs Club Náutico de Porto Colom at the northwest corner of the harbour has a bar, lounge, terrace and showers. Club Náutico de Pescadores is northeast of the harbour.

Showers By the Port Authority office just north of the west mole, and at the Club Náutico.

Entrance to Porto Colom. Note buoys laid left of port on entry. More have been added on the E side. Anchoring is now prohibited except in the bay on the E side, close to the entrance

Porto Colom looking northwest. Mooring buoys, Club Náutico top and two Ports IB pontoons centre. The wide fuelling jetty left. Note fish farm not in place in 2017

Post office A mobile post office visits a site near the Ports IB office (*see plan*) between 1150 and 1220, weekdays only. Times appear to change periodically.

Hospital/medical services Medical services in the town, hospital in Manacor 11M away.

Transport

Car hire/taxis In the town. A list is displayed in the marinero's cabin at the entrance to the Club Náutico Marina.

Buses Bus service to Felanitx, Manacor and beyond. There is a bus stop at the root of the fuel dock mole.

Ashore

The Monastery of San Salvador four miles inland is interesting and has a fine view, as has the ruined Castillo de San Tueri three miles inland.

Local event

A fiesta in honour of the Virgen del Carmen is held on 16 July, when the local fishing boats parade around the harbour dressed overall.

Eating out

The usual range of restaurants, cafés and bars.

Anchorages from Porto Colom to Puerto de Cala Llonga

⚓ Cala Marsal and Caló d'en Manuell

39°24'·6N 03°15'·8E

A fairly large double *cala* with rocky cliffs close south of Porto Colom (*see plan on page 167 and below*). Cala Marsal has a sandy beach at its head. Anchor in 3–5m over sand off the beach, open to northeast and east, or tuck into Caló d'en Manuell which has a sand and rock bottom, open to the east and southeast. Both *calas* are surrounded by apartment blocks and hotels.

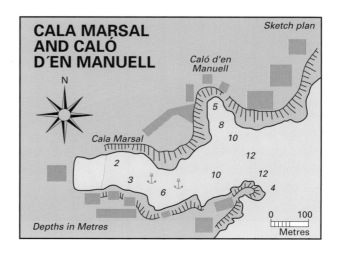

⚓ Cala Brafi

39°24'·2N 03°15'·5E

A small, narrow, dog-legged *cala* between rocky cliffs, with a stone boathouse at its head but no other buildings nearby. Anchor in 3–4m over sand, stone and weed. The small islet of Farayó d'es Fret lies close northeast of the *cala*. It consists of a flat shelf of rock just above sea-level, with a narrow, vertical-sided 11m high rock on the top. In time erosion will probably displace this and convert it into a dangerous breaking ledge.

⚓ Cala Arsenau (Cala sa Nau or Cala de Ras)

39°23'·6N 03°15'·2E

A narrow, angled *cala* offering relatively good protection, particularly near its head where there is a sandy beach, boathouse and café. There are

breaking rocks close to the headland north of the *cala*. Anchor in 3–6m over sand and weed, open to the east and (depending on position) northeast. One option is to take a sternline ashore to the northern bank behind the central promontory. In settled conditions Cala Arsenau makes a feasible overnight anchorage.

⚓ Cala Mitjana

39°23'·2N 03°15'E

A very attractive triple *cala* with two sandy beaches and room for at least ten yachts. A tall white flagstaff (often with flags) stands on the north side

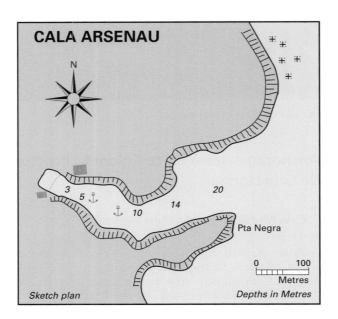

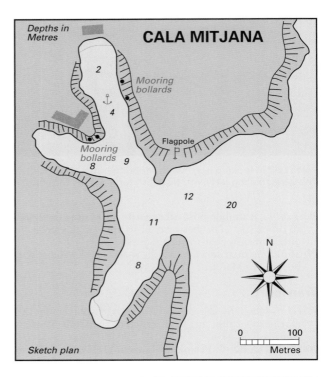

Cala Arsenau viewed from southeast

Cala Mitjana (one of the most attractive anchorages in the islands) looking north with Cala Arsenau beyond

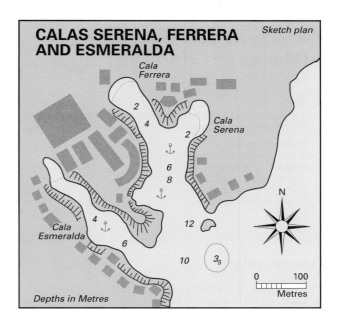

of the entrance and a pink-roofed building occupies the central headland. Swing wide of the rocky promontory below the flagstaff – a blind turn.

Anchor in 5m or less over sand and weed in the northern arm, setting a second anchor to limit swinging room, or take a line to the bollards set into the cliffs (*see plan*). This spot offers all-round protection.

Looking northwest into Cala Esmeralda (left) with Cala Ferrera (centre) and Cala Serena (right)

⚓ Calas Serena, Ferrera and Esmeralda

39°22'·5N 03°14'·6E

A triple *cala* with sandy beaches surrounded by hotels and apartments, with a prominent island off the northern headland and breaking rocks to the south. There is an isolated shoal patch carrying 3·5–4m in the centre of the entrance. Cala Serena appears to be permanently and totally buoyed-off.

Anchor in 3–6m over sand and weed, open (depending on position) to southeast and either east or south. Swell from anywhere in the east sector penetrates the whole area. Supermarkets and shops nearby plus innumerable restaurants and cafés.

III. MALLORCA

Puerto de Cala Llonga (Marina de Cala d'Or)

39°22'·1N 03°14'·2E

A well protected harbour, easy to enter in most conditions and with berthing for over 500 vessels in very pleasant surroundings.

Communications
Marina (Puerto Deportivo Marina) VHF Ch 09
Marina Cala d'Or ☎ 971 65 70 70
    Club Náutico de Cala d'Or ☎ 971 64 82 03
    info@marinacalador.es
    www.marinacalador.es

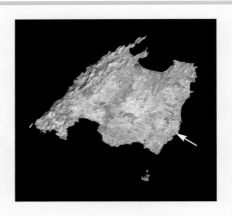

The marina

A single entrance from the sea leads to three *calas*: Cala Gran, Cala d'Or and Cala Llonga. Confusingly, the Marina Cala d'Or is located in the southernmost, Cala Llonga, rather than in Cala d'Or itself. Developers have not spoiled the very

special nature of the actual Cala d'Or: it retains much of its original charm, and is still counted amongst the most beautiful *calas* on this coast of Mallorca.

The 565-berth Marina Cala d'Or is well protected, with good facilities and helpful staff but, as in most of Mallorca, is expensive. It is usually full in summer and prior booking or at the very least a call on VHF Ch 09 prior to arrival would be essential. Approach and entrance are straightforward and good shelter is obtained, though in an east or southeast wind a heavy swell enters all three *calas*.

Pilotage

Approach

From south Low rocky cliffs broken by two small *calas* extend northwards from Porto Petro (*see plan on page 167*). The low, square pinkish-brown fort on Punta del Fortin with its nearby lighthouse (Fl(1+2)20s17m7M, round white column on square white base, both with vertical black stripes, 6m) are easily identified.

From north There are five small calas in the low rocky cliffs that extend from Porto Colom southwards (*see cala anchorages pages 171-173*). Again the fort and lighthouse are easy to identify.

Anchorages in the approach

- *Cala Gran* Anchor in 5–6m over sand and weed in the middle of the *cala*, opposite a small squarish *cala* on the starboard side, open to the south and to swell from the southeast and east. There is a fine sandy beach which is buoyed-off for bathing.
- *Cala d'Or* This *cala* is sometimes closed in the summer by means of buoys, when anchoring is prohibited. Otherwise anchor in the centre of the *cala* in 3–5m over sand and weed patches off a small sandy beach, open to east and southeast and to swell from the east. This is the least sheltered of the three *calas* to an easterly swell. There is a large white hotel at the head of the *cala*.

View west into Cala Llonga

Cala Gran anchorage just outside Marina Cala d'Or
Photohamburg / 123RF

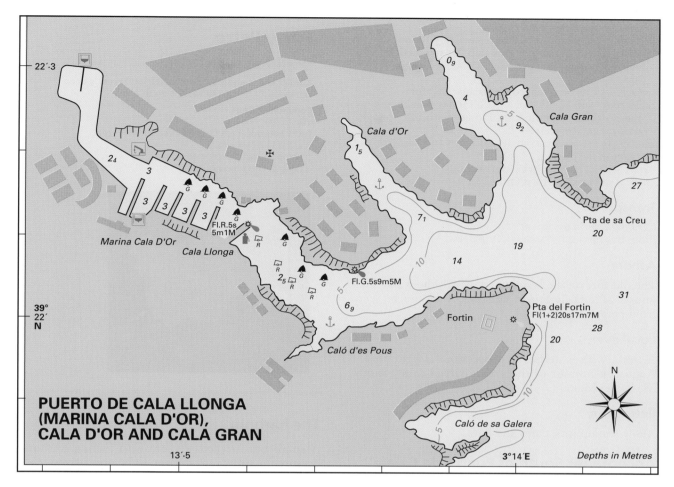

Map labels:
- 22'.3
- Cala d'Or
- 0₉
- 4
- Cala Gran
- 9₂
- 1₅
- 2₄
- 3
- 3
- 3 3 3 3
- G G G G
- G
- G
- Fl.R.5s 5m1M
- Marina Cala D'Or
- Cala Llonga
- R
- R R
- 2₅ G G
- R R
- R
- 6₉
- Fl.G.5s9m5M
- 7₁
- 10
- 14
- 19
- 27
- Pta de sa Creu
- 20
- 31
- Pta del Fortin Fl(1+2)20s17m7M
- 28
- 20
- Fortin
- 39° 22′ N
- Caló d'es Pous
- Caló de sa Galera
- 10
- 5
- N
- PUERTO DE CALA LLONGA (MARINA CALA D'OR), CALA D'OR AND CALA GRAN
- 13'.5
- 3°14'E
- Depths in Metres
- III. MALLORCA

• *Cala Llonga* Anchor in the entrance to Caló d'es Pous in 2·5m over sand and weed, well out of the marina approach channel, open to the east although somewhat surprisingly it seems to give the best protection in an east or southeast swell. Opposite Calo d'es Pous, near the flashing green light there is a large notice prohibiting anchoring 'in the *cala*' - it is not clear if this is intended to include Calo d'es Pous.

Entrance

The outer entrance is straightforward with good depths. After passing the light structure on the north side of the entrance to Cala Llonga (Fl.G.5s9m5M, green column on white base 6m) and crossing the 5m contour, the buoyed channel into the marina will open up. A minimum depth of 2·5m should be found in the channel.

Berthing

Secure temporarily to the fuelling berth at the end of the marina south mole, having already called on VHF Ch 09, in which case a berth may have already been allocated over the radio. Visitors are usually put on pontoon L at the head of the *cala*, which is open to the public and with little security.

Facilities

Water On the pontoons and the marina south mole (sometimes poor quality).
Electricity 220v AC points on all pontoons, some 380v points.
Fuel Fuel berth at the end of the marina south mole. Summer weekdays and Saturdays open 1000–1400 and 1600–1900; Sunday 0900–1430. Winter 24 hour self-service by credit card.
Provisions Supermarket and other shops nearby, with more at Porto Petro about a mile away. Produce markets on Wednesday and Saturday mornings in Santanyí, about 7 miles away by road.
Ice From the supermarket.

Cala Llonga Marina viewed from southeast

Chandlery In the marina complex.

Repairs A reasonable range of repairs to GRP and wood hulls and engineering jobs can be handled by the marina boatyard. There are 45 and 65 tonne travel lifts.

Sail repairs Can be arranged via the marina office.

Yacht club Club Náutico de Cala d'Or has a clubhouse on the northeast side of Cala Llonga with bar, lounge, terraces and showers.

Showers In the marina complex and the Club Náutico.

Laundry In the marina.

Banks Several in the nearby tourist complex.

Medical services In Cala d'Or and Santanyí.

Transport

Car hire/taxis In the town.

Buses Bus service to Santanyí, Palma, etc.

Ashore

The old fort on the headland is worth the walk. The unusual Punta de Fortin light structure can be seen from here.

Local event

A fiesta with waterborne processions is held on 15 August in honour of the area's patron saint, Santa Maria del Mar.

Eating out

Many restaurants, cafés and bars.

Anchorages South of Puerto de Cala Llonga

⚓ Cala d'Egos

39°21'·5N 03°13'·6E

A narrow, twisty, rocky-cliffed *cala*, surrounded by mainly luxurious detached houses plus a large white hotel overlooking the beach at its head. Anchor in 3–5m over sand and weed, open to southeast and south.

⚓ Cala del Llamp

39°21'·4N 03°13'·1E

A small *cala* between rocky cliffs on the northeast side of the entrance to Porto Petro (*see plan on page 177*). Anchor near the head in 3m over stone and weed, open to southeast and south. The area is also occupied by very luxurious detached houses, many with large gardens and pools.

Porto Petro

39°21'·2N 03°13'·5E

A small and friendly harbour which has recently been expanded to berth 230 vessels up to 15m.

Communications
VHF Ch 09, 16
Yacht harbour (Real Club Náutico Porto Petro)
☎ +34 971 65 76 57
rcnportopetro@rcnportopetro.es
www.rcnportopetro.com

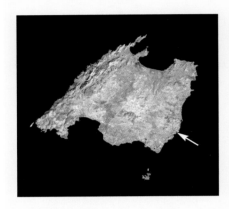

The harbour

A small but attractive yacht and fishing harbour occupying only one corner of a good-sized *cala* amidst relatively undeveloped surroundings and good anchorages (although these are now totally taken up by mooring buoys). Porto Petro yacht harbour can berth 230 or so vessels up to 15m. In the past depth was a problem with much of the yacht harbour having less than 2m, but dredging has approximately doubled previous figures (and charges have increased to match). A new mole has been built northeast from the rocky headland south of the harbour, increasing the number of deeper berths and blocking any southeasterly swell.

There is a sailing school and a branch of the Club Méditerranée in the *cala*. Facilities for visitors are still improving, but as usual the small yacht harbour is frequently crowded in summer. Pre-booking or at least a preliminary call on VHF Ch 09 is essential in summer, both for the marina and for a buoy, all of which are controlled by the Club Náutico.

Pilotage

Approach

From south Porto Petro lies 9·5M northeast of Punta Salinas, much of the coastline between comprising rough cliffs with few *calas* of any size until *Calas* Llombarts and Santanyí are reached (*see plan on page 167*). From Puerto de Cala Figuera with its conspicuous lighthouse (white octagonal tower with vertical black stripes, 6m) the coast is of low rocky cliffs. There is one small bay and a large deep *cala* before Porto Petro is reached. The Torre de Porto Petro and lighthouse (white tower on square base with two vertical black stripes, 9m) are obscured from west of south, and the entrance will be visible before they are seen.

From north From Cala Llonga and its low, square pinkish-brown fort and nearby lighthouse, Punta del Fortin (round white column on square white base, both with vertical black stripes, 6m), the coast is of low rocky cliffs broken by two small *calas*. The Torre de Porto Petro and lighthouse are very conspicuous from this direction.

Entrance to Porto Petro: Cala d'els Homos Morts and Cala de Sa Torre east on left, Cala del Llamp and Cala dels Mats right; Porto Petro centre

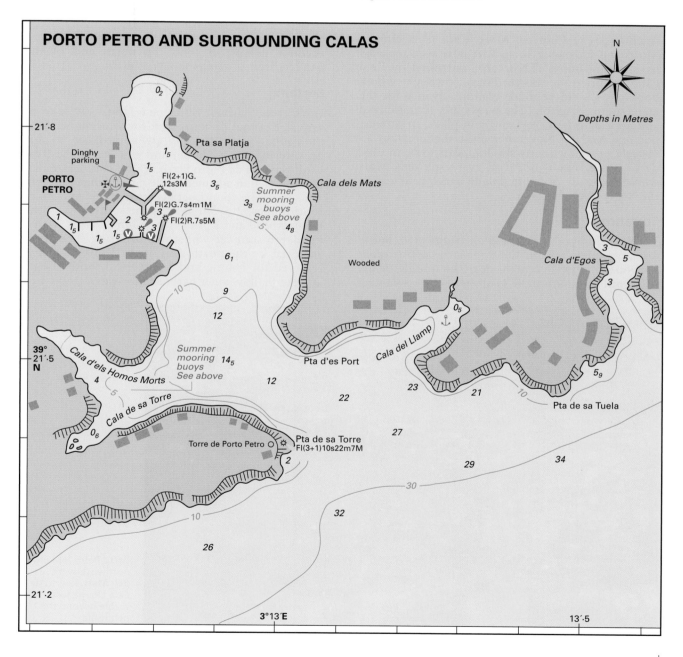

III. MALLORCA

Porto Petro entrance looking S across the laid moorings in
Cala del Mats administered by Club Náutico *Graham Hutt*

Anchorages in the approach

Anchorages in Cala del Mats, Cala d'els Homos
Morts and Cala se sa Torre have now been replaced
by mooring buoys. These are controlled by Real
Club Náutico de Porto Petro, through whom
bookings should be made well in advance for the
main summer season. The buoys are all numbered
and appear to be permanently in place, or at least
not removed by November. Best shelter from an
easterly or southeasterly swell appears to be in Cala
de sa Torre, but if north of east Cala dels Mats
would be better. A secure dinghy parking area is on
the N side of the harbour.

Entrance

The *cala* entrance is wide and unencumbered. Buoys
are sometimes laid in the approach to the yacht
harbour, otherwise remain near the middle of the
cala until the south mole is abeam before swinging
to pass between it and the hammerhead. On no
account venture beyond the north end of the
hammerhead as depths shoal rapidly.

Berthing

Contact the harbour office on VHF Ch 09 prior to
arrival, or if out of hours look for a vacant berth on
the visitors' quay (which is now immediately to port
on entering the harbour) and enquire at the Real
Club Náutico de Porto Petro. It is of course essential
to book well in advance in the peak summer period.
3m should be found between the outer and inner
south moles, 2·5–3m against the south arm of the
hammerhead and 2·5m in the visitors' berths. Watch
the depth-sounder whilst manoeuvring. The angle
enclosed by the north arm of the hammerhead is
reserved for fishing and commerical tourist boats
and the shallow inner harbour is private.

Porto Petro looking
northeast over Cala
dels Mats. Puerto de
Cala Llonga just
visible beyond the
peninsula

Facilities

Water All water connectors ashore are of the push-in adaptor type. It seems that the authorities do not like people visiting by dinghy and filling containers, but prefer them to berth to take on water (for which, of course, they make a charge).

Electricity 220v AC on quays plus a few 380v points. A deposit is normally required before the cable is connected.

Fuel No fuel available. Nearest is Marina Cala d'Or.

Provisioning Small supermarket nearby plus other shops in the village able to meet all day-to-day requirements. Produce markets Wednesday and Saturday mornings in Santanyí, some 5M away.

Ice From a café near the root of the mole and supermarket.

Repairs Basic work on engines, woodwork and GRP possible. Enquire at the Réal Club Náutico. A shallow slipway north of the hammerhead mole. 45-ton and 65 ton travel hoists are available.

Yacht club The Réal Club Náutico Porto Petro has a small clubhouse on the quay overlooking the yacht harbour.

Showers At the Réal Club Náutico. A small charge is made if not berthed in the yacht harbour.

Laundry In the shower block.

Banks In Cala d'Or and Santanyí, the latter about five miles away by road.

Medical services In Cala d'Or and Santanyí.

Transport

Car hire/taxis Enquire at the Real Club Náutico.
Buses Bus service to Santanyí, Palma, etc.

Ashore

A visit to the old town of Santanyí should prove interesting. A '*petit train*' runs between Cala d'Or, Porto Petro and Cala Mondragó.

Local events

Fiestas are held on 25 July in honour of San Jaime, with horseback processions, and on 30 November in honour of San Andrés.

Eating out

Several restaurants, cafés and bars.

Cala Mondragó viewed from southwest, showing nearby bays

Cala between Porto Petro and Puerto de Cala Figuera

⚓ Cala Mondragó

39°21'N 03°11'·7E

A wide, attractive and largely unspoilt *cala* between low rocky cliffs, Cala Mondragó has four arms, two of which are buoyed off in summer for swimmers. Anchor in 4–8m over sand and some weed. There are café/bars on both the tourist beaches.

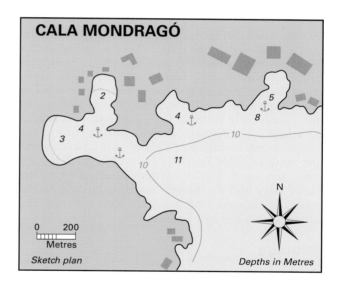

III. MALLORCA

Cala Mondragó *Susie Baggaley*

Puerto de Cala Figuera (de Santanyí)

39°19'·8N 03°10'·5E

A very tiny harbour offering good shelter but with visitors' berths for only six vessels. Isla de Cabrera is 15M from here.

Communications
Puerto de Cala Figuera ℰ 971 64 52 42

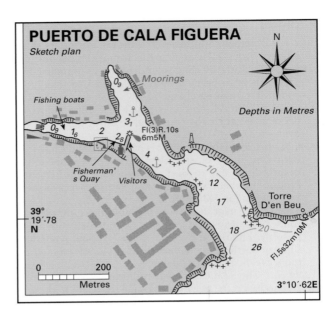

The harbour

A very small, attractive harbour devoted to fishing and a small day tourist trade. There is little space for yachts in the sheltered areas although six berths are reserved for visitors, stern-to at the short mole. These would become untenable with strong wind or swell from east, southeast or south. For this reason the *cala* is only suitable for a night stop in settled weather. The approach is straightforward but the entrance can be difficult to locate as it is narrow and lies between cliffs. Facilities are very limited, but the mole has been developed with lines tailed to the short quay and a *capitania* building erected on the mole. Yachts may be asked to move during the afternoon visit of a tourist ferry.

Pilotage

From south Puerto de Cala Figuera lies 7M northeast of Punta Salinas (*see plan on page 167*). Much of the coastline comprises rough cliffs with few *calas* of any size until Cala Llombarts is reached. The entrance to Cala Figuera can be identified in the close approach by the lighthouse, Torre D'en Beu (white octagonal tower with vertical black stripes, 6m) in front of a brownish stone watchtower on the northeast side of the entrance. A large radar scanner operates on top of the lighthouse.

From north From Porto Petro the coast is of low, broken rocky cliffs with a wide, deep indentation at Cala Mondragó. If sailing close inshore the lighthouse and tower at Cala Figuera are screened by hills and not visible until the closer approach.

Anchorage in the approach

Anchoring to the southeast of the mole is reported to be discouraged but if feasible anchor In 4–8m over muddy sand, weed and rock. This is not a good place to be with wind and waves from south to east. A number of small craft moorings are now present in this area which would limit swinging room for any anchored yachts. If space and draught permit, anchorage may be found north of the mole, but this area is usually taken up by large fishing boats. Holding is reported to be poor in places.

Entrance

The red column on the end of the mole can be seen from outside the entrance. Follow an S-shaped course, remaining near the centre of the *cala* and swinging wide of the foul ground extending from the two rocky points (*see plan above and photo opposite*). The wind can be fluky between the high cliffs and the seas heavy and confused, making it difficult for craft with limited auxiliary power.

Berthing

Six berths are reserved for visiting yachts on the southeast side of the mole and mooring lines have been installed. The inner end of the mole shoals to below 2m near the root and there is a rock with 0·3m over it close to the root. These berths are completely exposed to onshore winds from between east and southeast, which bring in a nasty swell and the *cala* is therefore only suitable as a night stop in very settled conditions.

Yachts are not normally permitted to berth at the fishermen's quay on the inside of the mole, though from Friday evening to Sunday evening it may be possible to lie alongside a fishing boat – which will probably wish to leave at 0600 on Monday morning. A small yacht can sometimes find a slot in the narrow northern arm. The western arm is very tight and is further obstructed by lines across the harbour.

Puerto de Cala Figuera: small harbour with little space for visitors

Moorings

There are a few moorings in the northern arm but they are private and usually occupied.

Facilities

Water Tap at the (wholesale) fish market near the root of the mole.

Electricity Not available.

Fuel Diesel from a pump near the root of the mole. Petrol by can from a filling station at Santanyí some 2½M inland.

Provisions Supermarket 10 minutes' walk up the hill south of the harbour. A few small shops provide everyday requirements. There are many more shops in Santanyí and an excellent market is held there on Wednesday and Saturday mornings.

Ice From one of the restaurants or supermarket.

Repairs A 5-tonne crane on the fishermen's quay. Small slipway at the head of the western arm.

Banks In Santanyí.

Medical services In the village and at Santanyí, 2½M inland.

Transport

Car hire/taxis In Santanyí.

Buses Summer service to Santanyí and beyond.

Ashore

See *Ashore from Porto Petro* on *page 179*.

Local events

Puerto de Cala Figuera is one of many harbours in Mallorca to honour Nuestra Señora del Carmen on 16 July with a fiesta including waterborne processions.

Eating out

Several restaurants and some cafés/bars near the harbour.

III. MALLORCA

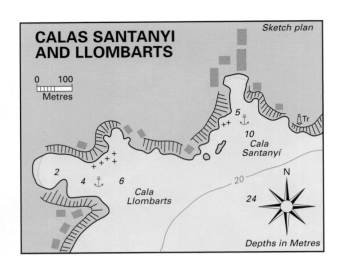

Cala Santanyí (right) viewed from southeast, with Cala Llombarts left

Anchorages between Puerto de Cala Figuera and Puerto Colonia de Sant Jordi

⚓ Cala Santanyí
39°19'·6N 03°08'·8E

A *cala* surrounded by houses and hotels, but nevertheless attractive, its sandy beach roped off in summer for swimming. There is a small tower on the east side of entrance and a small island on the west side, plus some breaking rocks inshore. Anchor in the middle of the *cala* in 5–10m over sand, open to east and southeast. In addition to the many swimmers there is a windsurfing school.

⚓ Cala Llombarts
39°19'·5N 03°08'·6E

A double *cala*, though the northern arm is much the smaller, with rocky sides and in summer a roped-off beach to the south. There is foul ground off the headland between the two. Anchor in 4–6m over sand and weed, open to east, southeast and possibly south.

⚓ Cala Marmols
39°17'·3N 03°05'·6E

A small and completely deserted *cala* between rocky cliffs, just over two miles northeast of Punta Salinas. If approaching from the north, two pairs of white transit posts will be seen, these presumably to confirm speed over a known distance. Cala Marmols is a short distance south of the southern pair of transits. Anchor in 3–6m over sand, open from east round to south.

Cala Llombarts *Susie Baggaley*

6. PUNTA (CAP) SALINAS TO BAHÍA DE PALMA

PUNTA SALINAS TO BAHIA DE PALMA

Close to Punta Salinas lie these salt pans, worked since before Roman times
Graham Hutt

Punta Salinas

39°15'·9N 03°03'·2E

A low, flat, wooded promontory edged by stony beaches and marked by a conspicuous lighthouse (white tower and building with narrow stone bands, 17m).

⚓ Cala Caragol

39°16'·5N 03°02'·5E

A wide bay one mile northwest of Punta Salinas and backed by pine woods, Cala Caragol has a particularly fine beach bounded to the southeast by the low rocky Punta Negra and to the northwest by Islote Caragol. Anchor in 2–5m over sand (some),

Punta Salinas looking northwest over the lighthouse, with Cala Caragol beyond

III. MALLORCA

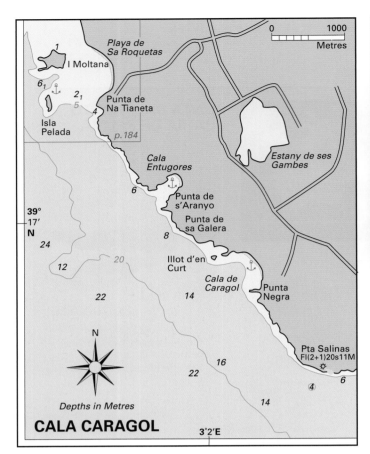

CALA CARAGOL

Depths in Metres

Playa des Carbó and Sa Roquetas (right-hand) with Islas Pelada and Moltana shown, viewed from south-southeast

weed (a little) and rock (lots), open to the south and west sectors. Even swell from the east seems to work its way round into the bay. The bay is often full of yachts during summer, but otherwise appears little visited. There is a house and a rough road and a track from Colonia de Sant Jordi which is popular with walkers and gives access to the beach.

⚓ Cala Entugores

39°17'·2N 03°01'·5E

Much smaller and narrower than its neighbour Cala Caragol, Cala Entugores has no beach and is very shallow. Enter carefully watching the depth-sounder – it is reported to shoal to below 2·5m not far from the entrance. Anchor as depth dictates, open to south and west.

Anchorages between Isla Pelada and Isla de na Guardia

⚓ Playa de sa Roquetas

39°18'·1N 03°00'·6E

⚓ Playa des Carbó

39°18'·5N 03°00'·5E

Less than 1M northwest of Cala Entugores lies a long sandy beach with a spit running out to several small islands and rocky shoals close to the shore. These are Isla Pelada, Isla Moltana and Isla de na

Guardia, the latter being the only one lit, marking the approach to Puerto Colonia de Sant Jordi. Do not attempt to pass between these islands and the mainland with a keeled yacht (*see plans below and opposite*).

Anchor in the northern bay (Playa des Carbó) in 3–4m over mainly sand, or further south (Playa de sa Roquetas) in 2–4m over sand and weed. There can be considerable disturbance from jet-skis and small speedboats in both anchorages.

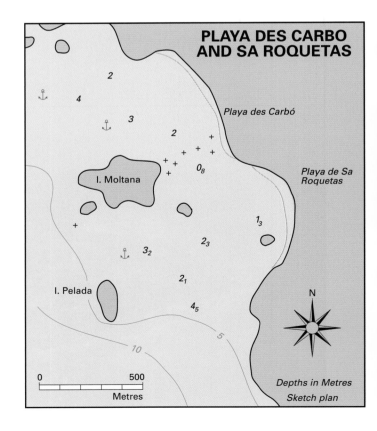

PLAYA DES CARBO AND SA ROQUETAS

Playa des Carbó

Playa de Sa Roquetas

I. Moltana

I. Pelada

Depths in Metres

Sketch plan

Puerto Colonia de Sant Jordi (Puerto de Campos)

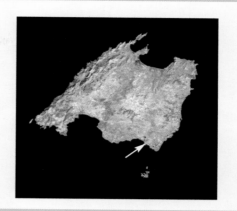

39°18'·8N 03°02'E

A small friendly fishing harbour with berths for over 300 vessels, usually full with local craft

Communications
VHF Ch 08
Puerto Colonia de Sant Jordi ✆ 971 65 62 24
  port.coloniasantjordi@portsib.es

The harbour

A medium-sized fishing and yachting harbour, with 322 berths, mostly for small vessels. Much of the harbour is shallow and occupied by local craft. This is still basically a fishing port with nets being mended on the quayside. Facilities are limited but do include fuel, water and reasonable shopping. The approach is between low islands, some unmarked, and care is necessary.

Tourist ferries taking visitors to Cabrera berth inshore of the fuel dock and leave the harbour at speed. This is a particular hazard if coming in by dinghy.

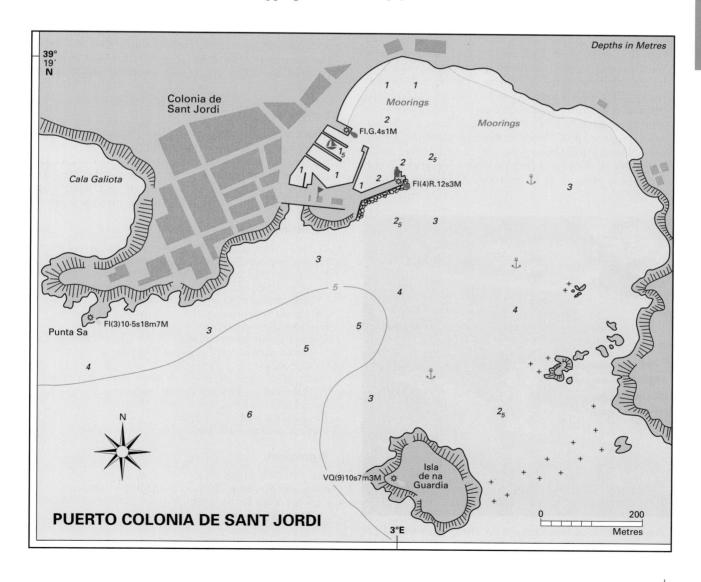

PUERTO COLONIA DE SANT JORDI

III. MALLORCA

Approaches to Puerto Colonia de Sant Jordi viewed northwest over Isla de na Guardia

Pilotage

Approach

From west From Cabo Blanco – a high promontory of steep light brown cliffs topped by a lighthouse (white tower and building, 12m) and an old watchtower which is more prominent than the lighthouse from some directions – the coast is of low rocky cliffs with a long sandy bay, Playa del Trench, followed by more low rocky cliffs and the houses and apartment blocks of Colonia de Sant Jordi (*see plan on page 183*). Punta Sa may be identified by its conspicuous lighthouse (white round tower with three black bands, 12m) on the very end of the headland, though it is partially hidden if viewed

from further north. The low and inconspicuous Isla Corberana some 550m offshore presents a potential hazard, particularly when sailing at night, though there is good water on either side (*see plan opposite*).

From east Round the low, tree-covered Punta Salinas with its lighthouse (Fl(2+1)20s17m13M, white tower and building with narrow stone bands 17m) and follow the coast past several sandy bays and low inconspicuous islands until south of the lighthouse on Punta Sa (*see plans on pages 183-185*). Do not attempt to pass inside either Isla Moltona or Isla de na Guardia.

Anchorage in the approach

The northeast part of the bay between the harbour entrance and Isla de na Guardia is occupied by moorings; anchor further southwest in 3–5m over sand and, mainly, weed, open to southwest and south, but with partial shelter from the southeast. Some areas of the bottom are foul and a trip line is advisable.

Entrance

From a point south of the lighthouse on Punta Sa, enter the bay on a northeast course leaving Isla de la Guardia to starboard. Depths shoal as the harbour is approached, so sound carefully. Note that the end of the southeast breakwater projects some distance beyond the light structure. Entry at night is not recommended.

Berthing

Much of the inner harbour has depths of less than 1·5m, though the fuel berth and the southern side of the marina south mole are reported to have 2m. It is claimed that there are 3m in the entrance. The marina is restricted to vessels of less than 10m. Secure at the fuel berth and consult harbour staff.

Facilities

Water Taps on quays and pontoons, and at the fuel berth.
Electricity 220v AC on quays and pontoons.
Fuel Diesel and petrol pumps inside the end of the south breakwater, but no more than 2m depth. Access can be difficult due to nearby tourist boats.
Provisions Supermarket and other shops in the town.
Ice From the fuel berth.
Repairs Small boatyard west of the Club Náutico. Two slipways, both very shallow. Engineer at the yard. 16 tonne crane.
Yacht club Club Náutico de Sant Jordi has a small clubhouse at the south end of the harbour.
Laundry In the town.
Banks In the town.
Medical services Basic medical services available.

Transport

Car hire/taxis In the town.
Buses Bus service to Ses Salinas and on to Palma, etc.
Ferries Ferries to the nearby island of Cabrera 12M south. See page 204.

Puerto Colonia de Sant Jordi and the anchorage east of the port

Ashore

There is a substantial area of saltings near the outskirts of the town, on the road to Salinas, which is still producing large volumes of sea salt after many hundreds, or perhaps thousands, of years. Otherwise it is an undistinguished little holiday resort, albeit with some good restaurants.

Anchorages between Puerto Colonia de Sant Jordi and Puerto de la Rápita

39°20'N 02°59'E to 39°21'·5N 02°57'·5E

The Ensenada de la Rapita, the open bay between Puerto Colonia Sant Jordi and Puerto de la Rapita contains what are claimed to be the finest beaches in Mallorca, particularly the Playa del Trench. The relatively sheltered southeast corner, to the east of Islas Llarga and Redonda and also protected by a mole with a launching slip on its northeast side, now has many small craft moorings and other buoys of indeterminate purpose. It may still be possible to anchor outside them but the bottom seems quite rocky. The rest of the bay consists of two long beaches, Playa del Trench (pronounced 'Trunk') and Playa de la Rapita. There is a point, Pta de Ses

Playa de la Trench: Isla Gabina can just be seen right of picture

Covetes, separating them which has been extensively developed. Anchor off either beach in 4m+ over sand with some patches of weed. Open south and west, and to swell from southeast and northwest.

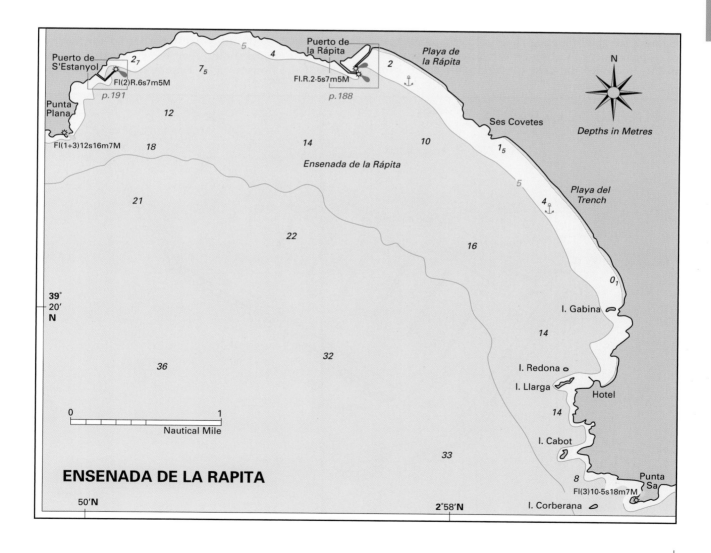

Puerto de la Rápita

39°21'·7N 02°57'·4E

A large, safe and friendly yacht harbour with berthing for 460 yachts just W of the finest beaches in Mallorca: Playa del Trench and Playa de la Rapita. It has comprehensive facilities, is well run and has particularly competent and helpful marineros. A good departure point for Isla de Cabrera.

Distances
Cabrera 12M

Communications
VHF Ch 09
Club Náutico de la Rápita
  Marina office (mobile manned 24hrs)
  ① 971 641 001 *Mobile* 676 337 357
  vela@cnrapita.es or administracion@cnrapita.e.telefonica.net
  www.cnrapita.com

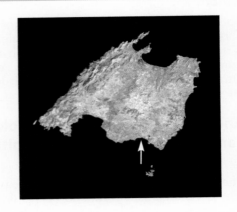

The port

Puerto de la Rápita is a large and modern artificial yacht harbour with 460 berths and excellent facilities, situated at the northwest end of the long Playa del Trench. It is easy to enter and offers good protection once inside.

Puerto de la Rápita is a favourite departure point for Isla de Cabrera, just 12M south, and the marina staff are happy to help visitors apply for the necessary permit. (For details of *Isla and Puerto de Cabrera* see the following chapter.) Perhaps because of its proximity to Cabrera it is relatively expensive - in late October the cost per night for a 13–14m

yacht was their mid-season price of €79 compared with €40 at the Real Club Náutico in Palma. Low season at La Rápita is from November to February, high season from June to September.

Pilotage

Approach

From west Round Punta Plana (white tower with black bands on building, 12m) and pass Puerto de S'Estanyol in the northwest corner of the bay; a northeast course should then be set towards the far end of the houses of La Rápita (*see plan on page*

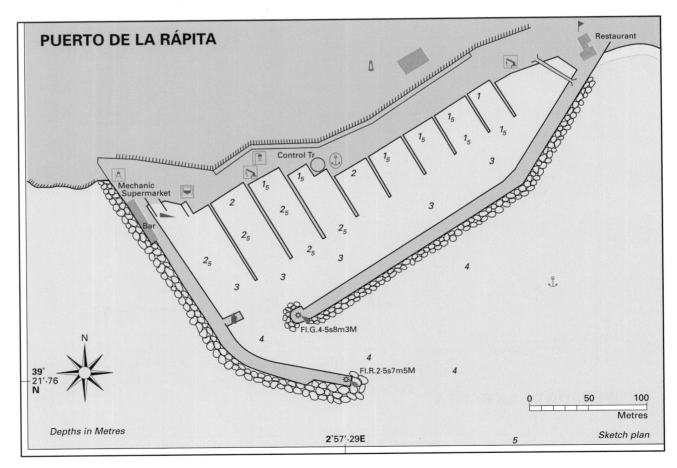

PUERTO DE LA RÁPITA

Restaurant

Control Tr

Mechanic
Supermarket

Bar

Fl.G.4·5s8m3M

Fl.R.2·5s7m5M

39°
21'·76
N

Depths in Metres

2°57'·29E

0   50   100
Metres

Sketch plan

Puerto de la Rápita looking northeast

187). On closer approach the harbour breakwater will be seen with an old watchtower (18m) behind.

From east Allow Punta Sa (white round tower with three black bands, 12m) an offing of at least ½M in order to clear Isla Corberana, then steer northwest into the wide Ensenada de la Rápita towards the houses of La Rápita. On nearing the harbour, the breakwater and watchtower will come into view.

Anchorage in the approach

In calm weather anchor in 4–5m over sand, 200–300m east or southeast of the harbour entrance off the Playa de la Rapita.

Entrance

The entrance presents no problems day or night, though a heavy swell from the southeast or south could make the final approach dangerous due to shoaling water. Minimum depth is 3m with best depths found in the starboard (N) side of the channel on entry. There is a 2kn speed limit in the harbour.

Berthing

Secure stern-to or alongside at the reception quay inside the southwest breakwater until allocated a berth. It is better to call the marina office on VHF Ch 09 before arrival and as usual advance booking is essential in summer. Transit visitors are usually berthed near the entrance just S of the fuel berth

The entrance to Puerto de la Rápita. Vistors' berths are in the entrance *Susie Baggaley*

where it can be uncomfortable, especially due to the long fetch, with wind or swell from northeast to southeast, and a fairly long walk to the office and town.

Facilities

Water Taps on the pontoons and quay, and at the visitors' berths. Note that there are two systems, one for drinkable (potable) water and the other for washing decks. Potable water is charged at €1 for 100 litres.

Electricity 220v AC and some 380v AC points on quays and pontoons, and at the visitors' quay.

Fuel Diesel and petrol at the fuel berth. Opening hours are 0800–2000 in summer, and 0800–1800 in winter, every day.

Provisioning Small supermarket at the west end of the harbour, more shops in the town ½M away.

Ice From a machine near the marina supermarket.

Chandlery Two at the west end of the harbour.

Repairs Boatyard in the northwest area of the marina. A 50-tonne travel-lift in the boatyard area and 7-tonne crane at the northeast end of the harbour. Lift out of a Swan 65 has been observed - a list had to be established to reduce draught in the approach but the lift was no problem!

Engineers Cosme Oliver ☎ 971 64 01 99 at the west end of the harbour are official service agents for Caterpillar, Honda, Perkins, Tohatsu, Vetus, Volvo Penta and Yamaha.

Yacht club Club Náutico de la Rápita has a large and well-appointed clubhouse with a bar and terrace restaurant at the east end of the harbour.

Showers Two shower blocks opposite the control tower and toilet facilities near the visitors' berths.

Bank In the town.

Medical services In the town.

Laundrette In the marina.

Blackwater pump-out

WiFi is claimed but does not appear to work anywhere in the marina let alone the visitors berths.

Transport

Car hire/taxis Consult the marina office.

Buses Bus service to Palma, etc.

Ashore

For those interested in ancient history and archaeological remains, this area is littered with interesting 'finds' such as Capicorp Vey, a prehistoric village, Sollerich (a burial cave) and Son Herue, a Bronze Age burial site. The village of Campos is well worth a visit, set in the countryside and surrounded by considerable agricultural activity and many beautiful restored windmills.

Local event

A fiesta in honour of Nuestra Señora del Carmen is held on 16 July.

Eating out

Several restaurants in the town, plus a restaurant with a good reputation at the road entrance to the Club Náutico and a café/bar at the west end of the harbour.

Puerto de S'Estanyol de Migjorn (El Estañol)

39°21'·7N 02°55'·3E

A small harbour less than 2M W of Puerto de la Rápita, but usually full with local vessels.

Communications
VHF Ch 09
Club Náutico de S'Estanyol ☎ 971 64 00 85 / 971 640 682
officina@cnestanyol.es
www.cnestanyol.es

The harbour

A small, square, artificial harbour close east of Punta Plana, occupied by fishing boats and a few yachts under 12m or so, with the possibility for up to 15m near the entrance. Approach and entrance are not usually difficult but would be dangerous in strong winds and swell from southeast or south due to shallow water in the approach. Facilities are fair and everyday shopping requirements can be met in the strip of coastal development which joins up with La Rápita to the east.

Pilotage

Approach

From west Once past Punta Plana (*see plans on page 183 and 187*), Puerto de S'Estanyol lies 0·6M north-northeast of the headland past a small, low-lying island which should be left to port.

From east Heading northwest through Ensenada de la Rápita, Puerto de S'Estanyol lies 0·6M north-northeast of the headland.

Entrance

Approach the eastern corner of the harbour heading northwest to round the head of the south breakwater at slow speed. The entrance is narrow and may be partially blocked by moored boats. There is a 2kn

PUERTO DE S'ESTANYOL

Depths in Metres

2°55'·17E

Fl(2)G.7s1M

Fl(2)R.6s5M

Sketch plan

speed limit. Note that the close approach and entrance are shallow, making it dangerous in heavy swell from south or southeast. Depth in the entrance is said to be 4m with depth inside 4m down to 1m. Vessels should contact the port on Ch 09 to establish depth as well as availability before entering.

Berthing

Secure to the inner side of the south breakwater as space permits and visit the harbour office for allocation of a berth. Depths are 4m near the breakwater head shoaling to 1m or less at the elbow.

Facilities

Water Taps on quays and pontoons.
Electricity 220v AC points at foot of lamp-posts and at normal supply points.
Fuel Diesel pump at the head of the north mole, petrol pump at its root (i.e. petrol by can only).

Puerto de S'Estanyol. Some development around the port, but plans for a much larger marina have been shelved for now, due to environmental concerns

Provisioning Everyday supplies from a supermarket and other shops in the nearby town.
Ice From the bar or supermarket.
Repairs A 12·5-tonne crane, and slipway near the root of the north mole. Motor mechanic available for engine repairs.
Yacht club Club Náutico s'Estanyol has a small clubhouse with restaurant, bar, terrace and two tennis courts.
Showers In the west corner of the harbour.
Bank In La Rápita, about 1½M away.
Hospital/medical services In Lluchmayor, 8M inland.

Transport

Car hire/taxis Consult the harbour office.
Buses Bus service to Palma, etc.

Eating out

A few restaurants and several café/bars.

Anchorages West of Puerto de S'Estanyol

⚓ Cala Pi

39°21'·6N 02°50'·1E (entrance to *cala*).

A beautiful and very popular *cala* between high cliffs, but extremely narrow and often crowded (avoid weekends when charter yachts are setting out or returning). *See plan on page 183 and below.* There is a conspicuous stone tower on the headland southeast of the entrance. There is a detached rock

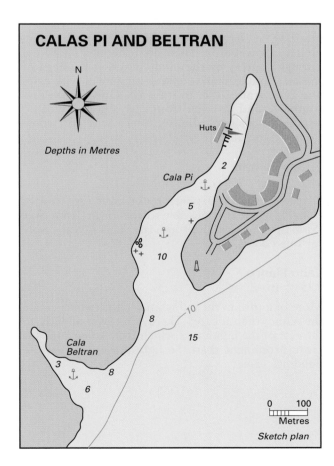

CALAS PI AND BELTRAN

Depths in Metres

Huts

Cala Pi

Cala Beltran

Sketch plan

Cala Pi is a delightful small anchorage *Hartmut Albert / 123RF*

to starboard (E) on entry and about 50m further in swimming buoys are in place. Anchor in 4–8m over sand and weed with a few rocks either using a stern anchor or taking a line ashore, to restrict swinging. At about the 3·5m depth line beware an isolated rock, with 1·3m clearance, close to the cliff where rope tails from old shorelines abound. There is also a substantial mooring block and ground tackle in the centre of the *cala* at this same depth, which may be a mooring in season but could be used as a swing limiter in low season. There are fishermen's huts and a rough slipway by the sandy beach at the head of the *cala*, and a small tourist development with cafés and restaurants, etc. to the east. Open south and southeast and to swell from east. On a day of no wind and almost calm sea there was still some rolling in the *cala*.

⚓ Cala Beltran
39°21'·5N 02°50'E

A very small *cala* between rocky cliffs just west of Cala Pi, where it is possible to anchor in 3–5m over sand, open to east and southeast. This is really only for small boats.

Cabo Blanco
39°21'·7N 02°47'·3E

More of a turn in the tall whitish cliffs (which create the name) than a cape. There is a tower slightly to the east of the lighthouse which from some angles is more prominent than the lighthouse itself (white building, 12m).

Bahía de Palma Marine Reserve

A marine reserve area has been created off Cabo Enderrocat. The four lightbuoys previously installed to define the area of the reserve are no longer in place, but their original positions are given below and the reserve should still be respected.

Buoys
34190(S) **Buoy A** 39°24'·7N 02°43'·8E Fl.Y.5s5M pillar with × topmark (S marker)
34191(S) **Buoy 2** 39°25'·5N 02°43'·6E Fl(2)Y.10s3M can with × topmark
34192(S) **Buoy 1** 39°28'·4N 02°42'·2E Fl(2)Y.10s3M can with × topmark
34193(S) **Buoy C** 39°29'·9N 02°42'·1E Fl.Y.5s5M pillar with × topmark. (N marker)

Cala Blava mooring buoys

Mooring buoys have been laid in Cala Blava, about 1·5km south of Puerto El Arenal in the Bay of Palma, which may be reserved in advance at www.balearslifeposidonia.eu for 1 June to 30 September. See plan below and the *Anchoring and moorings* section on *page 19* for further details. A very uncomfortable *cala* even in slight swell.

The buoyage situation is confusing, as Posidonia claims to have laid buoys but none have actually been in place. Marine reserves as marked on the Posidonia charts also are not indicated by yellow buoys as before.

Puerto El Arenal

39°30'·2N 02°44'·9E

A large yacht harbour at the southeast end of the Playa de Arenal, with berthing for over 600 yachts up to 25m

Communications
VHF Ch 09
Club Náutico El Arenal ☏ 971 44 01 42
   administracion@cnarenal.com
   www.cnamoorings.com

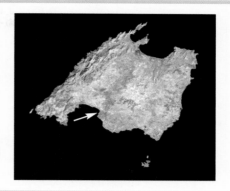

The harbour

A large, modern yacht harbour with 667 berths for vessels up to 25m and with 3m+ depths in the entrance and the outer areas of the marina. Built at the southeast end of another spectacular and popular beach, Playa de Arenal, the new harbour is built alongside the small old harbour which has now been improved.

To the south a low rocky coast is backed initially by large houses and, further on, by unspoilt open countryside.

The harbour offers first class facilities including a lovely clubhouse with restaurant and pool and is far enough away from the tourist areas not to suffer from traffic or other noise. The marina of Puerto El Arenal is now full of charter craft and has become expensive. This is a useful place for a crew change as the airport is close by.

Approach and entrance are normally without problem, but heavy winds and swell from the southwest quadrant could render the close approach and entrance dangerous.

Puerto El Arenal is one of many suitable departure points for Isla de Cabrera and the Club Náutico are happy to help visitors apply for the necessary permit (at a price!).

For details of *Isla* and *Puerto de Cabrera* see the following chapter.

Pilotage

Approach

For outer approach see plan on page 91.

From west Round the very prominent Punta Cala Figuera which has a lighthouse (white round tower with black diagonal stripes on building, 24m) and radio masts on its steep cliffs. Cross the Bahía de Palma heading just north of east towards Cabo Enderrocat, with an inconspicuous tower on its

III. MALLORCA

Puerto El Arenal, a well-run and helpful marina

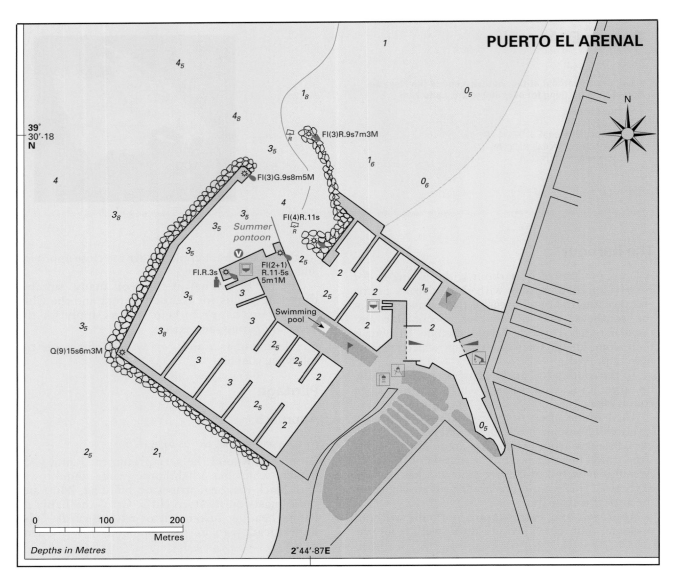

PUERTO EL ARENAL

summit, at the northern end of a line of high cliffs. El Arenal lies two miles northeast of this headland, at the southeast end of a sandy beach backed by solid high-rise development.

From east From Cabo Blanco follow the cliffs north-northwest round Cabo Enderrocat. El Arenal lies two miles northeast off this headland, at the southeast end of a sandy beach backed by a solid high-rise development.

Anchorage in the approach

Anchor either side of the harbour in 3m+ over sand and weed, open southwest–west–northwest.

Entrance

The entrance is easily seen and without hazards, other than those posed by stray bathers, snorkellers, sailboards and pedalos. The entrance suffers from continual sand silting and is regularly dredged to 4m+, with 3m throughout the yacht harbour. It is still wise to keep close to the southern breakwater head on entering. There is a 2kn speed limit. Note that in 2018 or later there may be a change in the marina layout involving moving the entrance to the southwest corner to reduce the silting problem.

Berthing

Visitors lie stern-to against the head of the central mole, between the slipway and the fuel berth. Lazy lines are provided, tailed to the quay. In summer an extra floating pontoon is installed from the northeast end of the visitors' quay adding 10 berths to give a total of about 40 available to visitors. Maximum boat length for visitors is 14m.

Facilities

Water Water points on the pontoons and quays.
Electricity 220v AC available on all quays and pontoons plus some 380v points.
Fuel Diesel and petrol from pumps at the west end of the central mole. There is a self-service facility enabling 24-hour availability.
Provisions Everyday supplies from nearby shops and supermarkets, with many more in Palma six miles away. Hypermarket less than five miles away on the road between Palma and the airport. A market is held in the town on Tuesday and Friday, with a clothes market on Thursdays.
Ice From the Club Náutico bar.
Chandlery Just outside the main gate to the harbour is Mar Blau (① 971 440 440).
Repairs Layup area on the central mole with some services available. Fully fledged boatyards in Palma. For repairs and general maintenance Renav is recommended locally. A 50-tonne travel-lift at the west end of the central mole. A smaller lift and 3-tonne mobile crane in the old harbour. Two slipways in the old harbour and one at the end of the central mole. Engineers available through the Club Náutico.
Yacht club Club Náutico El Arenal has an elegant clubhouse with restaurant, TV room, bar, terraces, large swimming pool and laundry. Use of the club facilities, including the pool, is a bonus here. The old clubhouse to the northeast also has a restaurant and is used by fishermen and dinghy sailors
Showers At the east and southeast corners of the harbour area.
WiFi Free WiFi available, said to be good.
Banks In the town.
Medical services In the town. Hospital in Palma 6M away.

Winter storage Storage ashore for about 40 yachts. Also, a warehouse on a Palma industrial estate for indoor storage of motor boats. (Enquire with Club Náutico.)

Transport

Car hire/taxis In the town.
Buses Frequent bus service to Palma.
Ferries From Palma to the other islands and mainland Spain.
Air services Busy international airport three miles away, with year-round international flights.

Ashore

Palma and all its charms are only a short bus ride away.

Eating out

Many restaurants, cafés and bars along the beach.

Anchorages northwest of Puerto el Arenal in the Bay of Palma

⚓ Bahía de Palma, northeast side

In settled weather it is possible to anchor off the shore virtually anywhere between El Arenal and Palma itself; the coast is in the main gently sloping, with wide sandy beaches (*see plan on page 91*). Anchor to suit draught off the open beach. If swimming buoys are laid, ensure you do not encroach on them. Vessels doing so are fined heavily.

III. MALLORCA

Bahía de Palma looking northwest over Puerto de San Antonio. Palma beyond

Puerto de San Antonio de la Playa (Ca'n Pastilla)

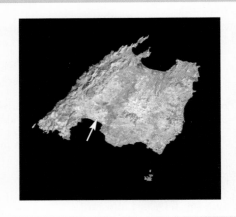

39°31'·8N 02°43'·0E

Offering excellent protection and facilities for nearly 400 berths up to 18m, this new marina is close to the airport and its accompanying noise, being directly under the flight path.

Communications
VHF Ch 09
Club Marítimo San Antonio de la Playa
℡ 971 74 50 76
cmsap@cmsap.com
www.cmsap.com

The harbour/marina

A good-sized yacht harbour with nearly 400 berths, handy for the airport (though paying the price with a good deal of aircraft noise) and with better than average facilities. It is easy to approach and enter in normal conditions though with strong onshore winds and swell it could become dangerous due to shallows in the close approach.

Puerto de San Antonio de la Playa lies very close to the large tourist resort of Ca'n Pastilla with its many high-rise hotels and apartment blocks, and is occasionally referred to by this name. An excellent sandy beach stretches for over two miles to the southeast.

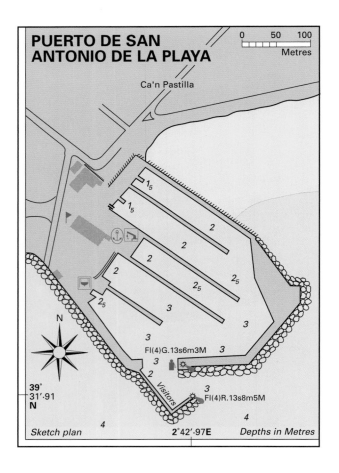

PUERTO DE SAN ANTONIO DE LA PLAYA

Ca'n Pastilla

0   50   100
Metres

1₅
1₅
2
2
2
2
2₅
2₅
2₅
3
3
3
Fl(4)G.13s6m3M
3
3
3
2
Visitors
3   Fl(4)R.13s8m5M
4   4

39°
31'·91
N

N

Sketch plan   **2°42'·97E**   *Depths in Metres*

Pilotage

Approach

For outer approach see plan on page 91

From west Round the very prominent Punta de Cala Figuera which has a lighthouse (white round tower with black diagonal stripes on building, 24m) and radio masts on its steep cliffs. Cross the Bahía de Palma on a northeast course; planes taking off and landing from Palma airport give a good indication of the position of this harbour. In the closer approach the long sandy Playa del Arenal, which is backed by a line of high-rise buildings, will be seen. Near the northwest end of this beach is a separate group of high-rise buildings with the harbour in front. The small, low Islote Galera which has reefs extending 100m southwest, lies 0·5M northwest of the harbour entrance.

From east Round cabos Blanco and Enderrocat into Bahía de Palma. Once past the Marine Reserve, Puerto San Antonio lies almost 3·3M distant.

Anchorage in the approach

Anchor southeast of the entrance in 5m over sand, or in nearby Cala Estancia (39°32'·1N 2°42'·8E), a small *cala* just west of the port. This is protected by two short breakwaters but is shallow (1–1·5m) and open to the south. A particularly large hotel overlooks it from the west and there is a busy road nearby.

Entrance

An extension to the end of the southwest breakwater has improved protection, particularly at the visitors' quay, but has turned the entrance into an S-bend. Observe the 2kn speed limit.

Berthing

Preferably call ahead on VHF Ch 09 to check that a berth will be available or, of course, book in advance. Otherwise secure to the inner side of the southwest breakwater and visit the harbour office at the Club Marítimo building. There is no more than 2·5–2·8m at the entrance and visitors' quay, shoaling

Puerto de San Antonio de la Playa looking north. It is very close to the airport

III. MALLORCA

to 1·5m in places deeper into the marina. They estimate about 20–25 visitors berths, being partly dependant on length.

Note The visitors' berth becomes virtually untenable in conditions likely to create a swell from the southerly quadrant due to reflection from the eastern breakwater. It is recommended that this port be avoided during strong south winds.

Facilities

Water Taps on all quays and pontoons, including the visitors' quay.

Electricity 220v AC points on all quays and pontoons, including the visitors' quay. 380v AC in the boatyard.

Fuel Diesel and petrol from pumps at the head of the east breakwater; the green column marking the starboard side of the entrance emerges from the fuel cabin's roof. There is a self-service facility giving 24 hour availability for fuel.

Provisions Many shops and supermarkets nearby, with more in Palma three miles away. Hypermarket about two miles away on the road between Palma and the airport. Market Tuesdays and Thursdays in Ca'n Pastilla.

Ice From the bar.

Chandlery Near the harbour. Several large chandleries in Palma.

Repairs Boatyard on the west side of the harbour, equal to most work. Otherwise large boatyards in Palma. A 60-tonne travel-lift in the boatyard, 6-tonne mobile crane and several smaller ones. A small slipway near the club Maritimo building.

Engineers, electronic & radio repairs at the boatyard. Several sailmakers in Palma.

Yacht club The Club Marítimo San Antonio de la Playa has a large clubhouse with restaurant, bar, terrace, showers, etc.

Showers Below the *Club Marítimo* building.

Laundrette In Ca'n Pastilla.

Banks In Ca'n Pastilla, directly behind the yacht harbour.

Medical services In Ca'n Pastilla. Hospital in Palma 3½ miles away.

Transport

Car hire/taxis In the town.

Buses Frequent bus service to Palma.

Ferries From Palma to the other islands and mainland Spain.

Air services Busy international airport three miles away.

Ashore

A short distance from Palma, with a regular bus service.

Eating out

Restaurant at the Club Marítimo and many more restaurants, cafés, and bars in the town.

Puerto de Cala Gamba

39°32'·8N 2°41'·8E

A small shallow well protected harbour with 275 berths, occupied with local vessels. Silting reduces depths in the marina to 1·4m.

Communications
VHF Ch 09
Club Náutico Cala Gamba ✆ 971 26 18 49
info@cncg.es
www.cncg.es

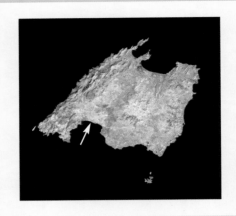

The harbour

The addition of new breakwaters and pontoons has turned this pleasant little fishing harbour into a flourishing yacht harbour with 275 berths, but both depth and facilities are still limited. Much of the harbour carries less than 2m, though 2·5m may be found against parts of the southwest breakwater. The entrance has been known to silt-up, reducing to 1·4m. It cannot be entered with any swell from southeast, south or southwest due to very shallow water in the approach, but otherwise approach and entry offer no difficulties. The noise generated by nearby Palma airport is considerable.

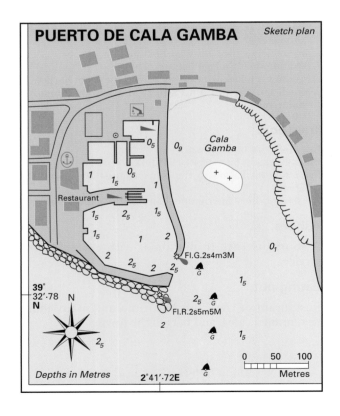

Pilotage

Approach

See plan on page 91

From west Puerto de Cala Gamba lies 1·3M northwest of Puerto de San Antonio de la Playa and slightly north of the airport main runway. A tall, solid, black and white buoy with an × topmark (Fl.Y.3s3M) 650m south of the harbour entrance marks the water inlet for a power station, the chimney of which will be seen. A west cardinal beacon marks the end of a short breakwater 550m northwest of the harbour, with a second west cardinal beacon, also a further 600m to the northwest. All three must be passed on the seaward side. Four small conical green buoys and a conical red buoy are the starboard entrance channel markers to the harbour.

From east Steer north-northwest from Cabo Enderrocat, being certain to leave both Islote Galera, 0·5M northwest of Puerto de San Antonio de la Playa, and the black and white buoy to starboard.

Anchorage in the approach

Anchor in 4m over stones 400m south of the entrance and some 250m north of the buoy mentioned above. Holding is poor.

Entrance

Approach cautiously heading northeast. Though dredged from time to time the entrance channel is narrow and subject to silting to 1·4M although the port claim 2m.

Berthing

Maximum size of vessel is 12m. Because of depth issues, yachts should call on VHF Ch 09 to establish the position on depth and berth availability before attempting entry.

Puerto de Cala Gamba: shallows to north of harbour can be seen clearly

Facilities

Water Taps on quays and pontoons.
Electricity 220v AC points on quays and pontoons.
Fuel Not available.
Provisions Some small shops nearby, supermarkets and more shops a little further inland and all the resources of Palma 2½M away. Hypermarket on the road between Palma and the airport.
Ice From the Club Náutico bar.
Repairs Local craftsmen can carry out simple work. Fully equipped boatyards in Palma. 5-tonne and 1-tonne cranes near the root of the east breakwater. A slipway on the central mole and another in the northeast corner.
Yacht club Club Náutico Cala Gamba has a clubhouse overlooking the harbour with restaurant, bar, showers, etc.
Showers At the Club Náutico.
Banks Nearby.
Hospital/medical services In Palma, 2½M away.

Transport

Car hire/taxis Locally or in Palma.
Buses Frequent bus service to Palma.
Ferries From Palma to the other islands and mainland Spain.
Air services Busy international airport two miles away.

Eating out

Numerous restaurants, cafés and bars nearby.

Puerto del Molinar de Levante (Caló d'en Rigo)

39°33'·4N 2°40'·5E

A small fishing harbour in a quaint old village, with berths for 140 craft drawing not much more than half a metre as the entrance is silted

Communications
Club Marítimo Molinar de Levante ☎ 971 27 34 79

The harbour

A very small fishing harbour built in Caló d'en Rigo, only suitable for craft drawing around half a metre (due to reduced depths in the entrance) and under 9m in length. It is almost exclusively occupied by small speedboats. Facilities are limited to everyday requirements. Approach and entrance are easy but would be dangerous with swell from the southern quadrant.

Pilotage

Approach

See *plan* on *page 91*. Puerto del Molinar de Levante lies 0·3M to the southeast of Puerto de Cala Portixol, a short distance east of Puerto de Palma.

Anchorage in the approach

Anchor in 2·5m over sand and mud, 400m southeast of the harbour entrance, open southeast–southwest–northwest.

Entrance

Approach the east side of the harbour at slow speed, watching the depth carefully, until the entrance opens up to port. The shallow nature of this harbour means that it is only suitable for small motor boats and even then the maximum length permitted is 6·5m.

Berthing

Seek a vacant berth and visit the Club Marítimo office for allocation of a visitors' berth.

Puerto del Molinar. Note silting in entrance

View northwest over Puerto del Molinar (bottom left) and Puerto de Cala Portixol. Puerto de Palma in background

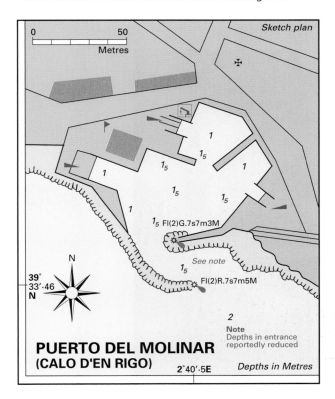

Facilities

Water Taps around the harbour.
Electricity 220v AC points around the harbour.
Fuel Not available.
Provisioning Shops and supermarkets in El Molinar.
Ice From the Club Marítimo bar.
Chandlery Small chandlery shop nearby.
Repairs Crane (5 tonnes) on the north side of the harbour and three slipways around the harbour. Mechanic available.
Yacht club The Club Marítimo Molinar de Levante has a clubhouse with restaurant and bar on the west side of the harbour.
Banks In El Molinar.
Hospital/medical services In Palma, 1½ miles away.

Transport

See *Puerto de Cala Portixol*, following.

Ashore

The surrounding area is, as yet, relatively unspoilt, with some attractive older houses and a lofty brick church directly behind the harbour.

Eating out

A wide selection of restaurants/cafés nearby.

Puerto de Cala Portixol

39°33'·5N 2°40'·1E

A large and very safe fishing and yacht harbour less than 2M east of Palma with berths for 300 vessels, but it is usually full with local boats and has little space for visitors

Communications
Club Náutico Portixol ☎ 971 24 24 24
  info@cnportixol.com
  www.cnportixol.com

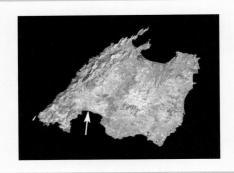

The harbour

An old fishing harbour just east of Palma, in a semicircular cove, converted into a combined fishing and yachting harbour by the addition of extra breakwaters and other facilities. Berthing available for 300 vessels, but restricted to not much more than 12m. No space is reserved for visitors. Much of the harbour has depths less than 2m. Traffic noise from the nearby motorway is distinctly audible, as is the nearby airport.

As with the harbours to the southeast, approach and entrance are straightforward other than in heavy swell from the south quadrant, when shoals in the approach could render it dangerous.

Pilotage

Approach

From west Round the very prominent Punta de Cala Figuera (*see plans on page 91 and 183*) with its lighthouse (white round tower with black diagonal stripes on building, 24m) and radio masts on its steep cliffs. Cross the Bahía de Palma heading northeast towards Palma Cathedral, a very large building with small twin spires. From a position 0·8M off Puerto de Palma south breakwater, the very much smaller breakwaters of Puerto de Cala Portixol will be seen 1·5M ahead.

From east Round Cabo Blanco, which is high with steep light brown cliffs topped by a lighthouse (white tower and building, 12m) and an old watchtower, and set a course northwest until the buildings of Palma come into view. Puerto de Cala Portixol will be seen to starboard when still a mile short of the entrance to Puerto de Palma.

Anchorage in the approach

See *Cala Portixolet* below.

Entrance

Approach and enter on a northerly course between the outer breakwaters and then the inner moles, to enter the main harbour. There is a 2kn speed limit.

Puerto de Cala Portixol: berthing for smaller yachts

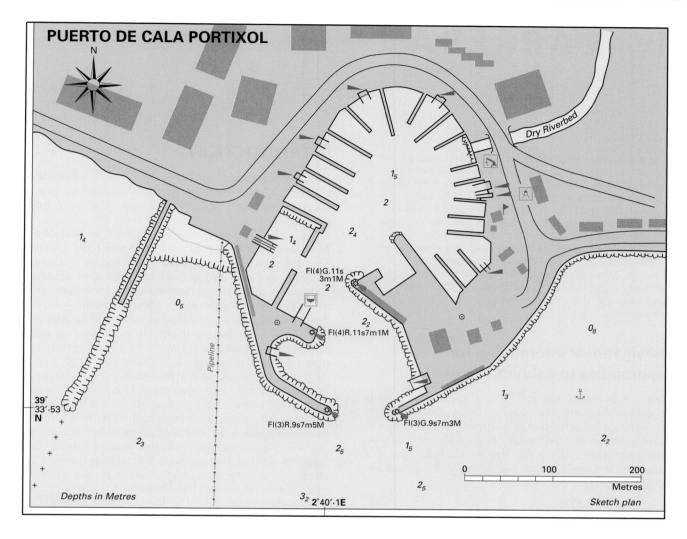

PUERTO DE CALA PORTIXOL

N

Dry Riverbed

Pipeline

Fl(4)G.11s
3m1M

Fl(4)R.11s7m1M

Fl(3)R.9s7m5M

Fl(3)G.9s7m3M

**39°
33'·53
N**

0   100   200
Metres

Depths in Metres   2°40'·1E   Sketch plan

Call the harbour in advance of entry to establish depths in the entrance and inside and berth availability.

Berthing

Local yachts berth on the west side of the harbour just inside the inner mole, but it is unlikely that there will be a space available.

Facilities

Water Water taps around the harbour.
Electricity 220v AC points around the harbour.
Fuel Not available.
Provisions Some shops nearby, with a vast range in Palma, less than two miles away.
Ice Ice machine at the Club Náutico.
Chandlery Two chandlery/fishing tackle shops on the road opposite the harbour gate.
Repairs Simple work possible. Fully equipped boatyards in Palma. A 4-tonne crane to the northeast of the harbour. Nine slipways, mostly very small.
Yacht club Club Náutico Portixol has a pleasant clubhouse on the east of the harbour with restaurant, bar, terrace, etc.
Showers At the Club Náutico.
Banks In Palma.
Hospital/medical services In Palma.

Transport

Car hire/taxis In Palma.
Buses Frequent bus service to Palma.
Ferries From Palma to the other islands and mainland Spain.
Air services Busy international airport three miles away.

Ashore

As for Palma.

Eating out

Many eating houses in the area.

⚓ Cala Portixolet

39°33'·6N 2°40'·4E

A shallow and somewhat bleak anchorage, with the rocky breakwaters of Puerto de Cala Portixol to the west and a road backed by houses at the head. Anchor in 1·5m over sand, open to the southern quadrant.

IV. CABRERA

As a National Park, Cabrera is a restricted zone of great natural interest due to its rich wildlife and several rare species of flora, fauna and birdlife unique to the archipelago. The island may only be visited if a permit has first been acquired through its offices in Mallorca. There are 50 buoys in the harbour, available to permit holders and limited to one or two nights. Unsupervised walks are limited to the foreshore and castle but other walks are conducted by the park ranger. There are virtually no facilities but the rugged beauty, rich wildlife and tranquillity of the island await those who are prepared to accept these inconveniences.

Navigational information for approaches to Cabrera

Since a permit obtained from the main islands is required to visit, approaches from the south are unlikely. The only dangers approaching from the south side are the unlit rocks around Islotes Estels on the southernmost tip. To the north, Isla Conejera and the passages between the island and Cabrera are described in this volume.

Magnetic variation

Less than 001°E.

Approach lights

Punta Anciola 39°07'·8N 02°55'·4E Fl(3)15s121m20M Red and white chequered tower on white building 21m 277·5°-vis-169°

Cabo Llebeig 39°09'·7N 02°55'·1E Fl(4)14·5s74m7M Black and white chequered angular tower 7m

Isla Horadada 39°12'·5N 02°58'·8E Fl(2)12s42m10M White round tower, five black bands, on white round house 13m 047°-vis-0001°

INTRODUCTION

Cabrera is a rugged and hilly island with numerous off lying islets, stretching north-northeast like giant stepping stones towards Mallorca, just over five miles away.

The archipelago was declared a National Maritime and Terrestial Park in April 1991 by the Spanish government in order to preserve the rare indigenous plant and animal life. The area around Cabrera is highly regulated: a national treasure and a frequently patrolled conservation zone. Administration for the island is with the Ministry of Agriculture. Anchoring is strictly prohibited in and around its shores except with a special permit as noted under Anchoring exceptions. (*See page 209*). Access is restricted and a permit must be obtained before visiting (*see below*). The main island measures some three miles in each direction, indented by several deep bays and rising to 172m at Alto de Picamoscas. There is an excellent sheltered bay on the northwest side, known as Puerto de Cabrera despite having no port facilities beyond a couple of short jetties. Anchoring is forbidden but fifty visitors' moorings have been laid.

The only other island in the group of any size is Isla Conejera, measuring about one mile by 0·6M and separated from Isla de Cabrera by a channel 0·7M wide and more than 20m deep. Seven smaller islands lie north of Isla de Cabrera, with others close inshore to the south. In general Isla de Cabrera and its islets are all steep-to, and in most places deep water runs close inshore.

No tourist developments, no jet-skis, no noise and only other seafarers for company: this place is heavenly.

Wildlife

There are several species of fauna, flora and lizards unique to the archipelago, which is also a haven for seabirds including the rare Audouins gull (see *Flora and Fauna* in the *General Introduction* on *page 9*) and birds of prey such as the osprey and both peregrine and Eleonora's falcon. The surrounding waters are home to fish, turtles, dolphins, whales and a variety of corals. Booklets describing the history and wildlife of the Cabrera group are available in several languages from the Cabrera National Park Office in Palma (*see details on page 206*).

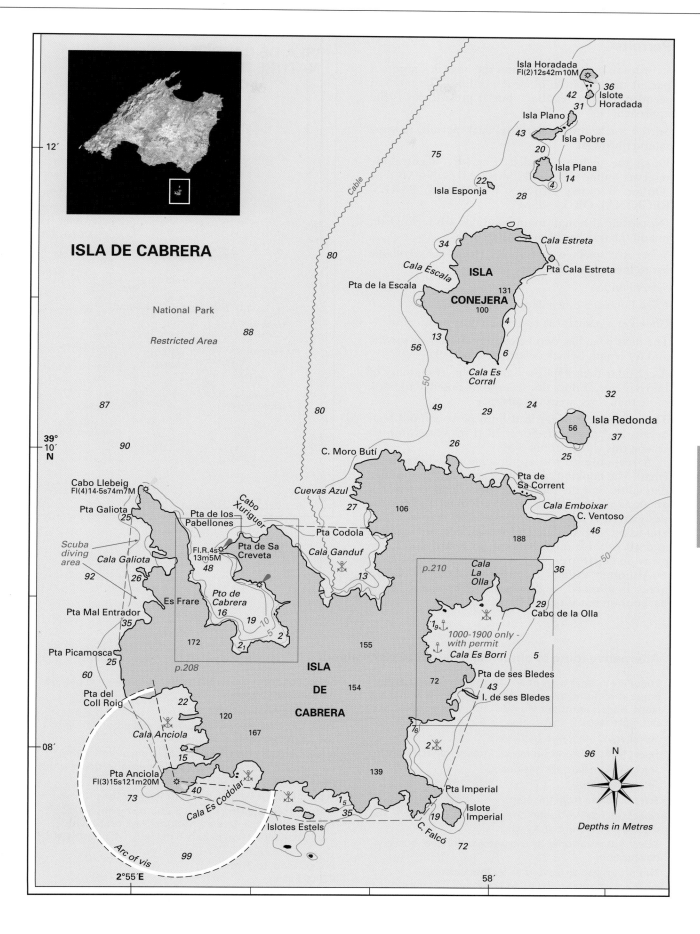

ISLA DE CABRERA

National Park

Restricted Area

88

Cable

80

75

Isla Horadada
Fl(2)12s42m10M
36
42 Islote
31 Horadada
Isla Plano
43 Isla Pobre
20
Isla Plana
14
22 28 4

Isla Esponja

34

Cala Estreta

Cala Escala
ISLA
Pta Cala Estreta

Pta de la Escala
CONEJERA
131
100
4

13
6
56

Cala Es
Corral

80

49 29 24 32

26

C. Moro Butí
56 Isla Redonda
37
25

87

39°
10´
N

90

Cabo Llebeig
Fl(4)14·5s74m7M

Pta Galiota
25

*Scuba
diving
area*

Cala Galiota
92 26

Es Frare

Pta Mal Entrador
35

Pta Picamosca
25

60

Pta del
Coll Roig

22 Cala Anciola

120

Pta Anciola
Fl(3)15s121m20M
40
73

Cala Es Codolar
35

Islotes Estels

Arc of vis

99

2°55´E

Cabo
Xuriguer

Pta de los
Pabellones

Fl.R.4s
13m5M
48

Pta de Sa
Creveta

Cuevas Azul

27

Pta Codola

*Pto de
Cabrera*
16

19

10
5 2

21

172

p.208

Cala Ganduf
13

106

188

ISLA

DE

CABRERA

155

154

167

15

1 5

139

19

Pta de
Sa Corrent

Cala Emboixar
C. Ventoso
46

p.210 *Cala
La
Olla*
36

29 Cabo de la Olla

1 9

*1000-1900 only -
with permit*
Cala Es Borri
5

72

Pta de ses Bledes
43
I. de ses Bledes

7 6

2

Pta Imperial

Islote
Imperial

C. Falcó
72

96 N

Depths in Metres

58´

IV. CABRERA

Permits

In order to moor or even enter the bays in Cabrera a permit must first be obtained online. The method seems to change regularly, but at present this is the approach:

Search for 'Cabrera National Park permit' in your internet browser

Open the website headed 'English - Central de reservas online - ORGANISMO AUTONOMO' or 'Online Booking Office - NATIONAL PARKS' REGIONAL ORGANISM'

(Note that although main headings are in English, not all the text has been translated)

Select Archipiélago de Cabrera (from the scrollable list to the right of the page)

Select Fondeo

Click Pulsar en este enlace

Click Per a realitzar la reserva en línia premi aquí

The next page has two boxes, for charter or private and for length (which determines charge).

A calendar then appears showing the availability of buoys. Note, it does not seem to be possible to book more than three weeks in advance.

The subsequent pages lead onto personal and boat details and payment. For a 12–15m vessel in high season this will be about 30€.

A response to the application will be sent by email. The booking can only be used on the specified date (although the local port officer may extend for an extra night if there are free buoys) and for the designated colour of buoy. Animals may not land and fishing is prohibited. Holding tanks are required and all rubbish must be kept on board and taken away on departure.

Although sailing around the island in certain areas is allowed, nights have to be spent in the harbour on the allocated buoy.

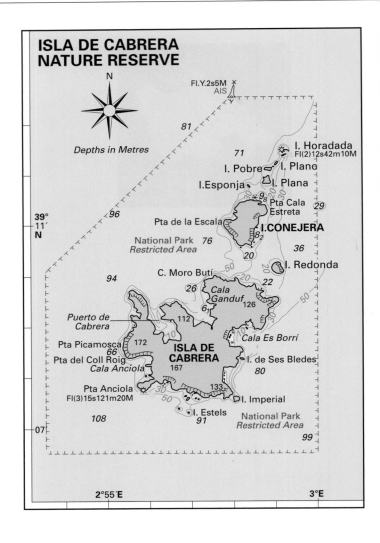

Alternative route to obtaining a permit to visit Cabrera

There are several ways of arriving at the online permit application form, all somewhat long-winded with many steps. Here is another method with fewer lengthy links but more steps:

Select www.magrama.gob.es/en/

Select National Parks (under Of interest, on the right)

Select Red de Parques Nacionales

Select Our Parks

Select Cabrera from the map

Select Guia del Visitante (under Accesos Directos on the right with a picture of a yacht)

Select Autorizaciones de uso público (fondeo, buceo y navegación)

This brings you to Govern de les Illes Balears

Under: AUTORIZACIÓN PARA FONDEAR, BUCEAR O NAVEGAR EN EL PARQUE NACIONAL DEL ARCHIPIÉLAGO DE CABRERA

Select Fondear en Cabrera (under Fondear en el parque nacional de Cabrera).

Select English (top right)

From there follow the instructions and enter details of the yacht and captain on the form.

It is worth the effort, which ends in payment for the permit with your credit card and a printable ticket which does not need to be printed out.

A phone app is being created to simplify the process.

Note If a scuba diving permit is also being applied for, then a visit to the Cabrera National Park office with original qualification papers is needed. Office located at:

Gremi de corredos
Poligon son Rosinyol
07009 Palma
℡ +34 971 177 647

Each permit is accompanied by a map with details of permitted daytime (1000–1900) anchorages – currently two areas in the entrance to Puerto de Cabrera and Cala Es Borri on the east coast – and prohibited areas, which at present include Cala Ganduf, Cala Anciola, Cala Es Codolar and others on the south coast: Cala La Olla and Cala Emboixar. Even so, brief details of these *calas* are included below in case the restrictions are lifted. There is a 5kn speed limit in the entire Maritime Park area and a 2kn speed limit in the harbour.

A permit can also be obtained in person by a visit to the National Park office in Palma at the address below taking ships papers, passport, and perhaps certificate of competence. If a scuba diving permit is also being applied for, then a visit to this office with original qualification papers is needed. Finally, we have found that staff in the marina offices in Mallorca have been happy to help obtain permits, particularly those at Ports IB marinas. The National Park office is located at:

Gremi de corredors 10, Piso1
Poligono de son Rosignol 07009 Palma
☎ +34 971 177 641
autorizacions@dgmambie.caib.es

History

It is probable that Isla de Cabrera (Goat Island) and Isla Conejera (Rabbit Island) were inhabited in prehistoric times: traces of an ancient building have been identified at Clot des Guix, and Roman and Byzantine ceramics and coins have also been found. The castle overlooking Puerto de Cabrera is thought to date back to the end of the 14th century and was probably built as a defence against pirates. During the Peninsular Wars some 9,000 French prisoners were interned on the island, where nearly two-thirds died of disease and starvation. They are buried near the castle and a memorial was erected in 1847 in the centre of the island.

Prior to the first world war the island was privately owned, but was requisitioned by the Spanish government in 1915 to prevent it falling into enemy hands. A small army garrison was established (which still exists) and at various times the area has been used as a gunnery range. Landing on any of the smaller islands could be dangerous, due to the presence of unexploded shells or other ammunition (as well as being contrary to the rules of the park).

Tourist offices

Sightseeing is limited on Cabrera as it is a National Park, but there is a Park Information Office in the harbour (*see harbour plan on page 208*). Their head office is in Palma, where permits are issued, details of which are above.

Puerto de Cabrera

39°09'·3N 02°55'·6E

This is a large sheltered bay laid with 50 buoys for which a permit must be obtained prior to entry (see notes on *Permits* opposite)

Communications
Cabrera National Park Office VHF Ch 09
☎ 971 17 76 41/17 66 13

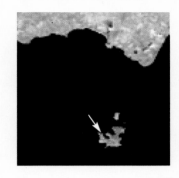

The harbour

A large natural harbour which can be entered in virtually any conditions apart from strong northwest winds, which are rare. Shelter is good, though a swell rolls in with north or northwest winds. Gusts blowing down into the harbour from the surrounding hills can also be fierce. However, in normal conditions it is a truly peaceful spot, though tourist ferries from Mallorca (Colonia de San Jordi) arrive daily in the summer.

Pilotage

Approach

From north When approaching from this direction the chain of islands running north/south does not appear separated from Isla de Cabrera itself until quite close (*see plan on page 205*). Leave these islands to port, heading for a position slightly east of Cabo Lleibeig (black and white chequered angular tower, 7m). The entrance lies close under this headland, with Punta de Sa Creveta (red and white chequered angular tower, 5m) to the east.

From west The hills of Isla de Cabrera can be seen from some distance away, with the line of smaller islands running towards the north visible on closer approach. Set a course to round Cabo Lleibeig, the northwest tip of the island, after which the entrance will open up beyond.

From east or northeast Pass either side of Isla Redonda to round Cabo Moro Butí and cross the wide and deep Cala Ganduf towards Cabo Xuriguer and Punta de los Pabellones. The entrance will open up on rounding Punta de Sa Creveta beyond.

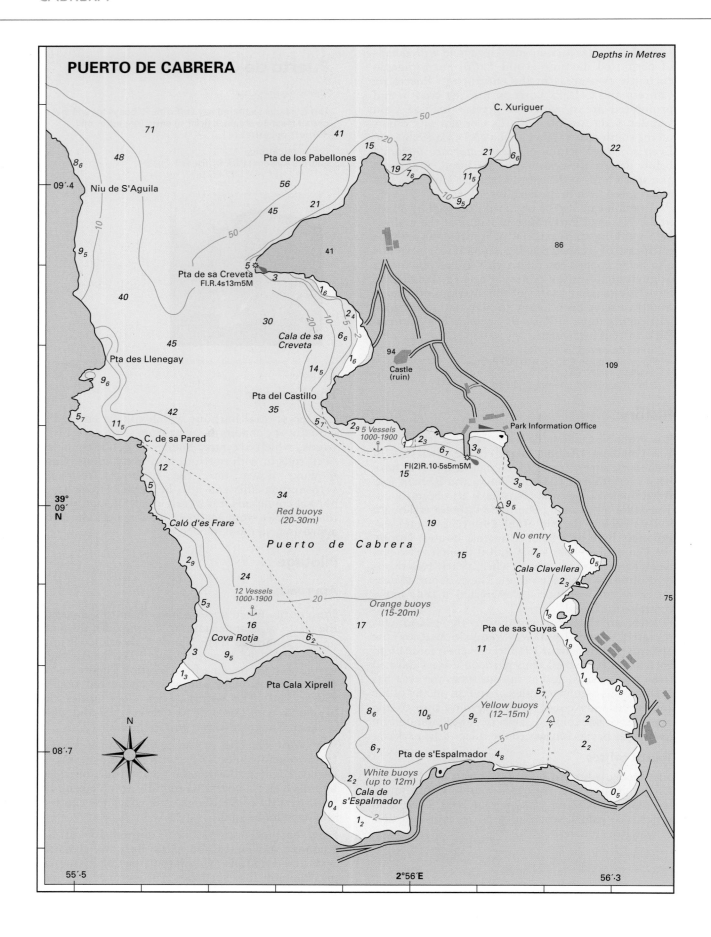

PUERTO DE CABRERA

Depths in Metres

C. Xuriguer

71

48

8₆

09´.4

Niu de S'Aguila

9₅

Pta de los Pabellones

41

56

45

21

50

15

20

22

19

7₆

21

6₆

22

11₅

10

9₅

86

40

30

Cala de sa
Creveta

20

10

2₄

6₆

1₆

14₅

Pta del Castillo

35

94

Castle
(ruin)

109

5

Pta de sa Creveta
Fl.R.4s13m5M

3

1₆

5

Pta des Llenegay

45

9₆

8₆

5₇

11₅

42

C. de sa Pared

12

5

**39°
09´
N**

5₇

2₉ 5 Vessels
1000-1900

1

2₃

6₇

3₈

Park Information Office

Fl(2)R.10·5s5m5M

15

3₈

3₈

9₅

No entry

7₆

1₉

0₅

Cala Clavellera

2₃

34

Red buoys
(20-30m)

Puerto de Cabrera

19

15

Caló d'es Frare

2₉

24

12 Vessels
1000-1900

5₃

16

Cova Rotja

6₂

20

Orange buoys
(15-20m)

17

11

1₉

Pta de sas Guyas

1₉

75

3

9₅

1₃

Pta Cala Xiprell

8₆

10₅

9₅

10

1₄

0₈

2

5₇

Yellow buoys
(12–15m)

2₂

N

08´.7

6₇

Pta de s'Espalmador

4₈

5

2₂

0₅

White buoys
(up to 12m)

Cala de
s'Espalmador

2₂

0₄

1₂

2

55´.5

2°56´E

56´.3

Currents

Strong wind-induced currents may be experienced around the islands, the direction and strength dependent on that of the wind.

Entrance

The entrance, which is deep but relatively narrow, lies between Cabo Llebeig and Punta de Sa Creveta. Wind conditions in both the entrance and harbour can be very fluky due to the high surrounding hills. Mooring buoys lie south of a line between Cabo de sa Pared and Punta del Castillo. As well as the 5kn speed limit in the entire Maritime Park area there is a 2kn speed limit in the harbour itself.

Berthing

Lying alongside the jetty is only possible with a military permit or in an emergency.

Moorings

Secure to one of the 50 visitors' moorings, colour-coded according to yacht size as follows:

White	up to 12m
Yellow	12–15m
Orange	15–20m
Red	20–30m

No charge is made for mooring use. Smaller yacht moorings are tucked into Cala de s'Espalmador and are the most sheltered but also furthest from the main (northeast) jetty, the only place where landing is permitted.

Secure to the mooring by putting a loop of line through the eye on the end of the mooring rope and paying out until the pick-up buoy is back in the water. If it is left out of the water the guard will correct it.

Anchoring exceptions

Anchoring in the harbour is generally forbidden. However, relaxation to the rule has been known, to allow 12 vessels to anchor between the hours of 1000 and 1900 on the west side of the harbour between C. de sa Pared and Pta Cala Xiprell and for five craft on the east side in the cove southeast of Pta del Castillo, as marked on the plan.

A third anchorage, possibly available between these hours, lies in Cala Es Borri (*described overleaf*). Recently, it has not been permitted to anchor anywhere on Cabrera, only to use a mooring buoy. But check with the National Park Office when applying for your permit before arrival, ② 971 17 76 41.

Formalities

A guard visits each yacht every evening to check that a valid permit is held. Landing by dinghy is only allowed at the main jetty, and the permit must be shown at the Park Information Office on embarking ashore. Scuba permits should also be presented before diving.

Puerto de Cabrera. The peace and tranquility is palpable

Facility

Water Small quantities of non-drinking water can usually be collected from the army *cantina* (take containers).

Ashore

It was once possible to roam over the island unsupervised, but yachtsmen, having landed on the main jetty, are now restricted to the road by the foreshore and a walk to the castle. All other walks (minimum four people) are conducted by Park Rangers at designated times available from the Park Information Office.

The walk up the steep track leading to the castle ruins will be rewarded with spectacular views and it is also possible to visit the memorial to the French prisoners of war.

The Cuevas Azul (Blue Caves) in Cala Ganduf some 600m south–southwest of Cabo Moro Butí are also most attractive but are only accessible by sea. Anchoring in the *cala* is not permitted, but at some 1·4M from the buoys in Puerto de Cabrera, a visit by dinghy may be feasible.

There are a few houses near the south mole, some used by the owners of the sheep and pigs pastured on the island which keep the vegetation down.

Eating out

The army *cantina* welcomes visitors and has a bar, though food is not available.

Isla de Cabrera Park buildings *Henry Buchanan*

IV. CABRERA

Anchorages around Cabrera

⚓ Cala Es Borri

39°08'·7N 02°57'·5E

This is the only anchorage which *may* be available to yachts, apart from those within Puerto de Cabrera. If permitted (see *Anchoring*), it will be restricted to use between 1000 and 1900 daily. Anchor in the central and southern parts of the bay. Cala Es Borri is actually the small inlet at its southwest corner. No more than twenty boats can be present at any one time in the *cala*.

Anchor as space permits in 5m+ over sand and rock, open to the east quadrant and to swell from the south. There is a fine sandy beach in Cala Es Borri itself.

Cala Es Borri looking north. Isla Redonda in view over peninsula with Isla Conejera top left of photo. Isla Plana and Mallorca just in view

Calas and features around Isla de Cabrera

Anchoring is prohibited in the *calas* listed below. Some, as noted, can be sailed in, whereas others can only be admired from afar. These brief details are included for interest.

Cala Ganduf

39°09'·2N 02°56'·7E

A protected and deep bay with several separate indentations, open for sailing, but nothing more.

Between Isla de Cabrera and Isla Redonda

An 800m wide passage with a minimum depth of 21m. Transit in a northwest–southeast direction.

Cala Emboixar

39°09'·6N 02°58'·3E

An attractive small bay under cliffs, with a rocky ledge looking like a breakwater to the northwest. Open for sailing, but not for anchoring. There are two small beaches, one rocky and one of sand.

Cabo Ventoso (Cap Ventós)

39°09'·5N 02°58'·6E

A high (188m), steep, rocky-cliffed promontory with good water at its base.

Cala la Olla

39°09'·0N 02°57'·9E

An interesting *cala* amidst wild scenery at the mouth of the eastern of two small *calas*, themselves at the northern end of a wide bay. Sailing (only) allowed in the *cala*. Several islets lie close to the west.

Between Islote Imperial and Isla de Cabrera

A 100m wide, 18m deep passage between dramatic cliffs, for use in settled weather.

Sailing is permitted along the south coast from Islote Imperial west to Punta Anciola.

Islotes Estels

39°07'·3N 02°56'·4E (Southernmost: Estels de Fuera)

Five scattered, rocky islands up to 750m off the south coast of Isla de Cabrera.

Punta Anciola

39°07'·7N 02°55'·3E (Lighthouse)

A rounded headland connected to Isla Cabrera by a low, narrow neck. The paintwork on its lighthouse (red and white chequered tower on white building, 21m) may well be unique.

North of Punta Mal Entrador
39°09'·1N 02°55'·1E

A small bay open to the western quadrant. This area is currently reserved for licensed scuba diving.

Cala Galiota
39°09'·2N 02°55'·1E

An attractive *cala* under high cliffs. As above, Cala Galiota is also part of an area restricted for licensed Scuba diving.

Cabo Llebeig
39°09'·7N 02°55'·0E

A large (60m) conspicuous rocky hummock with a not very prominent lighthouse (black and white chequered angular tower, 7m).

The smaller islands of the Isla de Cabrera group

Isla Redonda
Centred on 39°10'·1N 02°58'·6E

A roughly circular island some 450m in diameter and 56m high. No anchoring or landing allowed.

Between Isla Redonda and Isla Conejera

A 1,000m-wide passage with a minimum depth of 20m.

Isla Conejera (Illa des Conills)
Centred on 39°11'·1N 02°57'·9E

The second-largest island at 1M long by 0·6M wide and reaching 131m high. There are potential landing places on the east coast and several *calas* (see below) but their use is currently prohibited.

Cala Es Corral, Isla Conejera
39°10'·6N 02°57'·9E

Two small *calas* side by side at the south end of the island. There are two small offlying islets on either side.

Between Isla Conejera and Isla Esponja or Isla Plana

A passage 400m wide, with a minimum depth of 11m if midway between Isla Conejera and the two smaller islands.

Isla Esponja
39°11'·7N 02°57'·9E

200m by 40m, and 23m high, Isla Esponja is steep-to and inaccessible.

Isla Plana
39°11'·8N 02°58'·4E

400m by 125m, 26m high.

Between Isla Plana and Isla Pobre

A 150m wide pass with depths shoaling to 2·5m.

Isla Pobre
39°12'·1N 02°58'·4E

400m by 100m, 27m high.

Between Isla Pobre and Isla Plano

Foul.

Isla Plano (Illot Plá)
39°12'·2N 02°58'·6E

200m by 100m, 27m high.

Between Isla Plano and Islote Horadada

A passage 200m wide with 12m minimum depth.

Islote Horadada (Illot Foradada or Foradat)
39°12'·3N 02°58'·8E

100m by 80m, 12m high.

Between Islote Horadada and Isla Horadada

Foul.

Isla Horadada (Illa Foradada or Foradat)
39°12'·5N 02°58'·8E

210m by 120m and 42m high, with a lighthouse (white round tower with five black bands on white round house, 13m) on its summit.

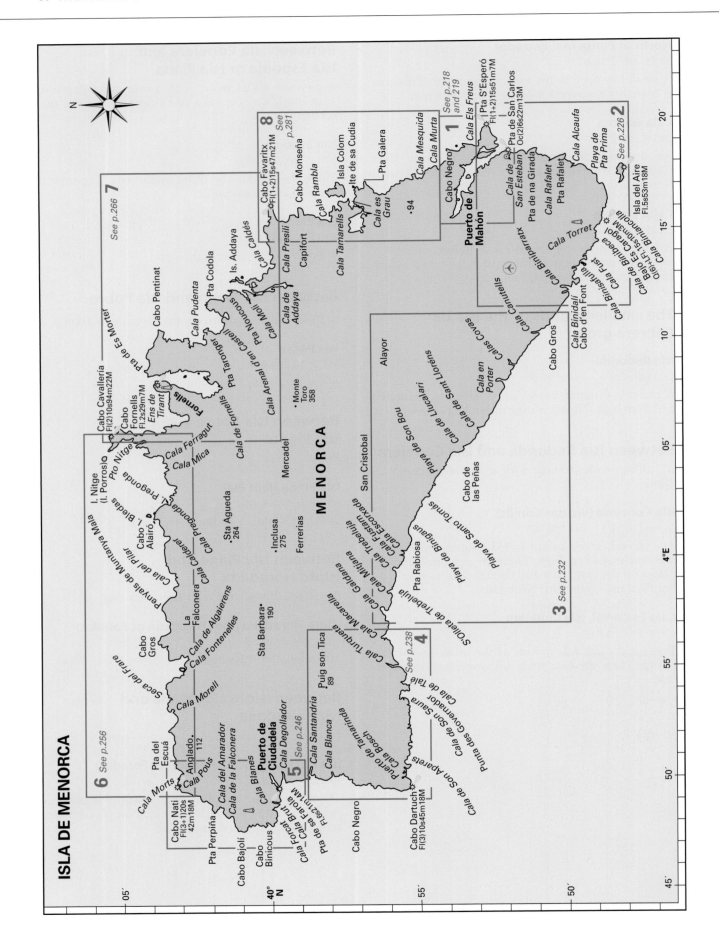

ISLA DE MENORCA

V. MENORCA

The earliest inhabited of the Islas Baleares, Menorca abounds in ancient monuments and relics. It also boasts one of the largest natural harbours in the world, Mahón, offering excellent berthing and nautical facilities as well as historical sites to visit. There are only three significant other ports, (Ciudadela, Fornells, Addaia) and numerous delightful bays in which to anchor, with only short distances between them. There is a strong British influence resulting from previous British occupations of the island and a preponderance of British retirees and holidaymakers over recent decades.

The coastline of Menorca is considered in a clockwise direction around the island beginning at Puerto de Mahón and divided into the following sections:

Ancient monastery with a church built in 1595 on the highest point in Menorca, Monte Toro

Navigational information for approaches to Menorca

Menorca is an excellent departure point when heading east and northeast to France, Italy or Corsica and Sardinia. Space for berthing in Puerto de Mahón while awaiting favourable winds is hard to find in summer. These days Menorca's harbours and anchorages are every bit as crowded as those of the other islands and there is little chance of finding a marina or harbour berth in summer without booking well in advance. Moreover, there may be difficulty in being able to anchor in Mahón when marinas are not full (see below) unless bad weather is being experienced.

Magnetic variation

Approximately 001°E.

Approach and coastal passage charts

(See *Appendix* for full list of Baleares charts).
Imray	M3
Admiralty	1703, 2833
Spanish	48E, 6A, 428A
French	5505, 7117

Approach lights

Punta S'Esperó 39°52'·7N 04°19'·7E Fl(1+2)15s51m7M
 White round tower, two black bands, on white building 11m

Punta de San Carlos 39°52'N 04°18'·5E Oc(2)6s22m13M
 White round tower, three black bands, on square white base 15m 183°-vis-143°

Isla del Aire 39°48'N 04°17'·6E Fl.5s53m18M
 White tower, black bands, on white building 38m 197°-vis-111°

Bajo d'es Caragol 39°48'·6N 04°15'·3E Q(6)+LFl.15s10m3M
 South cardinal beacon with s topmark 10m

Cabo Dartuch (D'Artrutx) 39°55'·4N 03°49'·5E
 Fl(3)10s45m18M
 White tower, three black bands, on white building 34m 267°-vis-158°

Punta de sa Farola Fl.6s21m14m
 White tower, black stripes on white dwelling, 13m

Cabo Nati 40°03'·1N 03°49'·5E Fl(3+1)20s42m18M
 White aluminium cupola over a pale limestone tower on a red-roofed building 039°-vis-162°
 Note The light and structural characteristics of Cabo Nati are very similar to those of Cabo Formentor, Mallorca

Cabo Cavallería 40°05'·3N 04°05'·5E Fl(2)10s94m22M
 White tower and building 15m 074°-vis-292° Racon

Cabo Favaritx 39°59'·8N 4°16'·5E Fl(1+2)15s47m21M
 White tower, black diagonal stripes, on white building 28m

INTRODUCTION

Menorca lies 25 miles eat-northeast of Mallorca. It is the most easterly of the Islas Baleares and is 34 miles long and 11 miles wide. It is not as mountainous as the other two main islands, being for the most part a low plateau with a few small hills near the north coast and the lone Monte Toro (358m) near the centre of the island. This 'mountain' can be seen from afar and makes a useful landmark, as well as being a magnificent viewpoint for almost all the island.

Geologically the island is interesting, in that it consists of two parts. That north of a line drawn from near Cala Morell to Mahón is the oldest part of the Islas Baleares and was apparently originally joined to Corsica, mainland Europe and Catalonia. The southern part of the island was created later by a process of overlaying and folding, part of the same upheaval which formed the Alps. Menorca was also the first of the Baleares to become separated as an island, but this was much later. It lies in the path of the northwest *tramontana* or *mestral* gales and is often and justifiably referred to as the 'Windy Isle'. The north coast is dangerous when this wind is blowing and should be given a wide berth.

Viewed from offshore many parts of Menorca, especially the north coast, have a barren appearance, due to the rocky cliffs and hilly brown coastal hinterland, despite a considerable amount of arable and wooded areas further inland. However, these cliffs are broken by many *calas* which offer protected and attractive anchorages.

Puerto de Mahón (Maó) on the east coast is the major port and can be entered under most conditions. On the west coast lies the much smaller (and often very crowded) Puerto de Ciudadela, which offers shelter in all conditions other than westerly or southwesterly gales. The two northern harbours should not be entered with strong onshore winds as their entrances can be downright

Magnificent prehistoric *talayot* and *taula* David Russell

dangerous at such times. Once inside, a well anchored yacht should be safe deep in Fornells, if a little uncomfortable, and Addaia is effectively a fine 'hurricane hole' to sit out anything in relative comfort.

Menorca has noticeably fewer tourist developments than the other main Balearic Islands, and is certainly less commercialised than the other islands. Mahón is, to a certain extent, an exception because it has been an important naval base for many years and has absorbed the influences, habits and behaviour of the various occupying forces (including the British who were there for much of the 18th century). The island population is currently some 95,000, of whom more than a third live in either Mahón or Ciudadela. Local industries of long standing include leatherwork (mainly shoes), jewellery, and agriculture, particularly in respect of the production of hard, mature cheeses which are enjoyed throughout Spain.

Although not as spectacularly beautiful as much of Mallorca, Menorca has its own attractions and has much to offer those who prefer to avoid major centres of tourism.

For the serious navigator interested in cruising around the coast of Menorca the book *Menorca; Atlas Náutico* by Alfonso Buenaventura is a useful adjunct to planning as it shows the coastline in 67 chartlets of extreme detail.

There is a growing tendency in some of the *calas*, as in mainland Spain, to exclude or limit pleasure craft by laying swimmer buoys in high season. In Menorca this applies to all of the popular beaches including those which are remote from hotels or indeed any development.

History

Menorca has the greatest concentration of prehistoric remains in the entire Mediterranean, including what is claimed to be the oldest building in Europe (the Naveta des Tudons near Ciudadela). There are a number of Neolithic caves and villages on the island and many megalithic monuments such as *talayots* (towers), navetas (burial mounds) and *taulas* (T-shaped monuments) – probably built for religious and funerary purposes by the Bronze Age civilisation which inhabited the land before the Iberians established themselves. Unfortunately very little has been discovered about this Bronze Age tribe, or about the construction and use of the 400 or so large buildings and monuments which are scattered around the island.

In due course, as in large parts of the Mediterranean basin, Menorca saw successive waves of invasion and colonisation by Phoenicians, Carthaginians, Greeks, Romans, Vandals, Byzantines, Visigoths and Moors. During the occupation by the Carthaginians the towns of Maguén (Mahón) and Yamma (Ciudadela) were founded, though doubtless both inlets had been used by seafarers since time immemorial. The period of Roman occupation from 123BC to AD427 was relatively peaceful and prosperous, Mahón becoming Municipio Flavio Magontano and Ciudadela, Lamnona. Amongst other legacies, the Romans built the island's first road system. The men of Menorca were famed for their prowess with the slingshot and many were co-opted into the Roman army.

The successive waves of invasion and colonisation by Vandals, Byzantines and Visigoths left fewer permanent traces. After many years of raids, the island was finally occupied by the Moors in about 913. They remained until driven out by King Alfonso III of Aragon in 1287, by which time Menorca was the last Muslim territory in eastern Spain, although in theory it had owed allegiance to the crown of Aragon since 1232. The common prefix 'Bini', as in Binidalí and Binibeca, is from the Arabic, meaning 'belonging to the son of'.

The following centuries were even more difficult for the islanders, with devastating pirate raids, droughts and epidemics. In 1535 Mahón lost much of its population to a raid by the Turkish pirate Barbarossa; in 1558 it was the turn of Ciudadela, which withstood a nine-day siege before being overrun and almost completely destroyed by a force of 15,000 Turks.

Due to the strategic position of Mahón as a naval base in the western Mediterranean, it was coveted by all maritime nations and Menorca changed hands frequently. In 1708 it was occupied by the British, who had supported the Carlist cause in the War of the Spanish Succession, and in 1713 the island was officially ceded to Britain by the Treaty of Utrecht (as was Gibraltar). One of their most lasting legacies was the road built by the Governor, Sir Richard Kane, from Ciudadela to Mahón – the first good road linking the two towns since Roman times – and his moving of the capital from Ciudadela to Mahón in 1722. The island remained in British hands for more than forty years, during which time Mahón grew as a fortified naval base and the island prospered.

In 1756 a French army landed near Ciudadela and marched across the island to lay siege to the fortress of San Felipe, near Mahón, which was eventually forced to surrender. It was following this episode that the unfortunate Admiral Byng was executed by firing squad at Portsmouth, on the quarterdeck of HMS *Monarque*, for failing to engage the numerically superior French fleet and thereby lift the siege. British ships of the time were expected to engage and win in all circumstances on the basis of superior gunnery. This event provoked Voltaire's famous quip 'Dans ce pays-ci, il est bon de tuer de temps en temps un amiral pour encourager les autres.' ('In this country, it is wise from time to time to kill an admiral in order to encourage the others'). However, the French only held the island until 1763 when it was returned to Britain by the Treaty of Paris.

Richelieu, who had commanded the successful French invasion in 1756, had a sauce called *mahonésa* – based on the local aïoli (alioli) sauce –

served at the victory banquet in Paris. This delicacy, which his chef had invented while on the island, has become the ubiquitous 'mayonnaise'.

In 1782 a Franco-Spanish force once more laid siege to the garrison, which after another heroic resistance was forced to surrender. Not surprisingly one of the first things the victors did was to demolish the fortress, first built in the 1500s as a defence against Corsairs. Sixteen years later the British recaptured the island but had to return it to Spain in 1802 under the Treaty of Amiens. A direct result of this ongoing rivalry was the construction of forts and other large defensive works in and around the port of Mahón, many of which are still to be seen. Although Spanish territory, after the resumption of the Napoleonic war in 1804 and the defeat of the combined French and Spanish fleet at Trafalgar in 1805, Mahón again became a major base for the British navy enabling it to maintain the blockade of the French fleet in Toulon and to dominate the whole of the western Mediterranean. After 1815 and under Spanish rule the island reverted to a simple pastoral and fishing existence, though in 1830 the French were permitted to establish a base at Mahón for use during their campaign in Algeria. The limited opportunities and employment for young people during the 19th century encouraged emigration, particularly to the west coast of America. The first Admiral of the American navy, David Glasgow Farragut, was the son of such an emigrant and in the American Civil War led a Union squadron to victory in the battle of Mobile Bay. There is a bust of Farragut near the Torre de San Nicolas at the entrance to Ciutadella harbour (*see page 252*). Each year a ship and representatives of the US Navy visit Menorca to pay their respects and hold a short service at this bust. During the Spanish Civil War Menorca was the last place in Spain to hold out against General Franco. Following the capture of the island much damage was done to the island's churches and a large number of the male population were killed or imprisoned.

Recent history

Tourism has developed steadily over the past fifty years but generally avoided the excesses of much of the coastal regions of the other islands and the Spanish mainland. It is now the dominant feature of Menorca's economy. The Consell Insular (Island Council) succeeded well in maintaining the infrastructure of Menorca in the aftermath of the financial crisis and unemployment grew by less than in many parts of Spain. With security fears affecting other Mediterranean countries, tourists have returned recently to Menorca, and indeed Spain generally, in large numbers and the present concern is more one of overcrowding in the peak holiday period.

Tourist information

Places of interest in Menorca

In addition to the places of interest described in the harbour sections there are many other sites inland which can be visited by taxi, bus or on foot. One not to be missed is Monte Toro, near the village of Es Mercadal, for the panoramic view, the church (built in 1595) and the restored 17th-century monastery founded by Augustine monks. The name Monte Toro comes not from the Spanish 'Bull Mountain', but from Arabic 'The Highest (point)' which indeed it is, at 358 metres. The prominent forest of aerials near the summit is vital for the island's communications.

Of the many Megalithic remains, the following are some of the many worth making an effort to visit:

- 1M south of Mahón, the *taula* and *talayot* of Trapuco: a megalithic tower and monument
- 2M southwest of Mahón, the *talayot* of Torellonet (near the airport)
- 5M west of Mahón, the Torralba group of *taulas* (T-shaped monuments) and So na Caçana
- 3M east of Ciudadela, the *naveta* burial mound at Nau d'es Tudóns (claimed to be the oldest building in Europe)
- 4M east of Ciudadela, the *poblado* and *taulas* of Torre Llafuda
- 4M south of Ciudadela, the *talayot* of Son Olivaret.
- Between the town of Alaior and the coastal resort of Son Bou, the extensive area of remains at Torre d'en Galmes

The Euro-Map of Mallorca, Menorca, Ibiza published by GeoCenter International shows many of the historic and prehistoric sites, as does a multilingual map available locally.
www.infomallorca.net
www.illesbalears.es

THE CAMI DE CAVALLS

The Cami de Cavalls is an ancient bridle path originating in the fourteenth century which essentially follows the coast around Menorca and was created to enable soldiers or militia to move rapidly around the island. With the passage of time some twenty defensive towers would be built along its route, some of which can still be seen in a fair state of preservation. The Cami also gave a right of way to all the people of the island through the large private estates.

The Cami de Cavalls fell into general disuse in the early twentieth century and many landowners effectively blocked the right of way. Awareness of the loss of a valuable recreational facility surfaced in the 1980s but it was not until the early part of the present century that a legal framework was established to reconstitute it. After lengthy negotiations with landowners the Cami de Cavalls was fully reopened in 2009 and has been awarded the European long-distance path designation GR223. The path is some 200kms long.

The nature of the path is that it passes close to many of the anchorages described in this Pilot Book and therefore gives the yachtsman a convenient opportunity to walk sections of the path which traverse interesting, diverse and beautiful parts of the Menorcan countryside. For those who enjoy a good walk, an investment in the guide to the Cami (*The Cami de Cavalls of Menorca*, ISBN 978-84-8478-505-7) is well worthwhile. It is available in several languages.

Cami de Cavalls trail marker post
David Baggaley

SAILING AROUND MENORCA

As noted above, Menorca is now as crowded as the other Balearic Islands in summer. The French flag is perhaps the most common, Italian yachtsmen are much in evidence, each year brings greater numbers of visiting yachts from the Spanish mainland, and almost every Menorcan family seems to have its own boat; the result is that the most popular *calas* are very crowded, at least in the daytime. Thankfully, peace is normally restored in early evening when many of the locals return to their marinas. However, it should be appreciated that there are no flotillas of the sort found in the eastern Mediterranean and bareboat charters are not numerous. Happily there are a number of small, little-known anchorages for those who prefer to get away from the crowds.

On the south coast most of the anchorages are small – Son Saura and Cala Galdana being the only ones of any size. Some of the smaller anchorages are particularly beautiful. On the north coast, meanwhile, there are many larger anchorages and finding room is less of a problem even in summer. However, much of the north coast becomes unpleasant if not untenable in northerly winds of any strength, with protection in these circumstances being limited to Fornells, Addaia and Presili.

The two main town harbours of Mahón on the east coast and Ciudadela on the west have marinas that are very expensive in summer, although there appears to have been some recent moderation. Furthermore, there are only limited nearby anchoring facilities, so do not rely on either harbour unless you have booked a berth.

In 2017 the island council expressed concern that in high season (early July to mid-September) some of the popular anchorages have effectively become marine caravan parks with yachts arriving and then not moving on for days or weeks. However, the

THE FIVE GREAT LIGHTHOUSES OF MENORCA
Clockwise from top:
Isla del Aire *Juano Pons / Triangle Postals*
Punta Nati *Juanjo Pons / Triangle Postals*
Favaritx *David Baggaley*
Artrutx (Dartuch) *Zhekos / 123RF*
Cavalleria *Juanjo Pons / Triangle Postals*

V. MENORCA

cruising yachtsman who is able to visit the Islas Baleares outside the peak period, will find near-empty anchorages and more reasonable prices in marinas. Weather is usually pleasantly warm and settled, and sea temperatures are good through to late October and (for the hardier) even into December. Periods of strong winds, principally *tramontanas*, are a little more frequent but rarely develop into the really strong gales that occur from January to April.

The most common wind directions in Menorca are from north to south via the eastern semicircle; a westerly element is relatively rare in summer. The usual Mediterranean complaint of too much or too little wind is often, and justifiably, heard but, of course the perfect wind strength, when it does occur, is even more appreciated!

Outside the main summer holiday period, Menorca is as fine a cruising area as can be found anywhere.

1. PUERTO DE MAHÓN

Puerto de Mahón (Maó, Mo)

39°52'·0N 04°18'·8E

A long and deep cala leads into a natural and well-protected commercial and cruise harbour, also hosting a naval base (now little used), fishing fleet and many yachting facilities along its shores, with berthing for over 1,000 vessels.

Communications
Pilots (Mahón Prácticos) VHF Ch 12, 14, 16, 20, 27
Port authority ① 971 22 81 50
Puerto de Mahón ① 971 35 48 44
portsdebaleares@portsdebalears.com
www.portsdebalears.com
See following text for communications information for marinas.

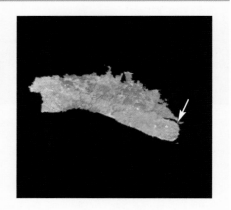

The port

An exceptionally attractive and interesting commercial, naval, fishing and yachting port up a long deep *cala* and one of the finest natural harbours in the world. Viewed from the water at night, it is quite breathtaking. The approach and entrance are straightforward and entry can be made in storm conditions, with good shelter available once inside. There are good and comprehensive facilities for yachtsmen including a yacht club. Because of the number of yachts visiting in summer, the need for more moorings has been addressed with the creation of floating pontoons forming two islands: Isla Clementina and Isla Cristina, to the east of Isla Pinto. These have water and electricity and are marked at night with a yellow flashing light. Two other floating pontoons, for larger vessels, are to the west of Isla del Rey.

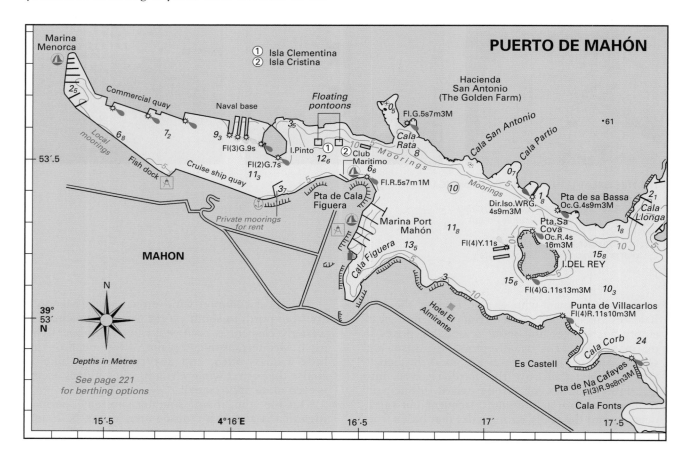

Pilotage

Approach

From south The tall lighthouse on Isla del Aire (white tower with black bands on a white building), 4M south of the *cala* entrance is easily identified and the island can safely be left on either side (*see plan on page 226*). The few hazards between Isla del Aire and Puerto de Mahón will be avoided by following a track at least 250m off Punta Rafalet and Punta de Na Girada. The lighthouse (white tower with three black bands on a square white base) and nearby radio towers on Punta de San Carlos are also conspicuous, and the high (78m) peninsula of La Mola ahead can be easily recognised. The harbour entrance lies between the two.

From north From Cabo Favaritx (white tower with black diagonal stripes on a white building) southwards the coast is very broken; Isla Colom may be recognised if sailing inshore (*see plan on page 281*). The high peninsula of La Mola (78m) with buildings on its summit and a lighthouse on Punta del Esperó (white tower with two black bands on a white base) are conspicuous from this direction. The entrance to Puerto de Mahón lies just beyond.

Currents

There is normally a slight southwest current past the entrance to Puerto de Mahón. North or northeast winds increase its speed while winds from south or southwest either slow or reverse the flow.

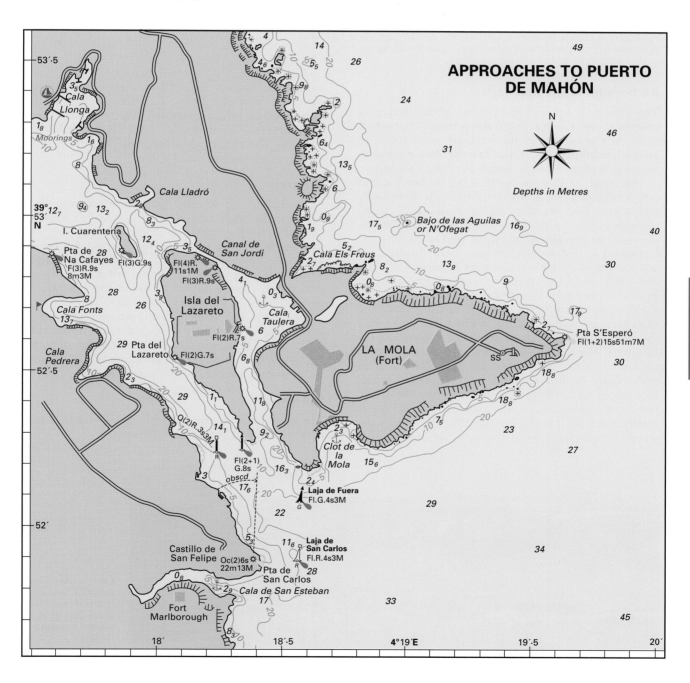

V. MENORCA

Approach to Mahón looking northwest. Pta de San Carlos left, La Mola right and Isla del Lazareto all clearly seen, along with buoys

Anchorages in the approach

The ebb and flow of anchoring permission is a continual one. Currently it is not normally permitted to anchor anywhere in the harbour apart from, in certain circumstances, Cala Taulera, but even here note the comment below under *Berthing options*.

Just south of the entrance lies Cala de San Esteban (see text page 226). To the north lie Clot de la Mola and Cala Taulera. Clot de la Mola is a small horseshoe bay with 10m over rock and stone, exposed to the south quadrant and with little to commend it as an anchorage. Cala Taulera, in contrast, is in a long narrow inlet between La Mola and Isla del Lazareto, offering almost total protection in 6m or less over sand and weed, though shallow along its north edge. If coming from the east, turn in close past Laja de Fuera buoy to avoid the spit running out from the south end of Isla del Lazareto. The *cala* can easily accommodate 20 or 30 yachts at anchor and is popular with both visitors and locals. Anchor in 3–6m over sand and weed. Holding is generally good, once through the weed, but more than one attempt may be needed. Water clarity is not great and it may be difficult to judge the weed-free patches. Avoid the west side of the *cala*

outside the line of channel buoys as this is used, at speed, by the tourist boats. An artificial channel, the Canal de San Jordi (sometimes referred to as Canal del Lazareto) provides a 'back door' into the harbour. The canal has a minimum depth of 2·8m and there are no overhead wires.

Entrance

Enter Puerto de Mahón on a northwest course between the high peninsula of La Mola, with its extensive fortifications, to starboard and the low rocky-cliffed Punta de San Carlos to port. Lit buoys mark the channel, which is used by commercial vessels of some size and should offer a yacht no difficulties, day or night, provided the buoyage is complied with. However, note that Mahón is a naval, ferry and commercial port and that these vessels have right of way over yachts and small craft. A 3kn speed limit is in force throughout the *cala* and harbour, but beware of speeding ferries, port officials and other craft who ignore it.

Sea levels

The sea level falls prior to and during strong winds from southwest, west and northwest.

Cala Taulera from La Mola, looking NW towards Canal San Jordi. Isla del Lazareto on left
Jane Russell

Floating pontoon islands Clementina and Christina to the east of Isla Pinto *Graham Hutt*

Berthing options

Port Mahón has several options for moorings. These include berths on the town quay (Moll de Llevant), floating pontoons, and an anchorage in Cala Taulera. Anchoring in Cala Taulera is officially forbidden. In practice, many yachts anchor there in summer with no problem. However, the harbour authority carries out daily inspections and often, but unpredictably, demands that yachts move on the basis that anchoring is only permitted when the marinas are full or in the event of bad weather (undefined) when it is regarded as an anchorage of refuge. The body setting the port regulations is made up of commercial interests, particularly the marinas, with no representation from the local sailing community. It is clearly unfortunate that a harbour with some claim to be one of the Mediterranean's major yachting centres should have no regular anchoring facilities. Note that the harbour authority do not seem to apply the rules outside the high summer season.

Finally note that in high season, when there are large numbers of visiting yachts in Menorca, if weather conditions are really bad, or forecast to be so, there may be insufficient room in Cala Taulera for the number of yachts seeking refuge. In these circumstances the Port Authority will allow anchoring to the west of Isla del Rey in 12 – 15m and upwards of fifty yachts have been seen sheltering there in these circumstances.

The government leasing concession to some established marina companies was recently reduced to just 2 years, bringing great uncertainty and confusion for long term investment in the port. Some marinas changed hands, along with name changes. The current situation is that there are basically 3 organisations holding the operating concession for the whole port of Mahón. Details of these are listed below. In addition there are many private moorings, particularly along the north side of the port. These are generally unavailable to visitors. The Spanish Navy has its own, little used, base and yacht club on the north side of the port to the west of Isla Pinto. Almost all moorings along the length of the quay are bows or stern-to using tailed lines. These are generally in excellent condition and very efficient *marineros* assist berthing, as strong cross winds often make mooring difficult.

There are no longer any public quay moorings available to visitors, as all are now in the hands of private companies, local residents and for the use of fishing boat owners.

The following are contact details for marinas within the port:

1. Marina Port Mahón

Marina Port Mahón pontoons and moorings are the first to come into view journeying west down the long harbour. These begin to the west of Isla del Rey (south side of the port) in Cala Figuera. The marina has 165 moorings on 5 pontoons with facilities for two 50m vessels. It has gated security and is close to several good restaurants along the shoreline.

C/o Moll de Llevant, 305 - 07701 Maó, Menorca, España
VHF Ch 09
☎ +34 971 366 787 or *mobile* +34 663 038 040
Marinero *mobile* +34 657 872 489
direccion@marinamahon.es
www.marinamahon.es

2. Club Marítimo de Mahón

Moorings begin at Punta de Cala Figuera and extend some 200 metres west to the first small floating pontoons, including what used to be Marina Estrella. There are 49 berths up to 35m. Most are for the use of visitors. All moorings are very busy in July and August and need pre-booking. These moorings are the cheapest option in the port. The Club Marítimo has ambitions to take over the concession to operate the pontoons of the Marina Port Mahón but at the time of writing had not been successful.

VHF Ch 09
☎ +34 971 365022 *mobile* +34 616953217
oficina@clubmaritimomahon.com
www.clubmaritimomahon.com

Between the Club Marítimo de Mahón moorings and the most western marina, Marina Menorca, is the cruise ship dock with some 'round the harbour' tripper boats operating from the eastern end and with no facilities for yachts. Between the cruise ship dock and Marina Menorca are the trawler fleet and smaller fishing boats and a section of harbour wall occupied by local yachts. Ferries and commercial vessels now operate from the north side of the

Mahón inner harbour looking west over Marina Port Mahón
Billy Hammond and Joanne Cotteril

Mahón Harbour from the west with Marina Menorca in the foreground *Juanjo Pons / Triangle Postals*

harbour near the power station. The haul-out facilities and hard-standing area used by Pedro's Boat Centre and others are on this northern section between the commercial dock area and Marina Menorca.

3. Marina Menorca

The largest (including its dispersed moorings) marina is based at the extreme western end of Puerto de Mahón. This marina also has the concession for the following: Isla Clementina and Isla Cristina; floating pontoons forming islands east of Isla Pinto; the 5 pontoons in Cala Llonga, with moorings for 100 vessels; and the two floating pontoons for larger vessels just west of Isla del Rey. There is a total capacity of 650 moorings for yachts up to 60m, of which 200 are in the marina itself at the extreme W end of the harbour. Floating pontoon moorings have water, electricity and rubbish collection, apart from a small number on the pontoons W of Isla del Rey. These pontoons have no facilities but can use the showers and toilets in the portacabin adjacent to the Marina Menorca office. All berths have mooring lines tailed to the pontoons.

Pontoons are lit at night with (Orange) Q(9)15s2m1M mounted on a 1m yellow structure.

The marina has a new office building which it shares with sister companies Nautic Centre (chandlery and motor boat sales - see below), Nautic Fun (yacht charter) and The Yacht Concierge (high-end personal service arrangements). It plans to replace all the marina pontoons and to build a new shower block in the winter of 2017/2018; there was no sign of this in early 2018.

VHF Ch 09
☎ +34 971 365 889
info@marinamenorca.com
www.marinamenorca.com

Note All moorings in the harbour suffer from the wash from speeding boats; large ferries, pilot boats and motor boats all appear to disregard the 3kn speed restriction.

Note also that vessels do not always manouevre as you might expect when passing. Larger ferries tend to use the north side of the harbour, whereas the military vessels use the deeper south side.

Mooring buoys

The mooring buoys on the northern shore are private moorings. Currently there are none available to visitors, though there are many private buoys for which there is a very long waiting list of local residents.

Anchorages

Anchoring is technically prohibited in the entire harbour, but see the *Berthing options* for Cala Taulera.

Facilities

Water and electricity Available at most berths, including on the floating islands, apart from those on the floating pontoons W of Isla del Rey.

Fuel Diesel and petrol available from the fuel dock at the south end of Marina Port Mahón/corner of Cala Figuera. In June, July and August it opens 0800 to 2000 each day. In September, 0800 to 1400 and 1600

Looking across to Mahón town, floating island 'Christina', centre, and Isla Pinto, right *Juanjo Pons / Triangle Postals*

to 2000 each day and the rest of the year 0800 to 1400 weekdays only. ② 971 354116 and 620 801859. The fuel dock is operated by the *Club Marítimo* whose website gives opening times which may contradict the information displayed in the fuel dock office.

Gas Camping Gaz is readily available in chandleries and hardware stores.

Provisioning Large supermarkets in the industrial estate outside of town, (Poligano) a very short taxi or bus ride. Smaller ones on Moll de Llevant near the fuel dock and up the hill from Cala Fonts. Excellent market place for fresh meat, fruit and vegetables, and local cheeses and charcuterie in the Claustre de Carme in town at the top of the steps and hill above the cruise ship dock. The supermarket under the Claustre (Cloisters) appears to have closed permanently. The fish market is 50m lower on the hill. There is also a fresh fish shop on the harbour near the trawler dock.

Shopping Alberto offers a delivery service to all yachts ② 655 46 38 62.

WiFi Free WiFi available from Club Marítimo de Mahón office, but this does not work well in all moorings along their concession, especially below deck. WiFi cards can be purchased from Mangalam (dress shop on the front) but Mo.net is unreliable at the artificial islands.

Ice From supermarkets or ask in marina offices.

Chandlery Pedro's Boat Centre has a chandlery opposite the trawler dock for practical items and one opposite Marina Port Mahón for clothing, smart gear and some basic hardware. Nautica Reynes (② 971 365952) in Carrer de Bajoli and Nautic Center (② 971 354499) in Carrer de S'Espero on the Poligano (industrial estate) have small chandleries in their showrooms and can often get items at short notice.

Charts From the chandlers; however, there is no official Spanish chart agent in Menorca.

Repairs Major repairs to wood, GRP and aluminium hulls can be undertaken by local yards. The haul-out facility and hard-standing area between Marina Menorca and the commercial/ferry dock is now operated by the Port Authority and a security barrier and guard deny access to all unauthorised persons. Concessions have been granted to Pedro's Boat Centre and others. Boats may

only come ashore or alongside for work to be done, and must leave when that is completed. Owners are not permitted to work on their own boats. There are two travel lifts of 50 and 35 tonne capacity. Boats are not allowed to be stored and this means that the only shore lay-up possibilities in Menorca are the very limited areas in Addaia and Cuidadela which are taken up entirely, or almost so, by local boats. This leaves a large and potentially income generating facility lying under-utilised in Mahón.

The best contact is Pedro's Boat Centre ② 971 366 968, info@pedrosboat.com, www.pedrosboat.com

Engineers Many around the harbour, including the English-run Marine & Auto Power ② 971 35 44 38 and MenMar ② 971 35 48 35.

Official service agents include the following:
Marina Estrella ② 971 35 33 20 – Volvo Penta;
Auto Recambios Union ② 971 36 01 13 – Yamaha;
Motonáutica Menorca ② 971 36 89 17 – Detroit diesel, Honda, Man, Mariner, Perkins; Nautic Centre Menorca www.nauticcenter.es ② 971 36 05 50 – Ecosse, Mercury/MerCruiser, Solé diesel, Yanmar;
Pedro's Boat Centre ② 971 36 69 68 – Mercury/ MerCruiser; Nautica Reynes www.nauticareynes.com ② 971 36 59 52 – Yanmar.

Electronic & radio repairs Enquire at the marina offices for information.

Sailmaker On the Moll de Llevant opposite Pantalan B of Marina Port Mahón is Wind Sails ② 971 36 19 99, windsailsmahon@hotmail.com, which specialises in covers, cushions, general canvas works and sail repairs. Velas Fonduco has a small canvas-working shop further to the west on Moll de Llevant near the Minerva floating restaurant and has a sail loft in Es Castell for more serious sailmaking and repairs ② 971 35 40 83, velasfonduco@gmail.com.

Both of these are helpful and have done good work for the authors.

Other canvas work can be carried out by Tapinautic Menorca ② 971 36 76 81 and 608 46 61 40, info@tapinauticmenorca.com.

Yacht clubs Club Marítimo de Mahón has pleasant facilities including a restaurant and bar on the 1st floor next to the office. Available to visitors and very friendly.

Showers and toilet facilities At the Club Marítimo de Mahón on the ground floor, also serving Marina Port Mahón. There are three showers and one toilet for men

Mahón even has its own Little Mermaid on the harbour
David Baggaley

and two showers and two toilets for women. Marina Menorca facilities are even more limited in a Portacabin but new facilities are planned. The facilities at both are currently seriously inadequate in quantity and quality for a major sailing centre, especially so considering the level of marina charges.

Launderette There is no convenient launderette but marina offices can arrange collection and delivery - reputedly expensive! There is also a new launderette, La Wash, near the bus station and football pitch at 46 Avenida José Anselmo Clavé, which will pick up from and deliver to yachts. The owner is English. ① 666242460 / 664781645, hola@lawash.es

Banks Several banks in the town with ATMs.

Water taxi A water taxi is available for yachts moored on the islands and pontoons in the *cala*. ① 616 42 88 91.

Hospital A relatively new and well equipped hospital, Mateo Orfila, on the southern edge of town.

Transport

Car hire All the major companies are represented and there are numerous local companies.

Taxis Radio Taxi ① 971 36 71 11

Buses A bus service runs every half hour between 0630 and 1830 along the S shoreline (Moll de Ponente/Moll de Llevant) from W to E. It continues to the bus depot, stopping for a few minutes before continuing to the industrial area and through the town centre, returning to the harbour to circuit again. This takes in all the local areas needed – the town centre, church, supermarket and market etc. Stopping points are not clearly marked, but local shops will tell you where they are. Bus services also run to the airport and all the island towns at varying frequency from the bus depot near the Esplanada square. Some only run in summer and frequencies are also seasonal.

Ferries To Palma and mainland Spain from Mahón (also from Ciudadela – worth comparing prices). Main ferry companies are Trasmediterranea (Mahón) and Balearia (Ciudadela) which serve all the islands.

Air services A good, modern international airport, just outside Mahón, with mainly May - October services direct to the main tourist originating cities and countries. Outside this period there remain several flights daily to both Palma and Barcelona with one daily to Madrid, all with numerous connections, the only direct international flight being weekly to the UK.

History

The whole area is steeped in history. This includes Bronze Age Talayotic sites and much from the 18th-century British occupation.

The ancient Portús Magonis (Mahón) was once thought to have been named after Mago, the younger brother of Hannibal, who founded it in about 206BC. There is, however, no evidence for this and the name could also have come from the Phoenician *maguén* meaning 'shield' or 'fortress', which would have been equally apt. Due to its excellent harbour and its position in the centre of the western Mediterranean, Mahón has been a prize that many nations have coveted, and traces of the long British occupation during the 18th century are unmistakable. Many of the older streets and houses with sash windows have a very English appearance, and various English words have gained a place in the

Menorquín language. There is even a gin distillery on the harbour and many cattle on the island are Freisans, descendants of those introduced during the British occupations. The island changed hands six times between 1708 and 1802 and each time it was Mahón that was the prize.

During the last period of British occupation, Horatio Nelson, who was in temporary command of the Mediterranean Fleet, spent a few days at the Golden Farm on the north side of the harbour, some time between 12 and 22 October 1799. Local tradition declares that Lady Hamilton was a guest in the house at the same time. Villa El Fonduco, near the southeast side of Cala Figuera and now a hotel, El Almirante, was the shore headquarters of Admiral Lord Cuthbert Collingwood while he was C-in-C Mediterranean in Mahón during the early 19th century. (Collingwood was Nelson's second-in-command at Trafalgar and took full control after Nelson was shot in the early stages; he is regarded by many as the true hero of that battle.)

Ashore

Among places of interest near Mahón, the Golden Farm, (which is now painted dark red, not yellow), should be visited for the view – the house is itself privately owned and not open to the public. Quite a few large houses are traditionally painted in this red colour. It is said that the British navy painted its lower decks with it to disguise shed blood – and that considerable amounts of the paint found their way into private hands to decorate houses. In Mahón itself the church of Santa María has a superb early 19th-century organ, built in Switzerland and transported from Barcelona by the British navy at the height of the Napoleonic war. The Casa Mercada Museum is also worth a visit. The old fortifications of San Felipe around the mouth of the harbour are good for exploring; there's not a lot to see above ground, but underground is an extensive network of three levels of tunnels. The fortress of Isabel II at La Mola is a must-see. It is open for guided walks, lasting two and a half hours, at 1000 and 1700. It is quite difficult to get to by road without a car, but for yachts anchored in Cala Taulera simply land on the small beach and walk the 100m to the ticket office. Depending on your interests, the Vickers cannons are said to be a highlight of the tour, but don't miss seeing the 'Loophole gallery'; a regular sequence of arches receding into the distance appears as an optical illusion stretching to infinity. Truly spectacular! Fort Marlborough in Cala Sant Esteve is also worth a visit as is Collingwood's shore base (Hotel El Almirante).

The prehistoric *taula* (T-shaped monument) and *talayot* (ancient tower) at Trepuco, about a mile to the south, are typical of many throughout the island. If prepared to stroll a little further, the village of San Lluis, founded by the French and still with a definite Gallic feel, is on the same road.

The first British Naval Hospital, Isla del Rey *Biel Puig / Triangle Postals*

Admiral Lord Cuthbert Collingwood (left) and Admiral Sir John Jennings (right) on Isla del Rey *David Baggaley*

Isla del Rey

Not to be missed is the Isla del Rey. This is the site of the Royal Navy's first hospital, created in 1711 at the iniative of Admiral Sir John Jennings (and in spite of initial skepticism from the Admiralty), which over the past ten years has been the subject of restoration by a large team of volunteers. There is still some way to go but the ground floor has been completed and a fascinating array of artifacts collected. In the grounds are bronze busts of Admirals Jennings and Collingwood, and an early Paleo-Christian religious site has also been found. The best time to visit is Sunday mornings on the 08·45 Yellow Catamaran from the east end of the cruise ship dock. Free tours, guided by very knowledgeable volunteers, are provided for about one and a half hours before a complimentary Menorquin breakfast is served (including wine and beer!) Donations to this worthwhile cause are politely suggested at the end of the visit. There are also guided tours on Thursday mornings. There is a good dock for dinghies on the north side – The Nuns' Dock. There is of course a story behind that name!

Local events

Fiestas are held on 5–6 January with the arrival by boat of Los Reyes Magos (the Three Kings) with toys for the children, followed by a procession. On Good Friday there is a procession and medieval parade. On 15–16 July a sea procession is held in honour of Our Lady of Carmen, and on 7–8 September the fiesta of Nuestra Señora de Gracia includes processions, music, sailing races and other sports. In the third week of September a fair is held to showcase local products.

Eating out

A wide selection of restaurants and many quayside bars and cafés. A walk up the steps near the cruise ship dock takes you into town where there are many excellent eating places, some friendly family run businesses and other more expensive restaurants.

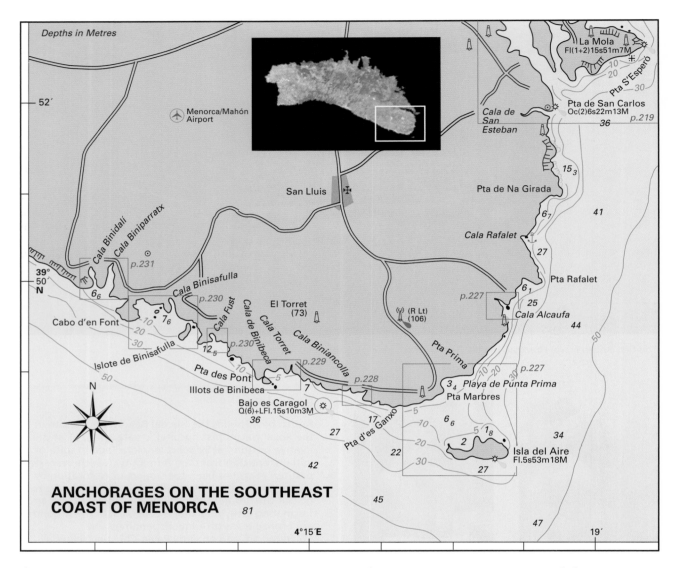

Depths in Metres

La Mola
Fl(1+2)15s51m7M

Pta S'Esperó

Pta de San Carlos
Oc(2)6s22m13M *p.219*

52′

Menorca/Mahón Airport

Cala de San Esteban

San Lluis

Pta de Na Girada

Cala Binidali

Cala Biniparratx

Cala Rafalet

39°
50′
N

Cala Binisafulla

El Torret
(73)

p.231

p.230

Cabo d'en Font

Cala Fust

Cala de Binibeca

Cala Torret

(R Lt)
(106)

Pta Rafalet

Cala Alcaufa

p.227

Islote de Binisafulla

p.230

Cala Biniancolla

p.229

Pta Prima

p.227

Pta des Pont

Illots de Binibeca

p.228

Playa de Punta Prima

Pta Marbres

Bajo es Caragol
Q(6)+LFl.15s10m3M

Pta d'es Ganxo

Isla del Aire
Fl.5s53m18M

ANCHORAGES ON THE SOUTHEAST COAST OF MENORCA

4°15′E

19′

⚓ Cala de San Esteban (Sant Esteve)

39°51′·8N 04°18′·5E

A narrow but deeply indented *cala* surrounded by a fringe of houses, just south of Puerto de Mahón and easily identified by Punta de San Carlos lighthouse (white tower with three black bands on a square white base) and two radio masts all close north of the entrance. Ruined walls, part of the old San Felipe fortifications are much in evidence to starboard on entry together with some buildings which are part of a modern military base. Further into the *cala* on the starboard (north) side is a small military social club. On the port (south) side, just before the houses begin, is the entrance to the hidden Fort Marlborough which is another of the old fortifications. Depths of 2m or more lead almost to the head of the *cala*: favour the deeper north side and sound carefully as the bottom is rocky. Good protection is gained deeper in the *cala*. However, there are many small craft moorings along the north

side, restricting swinging room and there are more such moorings towards the head of the *cala*. It will probably be necessary to anchor before reaching the level of the aforementioned club in 5m+ in mainly weed and rock.

Cala de San Esteban *Susie Baggaley*

⚓ Cala Rafalet

39°50'·4N 04°18'.1E

One of the most beautiful of the islands' small *calas*, narrow with steep rocky cliffs and ideal for a fantastic yacht photograph. Investigate by dinghy first and approach with great caution to anchor in 4–6m, open to the east quadrant. It is really only for small vessels – great to explore in such. The narrow valley running inland from the head of the *cala* is most attractive and shows signs of ancient cave dwellers. There is a track to the main road and a housing estate on the high ground several hundred metres to the south. A *talayot* (ancient tower) lies 1½M to the northwest.

⚓ Cala Alcaufa (d'Alcaufar)

39°49'·6N 04°17'·9E

One of the first *calas* to be developed, with many houses on the north side but virtually nothing to the south. Easy to identify by virtue of a large pale stone tower just south of the entrance. Enter leaving Illot d'es Torn to starboard and anchor in 4-6m over rock and sand, open to the southeast. Holding is said to

be poor, and certainly there is only a small area of sand outside the small craft moorings which occupy the greater part of the *cala* – it may be necessary to moor fore-and-aft or take a line ashore. There are a few shops, restaurants and bars in the village. On the south side of the entrance, not quite in the photograph, is Cala Roig, most attractive at its head, which would be fine for small craft.

⚓ Playa de Punta Prima (Ensenada Arenal de Alcaufa)

39°48'·8N 04°17'·0E

An exposed anchorage in a wide bay off a superb sandy beach. Anchor in 2m+ of turquoise water. Somewhat protected from the south by Isla del Aire, the bay is backed by houses and apartment blocks together with the usual shops, bars and restaurants. A submarine cable runs in a southeast direction from a point near the head of the bay.

The British landed here under Admiral Sir John Leake and General Stanhope when they captured the island in 1708. Later it was used again by Spanish

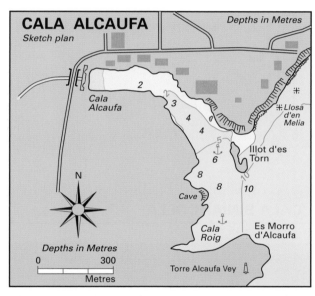

Playa de Punta Prima

Cala Alcaufa viewed from southeast. Often deserted even in summer

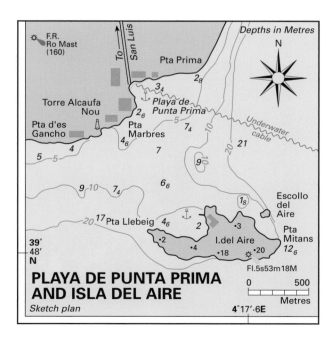

V. MENORCA

Rare black lizards said only to exist on Isla del Aire
David Russell

troops under the Duc de Crillon, landing in 1781 to recapture the island.

⚓ Isla del Aire

Bisected by 39°48'.1N 04°17'.4E

A low, flat island just over 1,000m long by 400m wide but much of it less than 4m high, with a couple of hillocks (18m) and (20m) to the southeast, one topped by a lighthouse (white tower, black bands, on a white building).

Anchor in the bay on the northwest side of the island in 4m+ over weed and rocks, about 150m west of the landing pier from which there is a track to the lighthouse. Watch for rocky pinnacles and use a tripline.

The island is uninhabited – other than by rabbits and a unique species of black lizards (*Lacerta lilfordi*) – but is visited by tourist boats during summer. It is said that the lizards particularly enjoy tomatoes and will approach quite close if pieces are offered.

Isla del Aire viewed from southeast.
Note anchorage north side of island

Admiral Byng's refused battle against the French fleet under Galissonnière took place off Isla del Aire in May 1756. This is where Byng failed to close and engage the enemy and fled to Gibraltar. He was court-martialled and executed, as Voltaire said: '*pour encourager les autres*' ('to encourage the others').

Passage between Isla del Aire and Menorca

An unimpeded passage 1,000m wide exists between Isla del Aire and Menorca with a minimum central depth of 6·6m. Yachts drawing 2·5m or less can follow the Menorcan coast at 200m. The sandy bottom can usually be seen quite clearly.

⚓ Cala Biniancolla

39°48'·6N 04°15'·6E

A small *cala* with low rocky sides and a village at its head, suitable for small yachts only. A large, conspicuous apartment block stands behind the

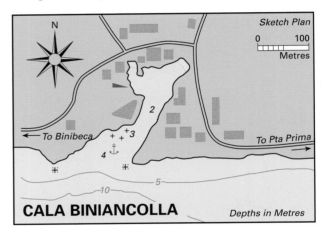

Biniancolla viewed from south. Rocky patches just visible

hamlet and can be seen from afar. If approaching from the west give the rocky Bajo Es Caragol a generous berth, and enter with care to avoid the outlying rocks on either side. Anchor in sand, rock and weed in ±3m. There are restaurants and cafés in the village.

Bajo Es Caragol

39°48'·6N 04°15'·2E

This breaking, rocky bank about 800m southwest of Cala Biniancolla is marked by a south cardinal beacon (*see plan on page 226*). Although there is good water about halfway between the beacon and the shore, the reef should be given a generous berth as rocks extend up to 100m east and south.

⚓ Cala Torret

39°48'·9N 04°14'·7E

A small, developed *cala* surrounded by houses, only suitable for smaller yachts in good weather. The El Torret tower on the skyline about ¾ mile northeast is a useful mark, as is a line of arched doorways

along the west side of the *cala*. Enter with care and anchor in the middle of the *cala*, open southeast through to southwest. The usual cafés, restaurants and small shops will be found ashore.

⚓ Cala de Binibeca (Binibequer)

39°48'·9N 04°14'·5E

A large, well-known 'developed' *cala* tucked behind Punta des Pont and the Illots de Binibeca, and overlooked by the tourist development of Binibeca Nou. Approach and entrance are straightforward: anchor near the middle in 3–7m over hard sand and weed, open from east to south. There is an excellent beach, very crowded in the season; with a pier, slipway and dinghy crane a short walk east. Restaurants, shops and a hotel will be found in Binibeca Nou. Anchoring has been restricted substantially by the extension of the swimming area

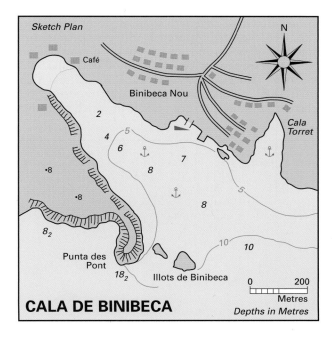

Cala Torret, far right, and Cala Binibeca, left, viewed from south

and with the placement of around 60 small craft buoys, most of which are occupied in the busy summer period.

⚓ Cala Fust (d'en Fust)

39°49'.2N 04°13'.7E

Occasionally, and confusingly, referred to as Binibeca Vell (the development at its head), Cala Fust is small with many houses and a conspicuous church spire to the east in the village of Binibeca Vell. It is suitable only for smaller yachts. There is an awash rock (Llosa d'en Fust) close east of the entrance. Local fishing craft are moored at the shallow head of the *cala*. There are the usual facilities ashore and some good examples of local rural architecture in Binibeca Vell.

⚓ Cala Binisafulla (Binisafuller)

39°49'.5N 04°13'.2E

A medium-sized *cala* with some adjacent houses but not overdeveloped. Approach with care because of a number of islets and awash rocks: a course from near the southwest corner of Illot de Binisafuller clears all dangers. The *cala* itself is totally taken up, at least in summer, with small craft moorings but there is an extensive area outside in which to anchor

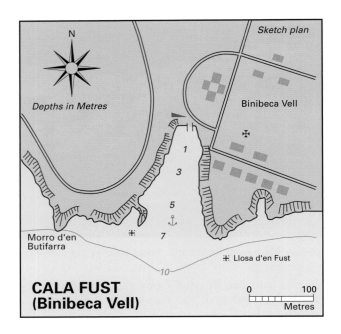

CALA FUST
(Binibeca Vell)

in 8-10m on sand with some areas of weed in the lee of Islote de Binisafuller and open south to west. Cala Binisafulla is close to being in line with the airport runway so it can be noisy.

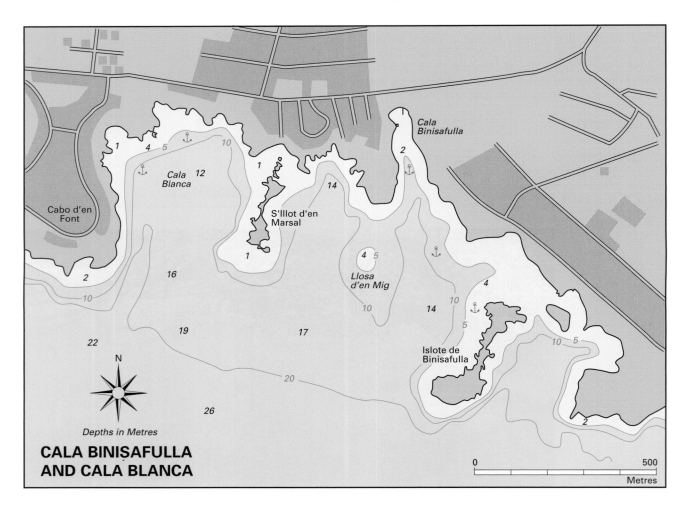

CALA BINISAFULLA
AND CALA BLANCA

Cala Binisafulla (with beach), Islote de Binisafulla (foreground) and Cap d'en Font from the east. Note anchorages outside the cala and also in front (east) of Cap d'en Font
Juanjo Pons / Triangle Postals

⚓ Cabo d'en Font (Es Cap d'en Font)/Cala Blanca
39°49'·5N 4°12'·6E

A low (12m) but prominent rocky-cliffed headland covered with houses. Several rocky islets lie to the southeast. Note that in westerly winds, yachts sometimes anchor to the east of Cabo d'en Font in Cala Blanca outside a number of small craft moorings. (34°49'·6N 04°12'·7E) Depths are considerable until close in and probably it will be necessary to anchor in 10–13m in sand, weed and rock. A number of very attractive houses adorn the cape in spite of aircraft noise as it is directly under the flightpath of the airport which is only a mile or so to the north.

⚓ Cala Biniparratx
39°49'·8N 04°12'.1E

An attractive little *cala* with high rocky sides, easy to approach and enter. Though the *cala* is inconspicuous from offshore, Cabo d'en Font (some 750m to the east) is prominent. Anchor just short of the 'elbow' in 4–6m over sand and rock, either with fore and aft anchors or a line ashore. There are rocky patches beyond the corner, and depths shoal rapidly towards the sandy beach. A few houses stand on the east bank of the *cala*, but there are no real facilities. Several (mostly unoccupied) permanent private moorings have been laid on the E side of the *cala*. These are not for the use of visitors. There are ancient rock dwellings in the valley.

⚓ Cala Binidalí
39°49'·9N 04°12'·0E

A pretty but very small *cala* just west of Cala Biniparratx, with high rocky cliffs, a sandy beach and a few houses well set back. Strictly a fair-weather anchorage but probably totally closed off by buoys

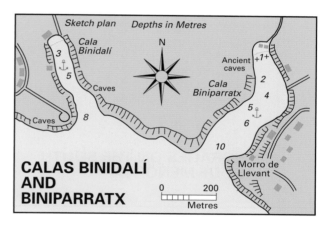

CALAS BINIDALÍ AND BINIPARRATX

Cala Biniparratx looking SW *David Russell*

for most of the summer. When open, the approach and entrance present no problems; use one or two anchors in 3–5m over sand and rock or with a line ashore. The head is shallow. There are no facilities.

3. CABO GROS TO CALA GALDANA

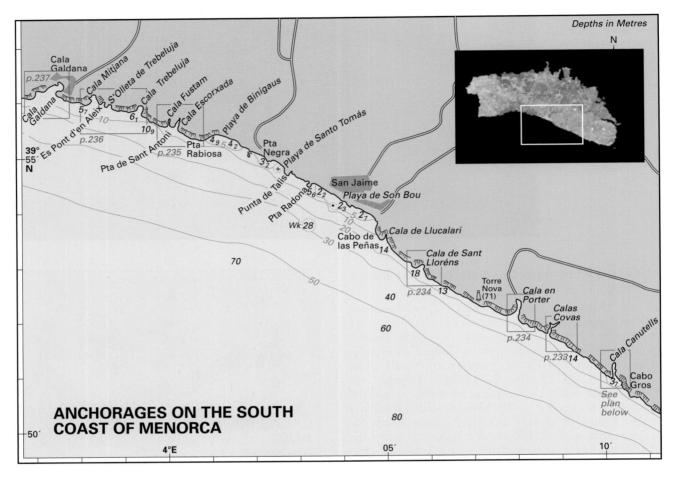

Depths in Metres

ANCHORAGES ON THE SOUTH
COAST OF MENORCA

Cabo Gros

39°50'·6N 04°10'·5E

A high (39m), rocky-cliffed headland with some houses on the top. Even so it is not very prominent and can only be seen if coasting close in. There are some prehistoric caves cut into the cliffs, including a very large one on the west face.

⚓ Cala Canutells

39°50'·9N 04°10'·1E

A large and attractive S-shaped *cala* between sloping rocky cliffs, with a large tourist development to the east and many local craft on permanent moorings. Apart from the entrance in 10m over sand, most of the *cala* is occupied with buoys for small local vessels, at least in summer. Enter down the centre of the *cala*, keeping well clear of the awash rock at the western entrance point, and anchor if, albeit unlikely, space permits in 4–6m over sand. The upper part of the *cala* is very shallow, with a shelving sandy beach at its head which is deservedly popular with tourists. There is a café/restaurant on the beach and at the top of the hill (200m past the café) there is a supermarket, hotel, post, car hire and an English-speaking doctor in attendance every day.

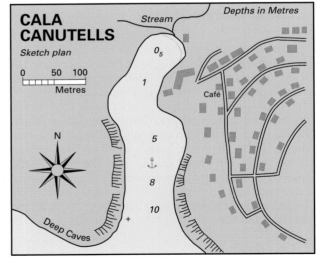

CALA CANUTELLS

Sketch plan

Depths in Metres

Cala Canutells viewed from southwest: caves visible left of picture

Calas Covas looking south. It is normally essential to anchor with a line ashore and sometimes yachts are as closely packed as in a marina! *David Baggaley*

The surrounding cliffs are riddled with caves, including two tall, arched recesses close west of the entrance and the Covas d'es Castella 800m to the east.

⚓ Calas Covas

39°51'·6N 04°08'·6E

Considered the most spectacular and beautiful anchorage in the Islas Baleares, Calas Covas is surrounded by nearly 150 caves, some of which were occupied during prehistoric times. The entrance, between two high rocky cliffs, lies ¾ mile east of Cala en Porter, which is easily identified by the huge housing development to its east. Anchor in 3–5m with two anchors or a line ashore to limit swinging: there are several convenient posts on the west side of the small central promontory (see plan),

Calas Covas looking east. The surroundings are dramatic and the prehistoric dwelling and funerary caves fascinating *David Baggaley*

but investigate first by dinghy as there are fringing rocks. Much of the bottom is rocky, making a tripline advisable. In summer it is not unusual to see perhaps twenty yachts anchored with lines ashore to the promontory, packed almost as tightly as in a marina. It could well lead to practising the technique to deal with fouled, crossed anchor chains, a technique essential for those heading on to the eastern Mediterranean! Yachts also anchor with a line ashore to the east or west cliffs in the outer section of the *cala* or free anchor even further out. The anchorage is open to southwest and south, depending on the spot chosen. Two pairs of 'no entry' buoys are placed at the entrance of both upper arms of the inner *calas*.

The *calas* are deserted except for two houses, but large numbers of tourists visit the small beaches every day in summer and litter has been a problem. There are several freshwater springs and a road inland, but no facilities.

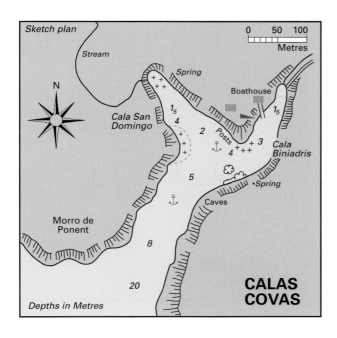

Sketch plan

0 50 100

Metres

Stream

Spring

N

Boathouse

Cala San Domingo

1·5

4

2

Posts

1·5

3

Cala Biniadris

4

Spring

5

Caves

Morro de Ponent

8

20

CALAS COVAS

Depths in Metres

V. MENORCA

Cala en Porter, buoys near the beach restrict anchoring

⚓ Cala en Porter (Calan Porter)

39°52'.1N 04°07'.8E

A fairly large *cala* lying between high (48m) rocky cliffs. The valley and hillside to the north and east are covered by holiday homes, hotels, shops, cafés, restaurants and discos, which make the *cala* easy to locate. The 8m Torre Nova tower stands about ¾ mile northwest.

Anchor in 3m+ over sand, open to the south and southwest. A line (sometimes two lines) of buoys may be laid to mark off the bathing area in front of the beach. Anchoring room is also restricted by a line of red buoys running along the E side of the *cala*, marking a submarine cable, so the area available to yachtsmen is substantially limited and it is likely that a yacht will have to anchor in around 10m. There are two beach cafés, and most everyday requirements are available in the tourist area.

It is worth walking along the cliffs on the eastern side of the entrance to Covas d'en Xoroi, a succession of natural caves with openings through the cliffs, now occupied by a bar and restaurant (and a nightly disco). It is fortunate that the caves face seaward and there is little noise from the disco in the anchorage. If space has not been available to anchor in Calas Covas it is well worth making a short walk, mainly on a section of the Cami de Cavalls from the top of Cala en Porter, to see the caves. There are several important *talayots* (towers) and other ancient ruins on the road to Alayor, the two most important being So Na Caçana and Torralba.

Torre Nova

39°52'.3N 04°07'.0E

A ruined ancient lookout tower 8m high on the edge of a 63m rocky cliff, about ¾ mile northwest of Cala en Porter. It is not very conspicuous.

⚓ Cala de Sant Lloréns (Sant Llorenç)

39°52'.9N 4°05'.6E

A very small, deserted *cala* surrounded by sheer rocky cliffs with a steep-sided river valley behind. Only suitable for use by small yachts in settled

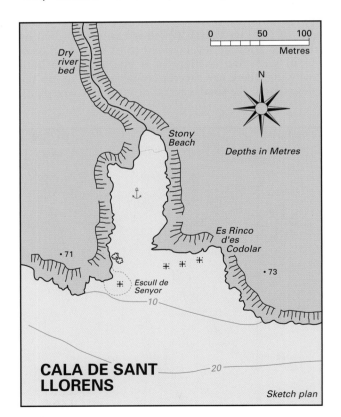

conditions and open southeast to southwest. Care is necessary in the approach due to several fringing rocks. Moor with two anchors over sand and rock, or with a line or lines ashore.

⚓ Cala de Llucalari
39°53'·3N 4°04'·9E

A very small, deserted *cala* similar to Cala de Sant Llorens, with high sloping rocky sides. It is tucked behind Cabo de las Peñas (Cap de ses Penyes; see plan on page 232) and backed by a dried-up river valley with a track inland. Its use is limited to small yachts in good weather. Anchor in the centre of the *cala* in 3–4m over rock and sand. There is a small rocky beach but no facilities and there is really nothing to commend the anchorage which is open to any wind from the southern semicircle.

⚓ Playa de Son Bou, Playa de Santo Tomás (Playa de Talis or Atalix) and Playa de Binigaus
Stretching from 39°53'·7N 4°04'·5E to 39°55'·2N 4°01'·1E

A 3-mile stretch of sandy beaches between Cabo de las Peñas (Cap de ses Penyes) and Punta Rabiosa, broken only by the low rocky promontories of Punta Radona, Punta de Talis and Punta Negra (see plan on page 232). They are backed by apartment blocks and hotels and a number of tourist developments, including those of San Jaime Mediterráneo and Santo Tomás.

The 10m contour runs some 400m offshore, making it possible to anchor over sand almost anywhere along this stretch of open and exposed coast, albeit in settled weather only. There are two small islands and some rocks close inshore.

The San Jaime Mediterráneo resort at Son Bou includes a bank amongst its facilities, as well as a supermarket and the usual bars and restaurants. Santo Tomás also has beach bars, restaurants, supermarkets and gift shops.

The ruins of an early Christian church dating from the 5th century overlook the eastern end of the Son Bou beach while two *talayots* (towers) lie near the road from Santo Tomás to Ferrerías, together with other ancient remains. There is a spring at the northwest end of Playa de Binigaus, which is totally free of buildings and delightfully unspoiled. A walk of about a mile up the valley behind Playa de Binigaus gives access to the huge Columbus (or Cathedral) Cave which is well worth visiting.

⚓ Cala Escorxada
39°55'·4N 04°00'.2E

A deserted *cala* with low rocky cliffs and a large sandy beach, about ¾M northwest of the end of Playa de Binigaus. Anchor in 2–5m over sand. The Cami de Cavalls path between Binigaus and Cala Trebalújer has been diverted inland but the previous very attractive track following the coast still seems open. There is a track inland to Es Migjorn Gran if the landowner grants access.

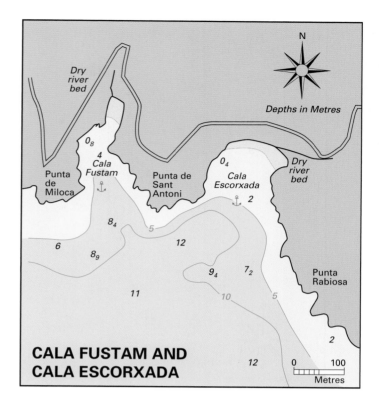

CALA FUSTAM AND CALA ESCORXADA

⚓ Cala Fustam
39°55'·5N 04°00'·0E

A smaller and narrower version of Cala Escorxada lying 300m further northwest, on the other side of Punta de Sant Antoni (see plan on page 232). Moor with two anchors in 3–4m over sand, open from southeast to southwest. The sandy beach is not as large as that at Cala Escorxada, but the *cala* is very pretty and totally deserted. It shares the coastal path and the track to Es Migjorn Gran with Cala Escorxada.

Calas Fustam and Escorxada *Juano Pons / Triangle Postals*

V. MENORCA

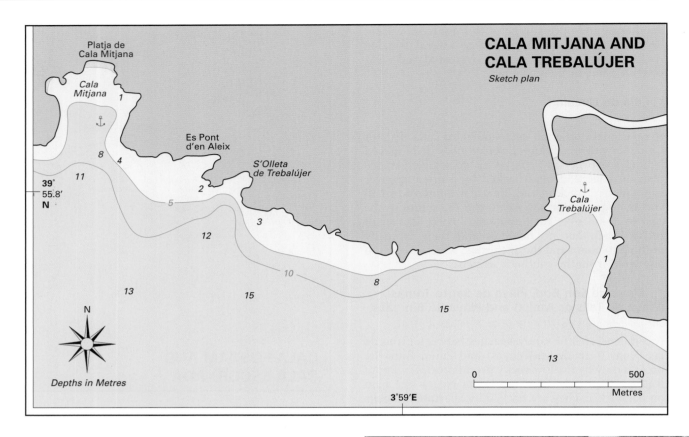

CALA MITJANA AND
CALA TREBALÚJER
Sketch plan

Platja de
Cala Mitjana

Cala
Mitjana

Es Pont
d'en Aleix

S'Olleta
de Trebalújer

Cala
Trebalújer

39°
55.8'
N

N

Depths in Metres

3°59'E

0   500
Metres

⚓ Cala Trebalújer

39°55'·7N 03°59'·3E

A larger, wide *cala* with a pinkish sandy beach. there are high (64m) sloping rocky caves on the southeast side and lower, tree-covered cliffs on the northwest side. Anchor in 4–6m over sand. A small freshwater river enters the northwest corner of the *cala*. It has a low sand bar over which a dinghy can be pulled or carried, allowing one to row a mile upstream with the chance of seeing turtles, fish and various birds. There is a track to Es Migjorn Gran and the Cami de Cavalls passes through but otherwise the *cala* is deserted.

Between Calas Trebalújer and Mitjana lie S'Olleta de Trebalújer and Es Pont d'en Aleix. These are little more than breaks in the cliff line rather than anchorages, with potential to explore by dinghy.

⚓ Cala Mitjana

39°55'·9N 03°58'·3E

A *cala* about 100m wide, surrounded by rocky cliffs but with two good sandy beaches, lying just under ¾M east of Cala Galdana (easily recognised by its large hotels and apartment blocks). It is a recognised beauty spot and hence justifiably popular. Swinging room is limited to perhaps five or six deep-keeled yachts with room for some more shallow draft vessels closer in. Anchor in 3–6m over sand and weed. A track connects with the road from Cala Galdana to Ferrerías and the Cami de Cavalls again passes through; these access routes mean that the beaches are popular and crowded.

Cala Trebalújer *Juanjo Pons / Triangle Postals*

Cala Mitjana *Paramotor Menorca*

Cala Galdana. As with many anchorages in the Balearic Islands, anchoring space
is substantially reduced by extensive buoyed-off swimming areas
Billy Hammond and Joanne Cotteril

⚓ Cala Galdana

39°56'·0N 03°57'·3E

Once one of the most beautiful large *calas* in
Menorca, and still one of the largest and most
sheltered anchorages on the south coast (*see plan on
page 232*). There are now a few high-rise hotels
which make it easy to recognise, especially if
approaching from the west. However, if arriving
from the east little is seen until abreast of the
entrance.

A series of buoys linked by a thin line stretches
from the central promontory across the *cala* to near
the end of the beach, protecting the bathing area but
seriously restricting the anchorage. Anchor as space

permits, probably in 5m or more, over sand and
weed. It may be necessary to lie to two anchors or
take a long line ashore when the harbour is crowded.
Note that in south and southwest winds the swell
rolls in and makes this a very uncomfortable
anchorage but then there are no anchorages on the
south coast with good protection from the southern
semicircle. The river from the barranca (gorge) of
Cala Galdana enters the northwest corner of the *cala*
and is navigable by dinghy for more than ½ mile. A
bridge some 10m long and 3m in height spans its
mouth, with small craft dock and moorings beyond.

The long sandy beach is crowded in season and
the shouts of the bathers echo around the
surrounding cliffs. There is also a lot of noise during
the evening from bars and discos, but these usually
cease around 2200. Restaurants, cafés, bars,
supermarkets and tourist shops flourish in the
resort.

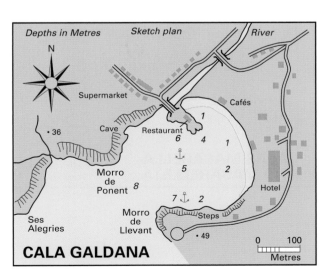

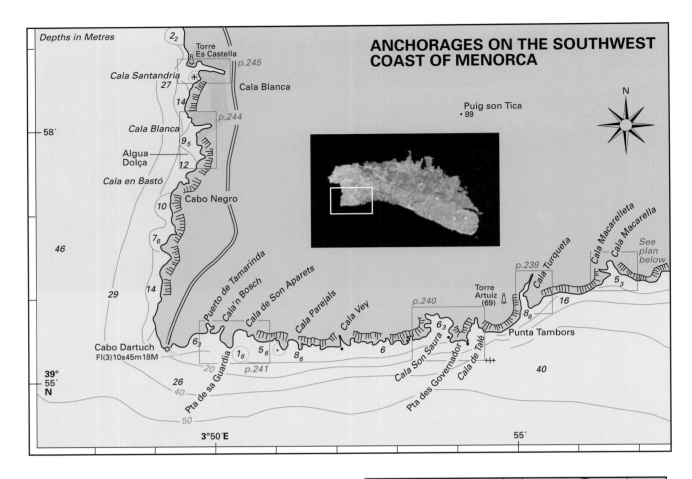

ANCHORAGES ON THE SOUTHWEST COAST OF MENORCA

Depths in Metres

Torre Es Castella
Cala Santandria 27
Cala Blanca
Puig son Tica • 89
14
Cala Blanca p.244
9₅
Algua Dolça 12
Cala en Bastó
Cabo Negro
10
7₆
46
Cala Macarelleta
Cala Macarella
See plan below
29 14
Puerto de Tamarinda
Cala'n Bosch
Cala de Son Aparets
Cala Parejals
Cala Vey
p.239
Cala Turqueta
5₃
16
8₆
p.240
Torre Artuiz (69)
Punta Tambors
Cabo Dartuch Fl(3)10s45m18M 6₃
1₆ 5₆ 8₆
6₃
6
Cala Son Saura
Cala de Talé
Pta de sa Guardia 20 p.241
26
40
Pta des Governador
Cala de Talé
40
39° 55' N
50
3°50'E
55'

⚓ Cala Macarella and Cala Macarelleta

39°56'·0N 03°56'·3E

A large double *cala* with two sandy beaches, surrounded by sloping rocky cliffs, scrub and trees, and easy to spot just under a mile west of Cala Galdana. It is particularly beautiful and therefore often crowded. Anchor in 3–6m over sand and a few weed patches; it may be necessary to use two anchors or to take a line ashore. Keep clear of the west end of the *cala* which is roped off for swimmers. The water is beautifully clear. The anchorage is open from southwest to southeast.

Part of the Cami de Cavalls from Cala Galdana, a track connecting with a car park and lane to Ciudadela brings in day tourists. The stream flowing into Cala Macarella is embanked with what could be Moorish masonry; the water appears clean and is recommended locally. The direct path round to Cala Macarelleta has been made easier but still a bit of a scramble at the Macarelleta end. This little *cala* is particularly beautiful and at times seems to be a favorite with nudists. There is a café/bar (Suzie's) behind the main, Macarella, beach and an ancient ruined village to the west. These *calas*, together with those further east, were used as hideouts by Barbary pirates in medieval times.

Dry river bed
0 200
Metres
Caves
Cala Macarella
• 48
4
Cala Macarelleta
Caves • 50
2 Pta de na Xuria
+ 6
• 45
Es Castellet
8
• 58
10
N

CALAS MACARELLA AND MACARELLETA

Depths in Metres Sketch plan

Above Calas Macarella and Macaralleta. Like most of the anchorages on the south coast, hugely popular and difficult to find room in high season
Billy Hammond and Joanne Cotteril

Right Cala Turqueta and the caves around its entrance

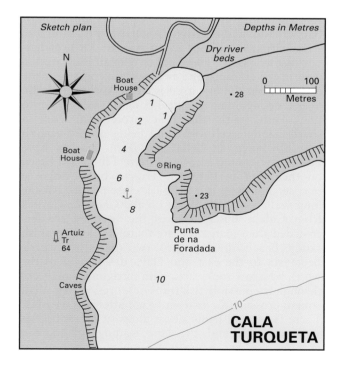

⚓ Cala Turqueta

39°55'·6N 03°54'·9E

A small, attractive and understandably popular *cala* surrounded by scrub and pine-covered rocky cliffs and with a sandy beach at its head. It lies a mile west of Cala Macarella and the same distance from Cala de Son Saura, and is again on the Cami de Cavalls. The conspicuous Torre de Artuiz lies just west of the entrance. Anchor in 3m+ over sand with weed patches, taking a line ashore if necessary; there is a mooring ring on the east side. A track at the head of the *cala* leads inland to connect with a car park and a lane to Ciudadela. Peace in the *cala* is somewhat spoiled in the middle of the day by a procession of tourist craft coming from Ciudadela and disgorging hundreds of tourists on to the tiny beach. Peace returns in the evening.

V. MENORCA

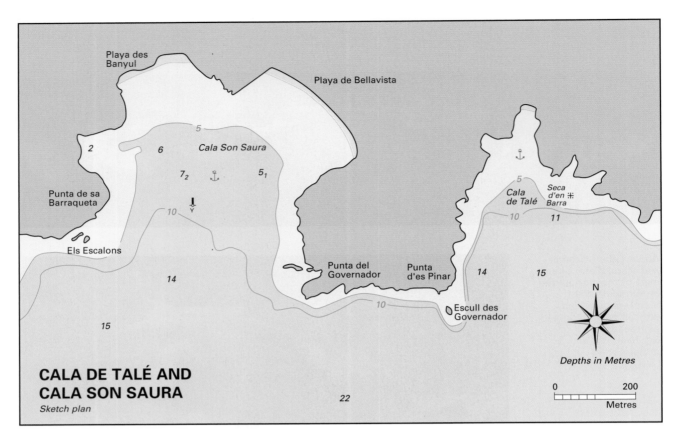

CALA DE TALÉ AND CALA SON SAURA
Sketch plan

⚓ Cala de Talé (d'es Talaier)

39°55'·4N 03°54'.2E

A small and once often deserted *cala* with a low rocky shore backed by scrub and pine woods, about ½M east of Cala Son Saura and separated from it by Punta des Governador, it is now another destination for day-tripper tourist boats. Enter with care as there is a small islet on the west side of the entrance and a lone rock awash close inshore to the east. Anchor in 5–8m over sand. The head of the *cala* is buoyed off for swimmers. Any slight swell rebounds from the rocks so it can be rolly. Space is very limited and it may be necessary to lie to two anchors. There is a sandy beach at the head of the *cala* and a track inland.

⚓ Cala Son Saura

39°55'·3N 03°53'·5E

A large, semi-enclosed bay surrounded by a low, sloping rocky foreshore with dark pine trees and scrub behind. It lies close west of Punta Governador (Gobernadó) and is easily recognised by its sheer size – the entrance is about 250m wide and it broadens out further inside. There are two small islets on the west of the entrance and two isolated rocks near the east side, but the bay itself is clear. Anchor in 3–8m over sand, avoiding a central bank of weed. Open to the south, with the best protection from a southeasterly swell and wind being on the eastern side off Playa de Bellavista. Both beaches have buoyed swimming areas and share a lifeguard based on the point in between. Tripper boats disgorge tourists and there is a car park close inland, but the long walk along the coast on the Camí de Cavalls from Cala'n Bosch ensures the beaches are less crowded than many. Ashore there is a long pinkish sandy beach divided into two parts (Playa de Bellavista to the east and Playa des Banyul to the west), by a low rocky area with intriguing canals cut through it - possibly fish traps or stores, with a small stream crossing the eastern beach after wet weather. There is a small fishing boat slipway, a few houses well set back and the lane leading inland, but nothing else. Son Saura is a popular anchorage for yachts arriving from, or departing for, Mallorca.

Cala son Saura with Cala de Talaier top right. Son Saura is the largest anchorage on the south coast and well placed for passages between Menorca and Mallorca
Paramotor Menorca

⚓ Cala Vey (de Son Vell) and Cala Parejals
39°55'·3N 03°52'.1E

Two small *calas* with rocky sides on the much-indented stretch of coast between Cala Son Saura and Cala de Son Aparets. There are numerous inshore rocks and islets, and the area should only be explored with considerable care and by experienced navigators. Cala Vey gives at least some protection from SW wind and swell.

⚓ Cala de Son Aparets (Playa de Son Xoriguer)
39°55'·3N 03°50'·6E

A large rounded bay surrounded by low rocky cliffs, behind which lie houses and some apartment blocks. The *cala* is easy to find, being a little under a mile east of Cabo Dartuch (*see plan on page 238*) and close east of Puerto de Tamarinda and Punta de sa Guardia. On the approach watch out for the isolated Bajo Dartuch, which lies 400m east of the west entrance point and has 1·6m depths. An uncharted rock has been reported in position: 39°55'·27N 003°50'·6E, approximately 185m S of Bajo Dartuch, with a depth of less than 2m. Navionics (ipad edition) reports an isolated danger, but there is nothing to mark either of the afore-mentioned hazards. Due to some positional uncertainty prudent navigators with no reason to close the coast might stay outside the 20m contour, as local charter skippers and the boatyard in Ciudadela report that yachts regularly strike this unmarked rock. Out of season, anchor in 2m+ over sand and weed. The beach is good but often very crowded and in season the swimmers' buoys are laid out to the 5m contour (the major part of the *cala*). There are several beach cafés and roads inland. The Puerto de Tamarinda tourist complex is a short walk away.

⚓ Cala'n Bosch (En Bosc)
39°55'·4N 03°50'.2E

A small *cala* with low rocky edges and a crowded sandy beach at its head, just east of Puerto de Tamarinda and west of Punta de sa Guardia (na Cap de Porc). Out of season, anchor in 2m+ over sand and weed. In season swimmers' buoys totally exclude craft from entry into this *cala* as they stretch from headland to headland. There are low-rise tourist apartments behind the *cala* and it is only a step across to the Puerto de Tamarinda tourist complex where there are shops and other facilities.

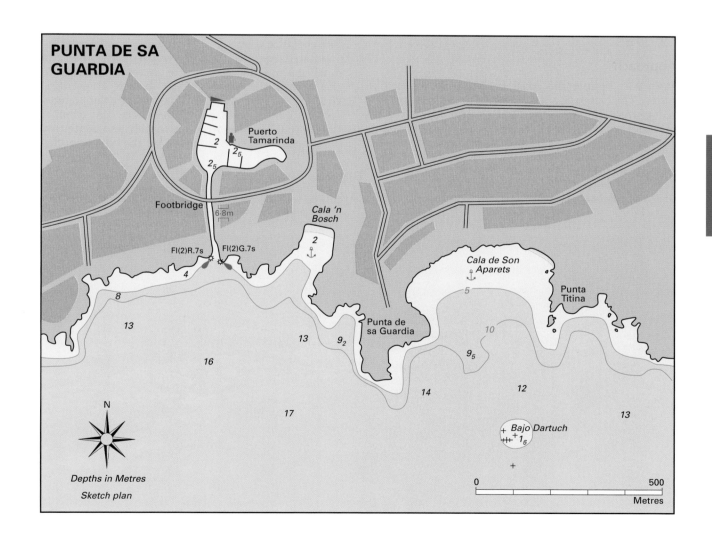

PUNTA DE SA GUARDIA

Puerto Tamarinda

Footbridge
6·8m

Fl(2)R.7s   Fl(2)G.7s

Cala 'n Bosch

Cala de Son Aparets

Punta Titina

Punta de sa Guardia

Bajo Dartuch

N

Depths in Metres

Sketch plan

0   500
Metres

Puerto de Tamarinda
(Marina Cala'n Bosch)

39°55'·5N 03°50'.1E

A small harbour with 264 moorings accessed via a narrow canal, but with a bridge restricting height to 6·8m. Only suitable for relatively small motor boats and dinghies, it has little relevance for the wider cruising population.

Communications
Club Deportivo Cala'n Bosch ☎ 971 38 71 70 / 38 52 38
darbosch@teleline.es

The harbour

A small man-made lagoon dredged from a low-lying area. Approached via a narrow channel spanned by a footbridge reminiscent of a willow-pattern plate, Puerto de Tamarinda is inaccessible to sailing vessels as the stated air height is only 6·8m, albeit with some publications reporting it as 10m. However, it makes an interesting visit by dinghy and is suited to medium-sized motor yachts, speedboats and smaller sailing craft. It is also used by sailboarders. The harbour is surrounded by a growing tourist development with all the related facilities.

Pilotage

Approach

From east Follow the coast past a series of small *calas*. The large Cala de Son Aparets is easily recognized, being separated by a low rocky promontory (Punta de sa Guardia, *see plan on page 238)* from the narrow Cala'n Bosch, behind which stands a group of apartment blocks. Beware the hazards mentioned above off Cala de son Aparets. The entrance to Puerto de Tamarinda is 200m west of Cala'n Bosch. The entrance is not obvious until close by.

From north and west Approach the prominent Cabo Dartuch with its black-and-white-banded lighthouse (34m) (*see plan on page 238*). The entrance to Puerto de Tamarinda lies around 1,000m east-northeast of the lighthouse and west of Cala'n Bosch, which will be recognised by its narrow sandy beach surrounded by apartment blocks.

Anchorages in the approach

Anchor in Cala'n Bosch or Cala de Son Aparets (*see page 241*) if possible; in the main holiday season the *calas* are closed off with swimmer buoys.

Entrance

The entrance is less than 10m wide – too narrow for anything larger than dinghies to pass each other, and much too narrow to turn. It is therefore essential to check that the way is clear before committing yourself. Approach heading north into the channel with its conspicuous white footbridge and enter at slow speed. The water is often muddy and depths are unreliable, so keep a close eye on the echo-sounder.

Cabo Dartuch (extreme left) viewed from the southeast. Cala de Son Aparets, centre, with Cala'n Bosch and Puerto de Tamarinda to its left *Graham Hutt*

Puerto de Tamarinda with its quaint bridge, Cala'n Bosch to right

If in any doubt about height clearance it would be wise to anchor in Cala'n Bosch and walk round to measure the bridge. In strong winds and swell from the southerly quadrant it would be dangerous to attempt entry into Puerto de Tamarinda.

Berthing

Secure in any vacant berth: the harbour is unlikely to be full. An official will allocate a berth in due course.

Facilities

Water At the base of some of the pontoons, otherwise from one of the cafés.
Electricity On some (but not all) of the pontoons.
Fuel Available.
Provisioning Small supermarket and other shops in the complex, a chemist and tourist shops.
Ice From the nearby bars and cafés.
Repairs A very wide slipway at the head of the harbour.
Bank In the tourist complex.
Hospital/medical services In Ciudadela, about 4½M away.

Transport

Taxis By telephone from Ciudadela, or enquire in the tourist complex.
Buses Buses to Ciudadela.

Ashore

There is a *talayot* (ancient tower) at Son Olivaret about a mile north on the road to Ciudadela.

Eating out

A choice of restaurants, cafés and bars within the tourist complex.

V. MENORCA

Puerto Tamarinda to Cala Santandria

Cabo Dartuch (Cap d'Artrutx)

39°55'·3N 03°49'·5E

A prominent headland of low (10m) dark cliffs surmounted by a conspicuous lighthouse (white tower with three black bands on a white building surrounded by a low white-topped wall). The headland is steep-to. *See plan on page 238.*

Cabo Negro (Cap Negre)

39°57'·1N 03°49'·4E

A relatively inconspicuous headland of black rock, 12m high and steep-to. Easily seen if coasting close inshore.

⚓ Cala en Bastó

39°57'·4N 03°49'·7E

A small *cala* close north of Cabo Negro and about 2M north of Cabo Dartuch, surrounded by low (8m) black rocky cliffs. A small breaking rock lies on the south side of the entrance. The *cala* is in a remote area with no beach and a rocky bottom and is open from west to north. Use with extreme caution.

⚓ Aigua Dolça

39°58'N 3°49'·9E

An almost right-angled corner in the low cliffs between Cala en Basto and Cala Blanca with no beach but a substantial area of sand in which to anchor in 5-8m. Open west and north it is otherwise well protected and is a quiet and pleasant anchorage, a short dinghy ride from Cala Blanca.

⚓ Cala Blanca

39°58'N 3°50'E

A narrow *cala* between low rocky sides, Cala Blanca is easy to identify due to an unusual building with deep verandas on its northern side and a huge white apartment block/hotel in the background. Anchor in

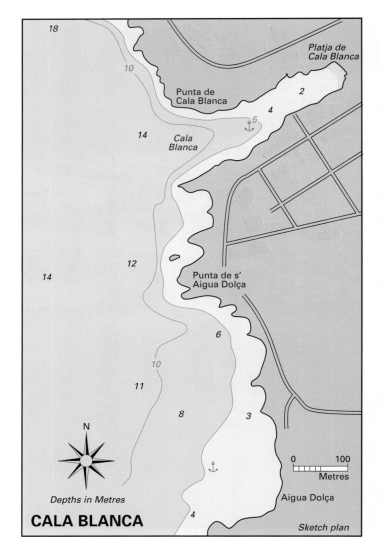

CALA BLANCA

4–8m over sand ideally with a line ashore; but in high season swimmers' buoys virtually exclude craft from this *cala*. The sandy beach at its head is often crowded, and there are hotels, restaurants, cafés and houses nearby. The Caves of Parella a few hundred metres inland are worth visiting.

Aigua Dolça. A quiet spot close to Cala Blanca, well protected from south or east winds *David Baggaley*

Cala Santandria viewed from west

⚓ Cala Santandria

39°58'·7N 03°49'·8E

A long *cala* with several shorter branches, Cala Santandria lies between low, pinkish, rocky cliffs about three quarters of a mile north of Cala Blanca (*see plan on page 238*). The entrance is not easily picked out, but the Torre Es Castella (a restored defensive tower) on the north headland helps. A small islet off the east side of the entrance, Escull de Santandria, is the only hazard on entering. Anchor in 3m+ over sand and weed as space permits, either lying to two anchors or taking a line ashore. Two cables run down the centre of the *cala*, so care is needed when picking a spot. This anchorage has been reported as uncomfortable even in light winds and it is difficult to keep clear of the cables.

In summer, lines of buoys mark off all three bathing beaches but there is still room for a few yachts to anchor in the mouth of the *cala* outside Caleta d'en Gorros in 6-8m over sand and weed. Supermarkets, hotels and restaurants are located slightly further back from the end of the *cala*. There are pleasant walks on either side of the *cala* and the Torre Es Castella is worth a visit. Maréchal Richelieu, commander of the French invasion, landed here with his troops on 18 April 1756, en route to capture Ciudadela.

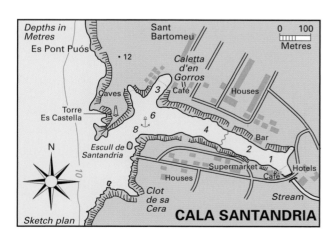

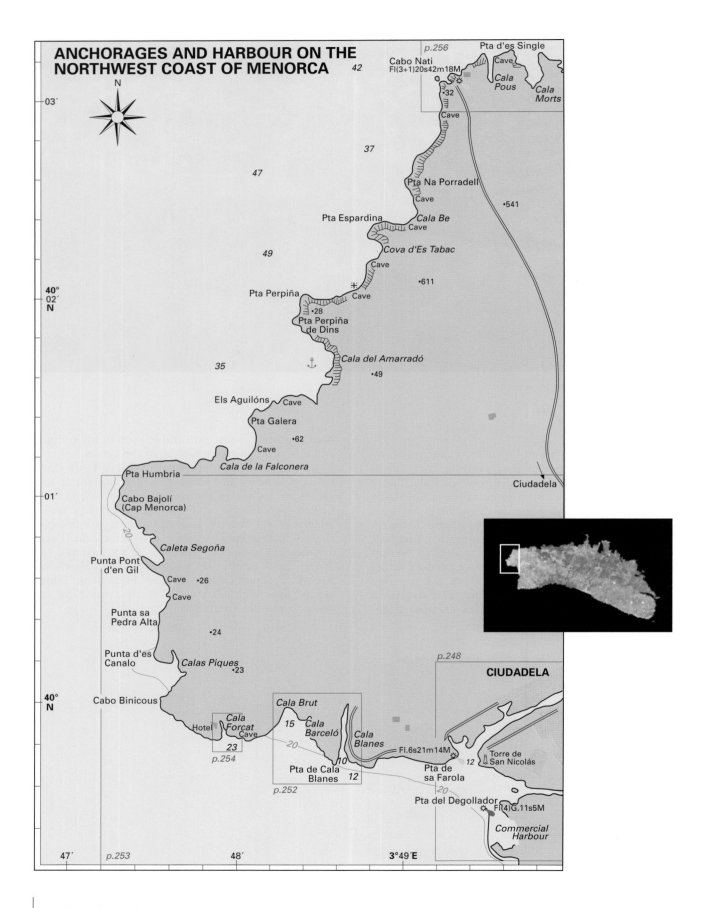

ANCHORAGES AND HARBOUR ON THE NORTHWEST COAST OF MENORCA

N

42

p.256

Pta d'es Single

Cabo Nati
Fl(3+1)20s42m18M

Cave

Cala Pous

Cala Morts

•32

Cave

–03´

37

Pta Na Porradell

Cave

•541

47

Pta Espardina

Cala Be

Cave

Cova d'Es Tabac

49

Cave

•611

40°
02´
N

Pta Perpiña

Cave

•28

Pta Perpiña
de Dins

Cala del Amarradó

35

•49

Els Aguilóns

Cave

Pta Galera

•62

Cave

Cala de la Falconera

Pta Humbria

Ciudadela

–01´

Cabo Bajolí
(Cap Menorca)

20

Caleta Segoña

Punta Pont
d'en Gil

Cave   •26

Cave

p.248

Punta sa
Pedra Alta

CIUDADELA

•24

Punta d'es
Canalo

Calas Piques

•23

40°
N

Cabo Binicous

Cala Brut

Hotel

Cala Forcat

Cave

15

Cala Barceló

Cala Blanes

Fl.6s21m14M

Torre de
San Nicolás

12

23

p.254

20

10

Pta de Cala
Blanes

12

Pta de
sa Farola

p.252

20

Pta del Degollador
Fl(4)G.11s5M

Commercial Harbour

47´   p.253

48´

3°49´E

View across the outer part of Cala Degollador to the new ferry harbour. Islote de la Galera behind foreground yacht
Susie Baggaley

⚓ Cala Degollador

39°59'·7N 03°49'·6E

A narrow *cala* just north of the entrance to the commercial harbour at Ciudadela, surrounded by low rocky cliffs and with two popular sandy beaches at its head. Islote de la Galera, a small islet 4m high, lies in the middle of the entrance with a 4·1m rocky shoal extending 80m northwards. Anchor in 4m+ over sand with weed patches. It may be necessary to use two anchors or a shore-line to restrict swinging room as the *cala* is very narrow (*see plan on page 248*). When it is busy it is necessary to anchor further out with a line ashore, usually to the N bank. In summer the entire narrow section of the *cala* from just east of Islote de la Galera is now closed off by swimming buoys. West of Islote de la Galera the bottom is mainly rocky and swinging at anchor is a noisy experience; better to take a line ashore!

Cala Degollador forms a useful alternative to Ciudadela when the latter is crowded, and has all its shoreside facilities within a short walk. Plans for turning the *cala* into a yacht harbour behind protective breakwaters have been shelved, probably permanently.

A commercial harbour with a ferry terminal has been constructed south of the *cala* (*see page 248*). Do not anchor further west than a line between Punta de Degollador and the Torre de San Nicolás to avoid encroaching on the ferry turning area.

V. MENORCA

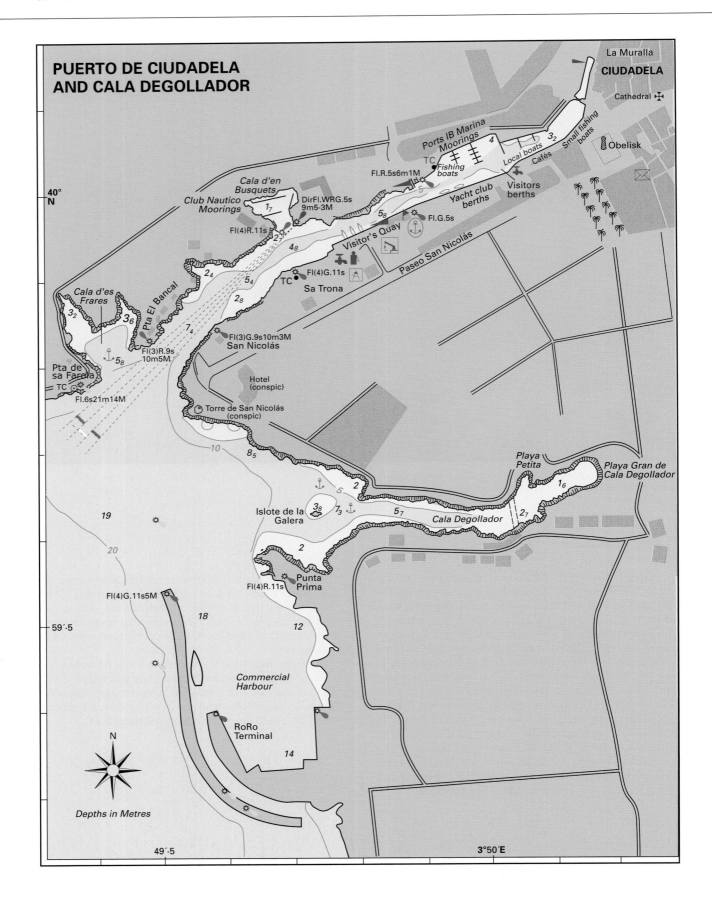

PUERTO DE CIUDADELA
AND CALA DEGOLLADOR

La Muralla
CIUDADELA

Cathedral

Ports IB Marina Moorings

Small fishing boats

4

3₂

Local boats

Cafés

Obelisk

TC
Fishing boats

Fl.R.5s6m1M

Visitors berths

Cala d'en Busquets

Club Nautico Moorings

DirFl.WRG.5s 9m5-3M

1₇

Yacht club berths

40°
N

Fl(4)R.11s

2₇

5₈

Fl.G.5s

4₈

Visitor's Quay

2₄

5₄

Paseo San Nicolás

Cala d'es Frares

Pta El Bancal

TC

Fl(4)G.11s

Sa Trona

3₂

3₆

2₈

7₄

Fl(3)G.9s10m3M
San Nicolás

5₈

Fl(3)R.9s 10m5M

Pta de sa Farola

Hotel (conspic)

TC

Fl.6s21m14M

Torre de San Nicolás (conspic)

Playa Petita

Playa Gran de Cala Degollador

10

8₅

1₆

2

19

5

3₈

7₃

5₇

2₇

Cala Degollador

Islote de la Galera

20

2

Punta Prima

Fl(4)R.11s

Fl(4)G.11s5M

18

12

N

Commercial Harbour

59´5

RoRo Terminal

14

Depths in Metres

49´5

3°50´E

Puerto de Ciudadela (Ciutadella)

39°59'·7N 03°49'·4E

A natural harbour up a long cala, with berthing for more than 100 vessels.

Communications
Ports IB (Puerto de Ciudadela) VHF Ch 08
✆ 971 484455
www.portsib.es
Club Náutico de Ciudadela VHF Ch 09
✆ 971 38 39 18 cnciutadela@cncuitadella.com
www.cnciutadella.com

The harbour

One of the most attractive and interesting harbours in the Baleares, Ciudadela is also the most ancient and should not be missed. Recently a new harbour and ferry terminal became fully operational outside the port, leaving the main harbour for the use of pleasure vessels and the small but very active fishing fleet. Restructuring the yachting facilities was soon accomplished with new moorings and floating pontoons added on the NW side of the *cala*, replacing the RoRo ferry terminal and now administered by Ports IB, which took over from the Port Authority. The Club Náutico moorings were changed from alongside, to fore-and-aft with lines tailed to the quay.

Outer part of the entrance to Ciudadela harbour
David Baggaley

Pilotage

Approach

From south or southwest Cabo Dartuch, a low rocky-cliffed promontory topped by a very conspicuous lighthouse (white tower with three black bands on a white building surrounded by a low white-topped wall), is easily recognised (*see plan on page 238*). The entrance to Puerto de Ciudadela lies 4·4M to the north and there are no offshore hazards. The buildings of Ciudadela (in particular the Torre de San Nicolás) and the large curved hotel behind can be seen from afar. Keep well clear of the ferry port entrance.

From north or northwest Cabo Nati and its conspicuous lighthouse (a white aluminium cupola on a pale limestone tower above a building with a red roof), Cabo Bajolí and Cabo Binicous further south, are all prominent headlands (*see plan on page 246*). Follow them round at 200m until heading east-southeast, at which point the buildings of Ciudadela will be seen less than 2M away.

Entrance

To navigate to the harbour, simply follow the centre line of the *cala*. Approach and entry are straightforward, although it is a little disconcerting to have such difficulty in identifying the entrance until very close. Even in the entrance of the narrow *cala* not much can be seen until well inside, when the spectacular ancient town suddenly appears along with the yachting facilities on both sides.

Sea levels

The level of the sea rises with a southwest wind and falls with north and northeast winds by as much as 0·5m. Under certain meteorological conditions, usually when a depression and spring tide coincide, a phenomenon known as resaca or seiche occurs, causing the level to rise and fall by as much as 1·5m every 10 or 15 minutes, an oscillation which may continue for several days. Local fishermen often give warning when they expect it to occur. The consequence of this oscillation is a very strong current, reversing every few minutes over a period of several hours, making mooring difficult.

V. MENORCA

Ciudadela viewed from southwest. Cala Degollador to right. The 17th-century Torre de San Nicolas seen centre of picture and Cala d'es Frares left

Berthing

Since the ferry terminal has moved from the inner harbour to south of Pta de Degollador, Club Náutico moorings are now bows/stern-to, with lines tailed to the quay, (rather than alongside) on the SE side of the *cala*. Limited mooring for larger vessels is alongside the Club Náutico office and clubhouse. More Club Náutico moorings (not generally used for visitors) are located on pontoons in Cala d'en Busquets, halfway up the *cala* on the N side. This was formerly an anchorage. Finally they also control an area for about 10 vessels to moor stern or bows to the quay just by the first restaurants, past the Club Náutico on the south side of the *cala*.

Beyond the Club Náutico moorings, on the north side where the RoRo ferry quay was located previously, are the Ports IB moorings on four pontoons which are partly taken up by local craft. In principle, these pontoons are for maximum 12m but this is often clearly exceeded particularly for the alongside berths on the hammerheads. Water and electricity are available at all berths. Ports IB moorings need booking at least 3 days in advance

The Club Náutico dock   *David Baggaley*

Looking across the inner harbour to the Ports IB pontoons
Susie Baggaley

during high season. Don't take a chance on finding a mooring available; it is almost impossible in July and August unless pre-booked online for a Ports IB mooring, or by phone with Club Náutico. Ports IB berths are less than half the price of the Club Náutico moorings in midsummer.

The larger fishing trawlers use part of the old commercial quay to moor. These leave noisily around 0400 daily.

Anchorage in the harbour

There is now no possibility of anchoring in the harbour. However, there is a very small anchorage in Cala d'es Frares, a small Y-shaped *cala* on the port side of the entrance. With an anchor laid towards the entrance and stern lines secured to the shore to avoid swinging, 2 yachts can possibly anchor here, otherwise just one. There is some dispute about attaching lines to rings ashore, as some yachts have been informed that it is no longer allowed, whilst others have done so without being challenged. Certainly it is no longer permissible to attach lines to the E side of the *cala*. The western arm of the *cala* is totally buoyed off for swimmers, at least in the summer.

Depth is around 5·5m over sand, but note that there is an isolated rock towards the W end of the rock cliff (with around 2m of water) along with many old moorings on the seabed. The water is clear enough to see the bottom and avoid these obstructions.

A better and much larger anchorage is in Cala Degollador, on the SE side of the entrance, keeping well clear of the ferries turning into the new port. (*See plan page 248.*) This anchorage gets crowded in summer, especially approaching nightfall, and the position is worsened now that virtually all the *cala* is buoyed off for swimmers (*see page 247*).

Facilities

Water & electricity Available at all berths.

Fuel Fuel dock for diesel and gasoline on the Club Náutico quay. July and August open every day 0915–1330 and 1500–1900. June and September open Monday to Saturday 0915–1330 and 1500–1800. Rest of year, mornings Monday to Friday only.

Provisions A good selection of small supermarkets and specialist food shops (large supermarkets on industrial estate on the edge of town). The nearest small supermarket to the yacht club is SUMA, virtually on the junction of Paseo San Nicolas and Paseo Republica Argentina across from the police station. Paseo San Nicolas is the next road back from the yacht club. There is a good but small open-air market in the middle of the old part of the town, with a fish market in its centre.

Ice From supermarkets.

Chandlery Nautica Ponseli on Paseo San Nicolas next door to the police station. ☎ 971 382542.
Menorca Yachting ☎ 971 48 20 44 on the waterfront above the restaurant Sa' Figura is also willing to assist yachtsmen in need.

Repairs Small boatyard, Astilleros Llompart, by the slipway west of the trawler quay. Cranes at Astilleros

The large trolley at Astilleros Llomparts for hauling shallow draught vessels – presumably a successor to the 'slightly rustic cradle' referred to in previous editions! *Susie Baggaley*

Llompart (12·5 tonnes) and at the Club Náutico (5 tonnes). Slipway at the west end of the Astilleros Llompart yard with a trolley which can haul out fishing vessels and other shallow draught motor craft of up to about 40 feet. There is room for only three or four modest- sized vessels in the yard at any one time, but there have been good reports on the quality of work, particularly carpentry. *Mobile* 650 957454, ☎ 971 380675, astillerosllompart@gmail.com

Engineers Centre Nautic Ciudadela ☎ 971 38 26 16 are agents for Ecosse, Volvo Penta and Yanmar.

Yacht club The Club Náutico de Ciudadela has a fine clubhouse fronting the harbour with bar, lounge, terrace, restaurant and showers.

Showers Good showers at the Club Náutico. There is no charge to those using the club moorings. Rather more basic showers at the PortsIB premises.

Launderette In the town – Calle Evissa and a particularly large one in Calle de Mallorca at the roundabout near the head of Cala Degollador. Also the Club Náutico has a small launderette.

Banks Several in the town, with credit card facilities.

Hospital/medical services In the town.

WiFi Reports of good WiFi hotspots at Ports IB marina

Transport

Car hire/taxis Available in the town.

Buses Bus service to Mahón, Fornells and elsewhere.

Ferries Car ferries to Alcudia (Mallorca) and Barcelona.

History

Ciudadela harbour has been in use since prehistoric times, long before the Phoenicians settled in 1600–1200BC and gave it its first name, Yamma, meaning 'western' or 'west town'. The Greeks and Romans

Bust of David Glasgow Farragut, first Admiral of the United States of America navy, near the Torre San Nicolas at the entrance to Ciudadela harbour (*see page 215*)
David Baggaley

followed, and Pliny the Elder referred to it as Iama or Iamnona. The next name on record was that of the Moors, to whom it was Medina Minurka. With the expulsion of the Moors by the Aragonese it received its current name of Ciudadela meaning 'little city', though very little from that time remains due to repeated attacks by pirates and corsairs. The most notorious assault was led by the Turkish pirate Barbarossa who, in 1558, laid siege to the town and, when it fell, destroyed its buildings and took most of the surviving inhabitants away as slaves. Even so, Ciudadela remained the capital of the island (and the see of a bishop) until 1722 when the British transferred the administration to Mahón, the bigger and better natural harbour.

Ashore

The fascinating old town is unspoilt and can answer most needs. It is a delight to explore, with pavement cafés under the arches of Ses Voltes and a contrast between the palaces of the old families fronting the open squares and the tiny houses of the artisans, packed apparently at random (intended, it is said, to confuse the all-too-frequent intruders with a succession of blind alleys and unexpected turns). The excellent market area 'lost' in the back streets of the old town is worth a visit not just for the meat, fish and fruit and vegetable sections but also for the surrounding small bars and restaurants. The 14th-century cathedral merits a special visit, but Ciudadela is a town oozing antiquity and interest on every side. This is also a good base to explore the bronze-age talayotic megalith sites around the island.

Three miles out of Ciudadela, just off the road to Mahón, lies the Naveta d'es Tudóns, which lays claim to being the oldest building in Europe and is undoubtedly the oldest in Spain. The Naveta (so-called because the ground plan resembles a ship) is built of large stone blocks and has two storeys. It measures 14m by 6·5m and was used over many centuries as a communal tomb.

Local events

Ciudadela's final distinction lies in its fiesta of San Juán on 23–24 June, famed for its daring equestrian displays to which the usual drinking and merrymaking are only a sideshow. The build-up to the fiesta begins the previous Sunday and it can be guaranteed that there will not be a free berth in the harbour. On 2 July the Fiesta Patriótica is celebrated, commemorating the town's resistance to Turkish pirates in 1558.

Eating out

Many restaurants, cafés and bars.

Anchorages west and northwest of Puerto de Ciudadela

⚓ Cala Blanes
39°59'·7N 03°48'·7E

A long narrow *cala* between low (9m) undercut cliffs leading to a crowded sandy beach, about ½ mile west of Punta de Sa Farola lighthouse and the entrance to Puerto de Ciudadela. There is a large hotel with a small white tower on its roof near the head of the *cala* which can be seen from the entrance. Anchor in 5m+ over sand and weed, open to the south: it may be necessary to use two anchors or to take a line to one of the rings ashore. In summer a line of buoys marks off the bathing area and virtually excludes craft from using this *cala*.

A tourist resort is growing around Cala Blanes, complete with the usual hotels, restaurants, beach bars, etc. Most day-to-day items can be purchased in the resort, though it may be simpler (and cheaper) to go into Ciudadela.

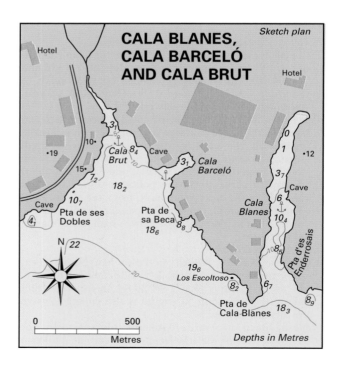

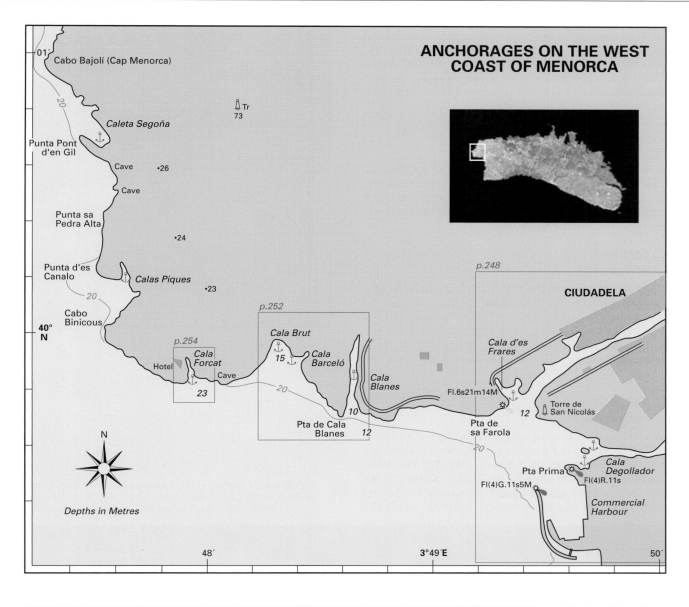

ANCHORAGES ON THE WEST
COAST OF MENORCA

01'
Cabo Bajolí (Cap Menorca)

20

⌀ Tr
73

Caleta Segoña

Punta Pont
d'en Gil

Cave   •26

Cave

Punta sa
Pedra Alta

•24

Punta d'es
Canalo   Calas Piques

•23

20

Cabo
Binicous

**40°
N**

p.254

p.252

Hotel   Cala
Forcat

Cala Brut

p.248

CIUDADELA

Cave

23

15   Cala
Barceló

Cala
Blanes

Cala d'es
Frares

20

10

Pta de Cala
Blanes   12

Fl.6s21m14M

Torre de
San Nicolás

12

Pta de
sa Farola

20

Pta Prima

Fl(4)R.11s

Cala
Degollador

N

Fl(4)G.11s5M

Commercial
Harbour

Depths in Metres

48'   **3°49′E**   50'

Cala Brut (left of
centre), Cala Barceló
(centre) and Cala
Blanes (right)
viewed from south

V. MENORCA

A strange night time phenomenon is experienced in this *cala* whereby even in a very flat calm sea, wavelets develop and slap under the cliffs and on the hull for several hours. Although it is not uncomfortable, it is noisy. It is possibly a mini seiche as described in the introduction.

⚓ Cala Barceló

39°59'·9N 03°48'·5E

A very small, almost circular and rather spectacular *cala* surrounded by 10m rocky cliffs, open to the southwest. Mooring buoys occupy most of the space available. There is no beach or other attractions. Suitable for small vessels only.

⚓ Cala Brut

40°00'N 03°48'·4E

A small narrow and spectacular *cala* at the head of a wider inlet about 0·75M west of the entrance to Puerto de Ciudadela. Anchor in 5–10m over sand in the entrance to the *cala* if not prevented by the swimming area buoys. There are rocky bathing terraces on either side and a large hotel near the head.

⚓ Cala Forcat

39°59'·8N 03°48'.1E

A very small Y-shaped *cala* dwarfed by an immense yellow hotel, Cala Forcat is suitable only for smaller yachts and dinghies. It is surrounded by low (10m) rocky cliffs and is open to the south. Anchor in 4–5m over sand and rock, using two anchors. All the usual facilities of a large modern hotel are available.

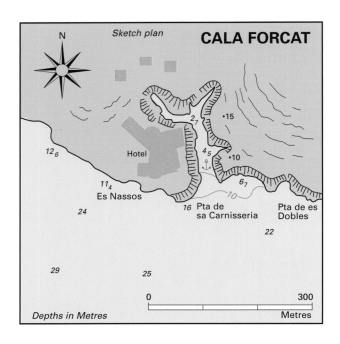

Cala Forcat bottom right, looking northwest over Cabo Binicous (left). Calas Piques and Caleta Segoña on far side of peninsula. Cala S'Amarrador at extreme top right

Cabo Binicous (Cap de Banyos) to Cabo Nati

40°00'·0N 03°47'·6E

Most anchorages between Cabo Binicous (Cap de Banyos) and Cabo Nati should not be attempted in anything less than settled weather and by experienced navigators. Most are deep and surrounded by high rocky cliffs (24–64m) and there are no beaches, houses or roads. The bottom is mostly rocky. The exception is Cala del Amarrado (S'Amarrador). In practice, these bays and inlets, and indeed those round the corner on the north coast before Cala Morell, are really just spectacular areas to nose into, admire, and move on.

Calas Piques

40°00'.2N 03°47'.7E

Two small but pretty *calas*, suitable only for small boats. The more southerly is fully buoyed off for swimmers in summer, but the northern arm may be clear. The *calas* are narrow and shore lines or fore and aft anchors are necessary.

Punta Pont d'en Gil

40°00'·7N 3°47'·6E

A long, thin, rocky-cliffed point with a large natural arch leading through into Caleta Segoña. The arch is about 10m high and 8m wide and can be used with care by dinghies and small motor boats.

Cala del Amarradó. A little known but useful anchorage (photo taken mid-day on a Saturday at the end of July!)
David Baggaley

⚓ Caleta Segoña (Cigonya)

40°00'·7N 3°47'·7E

The caleta is approached immediately to the north of Punta Pont D'en Gil which is pierced by the arch referred to above. The water is deep and the bottom mainly rocky.

Cabo Bajolí (Cap Menorca)

40°01'·0N 03°47'·4E

A large headland, high inland (72m), sloping down in a west direction to dark, rocky, steep-to cliffs. A disused semaphore signal station is located on the highest point. This is the most westerly point of Menorca.

⚓ Cala del Amarradó (Raco de S'Amarrador)

40°01'·7N 03°48'·4E

A fairly large open *cala* in a remote and attractive location with very clear turquoise water over a large expanse of sand. Anchor in 6-10m. There is no beach but there are deep caves and gullies especially in the southeast corner and the snorkelling should be good. The *cala* is open southwest to north. (See page 246.)

6. CABO NATI TO ISLA NITGE

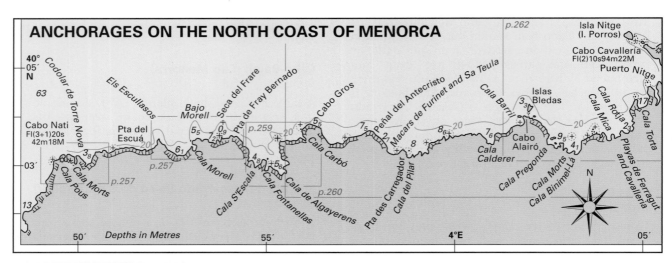

ANCHORAGES ON THE NORTH COAST OF MENORCA

Depths in Metres

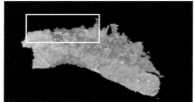

Cabo Nati

40°03'.1N 03°49'.2E

A prominent 32m headland of dark cliffs sloping to the northwest, with a conspicuous lighthouse (white aluminium cupola on a light limestone tower above a building with a red roof) set inside a white-topped wall a hundred metres or so inland. The cliffs are steep-to, but with several small rocky islets close inshore. A road runs from the lighthouse to Ciudadela.

⚓ Cala Pous

40°03'.2N 03°49'·6E

A small, narrow, rocky *cala* in rugged surroundings 300m northeast of Cabo Nati lighthouse, with a small islet on the east side of the entrance. The inlet lies between 30m sloping cliffs and has a small stony beach at its head. Anchor in 10–15m over rock, weed and sand, with shore-lines.

⚓ Codolar de la Torre Nova

40°03'.1N 03°50'.2E

A large, open deserted *cala* with 40m rocky cliffs, some rocky beaches and several caves, one of which can be entered by dinghy. There are several rocky islets off Punta d'es Llosar on the east side of the entrance and two *talayots* (ancient towers) on the skyline. Anchor in about 20m over sand, rock and

Rugged north coast looking east from Cabo Nati

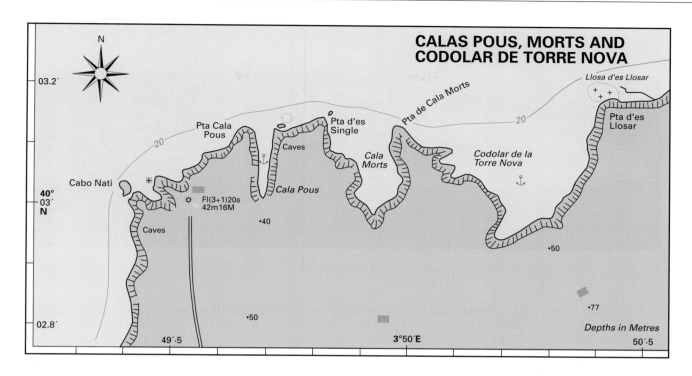

weed; however there are several gullies in the *cala* into which a small vessel might squeeze to moor either to anchor or to multiple lines ashore. Open to the north.

Punta del Escuá and Els Escullasos

40°03′·6N 03°52′·0E

Three small rocky islets lie close inshore under the high (79m) sloping cliffs of Punta del Escuá (Punta de s'Escullar). 100m to the north lie two breaking rocks (Els Escullasos) with foul ground extending for 100m around them.

⚓ Cala Morell

40°03′·4N 03°52′·9E

This small, almost landlocked *cala* with sloping rocky cliffs gives a very beautiful anchorage. The entrance is difficult to spot until well into the outer bay. If coming from the west, on rounding Els Escullasos a group of white houses will be seen above Punta d'es Elefant on the southwest side of the entrance. Coming from the east a few houses on Punta de Cala Morell will be seen. The *cala* only opens after this point is astern. Allow generous clearance to Seca del Frare and Bajo d'en Morell rocks (see plan).

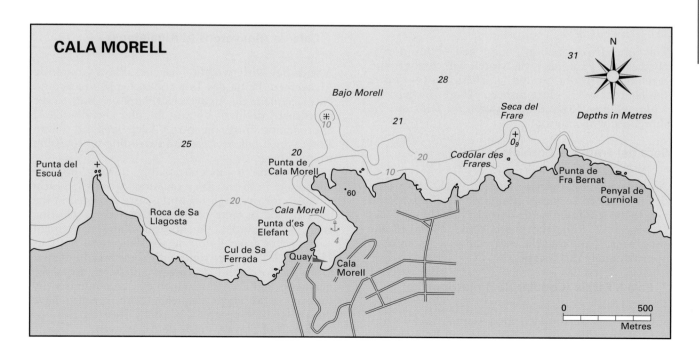

Cala Morell, rather limited for space as much of the cala is taken up with small craft moorings in summer
Juanjo Pons / Triangle Postals

Swimming buoys and a large number of small craft mooring buoys restrict anchoring to an area close to the mouth of the *cala* in about 8m over sand and weed where there is room for a few yachts to swing. If at any time it is possible to anchor closer in, it may be necessary to take a line to the western shore. Holding is said to be patchy. If winds from the north sector are forecast it is advisable to leave immediately, as a nasty swell rolls in and it could quickly become untenable (as is the case with most north coast anchorages).

There is a small sandy beach at the head of the *cala* where a seasonal stream enters, and a miniature quay, slipway, crane and boat park for dinghies. A restaurant and basic shopping can be found in the village. There are a large number of prehistoric cave dwellings and necropolis caves in Cala Morell which are second only in importance to those at Calas Covas. A main road leads to Ciudadela.

Bajo (Baix d'en) Morell
40°03'·7N 03°53'·0E

This uncharted breaking rock lies 400m north–northeast of Punta de Cala Morell with foul ground reaching for 100m around it. There are two other similar rocks very close inshore. There is a passage 150m wide and 16m deep between the *bajo* and the shore; use with caution.

Seca del Frare (de Corniola)
40°03'·7N 03°53'·7E

An isolated rock, carrying less than 1m, 250m west of Pta de Fray Bernardo (Punta de Fra Bernat) and not to be confused with a rocky islet, Escull des Frares, 50m from the shore some 200m to the southwest. (Note that the chart shows a 3m patch in approximately this location.)

⚓ Cala S'Escala (Codolar de Biniatram)
40°03'·1N 03°54'·7E

An open bay surrounded by a sloping rocky shore with a stony beach, Cala S'Escala can be identified by the bleak Escull de ses Vinjoles island (14m) off the headland to the east. Anchor over sand and rock, open to the north quadrant. There is a track leading inland but otherwise the bay is deserted.

⚓ Cala Fontanellas
40°03'·0N 03°55'·0E

A pleasant anchorage surrounded by green shrub-covered hills, with a small sand and rock beach. Escull de ses Vinjoles (14m) lies on the northwest side of the entrance. Anchor over sand, rock and weed near the head of the *cala*, which is open to the north but also feels swell from northwest and northeast. A few seasonal moorings may be laid for local boats.

There are one or two houses in the vicinity and fishermen's huts on the north side. Much of the beach at the head of the *cala* is taken up by a short stone quay and slipway for the use of small motorboats kept on the foreshore.

⚓ Cala de Algayerens (d'Algaiarens)
40°03'N 03°55'·2E

A wide bay with two good beaches, Playa Grande de Algayerens (Platja des Tancats) to the southeast and Playa Pequeña de Algayerens (Platja des Bot) to the northeast, divided by an angular headland. If approaching from the north keep well off Punta Rotja which has foul ground extending up to 200m from its base.

Algayerens is understandably a very popular anchorage both for day excursions from Ciudadela and also for overnighting and is very crowded in the peak period in spite of the fact that the anchoring area is substantial. Anchor anywhere convenient inside a line from Escull de ses Vinjoles to Pta d'es Lland in 2-11m over sand with some weed patches. Open to north and northwest and swell from the northeast and even east which can be minimised by tucking in to Playa Pequeña. Both beaches have buoyed swimming areas. A rocky reef lies close to the beach of Playa Grande de Algayerens.

The large anchorage of Cala Algayerens with Calas Fontanellas and S'Escala on the left *Paramotor Menorca*

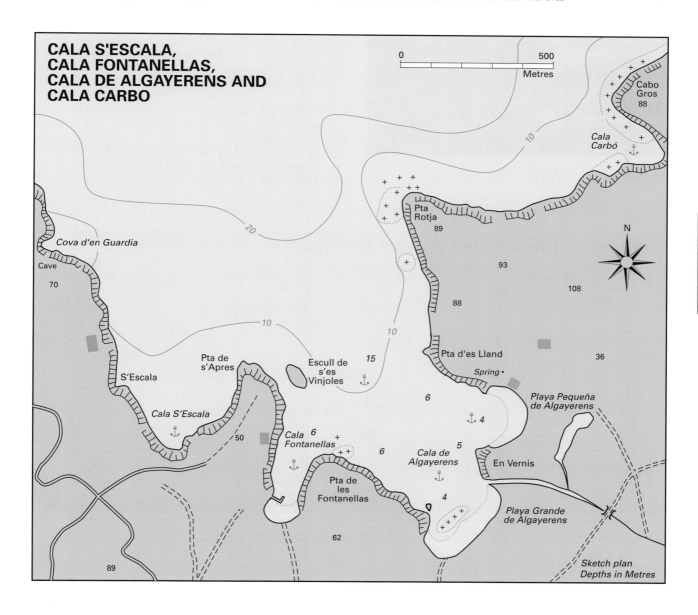

CALA S'ESCALA,
CALA FONTANELLAS,
CALA DE ALGAYERENS AND
CALA CARBO

V. MENORCA

There is a boathouse on Playa Pequeña de Algayerens with a spring, the Font d'en Cumar, nearby, but no houses. Several roads and tracks allow visitors to reach the beaches which are busy in summer. A large lagoon with much wildlife lies inland.

⚓ Cala Carbó (Carabó)
40°03'·5N 03°55'·7E

A small rocky *cala* tucked under the west side of Cabo Gros (*see plan on page 259*). Enter with care as awash rocks line most of the northeast side and parts of the southwest. Anchor over sand, stones and rock. The ruins of an important prehistoric village are ashore.

Cala Carbó

Cabo Gros
40°03'·8N 03°56'·1E

Cabo Gros (96m) has steep cliffs and several small islets and awash rocks close in (*see plan on page 259*). Both it and Peñal del Anticristo 1·2M further east are composed of the same distinctive rust-red rock as Punta Rotja. It is sometimes erroneously referred to as Falconera, which is actually the high peak (205m) which lies a mile south-southeast. A ruined prehistoric village and wall lie south of the headland, not far from Cala Carbó.

North Menorca Marine Reserve

Since 1999 there has been a marine reserve (limiting fishing) between Cabo Gros and Punta de Es Morter, just east of Fornells and, within that, shown on charts as marked by three lit yellow buoys, a *Reserva Integral* which included a prohibition on anchoring; some documents restrict this prohibition to anchoring on seagrass. There is also an area within Fornells in this category. The buoys are no longer in position and numerous vessels have been seen anchored in the following four anchorages which could have been affected (although they do have seagrass-free sand areas) and it appears that anchoring, as such, is not now a problem. A notice board by the harbour in Fornells (and elsewhere) describes the three zones which are shown in the plan below, which also gives the appropriate co-ordinates.

- Between Penal de Antichristo and Isla Bledas and about half a mile off each, all forms of fishing are prohibited.

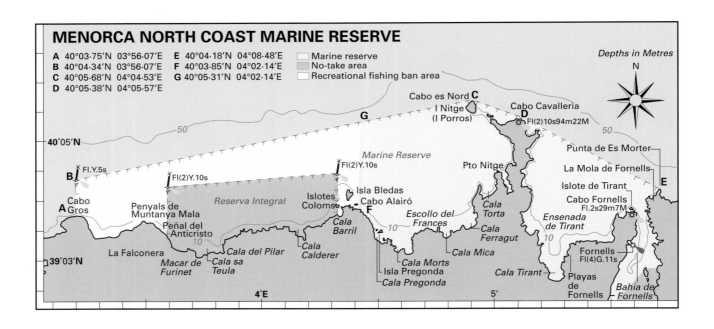

MENORCA NORTH COAST MARINE RESERVE

A 40°03·75'N 03°56·07'E   E 40°04·18'N 04°08·48'E
B 40°04·34'N 03°56·07'E   F 40°03·85'N 04°02·14'E
C 40°05·68'N 04°04·53'E   G 40°05·31'N 04°02·14'E
D 40°05·38'N 04°05·57'E

Marine reserve
No-take area
Recreational fishing ban area

Depths in Metres

Cala del Pilar *Paramotor Menorca*

- In the area from about half a mile off Cabo Gros to the north point of Isla Nitge, recreational fishing is prohibited.
- From Isla Nitge to Punta es Morter, trawl fishing and underwater fishing are prohibited.

If in doubt, don't!

⚓ Macars de Furinet and Sa Teula
40°03'·3N 03°58'·3E

Two ends of a rather unattractive open bay surrounded by sandy and rocky cliffs, to be used with care. There are rocks off the west beach (Macar de Furinet), while Punta des Carregador to the east has rocks and islets extending at least 100m northwest. Anchor off either beach over sand and rock, open to the north quadrant. There is a hut behind the stony east beach but otherwise the area is deserted.

⚓ Cala del Pilar
40°03'·2N 03°58'·7E

A small bay between high (69m), sloping and rather spectacular reddish cliffs. Numerous awash rocks and small islets line the coast to the east, but an approach on a southerly course leaving Illa d'es Pilar 150m to port clears all dangers. Anchor over sand and rock, checking holding carefully. Open northwest round to northeast and to swell from west through north to east. A long walk in means that the beach is usually very quiet even in the peak holiday season.

The ancient hill fortress of Santa Agueda can be accessed from here by following the Cami de Cavalls east for about a kilometre before bearing right onto the Cami dels Alocs for about five kilometres to where the signposted path up the hill appears on the left and takes you on for another kilometre. The fortifications were built by the Moors on an old Roman site and it was here that they made their last stand in 1287. And the hike is worth it for the view.

⚓ Cala Calderer
40°03'·6N 04°00'·9E

A small *cala* with sloping reddish cliffs on either side and scrub-covered hills (57m) above. There are two awash rocks close inshore, one each side of the *cala*, and at its head a sandy beach crossed by a stream bed. Anchor in the entrance where there is adequate swinging room over sand, weed and rock, open to the northwest and north. There is a track leading inland with the buildings of the old Sant Jordi farm and estate house and two prehistoric navetas (burial mounds) about ½ mile away. However, access into the Sant Jordi estate may be prohibited other than where the Cami de Cavalls passes through.

⚓ Cala Barril
40°03'·9N 04°01'·7E

An anchorage off a rock and sand beach close west of Cabo Alairó (Cap de s'Alarió) and the Isla Bledas (Illa Bledas), easy to locate by a track embanked with a stone wall. Careful navigation is necessary due to a small island, an awash rock and an islet to port of the approach. From a position 200m north of Isla de's Coloms, avoiding an awash rock (Baix d'es Coloms) 120m to the northwest of the isla, enter on a southerly course between the island and Cabo Alairó, aiming for the centre of the beach at the head of the *cala*. A small, spectacular anchorage, but approach with care.

V. MENORCA

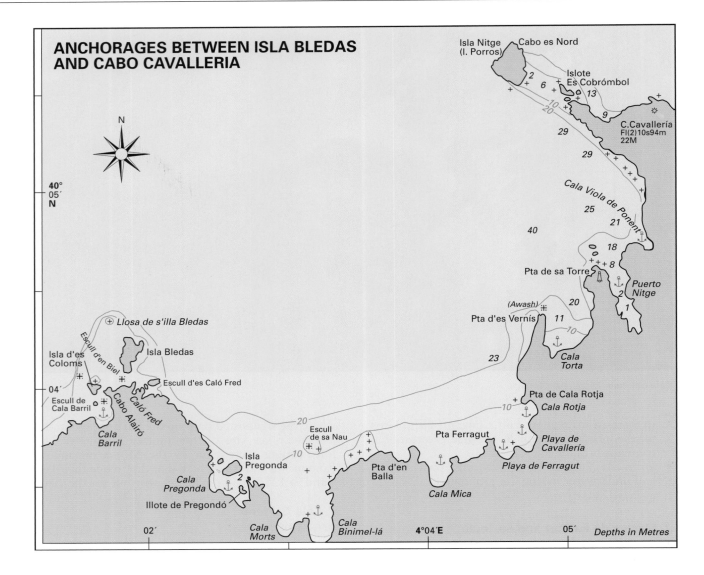

ANCHORAGES BETWEEN ISLA BLEDAS
AND CABO CAVALLERIA

Isla Bledas

40°04'.2N 04°01'.9E

An offing of at least 250m will clear the isolated
Llosa de s'illa Bledas, which lies 120m northwest of
the north-western point of Isla Bledas.

There is said to be a fair-weather passage 100m
wide and 5m deep inside Isla Bledas but this area is
reported as a maze of barely submerged rocks. Rock
hoppers should rely on eyeball navigation if
attempting this passage which certainly cannot be
recommended for deep-keeled vessels.

⚓ Caló Fred

40°03'.9N 04°02'.1E

A very small *cala* hidden away behind the Escull d'es
Caló Fred, only for use by experienced navigators in
good weather. More a place to explore than to
anchor, the *cala* is open to the northeast, has a rocky
bottom and no beach. There are just a few isolated
houses and a road ashore.

⚓ Cala Pregonda

40°03'.5N 04°02'.7E

A beautiful anchorage in a large bay substantially
protected by rocky islets, Cala Pregonda has become
over-popular in summer, both with day visitors and
overnighters. If coming from the northeast, having
rounded Isla Nitge (Porros), a direct course for the
entrance clears Escull de sa Nau – an awash rock off
Cala Binimel-lá. Enter the *cala* on a southwest
course between Isla Pregonda and the smaller Illot
de Pregondó. Anchor off the beach in ±4m over
sand. The wide sandy beach has three houses and a
road behind, and there is a second smaller beach to
the east. Both beaches have extensive buoyed areas
for swimmers. If tucked in behind Isla Pregonda, the
only real exposure in normal circumstaces is to the
northeast although the nearly two mile fetch to the
east would be uncomfortable in fresh easterlies.

The creamy white rocks of Isla Pregonda are
spectacular in early morning or evening light.

Cala Pregonda. In some lights the colour of the rocky islets is spectacular. An understandably popular and, therefore, usually crowded anchorage *Paramotor Menorca*

⚓ Cala Morts and Playa de Binimel-lá

40°03'·3N 04°03'·0E

A wide bay with two sandy beaches divided by a rocky promontory. The west bay (Cala Morts) has two islets and an awash rock at its mouth and is not recommended. The east beach has some small rocks close inshore near its centre but is otherwise clear. Most yachts approach from near to Isla Pregonda keeping at least 100m off the shore. An approach to the east of Escull de sa Nau is not recommended as a rock with less than 1·8m cover has been hit about 150m SSE of the Escull and rocky shallows to the east, in the area where two rocks are shown on the chartlet on page 262, appear to extend further out. To anchor, favour the east side of the bay, taking care to avoid a shallow patch extending northeast from the promontory which divides the two beaches. Anchor over sand and weed in 4m or less.

There is a lagoon behind the beach backed by sloping, scrub-covered hills, with one or two houses, a beach bar/restaurant and a track inland.

⚓ Cala Mica

40°03'·5N 04°04'·0E

A wide and deep *cala* with a sandy beach. It has a number of islets and awash rocks both in the approach (up to 200m from the shore) and fringing either side of the entrance. Anchor near the middle of the *cala* in 5-6m over sand, weed and rocks. There is very little ashore: a house and a track inland, and some of the surrounding hills are terraced.

⚓ Playa de Ferragut, Playa de Cavallería and Cala Rotja

40°03'·7N 04°04'·4E

Three possible anchorages in a large bay broken by rocky outcrops. Approach Playa de Ferragut on a south course to anchor off the beach over sand and weed. At the east end of the beach there are two small rocky islets dividing it from Playa de Cavallería. Take care on final approach to this latter as there is an isolated awash rock 200m off the middle of the beach (see plan on page 262) – favour the east end, to anchor over sand and rock. (Editors' note: we could not find the rock referred to above but there is an awash rock about 20m off Cavalleria beach, which even in the absence of swimming buoys would be unlikely to inconvenience any vessel.) There are some rocky patches but none appear troublesome, except that the water shoals quite rapidly towards Punta de Cala Rotja with a bottom that looks more substantially rocky. In general, anchor on sand, typically in 4–6m. The three beaches are very popular in summer, with a very large car park only five minutes walk away.

Beyond the distinctive reddish point known as Punta de Cala Rotja (Rotja means 'red'), lies the *cala*

Playa de Binimel-lá with Cala Pregonda and Isla Bledas behind *Ricard Pla / Triangle Postals*

V. MENORCA

Playas Cavalleria and Ferragut looking towards Isla Bledas
David Baggaley

Puerto Nitge. The old Roman port of Sanicera and before
that believed to be a Phoenician settlement *David Baggaley*

of that name. Approach cautiously, watching the depth sounder, on an easterly course. Anchor off the beach, avoiding a patch of rocky islets. If approaching from the north, beware of the awash rock (*accurately shown on the chartlet on page 262*) off the northwest point of Cala Rotja.

The large combined anchorage area is open west to north but gives good protection from the northeast and east winds and swells which are so common in summer.

There are no facilities ashore, just tracks leading to the large car park, and the Cami de Cavalls.

⚓ Cala Torta

40°04'.2N 04°04'.9E

A large open *cala* between dark rocky cliffs, with a large conspicuous tower built by the British in the 18th century on Punta de sa Torre, to the east. On the west side Punta d'es Vernís has an islet and an awash rock off its point. Approach and entrance are straightforward and depths are substantial until close in. The southwest corner has a small stony beach and gives the only practicable anchorage in the entire bay in perhaps 8–10m over sand, weed and rock, with a line taken ashore as swinging room is limited. It is a delightful, deserted location and rarely used. The snorkelling should be good with rocky ledges around the base of the cliffs.

⚓ Puerto Nitge (Port sa Nitja)

40°04'.6N 04°05'.2E

Not a port, but a long, narrow inlet on the west side of the peninsula of Cabo Cavallería. It is believed to have been a Phoenician harbour around 1600BC and is typical of the sites they often chose: a low, defensible promontory with the possibility of launching or anchoring boats on both sides, so that irrespective of wind direction they could escape, defend or attack as necessary. The eastern element of the settlement may well have been Cala en Saler. The Romans occupied the *cala* in their turn, beginning with the conquest of Menorca by Metellus between 123 and 121 BC. The settlement grew over subsequent centuries but was never large. Known as

Sanicera, it was mentioned by Pliny in his Natural History. Several areas have been excavated and it has been a popular educational dig site.

Puerto Nitge is tucked in on the west side of Cabo Cavalleriá with Pta de sa Torre and its large round tower just west of the entrance. On the eastern side are the remains of a rather more modern gun emplacement. Approach and entrance are straightforward, but without local knowledge it is advisable to pass outside the two islets lying off Punta de sa Torre even though a 50m passage carrying 5m depths exists between the islets and the point.

Favour the east side of the entrance as rocks fringe the west point, and watch the echo-sounder carefully – the inner part of the inlet has silted up – though 2m can usually be carried for 200m. Two conservation buoys prohibiting anchoring further in are now in place at this point. Anchor in 2m+ over sand, weed and rock, open between northwest and north only. The sides of the *cala* are of dark rock and the surroundings somewhat low and windswept.

There are three short piers or jetties in the upper part of the *cala*, and two more even further in, used by small motor and fishing boats, and some seasonal moorings are laid. A stream, largely blocked by a sandbank, flows into the southwest corner. A few houses and fishermen's huts lie to the east with a large farm, Santa Teresa, to the south. There is a road out to the lighthouse on Cabo Cavalleria. A large-scale plan of Puerto Nitge appears on Spanish chart 4262.

⚓ Cala Viola de Ponent

40°04'.7N 04°05'.3E

This tiny *cala*, which lies near the east side of the entrance to Puerto Nitge, might be visited by experienced navigators in good conditions, but has a number of isolated rocks, on the northeast side of the *cala*. The inner part of the *cala* has limited swinging room. Some yachts anchor just outside the narrows of the entrance in up to 8m over sand, weed and rock. Open to the west and northwest. The head of the *cala* seems to have become popular in summer with motorhomes, although there are no facilities.

Looking NW over the pass inside Isla Nitge. Keep to the middle and all will be well! *David Baggaley*

Pass inside Isla Nitge
(Illa d'els Porros)

40°05′·5N 04°04′·7E

In settled conditions there is a pass 150m wide with a minimum depth of 6m between Isla Nitge and Cabo Cavallería with its offlying rocks and islets. Head north-northeast (or south-southwest), equidistant between Isla Nitge and Islote Es Cobrómbol, keeping to the centre of the pass as the sides are lined with just-covered and awash isolated rocks. (*See plan on page 262.*)

A very narrow fishermen's pass, the Pas d'es Cobrómbol, exists between the islet of that name and Menorca. However, it should not be attempted without local knowledge or first making a detailed recce by dinghy.

Looking west from Ensenada de Tirant towards Isla Bledas and Cabo Gros, Cala en Saler is right foreground, and *calas* from Cavalleria to Pregonda in top centre

V. MENORCA

7. CABO CAVALLERÍA TO CABO FAVARITX

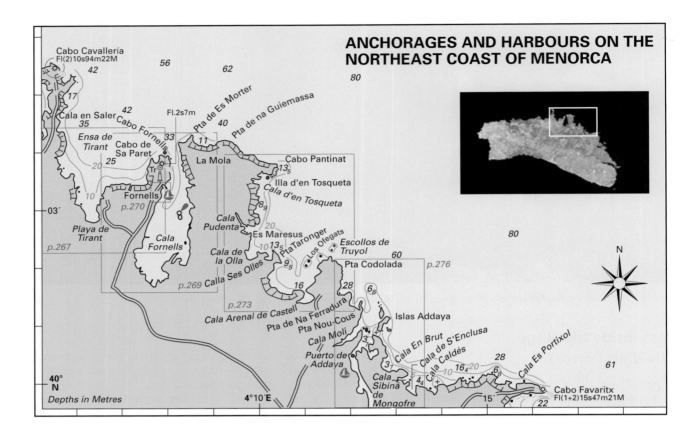

ANCHORAGES AND HARBOURS ON THE NORTHEAST COAST OF MENORCA

Depths in Metres

Cabo Cavallería

40°05'·4N 04°05'·5E

A very prominent and conspicuous peninsula and bold headland of approaching 100m. A lighthouse (Fl(2)10s94m22M, white tower and building) stands on the northeast point. There is very deep water up to the cliffs but watch out for the one 6·5m outlier, Llosa dels Ocelliers, just north of the lighthouse (*see plan on page 262*).

Anchorages between Cabo Cavallería and Puerto de Fornells

There is a series of potential anchorages open to northeast through to southeast, on the east side of the peninsula of Cabo Cavallería. All have isolated rocks close inshore and a rock and sand bottom, and should be used only with great care in settled conditions.

Cala en Saler

40°03'·8N04°05'·6E

Possibly the eastern site for the Phoenicians and a delightful location, it is a small bay with three small gullies opening off it, one of which has a little sandy beach. It is easy to imagine galleys tied up in two of the gullies! Ashore someone has built a permanent sun-shelter. Land access is via a section of the Cami

de Cavalls from some Roman remains a little to the north of Santa Teresa farm. Open north-northeast to southeast. A rock and weed bottom makes anchoring difficult, but fairly small motor boats might moor carefully in the gullies with lines to the shores. The *cala* can be seen in the right foreground of the photograph on *page 265*.

⚓ Cala Macar Gran

40°03'·6N 04°05'·7E

A wide shallow bay with some offshore rocks, open from north to northeast.

⚓ Cala Macar de sa Talayeta (Tailera)

40°03'·0N 04°06'·0E

A wide bay with a large sandy beach backed by houses, open to north through east. (Cala Macar de sa Talayeta is incorrectly identified on BA chart 2761 inset as Cala Es Macar Petit).

⚓ Playa de Tirant

40°03'·0N 04°06'·3E

A large deep bay surrounded by low scrub-covered hills and extensive housing developments. There is a sandbank with some 5m over it stretching across the *cala* for about 100m, at about the latitude of Cala Macar de sa Talayeta, which gives good anchoring.

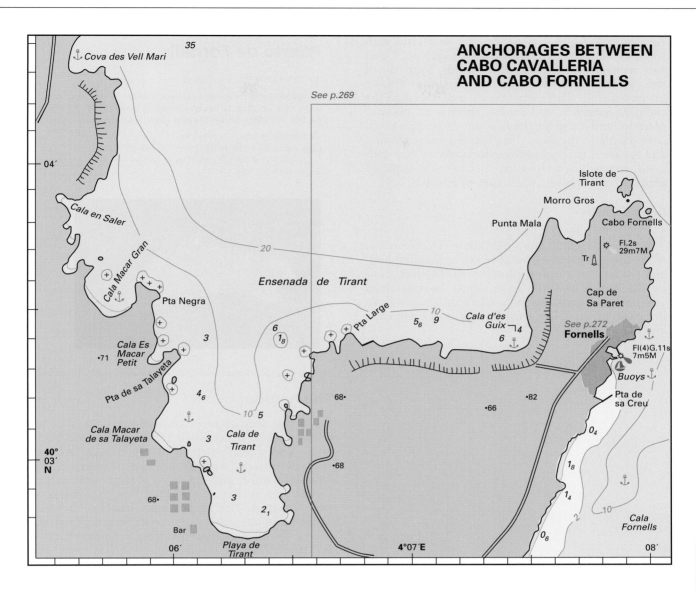

ANCHORAGES BETWEEN
CABO CAVALLERIA
AND CABO FORNELLS

Cala d'es Guix, a quiet little anchorage just round the corner from Fornells *David Baggaley*

Beyond this depths increase again to 7m+ mixed sand and weed shelving gently towards the buoyed swimming area. The water is less clear than many places. Altogether there is a very large anchoring area and it is surprising that it is not more popular, especially at times when some other north coast anchorages are overcrowded. Approach on a south course towards the centre of the beach and anchor anywhere over sand, open to the north with swell from the northeast. In strong north or northeast winds the whole *cala* can be filled with breakers. The long sandy beach is sometimes crowded – there are restaurants, a supermarket and a good road inland. The huge lagoon behind has much wildlife.

Cala d'es Guix

40°03 ·4N 04°07 ·4E

Not so much a *cala* as the right-angled corner on the west side of the Cabo Fornells peninsular south of Punta Mala, surrounded by low cliffs. A pleasant little anchorage, albeit popular with small day-boats from Fornells, which disappear in early evening.

V. MENORCA

Anchor in 4–8m in very clear water over sand with some well covered rocky areas closer inshore. Open and generally untenable with winds from north through west, and swell from northeast may also be uncomfortable. There is no beach and although the cliffs are very low and broken there is no obvious place to land a dinghy, the best option being a small cove a little to the west. This is still a stony landing and is easiest with a lightweight dinghy or one with good attached wheels. From here it is a walk of about 15 minutes into the centre of Fornells.

Cabo Fornells

40°03'·9N 04°07'·9E

This rocky headland has a lighthouse (Fl.2s29m8M, white tower with black band on white building 6m), and a small fort a little further inland. The fort, built by the British in 1801, has recently been restored and houses a small museum. Islote de Tirant (20m) lies close off its point with foul ground between it and the headland.

Puerto de Fornells

40°03'·9N 04°08'.1E (entrance)

A narrow entrance gives excellent shelter in this long and wide cala, leading to several mooring possibilities for yachts, including 88 berths and several anchorages.

Communications
Club Náutico de Fornells ① 971 37 63 28
nauticfornells@compusoft.es
www.cnfornells.com

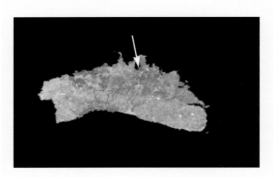

The harbour

A narrow, deep entrance channel gives access to an inland area of water some 2M long by up to 0·7M wide, with a small harbour (dredged to 2–3m) near the entrance. Approach and entrance are straightforward and there is a large area where yachts can anchor in solitude, though holding is poor in places. Two anchorages – one on either side of the harbour – are now laid with summer mooring buoys. See plan opposite and the *Anchorages* section on *page 270*. A swell finds its way into the anchorage with strong winds from north and northwest, but the effect may well be mitigated deep into the bay.

Fornells viewed from north over Islote de Tirant.
Isla Sargantana centre

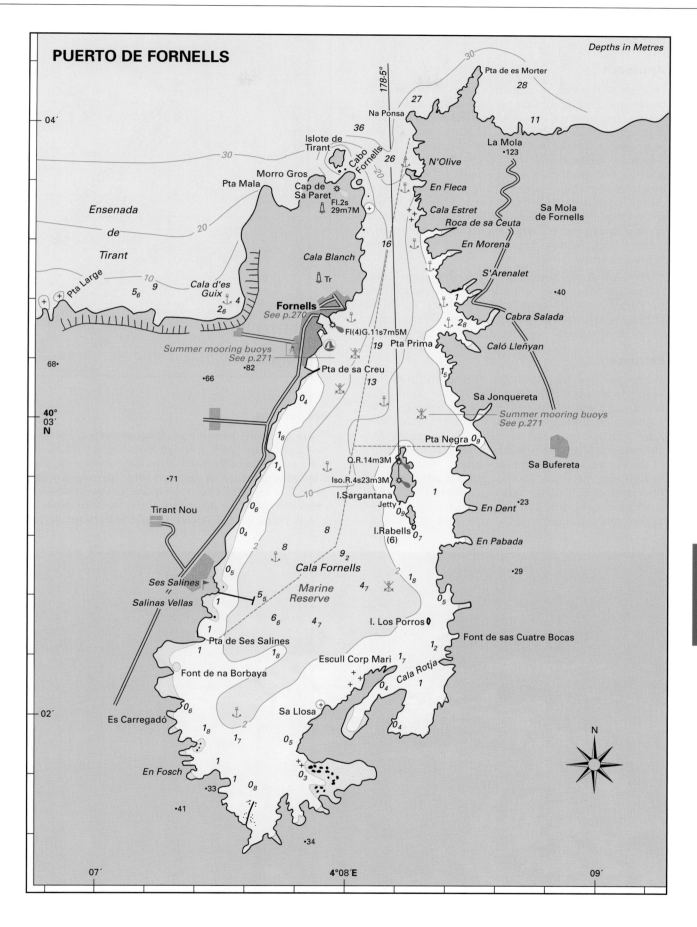

PUERTO DE FORNELLS

Depths in Metres

Pta de es Morter
28

27

Na Ponsa

36

11

Islote de
Tirant

La Mola
•123

Cabo
Fornells

26

N'Olive

Morro Gros

En Fleca

Pta Mala

Cap de
Sa Paret

Cala Estret

Sa Mola
de Fornells

Fl.2s
29m7M

Roca de sa Ceuta

Ensenada

16

En Morena

de

Cala Blanch

S'Arenalet

Tirant

Tr

•40

Pta Large

10
9

Cala d'es
Guix

1

Cabra Salada

5₆

4

2₈

Fornells
See p.270

2₆

Caló Lleñyan

Fl(4)G.11s7m5M

Summer mooring buoys
See p.271

19

Pta Prima

1₅

Pta de sa Creu

13

Sa Jonquereta

•66

•82

Summer mooring buoys
See p.271

68•

0₄

40°
03′
N

1₈

Pta Negra 0₉

•71

1₄

Q.R.14m3M

Sa Bufereta

0₆

Iso.R.4s23m3M

1

Tirant Nou

0₄

I.Sargantana

En Dent •23

2

8

Jetty

0₉

Es Carregadó

9₂

I.Rabells
(6)

0₇

En Pabada

Cala Fornells

2

1₈

•29

Ses Salines

0₅

Marine
Reserve

4₇

0₅

Salinas Vellas

1

5₅

6₆

4₇

I. Los Porros

Pta de Ses Salines

1

1₈

1₂

Font de sas Cuatre Bocas

Font de na Borbaya

Escull Corp Mari 1₇

Cala Rotja

1

0₆

2

Sa Llosa

0₄

1

02′

Es Carregadó

1₈

1₇

0₅

0₄

En Fosch

1

0₈

0₃

•33

•34

•41

07′

4°08′E

09′

Pilotage

Approach

From west The very prominent Cabo Cavallería with its conspicuous lighthouse projects nearly 2M out to sea and has two outlying islands to its northwest (*see plan on page 262*). Immediately to the east of this promontory lies the deeply indented Bahía de Tirant which is separated from Puerto de Fornells by another promontory, Cabo Fornells (41m). This is much smaller than Cabo Cavallería and has a very conspicuous isolated tower on its top. To the east of the entrance lies La Mola (123m) and Punta de Es Morter, composed of steep, angular cliffs falling to a gentler slope below. Approach when the entrance bears due south.

From east After rounding Cabo Pentinat (25m) follow the coast past Punta de na Guiemassa (50m) to Punta de Es Morter with the lofty La Mola (123m) behind (*see plan on page 266*). On rounding Punta de Es Morter the entrance lies to the south.

Entrance

When positive identification of the entrance has been made, approach on a course due south. Isla Sargantana with its two white beacon towers will be visible in the middle of the bay just over a mile away. Line up the towers on 178·5° to enter (or alternatively keep the island bearing 180°). The sides of the entrance channel are steep-to.

Entrance at night should present no problems providing the leading lights are identified before entering the channel and followed until opposite or beyond the small harbour.

PUERTO DE FORNELLS HARBOUR

Depths in Metres

Fishing boats

Yachts

Fl(4)G.11s7m5M

Yachts Pontoon

Fish and Lobster Pots

0   50   100
Metres
Sketch plan

Anchorages

There are many possible anchorages in Cala Fornells (*see plan page 269*), though holding is said to be poor in the more popular areas due to over-use and elsewhere because of beds of long, dense, slippery weed. For close access to the town, anchor over sand immediately to the northeast of the harbour mole or about 100m east or southeast of the harbour in 5m

Puerto de Fornells harbour looking northeast, with yachts anchored off. Shallows in the area can be clearly seen

Fornells viewed from the south *Juanjo Pons / TrianglePostals*

over soft mud and weed. These are untenable in strong north or northeast winds. An area just south of the harbour is sometimes used to moor lobster keep-boxes, which float just level with the water and are difficult to see.

South and southwest of the harbour is an extensive area of summer mooring buoys, stretching down to the latitude of Isla Sargantana, which may be reserved at www.balearslifeposidonia.eu between the 1 June and 30 September. See plan on *page 269* and the *Anchoring and moorings* section on *page 19* for further details. Anchoring is feasible outside this buoyed area and further south. Closer to the shore are permanent moorings which are not generally available for visitors.

The first four anchorages shown to port on entrance to Fornells on the plan on *page 269* are small and rocky and really only suitable for small vessels with a line taken shore. Elsewhere in Fornells the bottom is almost entirely weed over mud or sand, but holding is generally good once the anchor is through the weed, which may take more than one attempt. The area off S'Arenalet, Cabra Salada and Cala Llenyan is popular as is the area to the south and southwest of Isla Sargantana. The latter is much quieter than the buoyed areas and anchorages closer to the harbour and once through the weed the mud is of a quality much appreciated in stronger wind conditions! Indeed, this is probably the best place to anchor in Fornells in a northerly blow. Vessels anchoring off Punta Negra and Sa Bufereta are usually asked to move. The area between Punta Prima and the Isla Sargantana, previously taken up with fish farms, is also now taken up with mooring buoys, although (in May 2017) seemingly fewer than previous years, which can be reserved via the website above. (*See the plan on page 269.*)

The Club Náutico de Fornells has its clubhouse and dinghy jetty at Ses Salines in the southwest part of the bay, near which there are further anchorages particularly favoured by those who carry sailing dinghies or windsurfers. Ses Salines is a major

dinghy sailing centre. The lit yellow buoy southwest of Isla Sargantana no longer exists but there may be various racing marks to confuse the unwary.

If entering and anchoring after dark, follow the leading lights until the single harbour light (Fl(4)G.11s7m5M) bears 230°, alter course onto 215°, and drop anchor in 8m or so when the light bears due west.

Berthing

The harbour is small with room for fewer than 20 visiting yachts, maximum 12 metres – and a squeeze at that. It becomes very crowded in summer with little chance of a berth. Berths can only be reserved by email at www.portsib.es. The harbour has been dredged to 3m at least in the outer part and 2·5m about half way in. There is 2·7m alongside the fuel dock on the end of the southwest quay. The harbour office is about 100m north of the harbour. The pontoon extending from the southwest quay is for visitors. If space permits, berth stern-to the northeast mole or on the pontoon. Several buoys previously laid just north of the stone mole were not present in 2016 or 2017 but the area was used to anchor over sand; from here it is only a very short row into town. There are six new summer pontoons for smaller boats to the south of the harbour, the two southernmost being gated. Berths on these which would take small to medium motor cruisers can be reserved through Amarres Fornells on ☎ 971 154 620 or 646 964 520. The inner ends of the others seem to be used as dinghy docks.

Facilities

Water and electricity On the southern pontoon and all berths.
Fuel There is a fuel dock in the harbour but it is small (about 9m) and difficult to access (or more particularly claw off) in strong northerly winds. It is claimed that vessels up to 15m can use the dock but this may depend on whether there are long vessels in adjoining berths. Diesel and gasoline are supplied. Open every day in July and August from 0800 to 2000, mornings only in June and September and closed at other times.
Provisions Two supermarkets and other shops in the village.
Ice At the supermarkets.

Fornells harbour and the small fuel dock *David Baggaley*

V. MENORCA

Restaurants A wide range of restaurants, cafes and bars in the village.

Chandlery A small chandlery, Vivelmar at 34, Passeig Maritim (Paseo Marítimo) south of the harbour. ☎ 971 15 84 90 / 605 885 336 www.vivelmar.com

Repairs Carried out on local craft at the head of the wide shallow slipway which lies southwest of the harbour. Crane available but no information on specifications.

Yacht club The Club Náutico de Fornells, located at Ses Salines about 1¼M south of the harbour and main anchorage, has a bar, restaurant, lounge, terrace and showers.

Bank In the village (open mornings only).

Post office In the village.

Transport

Car hire/taxis One car rental company in the village.
Buses Buses to Mahón and Ciudadela.

History

The fishing village of Fornells (pronounced Fornays) dates back to time immemorial, but its claim to historic fame comes from having been used as one of the secondary invasion ports during the first British expedition of 1798. They had intended to land at Fornells, but a headwind prevented this so the first landing took place at Addaya. When the wind changed the following day Commodore Duckworth captured Fornells.

Ashore

Most of the surroundings are of unspoilt natural beauty and development is restricted to a few areas, although there has been gradual expansion to the south of the village in recent years. The village itself is small and picturesque but offers simple facilities.

The anchorage is surrounded by some enjoyable walks, such as to the defence tower and museum on Cabo Fornells or, for the moderately energetic, up to La Mola (123m) on the east side of the entrance. Both offer excellent views. Isla Sargantana makes an interesting dinghy expedition, partly to observe the unique breed of lizard which has evolved there (though you have to be an expert to know the difference). At the south end of Cala Fornells are the ruins of an ancient Christian church.

Local event

A fiesta is held in Fornells during the last week of July in honour of San Antonio.

Eating out

Many restaurants and cafés. Fornells has long been famous for its lobsters, served either with mahonésa or as caldereta de langosta (lobster stew). Es Cranc restaurant is well-known and is in the road behind the waterfront on C/ Escoles No.31.

Anchorages and features east of Puerto de Fornells

Punta de Es Morter (des Murter), Punta de na Guiemassa and Punta Pantinat

(See plan on page 266)
40°04'.2N 04°08'·5E to 40°03'·7N 04°10'·4E

A 1·7-mile-wide promontory with three distinct headlands, the westernmost backed by the heights of La Mola (123m). As a whole the headland slopes downwards from west to east and is steep-to other than two rocks awash close inshore off Punta Na Guiemassa. However, when rounding Punta Pantinat (Punta d'en Pentinar), you should give the point a berth of at least 200m to avoid Lloses d'en Pentinar, awash rocks that lie 100m northeast of the point and two smaller awash rocks east of the point. There may be some turbulence around the headland.

Note The authors round this point regularly but have never seen any awash rocks off the point or any other dangers. Nevertheless we are wary of removing such a clear warning from earlier editions. Feedback from others who have sailed in the area would be welcome!

⚓ Cala d'en Tosqueta

40°03'·4N 04°10'E

A well-protected *cala* tucked away under Punta Pantinat, with a sand and shingle beach and rocky cliffs. Approach leaving Illa d'en Tosqueta to starboard (rocks also extend off the headland to the northeast) to anchor off the beach over sand and rock, open to the southeast. There is really only room for two or three deep-keeled yachts to swing at anchor in 4–6m over sand close to the entrance to the *cala*, but room also for a good number of small shallow-draught vessels further in to anchor, perhaps with a line to the low cliffs. It is popular with small dayboats and some larger motor boats may overnight with a line ashore. It is also possible to anchor just outside the *cala* but this sacrifices shelter from the northeast and east. It is exposed to a fetch from east

Cala Tosqueta *Susie Baggaley*

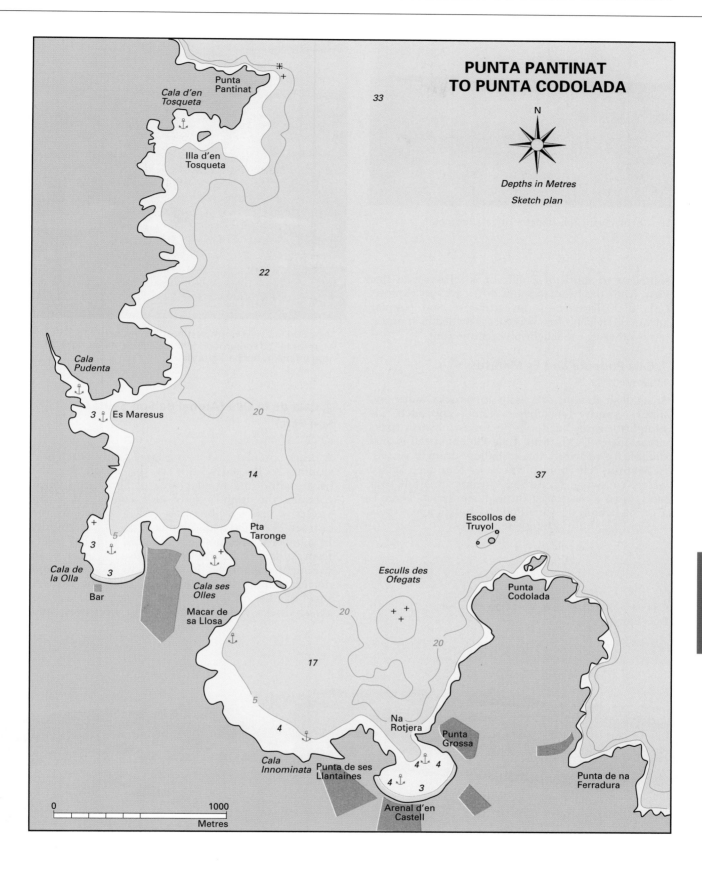

**PUNTA PANTINAT
TO PUNTA CODOLADA**

N

Depths in Metres

Sketch plan

Punta Pantinat

Cala d'en Tosqueta

Illa d'en Tosqueta

33

Cala Pudenta

22

3 Es Maresus

20

14

Cala de la Olla

3

3 5

+

Bar

Pta Taronge

Cala ses Olles

Macar de sa Llosa

Escollos de Truyol

37

Esculls des Ofegats

Punta Codolada

20

17

+ +
+

5

20

4

Na Rotjera

Punta Grossa

Cala Innominata

Punta de ses Llantaines

4 4

4 3

Arenal d'en Castell

Punta de na Ferradura

0   1000

Metres

V. MENORCA

Look behind you! The alligator of Cala Tosqueta
David Baggaley

View looking west-northwest over Peninsula La Mola. Es Maresus in the foreground with Cala Pudenta on right, Isla Sargantana in the background

southeast to south of a mile or so. There is a fine view from the headland and two caves to explore. Cala d'en Tosqueta is an attractive and popular anchorage which often becomes crowded in summer, but is otherwise a delightfully remote spot.

⚓ Cala Pudenta and Es Maresus

40°02'·5N 04°09'·8E

A smallish double *cala* with low rocky sides and small sandy beaches. The approach is straightforward, but look out for two awash rocks either side of Es Maresus. Cala Pudenta itself is only suitable for relatively small, shallow-draught vessels. Es Maresus has room for three or four deep-keeled yachts to swing at anchor. Anchor in 5-8m over sand, open to northeast through southeast. There is a spring behind the Cala Pudenta beach, and a track to Son Parc, but nothing else.

⚓ Cala de la Olla (Arenal de Son Saura/ Son Parc)

40°02'·2N 04°09'·8E

A nearly circular *cala* with a large sandy beach and sloping rocky sides, this is the beach for the urbanisation and holiday area of Son Parc (which contains the island's only golf course). It is an attractive and spacious *cala* rather spoiled by the barrack-like holiday development on its eastern side. In summer it becomes very crowded with day boats from Addaia and Fornells but is usually quiet as an overnight anchorage. It is open to the north and northeast and affected by swell from the east. A small islet lies off the northwest corner, and there are awash rocks close inshore on the northwest and

Cala de la Olla (Arenal de Son Saura / Son Parc)
David Baggaley

southeast sides. Anchor in 3–7m over sand. There are fine walks across to the eastern shores of Fornells and out to the cliffs between Punta de Es Morter and Cabo Pentinat. There is a restaurant in the southeast corner of the *cala* and a café/bar in the southwest corner. There are some shops and restaurants in Son Parc, about half a mile inland.

⚓ Cala Ses Olles

40°02'.2N 04°10'.1E

A small, rounded *cala* close east of Cala de la Olla, surrounded by low cliffs and with no beach. Enter with care sounding carefully: an awash rock, Escull d'en Tarouger, and several islets lie up to 150m off the point on the east side of the entrance and there are some small rocks close to the shore to the southwest. Anchor in 3–6m over rock, open north and northeast and to swell from the east. There is a large tourist development between the two *calas*.

Cala 'Innominata'

40°01'.6N 04°10'.5E

This is the long, open *cala* between Cala ses Olles and Arenal D'en Castell which is not named on the charts although its smaller, northern part, beyond a rocky headland, is known as Macar de sa Llosa. Its southeastern part is quite literally just round the corner from Arenal so that it provides a convenient escape from the hurly-burly of Arenal, in a quiet anchorage with a large expanse of sand over which to anchor in 4–6m. There is no beach and there are a few rocky patches close in under the cliffs which should not pose a problem. The corner round to Arenal has a number of detached rocks which are obvious - probably sensible to keep 100m or so offshore here. The anchorage is open north to east.

⚓ Arenal d'en Castell

40°01'.5N 04°10'.9E

A large, almost circular bay with a long sandy beach, surrounded by large apartment blocks, hotels and houses which would be very attractive were it not for two large, architecturally challenged, hotels. If approaching from the east, round Punta Codolada and continue due west until the entrance bears 160° before turning south. This avoids three small islets (Escollos de Truyol) off the headland, plus the awash rocks to the southwest known as Los Ofegats (Esculls d'es Augegats). In most conditions the latter's breaking crests will be clearly visible.

Anchor off the beach in 4–8m over sand and weed, open only to the north. It is this almost all-round protection which makes it an attractive anchorage in most conditions and especially outside the main season. There are a few small-craft moorings on the west side of the bay and a large area buoyed-off for swimmers (there are channels identified to access the shore by dinghy) and the north part has a rocky bottom. There is a

Cala 'Innominata' – a useful, quiet anchorage just round the corner from Arenal d'en Castell *David Baggaley*

Arenal d'en Castell

considerable amount of development behind the beach, with all the usual tourist shops, restaurants and cafés and a small supermarket. At night there is some noise from the bars and restaurants ashore, but it is not hugely intrusive and seems to die down at a reasonably early hour.

Punta Codolada

40°01'.9N 04°11'.8E

A low rocky, but steep-to headland with outlying rocks and islets which can be identified when coming from the east by an isolated white house 200m from the point. The Isla na Joanassa lies close north of the point, with three rocks, Escollos de Truyol, some 350m north of the point. If rounding to visit Arenal d'en Castell keep well clear of Los Ofegats, awash rocks which may in fact be passed on either side, lying some 550m southwest of the point (see *Arenal d'en Castell* above).

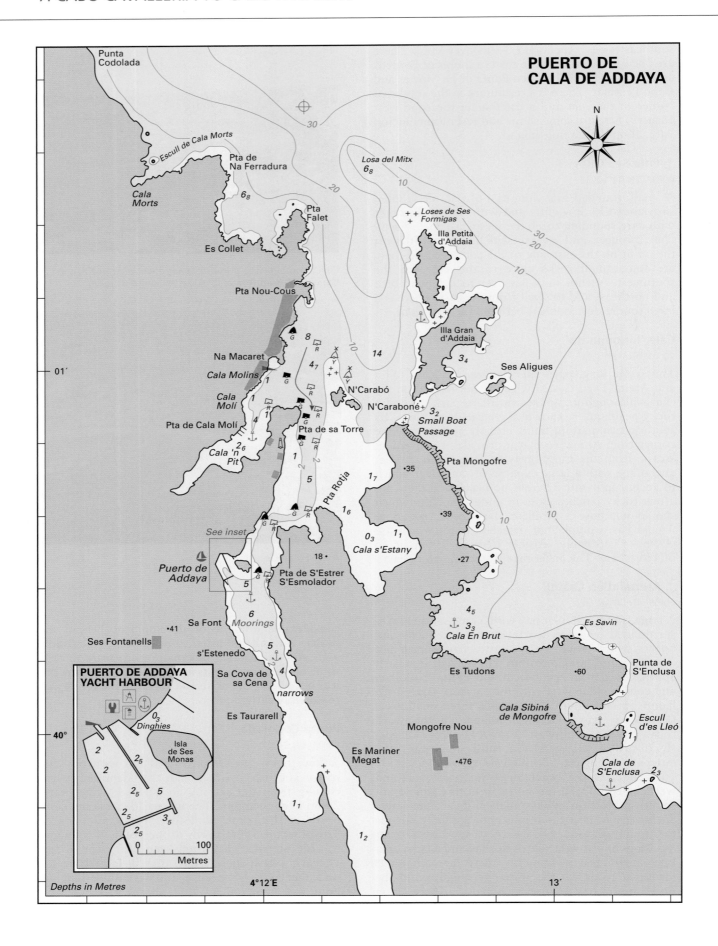

PUERTO DE CALA DE ADDAYA

N

Punta Codolada

Escull de Cala Morts

Pta de Na Ferradura

Cala Morts

6₈

Pta Falet

Es Collet

Losa del Mitx
6₈

Loses de Ses Formigas

Illa Petita d'Addaia

Pta Nou-Cous

G 8

R

Na Macaret

Cala Molins

4₇

Y

N'Carabó

14

Illa Gran d'Addaia

3₄

Ses Aligues

G

Cala Molí

1

N'Caraboné

3₂

Small Boat Passage

Pta de Cala Molí

R

4

G

Pta de sa Torre

1

Pta Mongofre

Cala 'n Pit

2₆

R

1

5

2

1₇

•35

Pta Rotja

G R

1₆

•39

0₃

1₁

Cala s'Estany

•27

See inset

G R

Puerto de Addaya

18 •

Pta de S'Estrer
S'Esmolador

5

Sa Font

6

Moorings

4₅

3₃

Cala En Brut

Es Savin

Ses Fontanells

•41

5

s'Estenedo

Es Tudons

•60

Punta de S'Enclusa

Sa Cova de sa Cena

4

narrows

Cala Sibiná de Mongofre

Escull d'es Lleó

Es Taurarell

Mongofre Nou

1

Cala de S'Enclusa

2₃

Es Mariner Megat

•476

1₁

1₂

PUERTO DE ADDAYA YACHT HARBOUR

0₃
Dinghies

2

2₅

Isla de Ses Monas

2

2₅

5

2₅

3₅

2₅

0   100
Metres

Depths in Metres

4°12′E

13′

Puerto (Deportivo) de Cala de Addaya

⊕ 40°01'·7N 04°12'·1E (entrance, ⊕ on plan opposite)
40°00'·4N 04°12'E (yacht harbour)

The nicest little marina in the Balearics – and beyond?
A very safe, beautiful and friendly harbour deep in a long cala, with berthing for 150 vessels up to 20m in the marina. Requires accurate navigation to enter with larger vessels.

Communications
Puerto Deportivo de Addaya VHF Ch 09
  Marina office ☎ +34 971 35 86 49
  puertoaddaya@puertoaddaya.com
  www.puertoaddaya.com

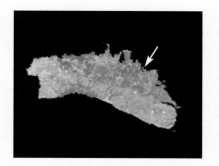

The harbour and anchorage

A long, narrow estuary, its entrance guarded by a line of islands, Cala de Addaya (or Addaia) is a very pleasant, secluded and sheltered anchorage with a small and helpful marina in one corner. Considerable development has taken place around the north and east end of the *cala* overlooking the marina, but this is not overbearing and is generally of good quality.

The entrance to the *cala* requires care and in some light conditions it is difficult to see. Entrance is sometimes impossible in strong winds from northwest round to east, though vessels already in the lagoon are both safe and comfortable. Indeed the lagoon could reasonably be described as a 'hurricane-hole'.

Facilities are adequate. There is a limited potential for on-the-hard wintering, with a lifting capacity of 25T. In summer, much of the hard standing is used as a car park but there is still room for a dozen or so hauled-out yachts. Note that Posidonia staff may sometimes patrol the *cala* to ensure anchors are in sand rather than in the sea grass, although the lack of clarity in the water makes it difficult to tell.

Pilotage

Approach

From northwest Round the wide promontory comprising Punta de Es Morter, Punta de Na Guiemassa and Punta Pantinat (*see plan on page 266*), then head south-southeast for Punta Codolada 1·8M away. There are a number of *calas* in the intervening bay (*see plan on page 273*). On rounding

Cali Moli, top centre and the approach to Puerto de Addaya which is on the far left

Punta Codolada, the Islas Addaya (Illes d'Addaia) will open up ahead, with Punta de Na Ferradura and Punta d'en Falet to starboard. In moderate to heavy weather Losa del Mitx (Losa d'Emmig), a rock with 6·8m depth, may break about 550m offshore and in these conditions the whole area between it and Loses de ses Formigas should be avoided. Aim to pass Punta d'en Falet at least 50m off, rounding the headland at this distance to take a south and then southwest course into the channel between Punta Nou-Cous (mis-spelt Punta Na Cous on BA 2833 and 2761, as well as being somewhat misplaced) and Illa Petita d'Addaia.

From southeast After rounding Cabo Favaritx (*see plan on page 266*), a low headland with a conspicuous lighthouse of black and white diagonal stripes, steer 300° towards a position off Punta Codolada. Stand on well past the Islas Addaia and the offlying Loses de Ses Formigas rocks, only heading in towards the coast when Punta d'en Falet bears 240° or less. Close the headland to a distance of about 200m before taking a south and then south-southwest course into the channel between Punta Nou-Cous and Illa Petita d'Addaia (*see plan on page 276*). As noted above, with strengthening onshore winds wave heights build rapidly across the whole distance from Loses de ses Formigas to Losa del Mitx. In these circumstances a vessel approaching from the east will find a more comfortable passage by first heading well to the north and west of Losa del Mitx and then heading for the 'entrance location' of 40°01'·7N 04°12'·1E before entering on a course of about 170° for almost 0·5nm, clearing Punta Falet by 100m. The 'entrance location' is intended to support these heavy weather circumstances but normally the area around Losa del Mitx is not a problem and a more direct line can be taken quite comfortably.

Although fishermen use the passage between Punta Mongofre and the Islas Addaia as a short cut if heading or coming from the east, it is far from straightforward and requires local knowledge.

Anchorage in the approach

There is an anchorage just west of the gap between Illa Gran d'Addaia and Illa Petita d'Addaia in 5m+ over rock and weed, open to the north and northwest.

Entrance

A new and comprehensive buoyage arrangement has been put in place which greatly eases the approach to Addaia and which stays in place throughout the year, with the proviso that the frequent winter storms which hit the north coast of Menorca may result in a buoy being off-station. Indeed in 2017 it seems as though the green buoy very close off Punta de sa Torre (numbered No.7 on the latest Navionics chart) may have shifted a metre or two closer to the point – certainly there is a shallow area of 3m or less immediately to its south. After passing Punta Nou-Cous, the first pair of red and green buoys mark the wide channel about half way to the crucial 'gate' shown clearly on the plan. These outer buoys are lit, flashing red and green although their reliability is a little uncertain. Two yellow buoys with a cross on top beyond the red buoy cover a rocky shoal which

Addaya marina and anchorage *David Baggaley*

Puerto de Cala de Addaya from northeast, tucked in behind Isla Monas

several boats have hit, but these are probably only of interest to those using the passage to the south of Illa Gran d'Addaia referred to above. The next red and green (which has a red band close to the top), close inshore to Punta de la Torre are the 'gate' requiring a sharp turn to port and then, after about 100m, to starboard. A least depth of about 3·7m will be found in the 'gate' on the port side of the channel; depths are a little greater on the starboard side. Three red and green pairs then mark the channel as far as Punta Rotga. Note that on the port side beyond the red buoys and parallel with them are a series of six can buoys which (confusingly to some) are also red albeit with white squares on them. These mark a conservation area which should not be entered, although in practice you could well be aground before you got there! In fact, although the channel typically has about 8–10m along this section, in places the depth decreases rapidly on both sides. Off Punta Rotja the buoys clearly guide round a sharp turn to starboard and then back to port for a straight run into the harbour. A 3kn speed limit is in force all the way from Punta de la Torre onwards. Night approaches, especially in poor weather, are not recommended without considerable local experience.

Berthing

Visitors should always call the marina for a berth on VHF Ch 09 and in high season it is desirable to book in advance. If unable to contact the marina, anchor off and dinghy in to the marina office. Visitors are usually directed to berth bow or stern-to the south pontoon (Pantalan 111) and assistance is normally available. Alongside berthing may be available on the hammerhead.

Anchorages

Anchor in 6m or less in the lagoon south of the marina, which has generally good holding and all-round shelter. There is a small pontoon directly in front of the harbour office where crews of anchored yachts may land by dinghy. There is no charge for anchoring. It is also possible to anchor further into the *cala* (*see plan page 276*) in 4–6m, north of the narrows. (Note: a mud bank sticks out from the east shore almost to the centre of the narrows so keep to the west side). The inner lagoon south of the narrows is silting and depths are now reported as being less than 2m: proceed with caution and keep a good lookout at the bow. Much of the bottom is weed covered and holding is thus suspect and you would probably fall foul of the Posidonia officials. The land around the *cala* is privately owned.

Owners of shallow-draught yachts may wish to investigate Cala Molí (Molins) on the west side of Punta de la Torre. Proceed with care (the bottom is uneven and there are many moorings). The birdwatching was said to be excellent but in September 2016 the area was devastated by a forest fire.

Moorings

There are a number of mooring buoys in the lagoon but all are private.

Facilities

Water On the pontoons; yachts anchored off are charged to come in and fill tanks. There is a coin operated system on the hammerhead. (80L for €1, 2017.)

Electricity 220v AC points on the pontoons.

Fuel Not available, though it may be possible to arrange small quantities via the harbour office.

Provisions The small but well-stocked supermarket up the hill to the west of the harbour, plus shops at Na Macaret (west of Cala Molí) can provide everyday requirements.

Chandlery Dinautica have a small but very helpful chandlery on site and seem able to obtain most items not stocked on a same or next day basis.
①971358185 / 628620891 / 699061990 (the latter number for English language and also emergencies), dinauticamenorca@gmail.com
Nautica Puig chandlery in Addaya village centre
① 971 351106 / 669 440713, nauticapuig@gmail.com

Repairs Most marine services are available reasonably locally. The staff of the marina office are a good source of advice and are also helpful where language is a problem.
Dinautica in the marina can undertake a range of basic repair and maintenance activities. (See *Chandlery* above for contact details.)
Mechanic David Carr ① 676 926631, dgcarr@hotmail.co.uk
Rig, fibreglass and general marine problem-solving. Sailpower Menorca (Lawrence Vinnie)
① 679 516829, info@sailpowermenorca.com

Showers Next to the marina office. Free if berthed in the marina but otherwise € 3·50 (2017).

Launderette In the shower block (obtain pack of 50 cent coins in marina office - 10 per wash needed).

Banks In Mahón. There are no ATMs in Addaia, the nearest being in Coves Noves some 2M away.

Hospital/medical services In Mahón (hospital) or Alaior (clinic with emergency function).

Transport

Car hire/taxis Available from several companies in nearby Arenal d'en Castel; hire cars will be delivered to the marina. Marina staff will help with arrangements. During the summer, motorscooters and bicycles are available for hire in the marina.

Buses Bus service to Mahón and elsewhere from in front of the supermarket.

History

The harbour has been in use since Roman times and many amphoras and other remains have been found. The last British expedition to Menorca landed near Na Macaret on 7 November 1798 under the command of General Sir Charles Stuart, mainly because the three frigates and troop transports were unable to enter Fornells in adverse winds. In five days the 3,000 British troops captured Menorca from 3,600 Spanish without the loss of a single British soldier. In 1861 three Dutch ships carrying bullion (the warship *Wasaner* and two escorts, the *Sint Laurens* and *Sint Joris*) were wrecked off Cala de Addaya.

Ashore

A particularly pleasant section of the Camí de Cavalls goes from Addaia to Cabo Favoritz passing through the extensive old salt workings at the innermost end of Cala Addaia.

Addaia is the closest berthing point to Son Parc golf course which is a 5-10 minute taxi ride for those aficionados who keep a set of clubs onboard.

Eating out

Two or three restaurants up the hill from the marina and a bar/café/restaurant (La Cantina) which is very popular in the marina itself.

Anchorages east and southeast of Puerto de Addaya

⚓ Cala en Brut
40°00'·3N 04°12'·8E

An open bay in rather barren surroundings on the east side and south of Punta Mongofre, surrounded by high sloping rocks, recognisable by a conspicuous white building with a tower on the hill behind. There are a few islets close inshore on the north side. Anchor in 4-6m over sand of which there is a large area (*see plan on page 276*). Open northwest to east-southeast.

⚓ Cala Sibiná (Sivinar, Savinar) de Mongofre and Cala de S'Enclusa
40°00'N 04°13'·3E

Twin *calas* surrounded by high (40–63m) rough hills and separated by a rocky point. Cala Sibiná is the smaller of the two and has rocks awash close inshore on both sides of the entrance. If approaching from the east it must be appreciated that the reef of Escull d'es Lleó extends further across the entrance than is at first apparent. There are spectacular slopes of sand at the back of the Cala. Anchor in about 5m taking care to check swinging room. Cala de S'Enclusa has an islet with an outlying rock, Llosa de S'Enclusa, east of the entrance and a single breaking rock in the southeast part of the *cala* itself. It is the larger of the two *calas* but becomes very shallow in the southern part. Both *calas* are mainly sand and are open to the north and northeast. A conspicuous white building (Mongofre Nou) with a tower and red roof, stands on the hill to the east. There are several sandy beaches and some tracks inland, but otherwise nothing.

8. CABO FAVARITX TO PUNTA S'ESPERÓ

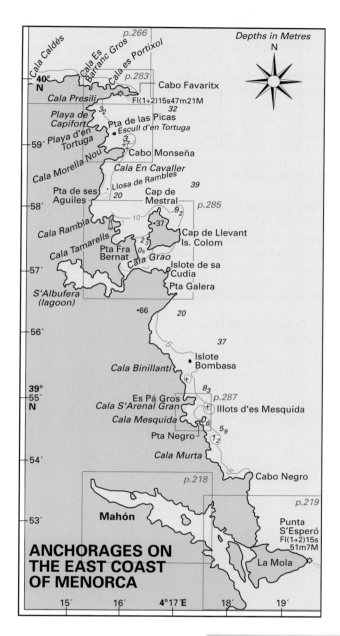

Map labels:

Cala Caldés
p.266
Cala Es Barranc Gros
Cala es Portixol
p.283
40° N
Cala Presili
Cabo Favaritx
Fl(1+2)15s47m21M
32
Playa de Capifort
Pta de las Picas
Escull d'en Tortuga
59' Playa d'en Tortuga
Cabo Monseña
Cala Morella Nou
Cala En Cavaller
Llosa de Rambles
39
Pta de ses Aguiles
20
Cap de Mestral
p.285
9₂
58'
10
Cala Rambla
•37
Cap de Llevant
Is. Colom
Cala Tamarells
2₃
Pta Fra Bernat
0₅
Cala Grao
57'
Islote de sa Cudia
Pta Galera
S'Albufera (lagoon)
•66
20
56'
37
Cala Binillantí
Islote Bombasa
39° 55' N
Es Pá Gros
8₃
p.287
Cala S'Arenal Gran
Illots d'es Mesquida
Cala Mesquida
0₆
5₉
Pta Negro
1₂
54'
Cala Murta
Cabo Negro
p.218
Mahón
p.219
53'
Punta S'Esperó
Fl(1+2)15s 51m7M
La Mola
ANCHORAGES ON THE EAST COAST OF MENORCA
15'   16'   4°17'E   18'   19'

Depths in Metres
N

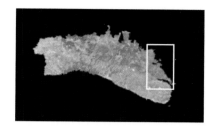

Anchorages on the north side of Cabo Favaritx

⚓ Cala Caldés

39°59'·9N 04°13'·7E

A small *cala* at the mouth of a narrow valley with high (30–70m) hills each side and a small stony beach. A group of five rocky islets lies to the west of the entrance and four awash rocks plus an islet to the east. Enter on a south course midway between the two groups to anchor off the beach over sand and rock, open to the north. Swinging room is probably restricted to two deep keel yachts. There is one small house in the valley with a track inland.

⚓ Cala es Barranc Gros (S'Escala)

40°00'·0N 4°15'.2E

A large open *cala* amongst rocky cliffs and hills, with a smaller *cala* in the southwest corner in which there is a sand and stone beach. Several islets lie close inshore on either side of the entrance. Anchor off the beach over rock with sand patches. The road from Cabo Favaritx to Mahón lies only 200m inland.

⚓ Cala es Portixol

40°00'N 04°15'·5E

A small round *cala* with an islet in the middle of the entrance, surrounded by low rocky cliffs and sloping hills (15–21m) (*see plan page 283*). Inshore islets line

View southeast over Cabo Favaritx, Cala Portixol in centre foreground

V. MENORCA

either side of the entrance; enter with care favouring the east side, and anchor off the beach, taking care to avoid three awash rocks in the south centre of the *cala*. The anchorage is probably only suitable for smaller shallow draft vessels. Open to the north. There is a small sandy beach backed by sand dunes in the southeast corner, and the road to Mahón 100m inland. (*See photograph page 281.*)

Cabo Favaritx

39°59'·8N 04°16'.2E

A very prominent low (12m), broken rocky headland with a conspicuous lighthouse (white tower with black diagonal stripes on a white building, 28m) set slightly back from the point itself. It is steep-to but with two islets on its south side.

⚓ Cala Presili / Playa De Capifort / Playa d'en Tortuga

39°59'·5N 04°15'·4E

(Incorrectly identified as Cala Algaret on BA 2833)

A very large triple open *cala* with two sandy beaches and a third, Playa d'en Tortuga, which is stony. There are dunes and small sloping hills behind and rocky cliffs between each section. The bottom is mainly sand with a few patches of easily seen rock and weed with one extensive such area off the northern end of Playa Capifort and between it and Playa Presili. A less extensive area lies in the northwest corner of Cala Presili about 100–150m off the north end of the beach which has several points with little more than 1m water over them. Sand and anchoring depths extend well off shore. Swimming area buoys are now installed off both beaches but the anchoring area is so large that this

does not detract. This is an excellent anchorage but its greatest importance is that it provides the only real protection from northerly winds on the north and east coasts apart, of course, from Fornells and Addaia which may become difficult to exit. From Presili there is no impediment to running off to Mahón or the south coast. If the wind veers to northeast, a swell may curve round Favaritx causing some discomfort. Anchor off one of the beaches over sand, typically 5-8m, or close in to much of the lee of the Favaritx peninsular, but watch out for some shallow rocky areas; open to the northeast through southeast. If approaching from the south see the note regarding Punta de las Picas and Cabo Monseña, below.

Punta de las Picas

39°59'.2N 04°15'·7E

Punta de las Picas (Cap de ses Piques) is a wide headland with offliers and awash rocks some 150m offshore. An islet, Escull d'en Tortuga (39°59'·1N 04°15'·8E), lies 350m to the east of the point with clear water all around it.

⚓ Cala Morella Nou

39°59'N 04°15'·7E

A *cala* with two sandy beaches separated by a rocky point. Enter on a southwest course between the islets and reefs off Cabo Monseña (Cap Monsenyar Vives) to port, and Punta de las Picas (Cap de Ses Piques) to starboard. The latter has a small island, Escull d'en Tortuga, some 350m offshore which should be left to starboard. Anchor off either beach in sand, the larger patches of which are well out in 6–7m. There is a track inland and a few houses.

Cala Presili and the peninsula of Favaritx which gives excellent protection from the north *David Baggaley*

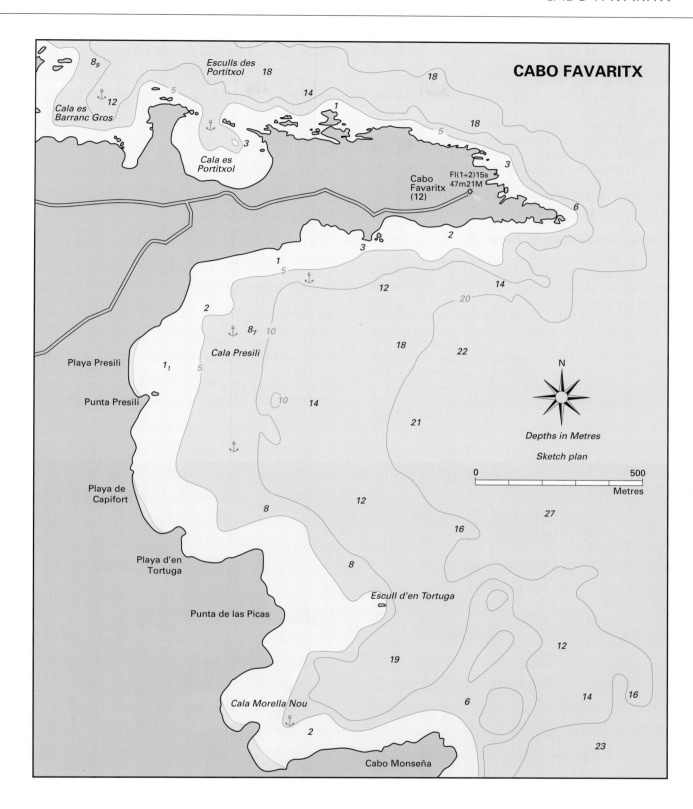

CABO FAVARITX

Esculls des Portitxol

Cala es Barranc Gros

Cala es Portitxol

Cabo Favaritx (12)

Fl(1+2)15s 47m21M

Playa Presili

Punta Presili

Cala Presili

Playa de Capifort

Playa d'en Tortuga

Punta de las Picas

Escull d'en Tortuga

Cala Morella Nou

Cabo Monseña

N

Depths in Metres

Sketch plan

0   500

Metres

Cabo Monseña

39°58′·9N 04°16′·0E

Cabo Monseña (Cap de Mossèn Vives) is a narrow headland with a reef of awash rocks, Baix des Ferros, running off some 450m to the northeast. It is advisable to keep at least 600m off this point especially in rough weather, to avoid the overfalls.

⚓ Cala en Cavaller
39°58'·7N 04°15'·7E

A small *cala* just south of Cabo Monseña, with a sand and shingle beach and a small islet on the south side of the entrance. Enter on a northwest course, keeping to the middle. A shallow rocky area extends from the south side and there are awash rocks on the north of the entrance approach. Anchor off the beach, mainly on weed and rock, open to east and southeast. A tree-lined valley with sloping rocky sides runs inland. If approaching from the north, see Cabo Monseña and Punta de las Picas, above.

⚓ Cala Rambla (Cala sa Torreta)
39°57'·8N 04°15'·4E

A large double *cala* with low rocky cliffs on either side and the Llosa de Rambles reef some 400m north of the entrance. A nice, quiet anchorage if the hustle and bustle of the Isla Colom area becomes too much. The shallow area shown on the chartlet south of Llosa des Rambles (*page 285*) extends further to the south-southeast than is apparent. Enter on a west-southwest course to anchor over sand off the west beach, open to north and northeast. The east side of the *cala* has some awash rocks scattered across its entrance though there is a good sandy beach behind.

There is a single house between the beaches and a track inland. A standing *taula* and a *talayot* (ancient monument and tower) and burial ground will be found just over 0·5M inland, together with a ruined village at Sa Torre Blanca.

Isla Colom
39°58'·0N 04°16'·6E (North end)

An almost deserted island with rocky cliffs, Isla Colom is 0·6M long by 0·5M at its widest point and up to 42m high. The northeast coast between Cap de Mestral and Cap de Llevant has many rocky outliers, many just below the surface. One, Llosa des Cap de Mestral, is no less than 450m north of the central headland and a similar distance north-northeast of Cap de Mestral itself. Some 75m north of Cap de Llevant, (although it has been reported further offshore by several people who have grounded there) lies Llosa de ses Eugos, a rock with only 1·3m over. It is recommended that an offing of at least 550m is maintained along this section of the island coast. There are two attractive small beaches to which frequent daily boat trips are run from Es Grao, and one large house, Lloc de s'Illa, plus a hut. Inevitably, the island has its own unique species of lizard.

Dangerous rock

Es Grau and Isla Colom. The dangerous rock off Cala Avellana, right centre, can just be seen *Juanjo Pons / Triangle Postals*

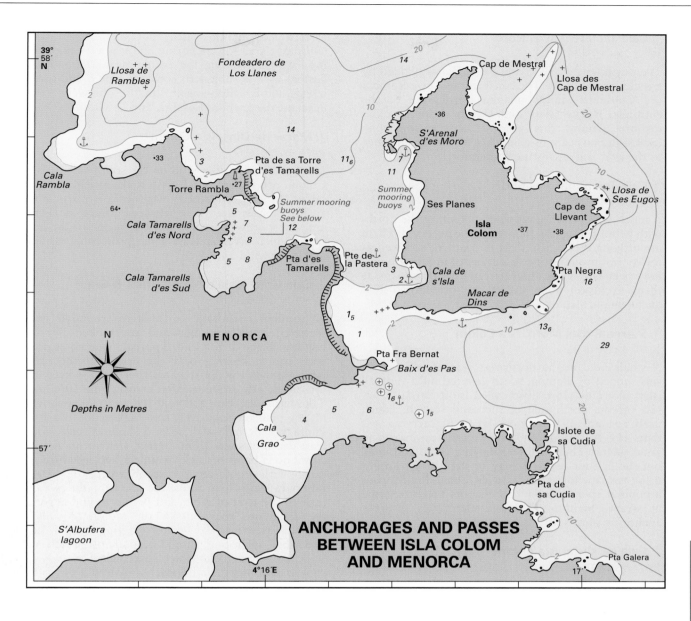

ANCHORAGES AND PASSES BETWEEN ISLA COLOM AND MENORCA

Pass inside Isla Colom

A dog-legged passage between Isla Colom and Menorca, little more than 1m deep and about 100m wide makes a short cut for shallow draught vessels. However, the passage is prone to shifting sands following gales and reported depths are therefore unreliable.

Anchorages behind Isla Colom

Apart from Mahón and Addaya, the anchorages behind Isla Colom offer the best shelter from easterly winds on the northeast coast. They are, however, open to the northwest through to northeast and are therefore not suitable in heavy weather or in winds with a north component, since the two anchorages that might be thought to give all-round shelter (Cala Tamarells d'es Nord and S'Arenal d'es Moro) are too small to provide adequate swinging room in a blow. In any event summer mooring buoys have been placed south of Punta de sa Torre d'es Tamarells and east of Punta d'es Tamarells, which can be reserved in advance for 1 June to 30 September at www.balearslifeposidonia.eu. See plan above and the *Moorings* section on page 19 for further details.

The next four anchorages all have an interesting phenomenon: sandy weed-covered tufts stick up abruptly giving unreliable depth readings. Clumps of weed can be as high as 3m, reducing depths displayed on the echo-sounder to practically nothing. For reliable depths avoid these areas.

⚓ Cala Tamarells d'es Nord
39°57'·7N 04°15'·9E

The north, and smaller, of a pair of *calas* divided by a rocky promontory. The conspicuous Torre Rambla (Es Colomar) stands on the north side of the entrance. Rocky islets and awash rocks lie close inshore around this point. Conservation zone exclusion buoys are now in place across the entrance to the *cala* and anchoring is therefore forbidden.

⚓ Cala Tamarells d'es Sud
39°57'·6N 04°15·9E

A much larger anchorage than its twin to the north, with better protection than might be expected. There are offlying rocks around both headlands as well as the central promontory. A number of mooring buoys have been laid in the outer part of the *cala* and inside them exclusion zone buoys are present so that anchoring is forbidden.

⚓ S'Arenal d'es Moro, Isla Colom
39°57'·8N 04°16'·4E

A small *cala* on the northwest side of Isla Colom surrounded by sloping, scrub-covered hills. A small islet, Illot d'es Moro (also called Islote Pardals), lies just off the north side of the sandy beach, which itself has an off-lying ridge of rock, carrying less than 1m. Anchor in 5–7m over sand and weed in good shelter. There is little swinging room and in all but the lightest winds it may be necessary to moor using two anchors at the bow. S'Arenal d'es Moro is a popular spot with daytime visitors but is deserted at night. Swimming buoys effectively prevent anchoring in this little *cala* in summer.

⚓ Cala de s'Isla, Isla Colom
39°57'·5N 04°16'·4E

A small, shallow, but very pretty *cala* just northeast of the passage between Isla Colom and Menorca, surrounded by low sloping hills and with a house set back from the northeast corner. A large rocky area just below water level lies in the central part of the anchorage, while the south side is fringed with rocks merging into those of the southwest headland. Approach the centre of the *cala* with care on an east course to anchor in the outer part of the bay in 2–3m over sand. Like the beach further north, Cala de s'Isla is a popular destination for tourist boats from Cala Grao but is very quiet at night.

⚓ Isla Colom, general anchorage
39°57'·6N 04°16'·3E

Virtually the whole area bounded by Punta de sa Torre, Punta de la Pastera, Cala de s'Isla and s'Arenal d'es Moro is one large anchoring area, mainly over sand with some small patches of weed and depths of 2–11m. A considerable number of mooring buoys have been laid over weed on the eastern side of this area, but there is still an enormous area for anchoring and it is very popular. It is worth avoiding the corner near Punta de la Pastera as it is subject to constant, noisy, and often irresponsibly high-speed, traffic between the beaches, the anchored yachts, and Es Grau.

⚓ Macar de Dins, Isla Colom
39°57'·3N 04°16'·6E

Strictly a fair-weather stop on the south side of Isla Colom, off a small beach with rocks awash near its centre. In settled northerly weather it is possible to anchor almost anywhere between Macar de Dins and the southwest promontory. It is one of the few spots which gives at least some protection from a northeast wind and swell.

⚓ Cala Grao (Cala de la Albufera & Grau)
39°57'·1N 04°16'·3E

A popular anchorage in a large, rounded *cala* scattered with moorings and overlooked by the holiday village of Es Grao. Approach and enter on a west course keeping near the centre of the *cala*, which shoals rapidly towards the beach – keep an eye on the echo-sounder after crossing the 10m line. Take particular care to avoid the rocky area shown on the plan on *page 285*, some 200m southeast of Punta Fra Bernat, with several shallow rocks with least depth of some 1·6m. In fact, there is an almost continuous band of rock, boulders and weed (most of it with good cover except where described otherwise) stretching across the *cala* from the point a little to the west of Punta Fra Bernat to and beyond the dangerous rock outside the mouth of Caleta Avellana (see below). Vessels entering Cala Grau, and when anchoring, should keep a close watch for these dangerous rocks which nevertheless are easy to spot in good light conditions.

Looking southeast over Isla Colom to Cala Grao and S'Albufera lagoon. Es Grao is on the left, Cala de s'Isla at bottom right

A very large area is effectively closed off by local small craft moorings and anchoring is likely to be in 5–8m outside these. Open to the east and swell from northeast to southeast.

There are slipways and quays for dinghies and small boats. Es Grao has a supermarket, restaurants and cafés (which also sell ice). Es Moll d'es Grau is a small and basic restaurant on the quay which was well known for the best sardines on the island and other seafood as well; it also does take-away paellas etc. ☏ 629 141638. This restaurant changed hands in 2017 and it is too soon to judge if the standards will be maintained. There is a summer water taxi service covering Cala Grau, Isla Colom, and neighbouring anchorages – ☏ 609 592150.

A broad stream leading from the vast Albufera lagoon drains into the southwest corner of the *cala* and would make an interesting dinghy excursion. The lagoon and marshes, which extend more than a mile inland, are a wildlife and nature reserve.

⚓ Caleta Avellana (Cala Vellana)
39°57'.1N 4°16'.4E

A small *cala* between sloping rocky sides close east of Cala Grao, with an isolated rock, with least depth of 1·5m, outside the middle of the entrance and about 100m further north than shown in earlier editions. Entry to Caleta Avellana can be made either side of this rock which has a diameter of about 20m and is clearly visible in good light conditions if a careful watch is maintained. Anchor over sand, weed and rock.

⚓ Cala Binillantí
39°55'.5N 04°17'.0E

A very small, deserted *cala* inshore of Islote Bombasa (En Bombarda) and north of Punta Sansá. Approach on a southwest course and anchor off the beach. Do not confuse Cala Binillantí with one of a series of five even smaller *calas* to the north (*see plan on page 281*).

⚓ Cala S'Arenal Gran (Grau)
39°54'.9N 04°17'.3E

This large *cala* lies immediately north of Cala Mesquida and Punta de sa Torre (topped by a large pale stone tower), and south of Punta Pá Gros. To the east lies Islota Mesquida. Punta Pá Gros has groups of offlying rocky islets of which the outermost, the Illots d'es Mesquida, are 400m offshore. Leave all these islets to starboard on the approach and head towards a white building in the centre of the beach to then anchor over sand off the north end of the beach in 4–5m, open to the east and southeast. Swimming buoys are in place during the summer. The south part of the beach has rocky outcrops running out into the *cala*. There are a few houses and a road, but no facilities.

⚓ Cala Mesquida
39°54'.8N 04°17'.3E

An angular *cala* with a small beach, close south of Cala S'Arenal Gran and Punta de sa Torre and its prominent tower (which has the proportions of a medieval castle keep). Leave the Illots d'es Mesquida to starboard and steer southwest towards the small beach, leaving Racó de sa Creveta and its associated rocks to port. If approaching from the south keep at least 500m offshore until due east of Punta de sa Torre before heading in. The Restaurant Cap Roig is prominent on the cliff to port and has probably the most dramatic view of any restaurant in Menorca. Anchor between Racó de sa Creveta and the tower in 5–6m mainly over sand.

Do not approach the beach without a previous recce by dinghy, as a reef runs most of the way across it in a northwest direction from the rocks near the further buildings. A shallow river flows into the head of the *cala*. There is a dinghy harbour and slipway in the southeast corner, in front of a café/restaurant backed by several streets of houses.

It was here that the heavy siege train of the Duc de Richelieu was finally landed in April 1756. It had originally been landed at Ciudadela, but was held up by the destruction of the road to Mahón and was re-embarked.

Punta Negro
39°54'.3N 04°17'.8E

A low (12m) headland with houses on its summit, not to be confused with the much more prominent Cabo Negro (37m) 0·7M to the southeast. Rocks lie southeast off the point.

Calas S'Arenal Gran and Mesquida, Mahón harbour in the background
Juanjo Pons / Triangle Postals

⚓ Cala Murta (Es Murtar)

39°54'.2N 04°17'.7E

A wide *cala* just south of Punta Negro, with a series of rocky beaches and many houses to the north. Approach the middle of the *cala* on a west course to anchor in the northwest corner over rock and sand, open to the east and southeast. Care is necessary because the coast is foul in parts.

Cabo Negro (Cap Negre)

39°54'N 04°18'.5E

A high (37m), prominent point of black rock with steep sides sloping seawards. A small islet and awash rock lie close to the promontory, which has some sea caves.

⚓ Cala Els Freus

39°52'.9N 04°18'.7E

A narrow *cala* on the north side of the isthmus of La Mola, which is foul on its south side. Bajo de las Aguilas (N'Ofegat), a low islet with awash rocks, guards the approach 500m to the east-northeast (*see plan on page 219*).

Punta S'Esperó

39°52'.6N 04°19'.7E

A high (78m), conspicuous, flat-topped promontory with sheer cliffs, sloping gently downwards towards Puerto de Mahón. A large fort (La Mola) and other conspicuous buildings occupy the plateau, with a lighthouse (white round tower with two black bands on a white base) at the eastern tip. There are two awash rocks close to the point but it is otherwise steep-to (*see plan on page 219*).

Appendix

1. Obtaining charts

Up-to-date information on chart coverage for Islas
Baleares with full details of chart schemes, titles and
scales can be found as follows:

Admiralty charts

British Admiralty charts at www.admiralty.co.uk/charts

French charts

SHOM (Service Hydrographique et Océanographique de
la Marine) charts at www.shom.fr
Note that SHOM chart numbers change and the SHOM
website should be checked for the latest details.

Spanish charts

Instituto Hydrografico de la Marina charts at
www.armada.mde.es/ArmadaPortal/page/Portal/ArmadaEsp
annola/cienciaihm1/prefLang-en/
Go to Products and Services > Nautical charts >
Paper charts (or > Electronic charts)

Imray charts

Imray M3 Islas Baleares 1:350,000
Includes 7 harbour inserts at 1: 10,000 to 1:30,000
Search www.imray.com for M3

Further Imray chart coverage is given at
www.imray.com

Imray Navigator

Imray charts, as well as those from other official
Hydrographic Offices, are available on Imray's new
navigation app for iPad and iPhone.

Download the free app Imray
Navigator from the App Store for
navigation software and
demonstration charts. Subscribe to
chart sets by area for updates
throughout the year.

The chart set covered by this book is:
ID50 Western Mediterranean

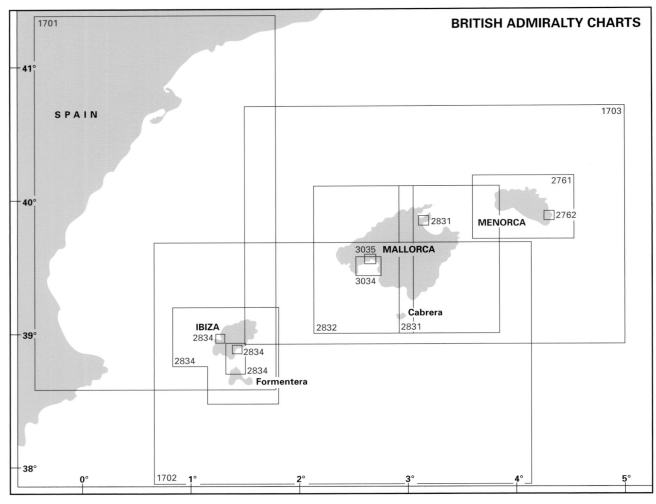

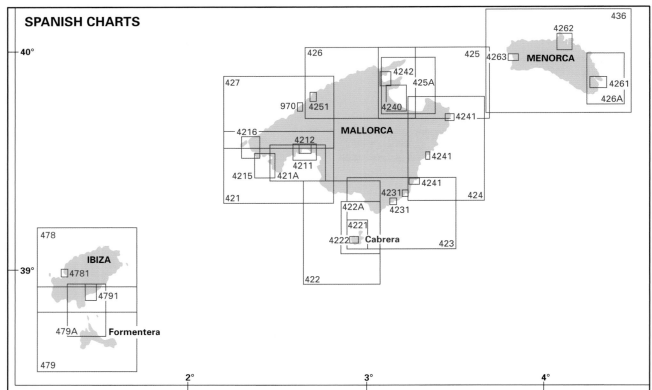

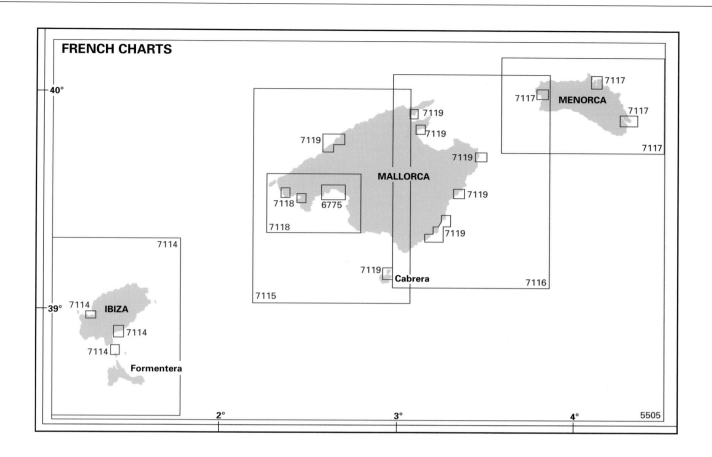

FRENCH CHARTS

40°

7119
7119
7119
7119

7119
MALLORCA

7118 6775
7118

7119
7119
7115

7117
7117 MENORCA
7117
7117

7116

7114
7114 IBIZA
39°
7114
7114
Formentera

2°
3°
4°
5505

2. Further reading

Pilots and tourist guides

There are literally hundreds of books available about different aspects of the Baleares Islands and more are published each year. These include books on the flora and fauna of the Islands, places to eat, general walking guides, history of the Islands, etc. Many are updated regularly, like the Rough Guides, whilst others soon become obsolete. For further reading, search online for latest titles. Often, historic editions may be available on the Amazon website.

Admiralty publications

Mediterranean Pilot Vol I (NP 45) and supplement covers the S and E coasts of Spain, the Islas Baleares, Sardinia, Sicily and the N coast of Africa

List of Lights and Fog Signals Vol E (NP 78) (Mediterranean, Black and Red Seas)

List of Radio Signals

Vol 1, Part 1 (NP281/1) Coast Radio Stations (Europe, Africa and Asia)

Vol 2 (NP 282) Radio Navigational Aids, Electronic Position Fixing Systems and Radio Time Signals

Vol 3 Part 1 (NP 283/1) Radio Weather Services and Navigational Warnings (Europe, Africa and Asia)

Vol 4 (NP 284) Meteorological Observation Stations

Vol 5 (NP 285) Global Maritime Distress and Safety Systems (GMDSS)

Vol 6, Part 2 (NP 286/2) Vessel Traffic Services, Port Operations and Pilot Services (The Mediterranean, Africa and Asia)

English language

Imray Mediterranean Almanac Lucinda and Rod Heikell (Imray Laurie Norie & Wilson Ltd). A biennial almanac with second year supplement, packed with information. Particularly good value for yachts on passage when not every cruising guide is likely to be carried.

Mediterranean Cruising Handbook Rod Heikell (Imray Laurie Norie & Wilson Ltd). General information on cruising areas, passages etc.

Menorca. Atlas Náutico Alfonso Buenaventure. A book of 67 double page chartlets showing the coastline of Menorca in extreme detail – a must for anyone thinking of cruising around Menorca.

Nuevos Aeroguias – El Litoral de Mallorca (Editorial Planeta S.A) It has aerial photographs of the whole coastline of Mallorca. Ensure you get a recent edition as most shops only hold the old one.

North Africa RCCPF/Graham Hutt (Imray)

French

Votre Livre de Bord – Méditerranée (Bloc Marine) French almanac covering the Mediterranean, including details of weather forecasts transmitted from France and Monaco. An English/French version is also published which translates some, though by no means all, the text. Published annually.

German

Spanische Gewässer, Lissabon bis Golfe du Lion K Neumann (Delius Klasing). A seamanlike guide and semi-pilot book, which includes sketch plans of most harbours. Harbour data is limited but it contains much good general advice on sailing in this area.

Balearen Gerd Radspieler. A useful book but with very basic plans and lacking in detail.

Background

The Birth of Europe Michael Andrew (BBC Books). An excellent and comprehensive work which explains in simple terms how the Mediterranean and surrounding countries developed over the ages from 3000 BC.

The First Eden, David Attenborough (William Collins). A fascinating study of 'The Mediterranean World and Man'.

The Inner Sea Robert Fox (Sinclair-Stevenson, 1991). An account of the countries surrounding the Mediterranean and the forces which shaped them, written by a well known BBC journalist.

Travellers' guides

Cami de Cavalls of Menorca (Triangle Postals, 2012) An excellent coastal walking guide for the GR223. *See page 216 for details.*

Yacht Insiders Guide: Balearic Islands (Shorelink Publications). An excellent booklet listing places to go, things to do, good eating places etc. with special reference to yachtsmen. Published annually.

The AA Map & Guide to Menorca, Twinpack (AA publishing 2015). Includes, 'Top 25 sights', 'Where to: eat, shop, etc.' and 'Practical Matters'. It comes with an OS map of the island. Highly recommended.

Landscapes of Ibiza and Formentera Han Losse; *Landscapes of Mallorca* Valerie Crespí-Green; *Landscapes of Menorca* Rodney Ansell (Sunflower Books, 2017, 2015 & 2016). Three pocket-sized volumes of car tours, walks and picnic suggestions, plus some public transport schedules.

The Rough Guide: Mallorca & Menorca Phil Lee (Rough Guides, 2016). Part of the worldwide series for land-based budget travellers, but useful to anyone wanting practical information, including town plans. The Islas Baleares are also included in the *Spain* volume (2015).

Mallorca Pocket Guide and *Menorca Pocket Guide* Berlitz. Published 2016 and 2015 respectively.

Period accounts

Jogging Round Majorca Gordon West (Black Swan Books, 1994). First published in 1929 when 'jogging' meant a leisurely stroll, this is a charming glimpse of the island before tourism arrived. Also available on cassette. Highly recommended.

A Cottage in Majorca Lady Margaret Kinloch (Skeffinton, 1936). Another mirror into the past written with great affection. Long out of print, so not an easy book to track down.

Majorca Observed Robert Graves and Paul Hogarth (Cassells, 1965). Probably the most famous author to live and write in Mallorca before mass tourism.

Road maps

Road maps are indispensable when making a journey inland. As usual, Michelin produce an excellent road map which is available throughout the islands.

Euro-Map – Mallorca, Menorca, Ibiza (GeoCenter International). Detailed but comprehensible road map giving contours, place names (sometimes both Castilian and local versions) historic sites, street plan of Palma, etc. Scale 1:150,000. Useful for any form of travel.

The Firestone road map of the Islas Baleares is also reported to be excellent, but may be difficult to obtain in the UK.

Cookery books

Mediterranean Seafood Alan Davidson. Prospect Books, 2012. A handbook with all the names of Mediterranean fish, crustaceans and molluscs in several languages and over 200 recipes from Mediterranean countries. Indispensable in markets and fishing harbours with their unfamiliar fish. The recipes are practical and do not require ingredients exotic to the Mediterranean.

Mediterranean Cookery Claudia Roden. It contains 250 delicious and easy recipes of traditional Mediterranean cooking prepared with locally available ingredients.

3. Spanish glossary

The following limited glossary relates to the weather, the abbreviations to be found on Spanish charts and some words likely to be useful on entering port. For a list containing many words commonly used in connection with sailing, see Webb & Manton, *Yachtsman's Ten Language Dictionary* (Adlard Coles Nautical) and *Spanish for Cruisers* by Kathy Parsons (Aventuras Publishing Company).

Weather

On the radio, if there is a storm warning the forecast starts *aviso temporal*. If, as usual, there is no storm warning, the forecast starts *no hay temporal*. Many words are similar to the English and their meanings can be guessed. The following may be less familiar:

Viento (wind)
calm calm
ventolina light air
flojito light breeze
flojo gentle breeze
bonancible moderate breeze
fresquito fresh breeze
fresco strong breeze
frescachón near gale
temporal fuerte gale
temporal duro strong gale
temporal muy duro storm
borrasca violent storm
huracán, temporal huracanado hurricane
tempestad, borrasca thunderstorm

El cielo (the sky)
nube cloud
nubes altas, bajas high, low clouds
nubloso cloudy
cubierto covered, overcast
claro, despejado clear
Names of cloud types in Spanish are based on the same Latin words as the names used in English.

El mar (sea state)
calma calm
marizada ripples
marejadilla slight sea (choppy)
marejada rough sea
fuerte marejada very rough
mar corta short seas
mar gruesa steep seas

Visibilidad (visibility)
buena, bueno, buen good
regular moderate
malo, mala, mal poor
calima haze
neblina mist
bruma sea mist
niebla fog
Precipitación Precipitation
aguacero shower
llovizna drizzle
lluvia rain
aguanieve sleet
nieve snow
granizada hail

Sistemas del tiempo (weather systems)
anticiclón anticyclone
depresión, borrasca depression
vaguada trough
cresta, dorsal ridge
cuna wedge
frente front
frío cold
cálido warm
ocluido occluded
bajando falling
subiendo rising

Lights and charts – major terms and abbreviations

A	*amarilla*	yellow
Alt	*alternativa*	alternative
Ag Nv	*aguas navegables*	navegable waters
Ang	*angulo*	angle
Ant	*anterior*	anterior, earlier, forward
Apag	*apagado*	extinguished
Arrc	*arrecife*	reef
At	*atenuada*	attenuated
B	*blanca*	white
Ba	*bahía*	bay
	bajamar escorada	chart datum
Bal	*baliza*	buoy, beacon
Bal. E	*baliza elástica*	plastic (elastic) buoy
Bco	*banco*	bank
Bo	*bajo*	shoal, under, below, low
Boc	*bocina*	horn, trumpet
Br	*babor*	port (i.e. left)
C	*campana*	bell
Card	*cardinal*	cardinal
Cañ	*cañon*	canyon
	boya de castillete	pillar buoy
cil	*cilíndrico*	cylindrical
C	*cabo*	cape
Cha	*chimenea*	chimney
Cno	*castillo*	castle
cón	*cónico*	conical
Ct	*centellante*	quick flashing (50–80/minute)
CtI	*centellante interrumpida*	interrupted quick flashing
cuad	*cuadrangular*	quadrangular
D	*destello*	flash
Desap	*desaparecida*	disappeared
Dest	*destruida*	destroyed
	dique	breakwater, jetty
Dir	*direccional*	directional
DL	*destello largo*	long flash
E	*este*	east
edif	*edificio*	building
	ensenada	cove, inlet
Er	*estribor*	starboard
Est	*esférico*	spherical
Esp	*especial*	special
Est sñ	*estación de señales*	signal station
ext	*exterior*	exterior
Extr	*extremo*	end, head (of pier etc.)
F	*fija*	fixed
Fca	*fabrica*	factory
FD	*fija y destello*	fixed and flashing
FGpD	*fija y grupo de destellos*	fixed and group flashing
Flot	*flotador*	float
Fondn	*fondeadero*	anchorage
GpCt	*grupo de centellos*	group quick flashing
GpD	*grupo de destellos*	group flashing
GpOc	*grupo de ocultaciones*	group occulting
GpRp	*grupo de centellos rápidos*	group very quick flashing
hel	*helicoidales*	helicoidal
hor	*horizontal*	horizontal
Hund	*hundida*	submerged, sunk
I	*interrumpido*	interrupted
Igla	*iglesia*	church
Inf	*inferior*	inferior, lower
Intens	*intensificado*	intensified
Irreg	*irregular*	irregular
Iso	*isofase*	isophase
L	*luz*	light
La	*lateral*	lateral
	levante	eastern
M	*millas*	miles
Mte	*monte*	mountain
Mto	*monumento*	monument
N	*norte*	north

Naut	*nautófono*	foghorn
NE	*nordeste*	northeast
No	*número*	number
NW	*noroeste*	northwest
Obst	*obstrucción*	obstruction
ocas	*ocasional*	occasional
oct	*octagonal*	octagonal
oc	*oculta*	obscured
Oc	*ocultación sectores*	obscured sectors
Pe A	*peligro aislado*	isolated danger
	poniente	western
Post	*posterior*	posterior, later
Ppal	*principal*	principal
	prohibido	prohibited
Obston	*obstrucción*	obstruction
Prov	*provisional*	provisional
prom	*prominente*	prominent, conspicuous
Pta	*punta*	point
Pto	*puerto*	port
PTO	*puerto deportivo*	yacht harbour
	puerto pesquero	fishing harbour
	puerto de Marina de Guerra	naval harbour
R	*roja*	red
Ra	*estación radar*	radar station
Ra+	*radar + suffix*	radar + suffix (Ra Ref etc.)
RC	*radiofaro circular*	non-directional radiobeacon
RD	*radiofaro dirigido*	directional radiobeacon
rect	*rectangular*	rectangular
Ra	*rocas*	rocks
Rp	*centeneallante*	very quick flashing
	rápida	(80-160/min)
RpI	*cent. rápida interrumpida*	interrupted very quick flashing
RW	*radiofaro giratorio*	rotating radiobeacon
s	*segundos*	seconds
S	*sur*	south
SE	*sudeste*	southeast
sil	*silencio*	silence
Silb	*silbato*	whistle
Sincro	*sincronizda con*	synchronized with
Sir	*sirena*	siren
son	*sonido*	sound, noise, report
Sto/a	*Santo, Santa*	Saint
SW	*sudoeste*	southwest
T	*temporal*	temporary
Te	*torre*	tower
trans	*transversal*	transversal
triang	*triangular*	triangular
troncoc	*troncocónico*	truncated cone
troncop	*troncopiramidal*	truncated pyramid
TSH	*antena de radio*	radio mast
TV	*antena de TV*	TV mast
U	*centellante* *Ultra-rápida*	ultra quick flashing (+160/min)
UI	*cent. Ultra-rápida interrumpido*	interrupted ultra quick flashing
V	*verde*	green
Vis	*visible*	visible
	vivero	shellfish raft or bed
W	*oeste*	west

Ports and harbours

Puerto is applied to any landing place from a beach to a container port

a popa stern-to
a proa bows-to
abrigo shelter
al costado alongside
amarrar to moor
amarradero mooring
ancho breadth (see also manga)
anclar to anchor

botar to launch (a yacht)
boya de amarre mooring buoy
cabo warp, line (also cape)
calado draught
compuerta lock, basin
dársena dock, harbour
dique breakwater, jetty
escala ladder
escalera steps
esclusa lock
escollera jetty
eslora total length overall
espigón spur, spike, mole
fábrica factory
ferrocarril railway
fondear to anchor or moor
fondeadero anchorage
fondeo mooring buoy
fondo depth (bottom)
grua crane
guia mooring lazy-line (lit. guide)
nudo knot (i.e. speed)
longitud length (see also eslora), longitude
lonja fish market (wholesale)
manga beam (i.e. width)
muelle mole, jetty, quay
noray bollard
pantalán jetty, pontoon
parar to stop
pila estaca pile
pontón pontoon
práctico pilot (i.e. pilot boat)
profundidad depth
rampa slipway
rompeolas breakwater
varadero slipway, hardstanding
varar to lift (a yacht)
vertedero (verto) spoil ground

Direction
babor port
estribor starboard
norte north
este east
sur south
oeste west

Around the port
aceite oil (including engine oil)
agua potable drinking water
aseos toilet block
astiller shipyard
duchas showers
efectos navales chandlery
electricidad electricity
gasoleo diesel diesel
hielo (cubitos) ice (cubes)
lavandería laundry
lavandería automática launderette
luz electricity (lit. light)
manguera hosepipe
parafina, petróleo, keroseno paraffin, kerosene
gasolina petrol
velero sailmaker (also sailing ship)

Phrases useful on arrival
Donde puedo amarrar? Where can I moor?
A donde debo ir? Where should I go?
Que es la profundidad? What is the depth?
Cuantos metros? What is your length?
Para cuantas noches? For how many nights?

Formalities
aduana customs
capitán de puerto harbourmaster
derechos dues, rights
dueño, propietario owner
guardia civil police
patrón skipper (not owner)
título certificate

Documentation

It has been found useful to have the following list available for registering at each port or marina to be visited:

Nombre de Yate Yacht's name
Bandera Flag
Lista y folio Yacht's number
Reg. bruto Registered weight
Tipo Type of vessel
Palos Number of masts
Motor, marca y potencia Engine make and capacity
Eslora total L.O.A.
Maga Beam
Calado Draught
Puerto base Home port
No. cabinas No. of cabins
Seguro Insurance company
Proprietario Skipper
Nacionalidad Nationality
Telefono Telephone
Pasaporte Passport
Tripulante y pasajero Passengers on board

4. Repair and maintenance facilities in Palma de Mallorca

Companies are normally listed alphabetically.
Chandleries
    Yacht Centre Palma ☎ 971 715612, info@ycp.com.es, at RCNP, Club de Mar, Santa Ponsa and Alcudia.
    La Central ☎ 971 731838 and others.
Liferaft servicing
    GDR ☎ 971 760798, www.gdrnautica.com
Charts Admiralty
    Rapid Transit Service ☎ 971 401210 / 629 464428.
    bruno@rapidtrans.com, aurelie@rapidtrans.com
    Spanish – Librería Fondevila ☎ 971 725616
Generators
    Salva Centro ☎ 971 730303
Repairs
    Audax Marina ☎ 971 720474 and 680 279280. Repair yard at the Réal Club Náutico, info@audaxmarina.com
    Astilleros de Mallorca boatyard ☎ 971 710645, info@astillerosdemallorca.com, a shipyard with four slipways able to take yachts up to 100m on the Contramuelle Mollet opposite the Réal Club Náutico.
    Boat Yard Palma ☎ 971 718302, info@boatyardpalma.com, and Carpinser ☎ 971 725079, administracion@carpinser.com, projects@carpinser.com on the Muelles Viejo and Nuevo near the root of the NE breakwater and several others.
    A 150-tonne travel-lift at Boat Yard Palma, 90 and 30-tonne lifts on the Muelle Viejo, 60-tonne lift at the Réal Club Náutico. A 9-tonne crane at the Réal Club Náutico, 5-tonne crane at Club de Mar, plus many others in the commercial areas of the port. A commercial slipway in the Dársena de Porto Pi able to handle 350 tonnes, for which a docking plan is required. Several in the shipyard E of the Réal Club Náutico.
Engineers
    C-Tec SA ☎ 971 405 712 / 609 222245, info@c-tec.org
    Marine Machine ☎ 971 462 660,info@marine-machine.com
    Talleres Guidet ☎ 971 718 643 / 670 303713, t_guidet@yahoo.es
Official service agents include:
    C-Tec SA (*see above*) – Caterpillar, Man
    Marine Machine (*see above*) Ford/Lehman, Perkins, Sabre, Volvo Penta
    Salva Centro ☎ 971 730 303
    Camber Marine ☎ 971 430 343, respuestos@cambermarine.com Volvo Penta main dealer
Metalwork
    Ruben Doñaque ☎ 971 760 796, info@rubendonaquewelding.com
    Talleres Guidet (*see above in Engineers*).

Electronic & radio repairs, autopilots, watermakers etc
    C-Tec SA (see above)
    Dahlberg (for AIS, radio etc.) ☎ 902 999 114/ 609 414492, info@dahlberg-sa.com
    Vetus Mallorca ☎ 971 713 050
    Yacht Engineering Solutions – including Gas/Refrigeration. Gas-certified for gas cooker safety check.
    ☎ 661 596 487, 678899038, info@yesyes.es
Canvaswork
    Valería Orion ☎ 971 757 688 / 607 755531, info@valeriaorion.com
Sailmakers
    Valera J Matheu ☎ 971 273 887, info@velasmatheu.com
Rigging
    A + Rigging
    Marko Bakker, Mallorca SL *mobile* 639 442 761, mbakker@aplusriggingmallorca.com

N.B. Noonsite also has a very full list of service companies

5. Official addresses

SPANISH NATIONAL EMBASSIES AND CONSULATES
UK 39 Chesham Place, London SW1X 8SB ☎ 020 7235 5555
Consulate 20 Draycott Place, London SW3 2RZ
    ☎ 020 7589 8989
US 2375 Pennsylvania Avenue NW, Washington, DC 20037
    ☎ 202 452 0100/728 2340
    embespus@mail.mae.es
Consulate 150 E. 58th St, New York, NY 10155
    ☎ 212 355 4080/2/5/6
    spainconsulny@mail.mae.es

BRITISH AND AMERICAN EMBASSIES IN MADRID
UK Calle Fernando el Santo 16, 28010 Madrid
    ☎ 91 700 8200/524 9700
    madridconsulate@ukinspain.com
US Calle Serrano 75, 28006 Madrid
    ☎ 91 587 2240/5872240

BRITISH CONSULATES IN ISLAS BALEARES
Mallorca British Consulate, Carrer Convent dels Caputxins, 4 Edificio Orisba B 4ºD 07002 Palma de Mallorca
    ☎ +34 933 666200, spain.consulate@fco.gov.uk
Menorca British Honorary Consul ☎ 933 666200
Ibiza British Consulate, Avenida Isidoro Macabich 45
    1º1ª (corner with Calle Canarias), 07800 Ibiza
    ☎ +34 933 666200, spain.consulate@fco.gov.uk

FRENCH REPRESENTATION IN ISLAS BALEARES
French Honorary Consulate, c/Caro 1, 1G, 07002, Palma de Mallorca, ☎ 971 730301, agenceconsulairepalma@gmail.com

ITALIAN REPRESENTATION IN ISLAS BALEARES
Italian Honorary Vice-Consul, Carretera de Porto Pi 8 - 6D, 07015 Palma de Mallorca, ☎ 971 405668, maiorca@esteri.it

DUTCH REPRESENTATION IN ISLAS BALEARES
Netherlands Honorary Consulate, c/San Miguel 36-60-C, 07002 Palma de Mallorca, ☎ 971 716493, nlgovpm@consulaatmallorca.com

SWEDISH REPRESENTATION IN THE ISLAS BALEARES
Swedish Honorary Consulate, San Jaime 7, Palma de Mallorca, ☎ 971 725492, consuladodesuecia@montisabogados.com

AMERICAN REPRESENTATION IN ISLAS BALEARES
United States Consular Agency, c/Porto Pi, 8-90-D, 07015 Palma de Mallorca, ☎ 971 303707, pmagency@state.gov

SPANISH NATIONAL TOURIST OFFICES
UK PO Box 4009 London W1A 6NB ☎ +44 020 74868077
    info.londres@tourspain.es www.tourspain.co.uk
US 666 Fifth Avenue, New York, NY 10103
    ☎ 212 265 8822/6577246
    oetny@tourspain.es
    www.okspain.org

Index